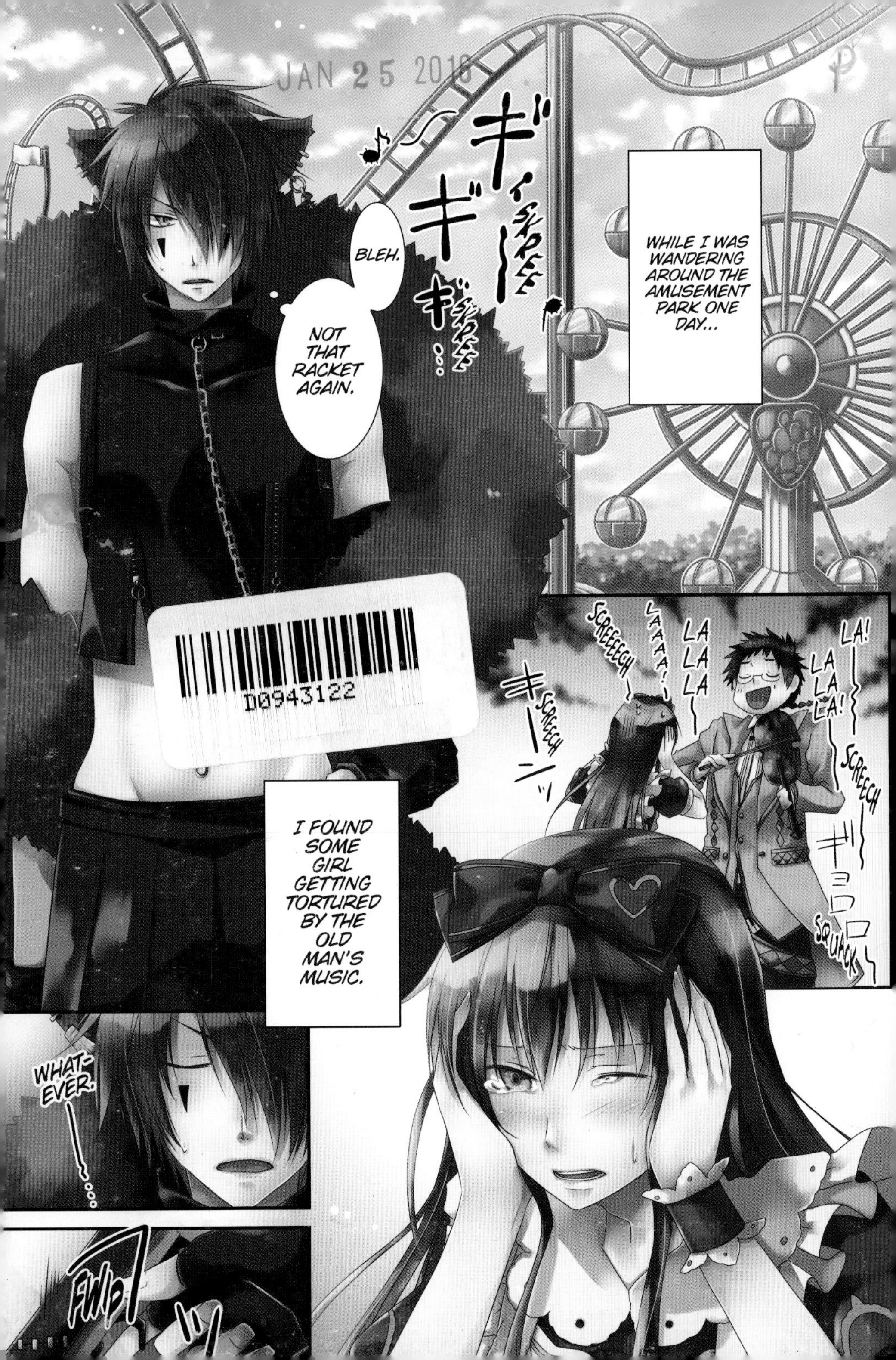
WHILE I WAS WANDERING AROUND THE AMUSEMENT PARK ONE DAY...
ギィ〜 SKREE
ギギ… SKREE
BLEH.
NOT THAT RACKET AGAIN.
LA! LA LA LA!
LA LA LA~
LAAAA!
SCREEEECH
SCREECH
キーッ SCREECH
ギョロロ〜 SQUACK
I FOUND SOME GIRL GETTING TORTURED BY THE OLD MAN'S MUSIC.
WHAT-EVER.
FWIP

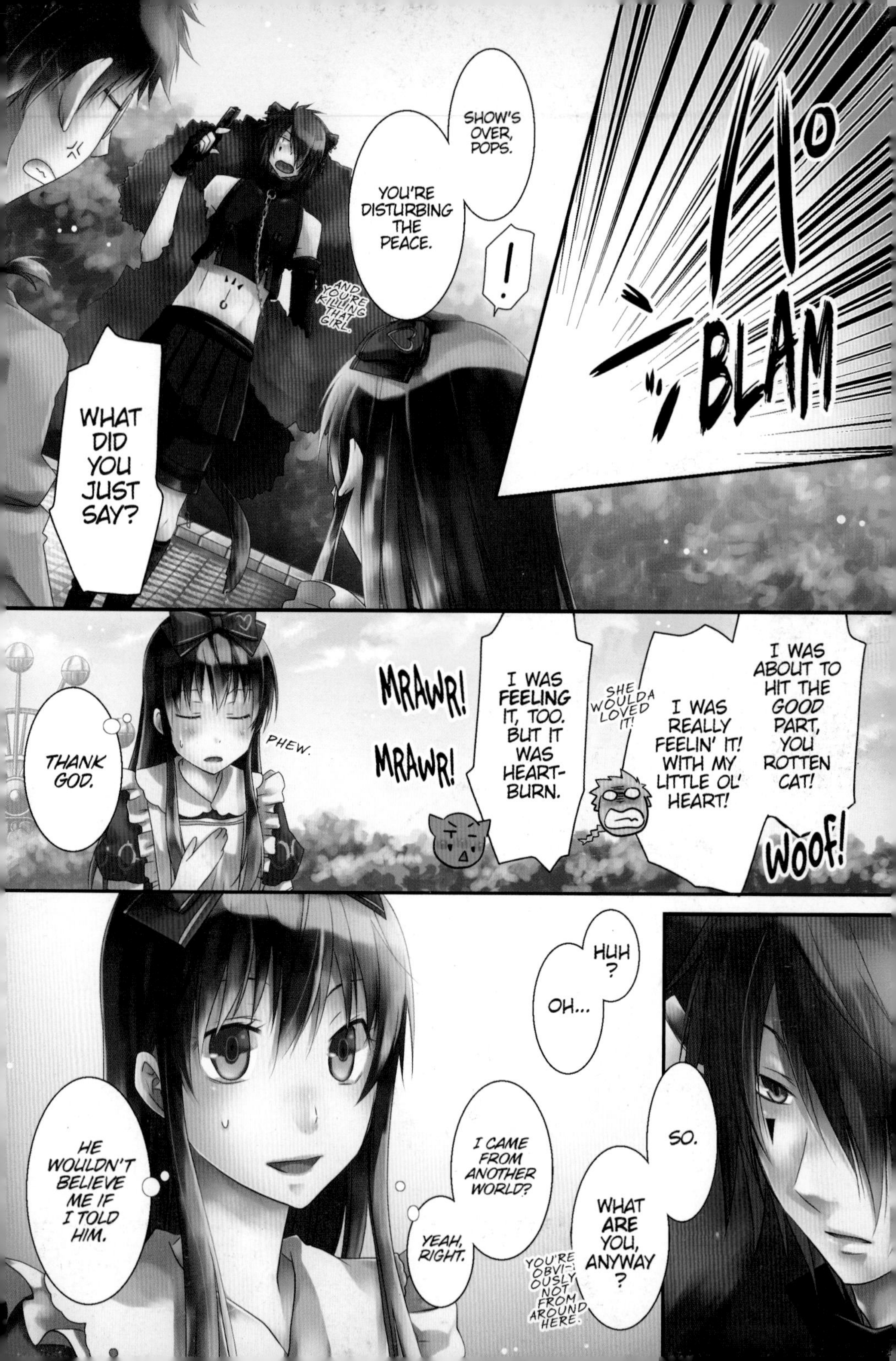
BLAM
SHOW'S OVER, POPS.
YOU'RE DISTURBING THE PEACE.
!
AND YOU'RE KILLING THAT GIRL.
WHAT DID YOU JUST SAY?
I WAS ABOUT TO HIT THE GOOD PART, YOU ROTTEN CAT!
WOOF!
I WAS REALLY FEELIN' IT! WITH MY LITTLE OL' HEART!
SHE WOULDA LOVED IT!
I WAS FEELING IT, TOO. BUT IT WAS HEART-BURN.
MRAWR!
MRAWR!
PHEW.
THANK GOD.
SO.
WHAT ARE YOU, ANYWAY?
YOU'RE OBVI-OUSLY NOT FROM AROUND HERE.
HUH?
OH...
I CAME FROM ANOTHER WORLD?
YEAH, RIGHT.
HE WOULDN'T BELIEVE ME IF I TOLD HIM.

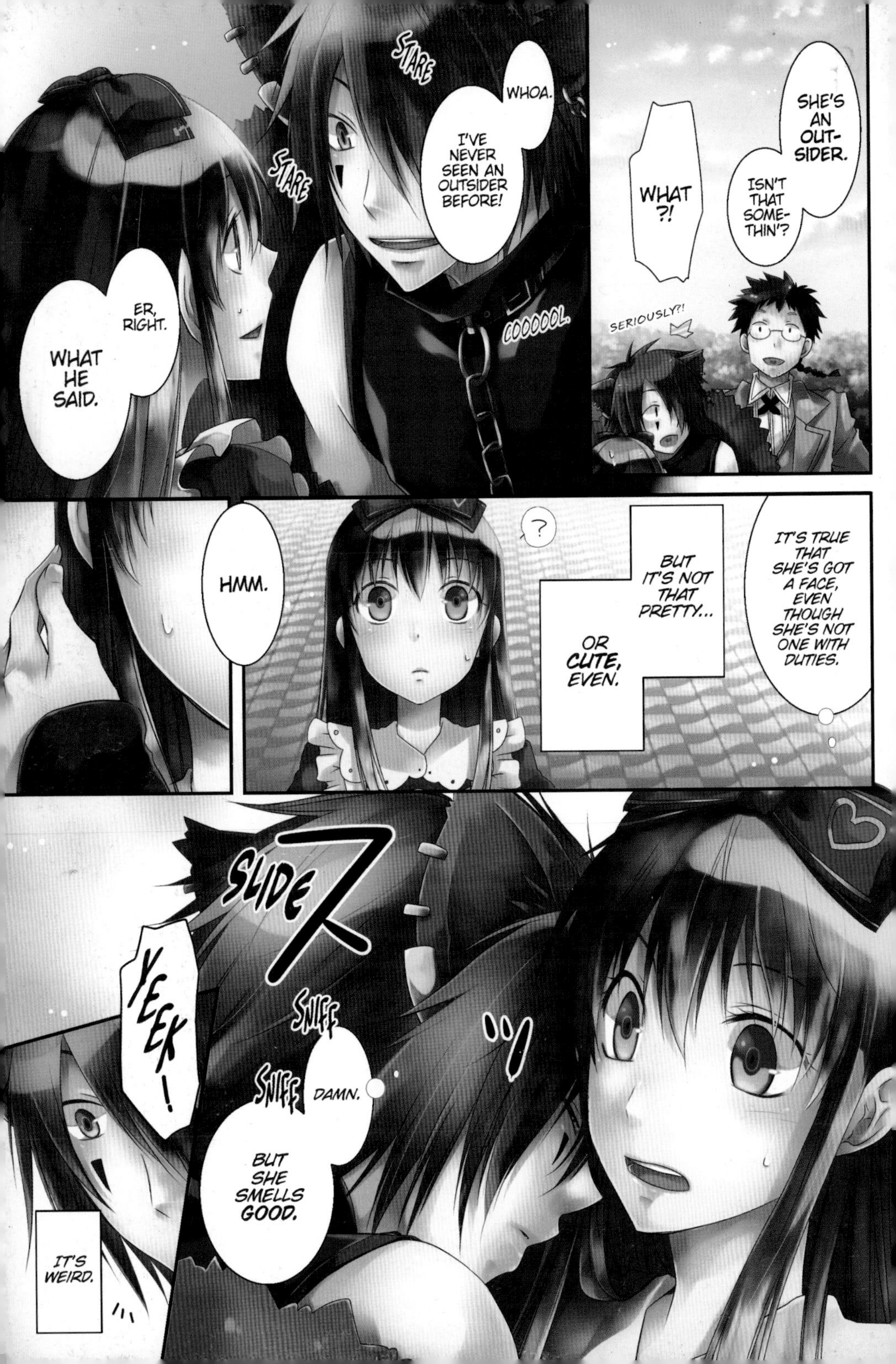
SHE'S AN OUT-SIDER.
ISN'T THAT SOME-THIN'?
WHAT ?!
SERIOUSLY?!
STARE
WHOA.
I'VE NEVER SEEN AN OUTSIDER BEFORE!
STARE
COOOOOL.
ER, RIGHT.
WHAT HE SAID.
IT'S TRUE THAT SHE'S GOT A FACE, EVEN THOUGH SHE'S NOT ONE WITH DUTIES.
BUT IT'S NOT THAT PRETTY...
OR CUTE, EVEN.
?
HMM.
SLIDE
SNIFF
SNIFF
DAMN.
BUT SHE SMELLS GOOD.
YEEK!
IT'S WEIRD.

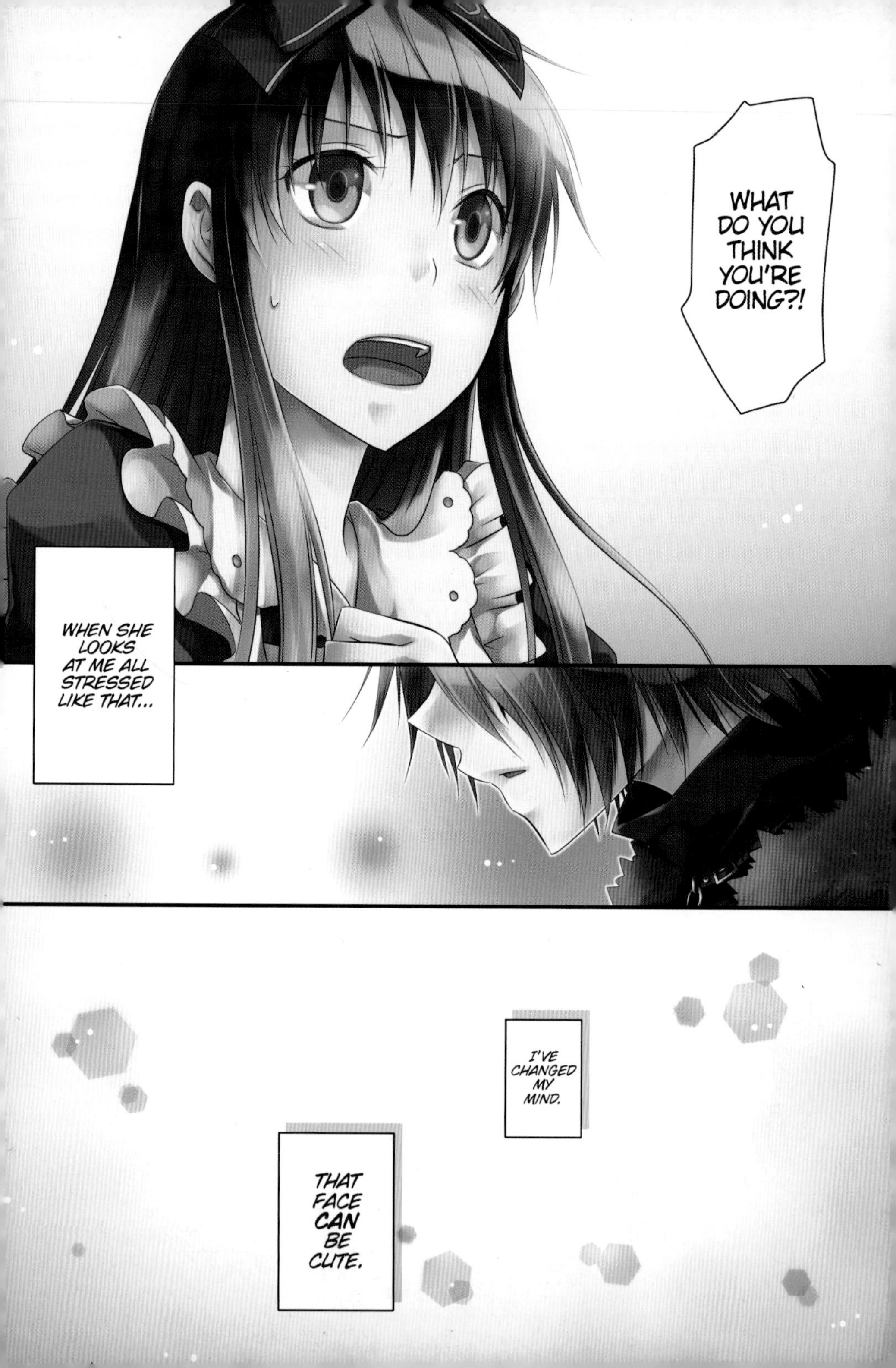
WHAT DO YOU THINK YOU'RE DOING?!
WHEN SHE LOOKS AT ME ALL STRESSED LIKE THAT...
I'VE CHANGED MY MIND.
THAT FACE CAN BE CUTE.

Alice in the Country of Clover
~Cheshire Cat Waltz~
1

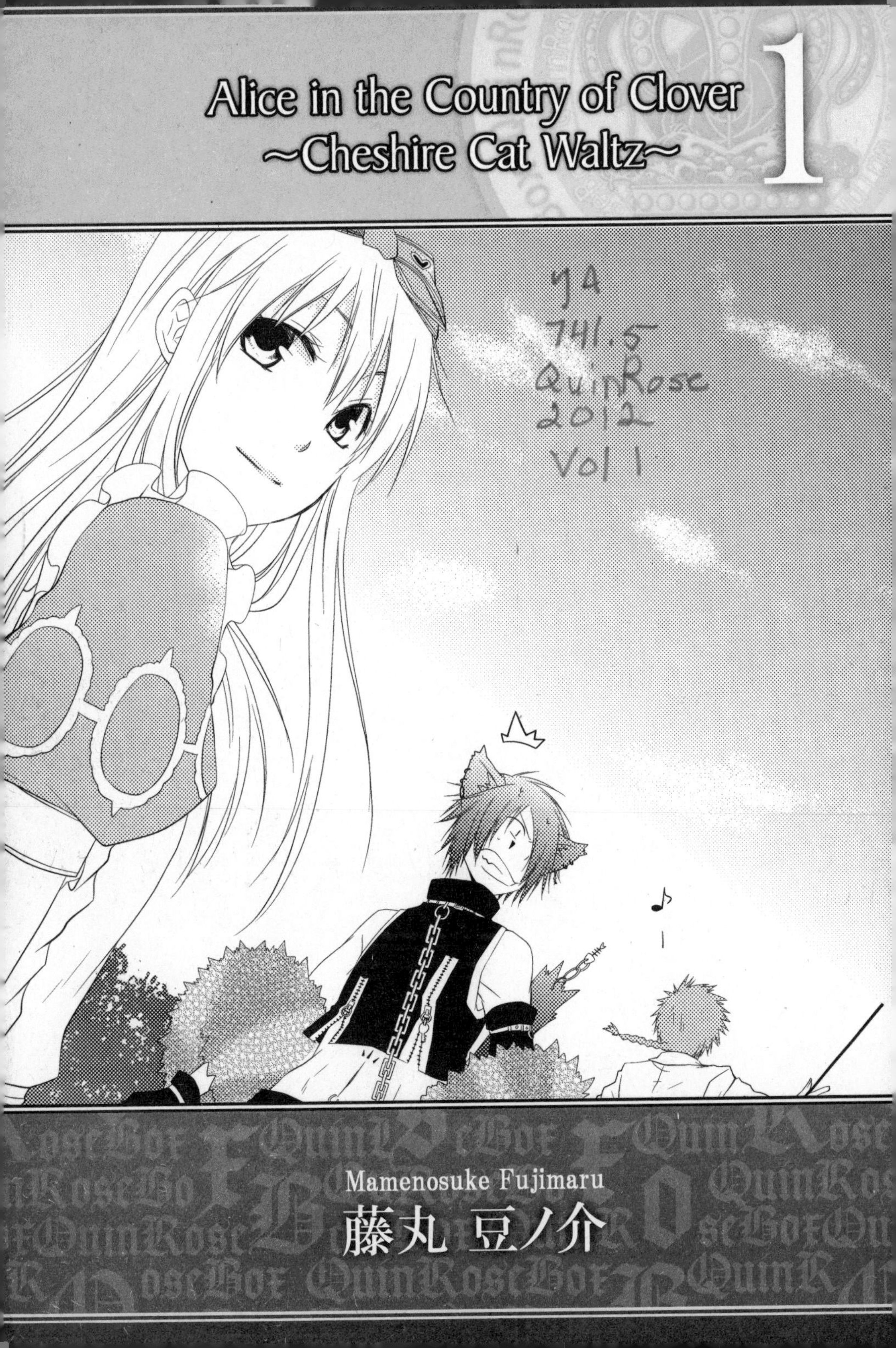

Mamenosuke Fujimaru
藤丸 豆ノ介

Alice IN THE COUNTRY OF Clover
CHESHIRE CAT WALTZ
VOLUME 1

story by **QuinRose**
art by **Mamenosuke Fujimaru**

STAFF CREDITS

translation **Angela Liu**
adaptation **Lianne Sentar**
lettering **Roland Amago**
layout **Bambi Eloriaga-Amago**
cover design **Nicky Lim**
copy editor **Shanti Whitesides**
editor **Adam Arnold**

publisher **Jason DeAngelis**
Seven Seas Entertainment

ALICE IN THE COUNTRY OF CLOVER: CHESHIRE CAT WALTZ VOL. 1
Copyright © Mamenosuke Fujimaru / QuinRose 2010
First published in Japan in 2010 by ICHIJINSHA Inc., Tokyo.
English translation rights arranged with ICHIJINSHA Inc., Tokyo, Japan.

ISBN: 978-1-935934-91-2

Printed in Canada

First Printing: July 2012

10 9 8 7 6 5

FOLLOW US ONLINE: *www.gomanga.com*

READING DIRECTIONS

This book reads from *right to left*, Japanese style.
If this is your first time reading manga, you start
reading from the top right panel on each page and
take it from there. If you get lost, just follow the
numbered diagram here. It may seem backwards
at first, but you'll get the hang of it! Have fun!!

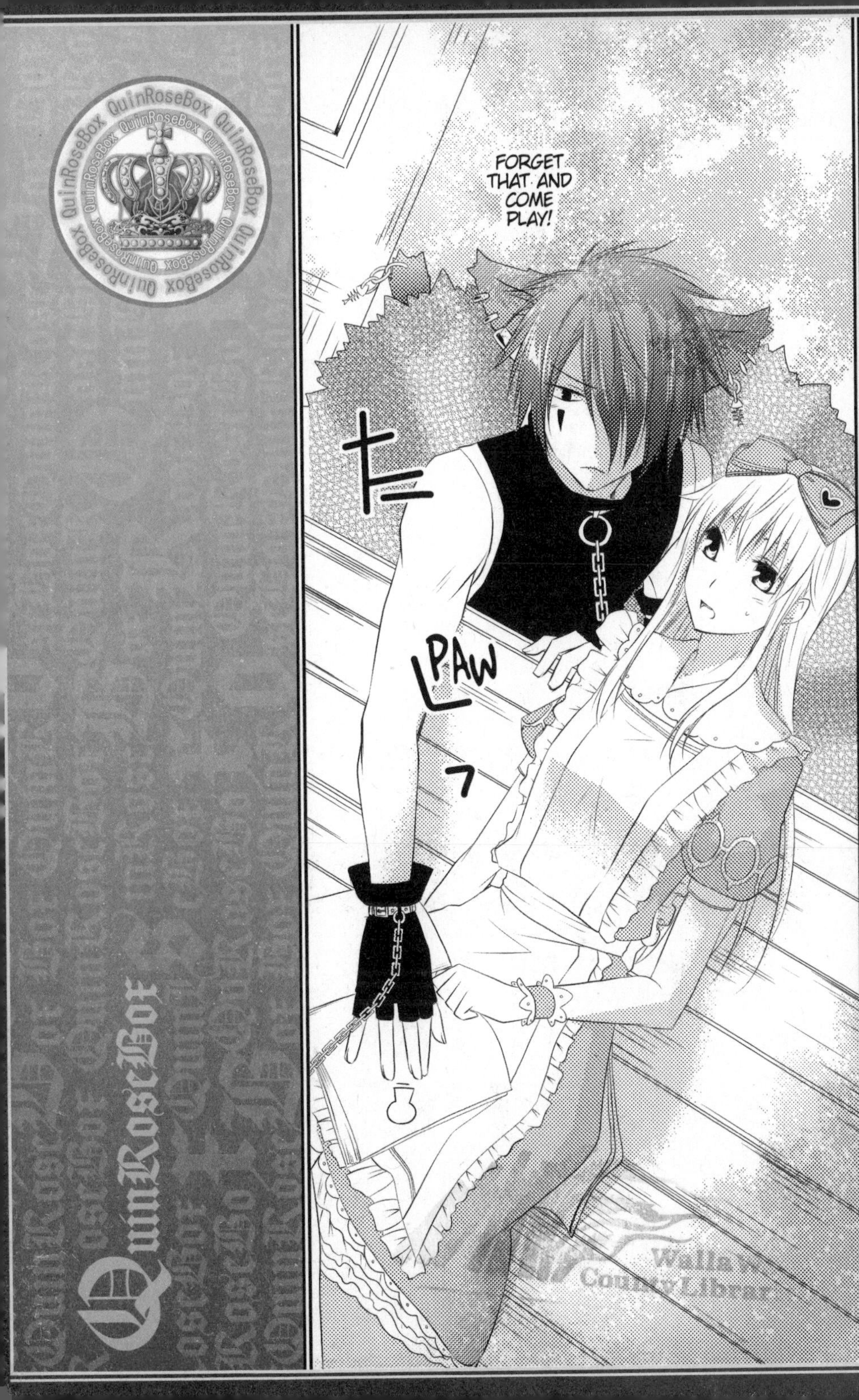
FORGET THAT AND COME PLAY!
PAW

Alice in the Country of Clover

クローバーの国の

アリス

~Wonderful Wonder World~

- STORY -

In *Alice in the Country of Clover*, the game starts with Alice having not fallen in love,
but still deciding to stay in Wonderland.

She's acquainted with all the characters from the previous game, *Alice in the Country of Hearts*.

Since love would now start from a place of friendship rather than passion with a new stranger, she can experi-
ence a different type of romance from that in the previous game. Her dynamic with the characters is different
through this friendship—characters can't always be forceful with her, and in many ways it's more comfortable
to grow intimate. The relationships *between* the Ones With Duties have also become more of a factor.

In this game, the story focuses on the mafia. Alice attends the suited meetings (forcefully) and gets involved in
various gunfights (forcefully), among other things.

Land fluctuations, sea creatures in the forest, and whispering doors—it's a game more fantastic and more
eerie than the first.

Will our everywoman Alice be able to have a romantic relationship in a world devoid of common sense?

Alice in the Country of Clover Character Information

Elliot March
VA: Tsuguo Mogami

Blood's right-hand man has a criminal past... and a temperamental present. But he's not as bad as he used to be, so that's something. Joining Blood has been good(?) for him.

Blood Dupre
VA: Katsuyuki Konishi

The head of the mafia Hatter Family, Blood is a cunning yet moody puppet-master. Alice now has the pleasure of having him for a landlord.

Alice Liddell
VA: Rie Kugimiya

A normal girl with a bit of a chip on her shoulder. Deciding to stay in the Wonderland she was carried to, she's adapted to her strange new lifestyle.

Vivaldi
VA: Yuuko Kaida

The beautiful Queen of Hearts has an unrivaled temper—which is really saying something in Wonderland. Although a picture-perfect Mad Queen, she cares for Alice as if Alice were her little sister...or a very interesting plaything.

Tweedle Dum
VA: Jun Fukuyama

The second "Bloody Twin" is equally cute and equally scary. In *Clover*, Dum can also turn into an adult.

Tweedle Dee
VA: Jun Fukuyama

One of the "Bloody Twin" gatekeepers of the Hatter territory, Dee can be cute when he's not being terrifying. In *Clover*, he sometimes turns into an adult.

Boris Airay
VA: Noriaki Sugiyama

This riddle-loving cat has a signature smirk—and in *Clover*, a new toy. One of his favorite pastimes is giving the Sleepy Mouse a hard time.

Ace
VA: Daisuke Hirakawa

The unlucky knight of Hearts was a former subordinate of Vivaldi and is perpetually lost. Even though he's depressed to be separated from his friend and boss Julius, he stays positive and tries to overcome it with a smile. He seems like a classic nice guy... or is he?

Peter White
VA: Kouki Miyata

The Prime Minister of Heart Castle—who has rabbit ears growing out of his head—invited (kidnapped) Alice to Wonderland. He loves Alice and hates everything else. His cruel, irrational actions are disturbing, but he acts like a completely different person (rabbit?) when in the throes of his love for Alice.

Gray Ringmarc
VA: Kazuya Nakai

Nightmare's subordinate in *Clover*. He used to have strong social ambition and considered assassinating Nightmare... but since Nightmare was such a useless boss, Gray couldn't help but feel sorry for him and ended up a dedicated assistant. He's a sound thinker with a strong work ethic. He's also highly skilled with his blades, rivaling even Ace.

Nightmare Gottschalk
VA: Tomokazu Sugita

A sickly nightmare who hates the hospital and needles. He has the power to read people's thoughts and enter dreams. Even though he likes to shut himself away in dreams, Gray drags him out to sulk from time to time. He technically holds a high position and has many subordinates, but since he can't even take care of his own health, he leaves most things to Gray.

Pierce Villiers
VA: Souichirou Hoshi

New to *Clover*, Pierce is an insomniac mouse who drinks too much coffee. He loves Nightmare (who can help him sleep) and hates Boris (who terrifies him). He dislikes Blood and Vivaldi for discarding coffee in favor of tea. He likes Elliot and Peter well enough, since rabbits aren't natural predators of mice.

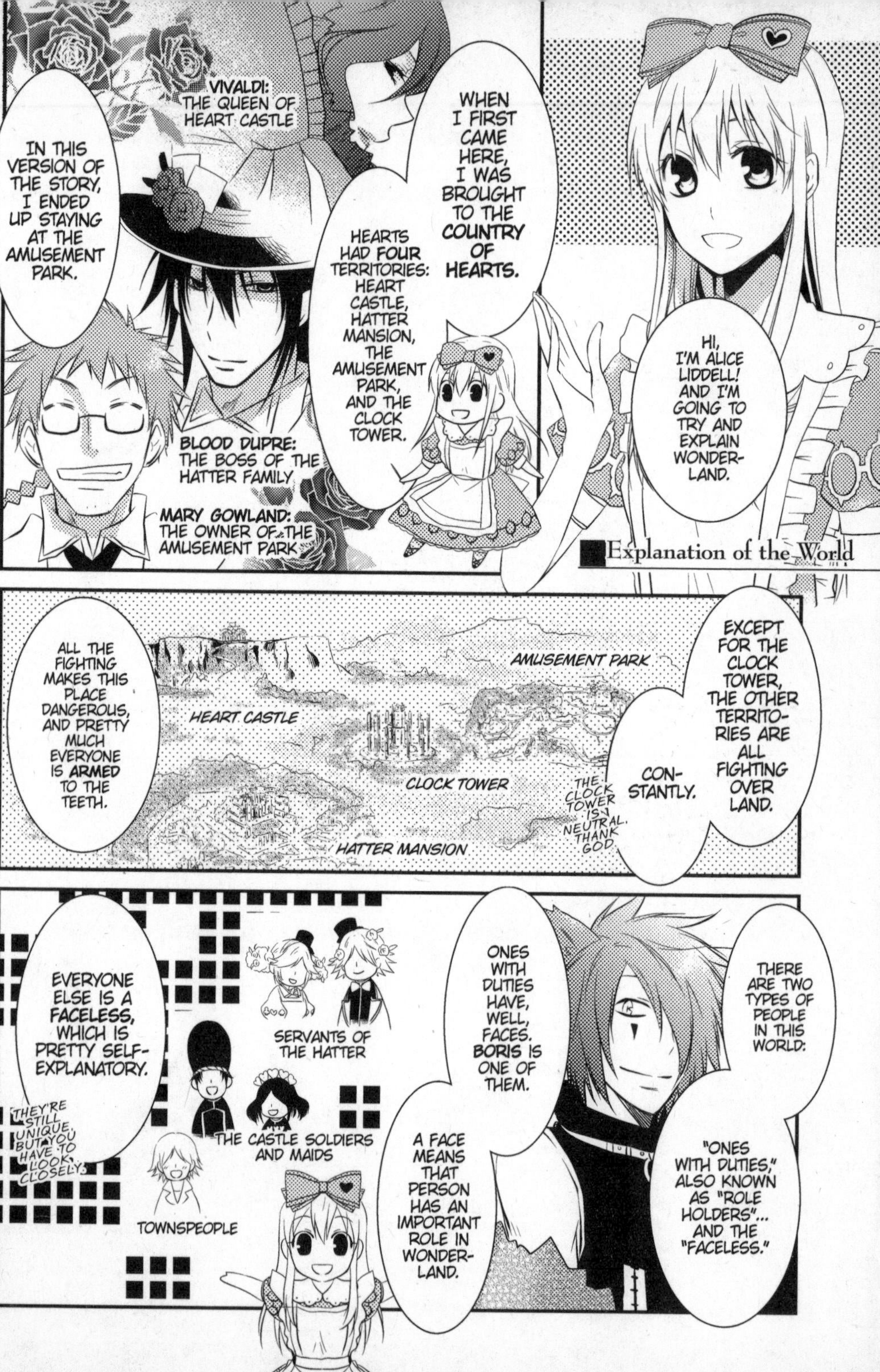
Explanation of the World
HI, I'M ALICE LIDDELL! AND I'M GOING TO TRY AND EXPLAIN WONDERLAND.
WHEN I FIRST CAME HERE, I WAS BROUGHT TO THE COUNTRY OF HEARTS.
HEARTS HAD FOUR TERRITORIES: HEART CASTLE, HATTER MANSION, THE AMUSEMENT PARK, AND THE CLOCK TOWER.
VIVALDI: THE QUEEN OF HEART CASTLE
IN THIS VERSION OF THE STORY, I ENDED UP STAYING AT THE AMUSEMENT PARK.
BLOOD DUPRE: THE BOSS OF THE HATTER FAMILY
MARY GOWLAND: THE OWNER OF THE AMUSEMENT PARK
EXCEPT FOR THE CLOCK TOWER, THE OTHER TERRITORIES ARE ALL FIGHTING OVER LAND.
CON-STANTLY.
THE CLOCK TOWER IS NEUTRAL, THANK GOD.
AMUSEMENT PARK
HEART CASTLE
CLOCK TOWER
HATTER MANSION
ALL THE FIGHTING MAKES THIS PLACE DANGEROUS, AND PRETTY MUCH EVERYONE IS ARMED TO THE TEETH.
THERE ARE TWO TYPES OF PEOPLE IN THIS WORLD:
"ONES WITH DUTIES," ALSO KNOWN AS "ROLE HOLDERS"... AND THE "FACELESS."
ONES WITH DUTIES HAVE, WELL, FACES. BORIS IS ONE OF THEM.
A FACE MEANS THAT PERSON HAS AN IMPORTANT ROLE IN WONDER-LAND.
EVERYONE ELSE IS A FACELESS, WHICH IS PRETTY SELF-EXPLANATORY.
SERVANTS OF THE HATTER
THE CASTLE SOLDIERS AND MAIDS
TOWNSPEOPLE
THEY'RE STILL UNIQUE, BUT YOU HAVE TO LOOK CLOSELY.

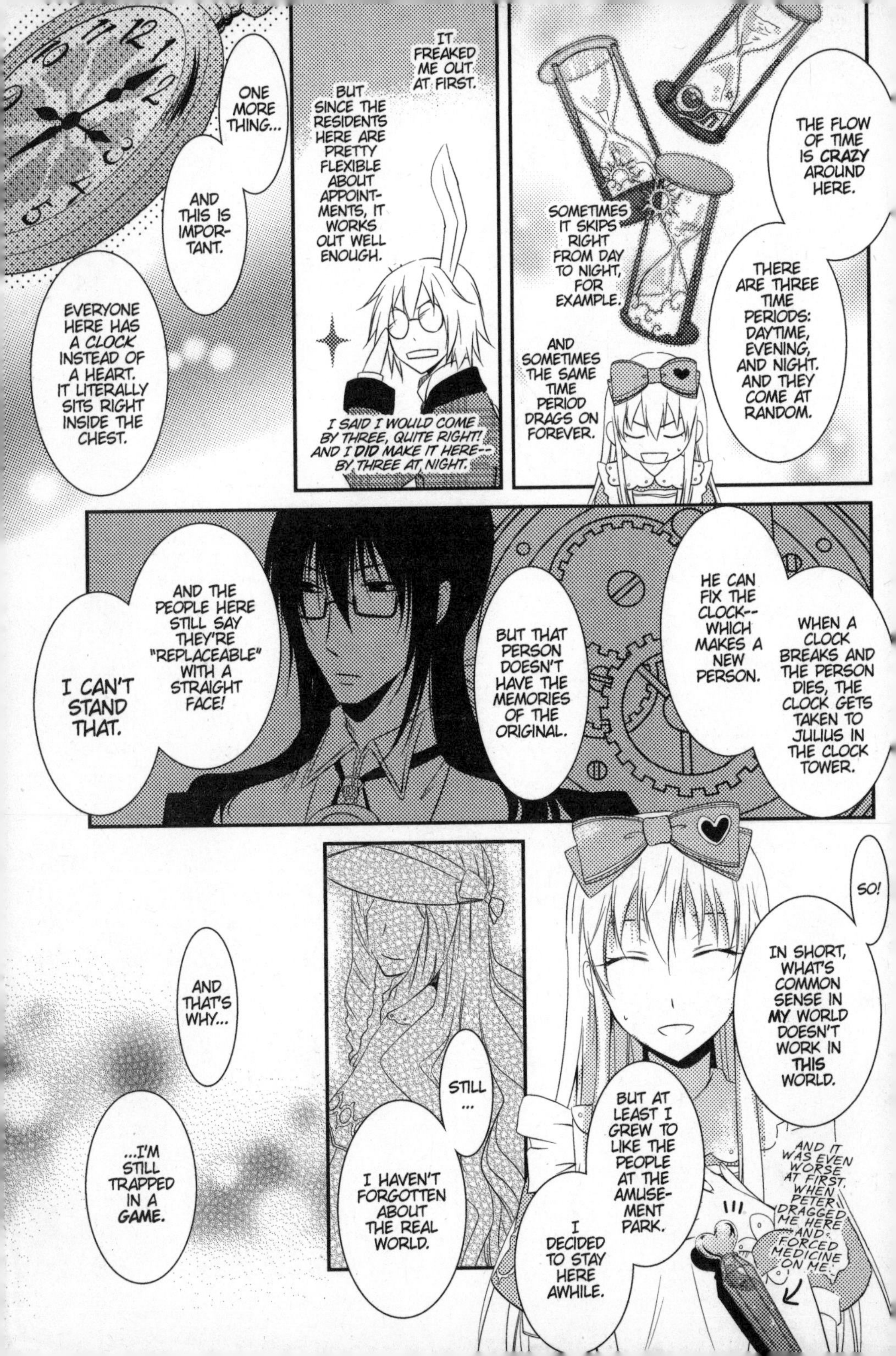
THE FLOW OF TIME IS **CRAZY** AROUND HERE.
SOMETIMES IT SKIPS RIGHT FROM DAY TO NIGHT, FOR EXAMPLE.
THERE ARE THREE TIME PERIODS: DAYTIME, EVENING, AND NIGHT. AND THEY COME AT RANDOM.
AND SOMETIMES THE SAME TIME PERIOD DRAGS ON FOREVER.
IT FREAKED ME OUT AT FIRST.
BUT SINCE THE RESIDENTS HERE ARE PRETTY FLEXIBLE ABOUT APPOINT-MENTS, IT WORKS OUT WELL ENOUGH.
*I SAID I WOULD COME BY THREE, QUITE RIGHT! AND I **DID** MAKE IT HERE-- BY THREE AT NIGHT.*
ONE MORE THING...
AND THIS IS IMPOR-TANT.
EVERYONE HERE HAS A *CLOCK* INSTEAD OF A HEART. IT LITERALLY SITS RIGHT INSIDE THE CHEST.
WHEN A CLOCK BREAKS AND THE PERSON DIES, THE CLOCK GETS TAKEN TO JULIUS IN THE CLOCK TOWER.
HE CAN FIX THE CLOCK-- WHICH MAKES A NEW PERSON.
BUT THAT PERSON DOESN'T HAVE THE MEMORIES OF THE ORIGINAL.
AND THE PEOPLE HERE STILL SAY THEY'RE "REPLACEABLE" WITH A STRAIGHT FACE!
I CAN'T STAND THAT.
SO!
IN SHORT, WHAT'S COMMON SENSE IN **MY** WORLD DOESN'T WORK IN **THIS** WORLD.
BUT AT LEAST I GREW TO LIKE THE PEOPLE AT THE AMUSE-MENT PARK.
AND IT WAS EVEN WORSE AT FIRST, WHEN PETER DRAGGED ME HERE AND FORCED MEDICINE ON ME.
I DECIDED TO STAY HERE AWHILE.
STILL ...
I HAVEN'T FORGOTTEN ABOUT THE REAL WORLD.
AND THAT'S WHY...
...I'M STILL TRAPPED IN A **GAME**.

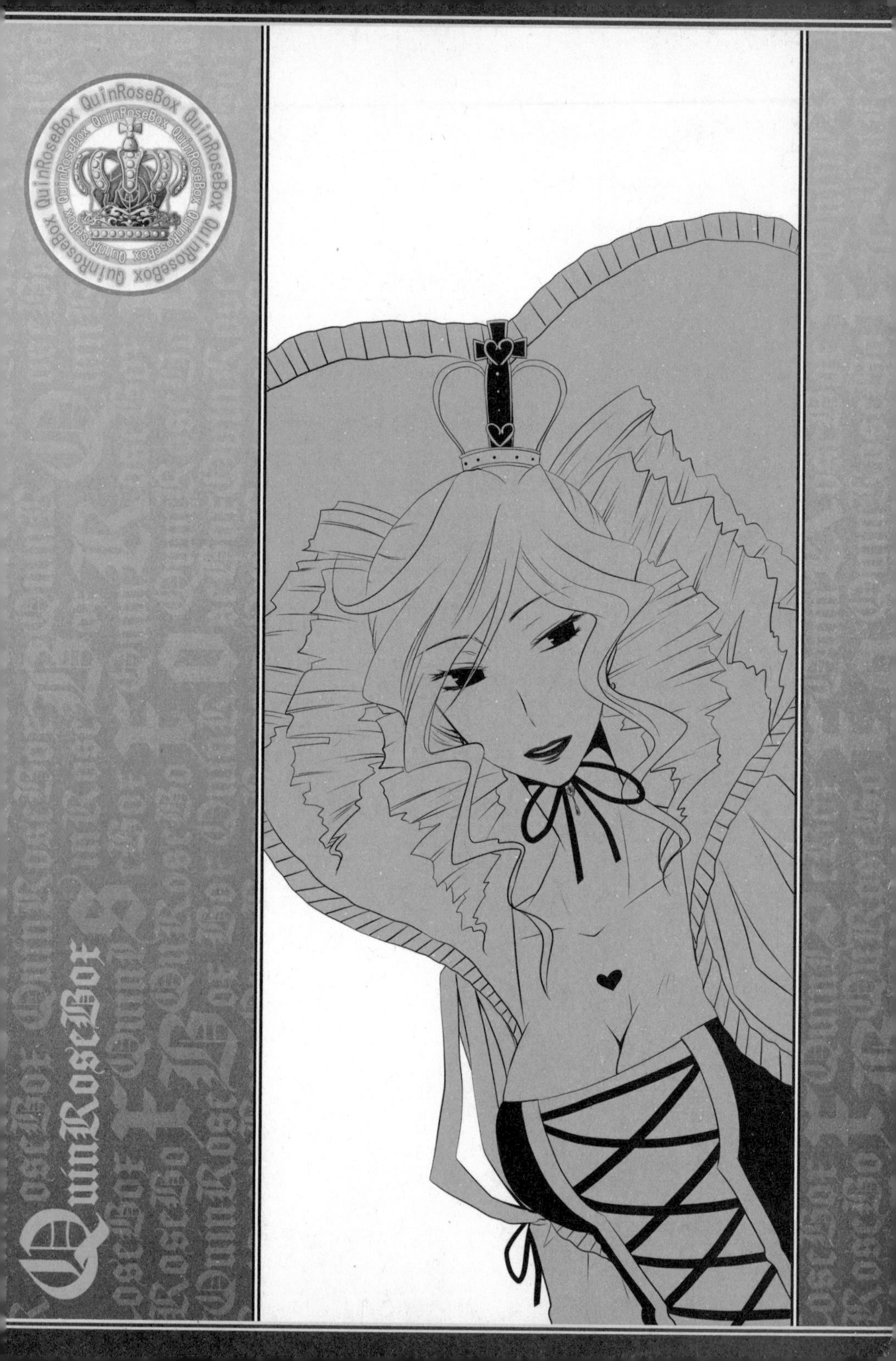
QuinRoseBox

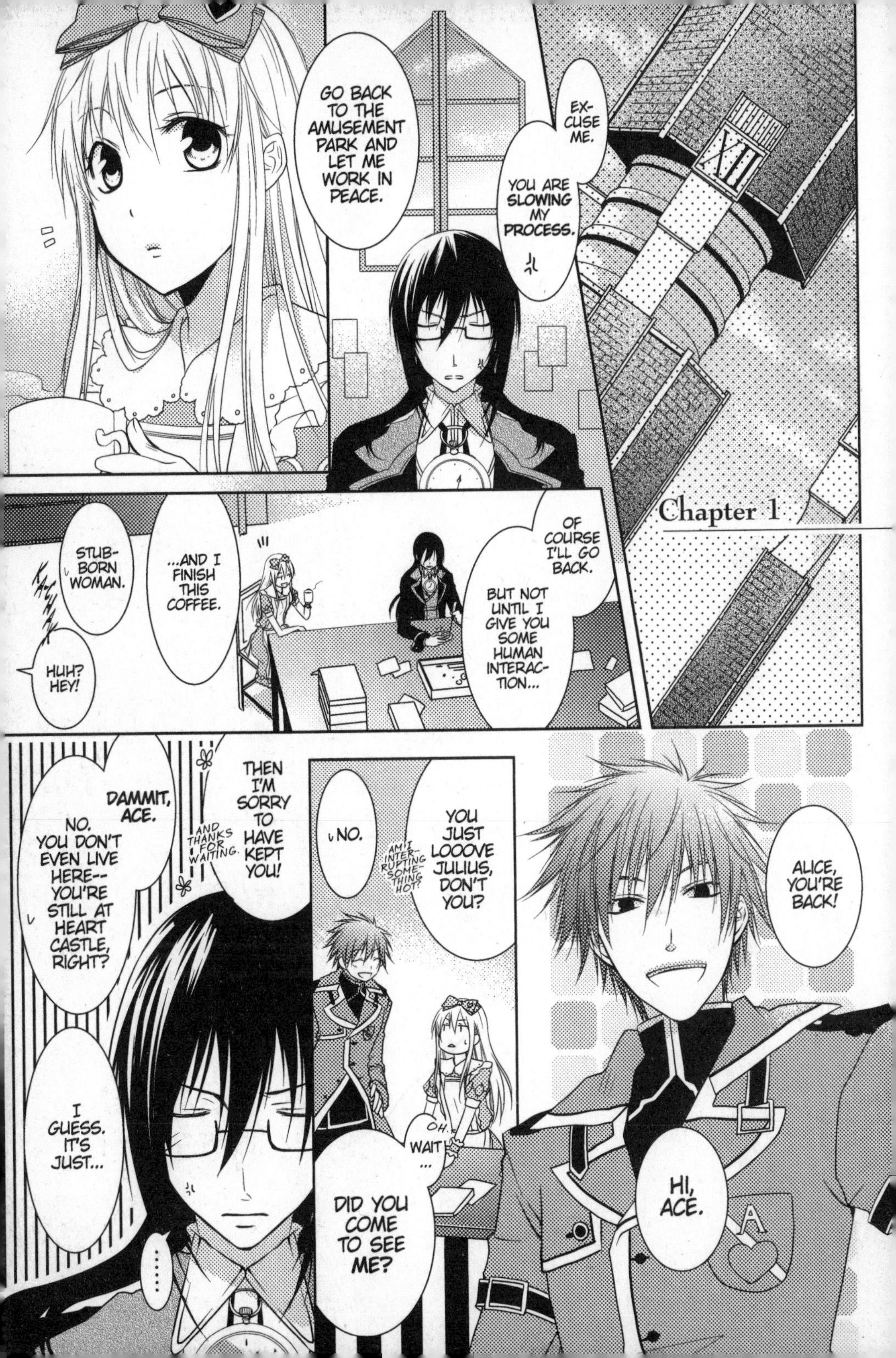
Chapter 1
EX-CUSE ME.
YOU ARE SLOWING MY PROCESS.
GO BACK TO THE AMUSEMENT PARK AND LET ME WORK IN PEACE.
OF COURSE I'LL GO BACK.
BUT NOT UNTIL I GIVE YOU SOME HUMAN INTERAC-TION...
...AND I FINISH THIS COFFEE.
STUB-BORN WOMAN.
KA-CHAK
HUH? HEY!
ALICE, YOU'RE BACK!
HI, ACE.
YOU JUST LOOOVE JULIUS, DON'T YOU?
AM I INTER-RUPTING SOME-THING HOT?
NO.
OH. WAIT...
DID YOU COME TO SEE ME?
THEN I'M SORRY TO HAVE KEPT YOU!
AND THANKS FOR WAITING.
DAMMIT, ACE.
NO. YOU DON'T EVEN LIVE HERE-- YOU'RE STILL AT HEART CASTLE, RIGHT?
I GUESS. IT'S JUST...
......

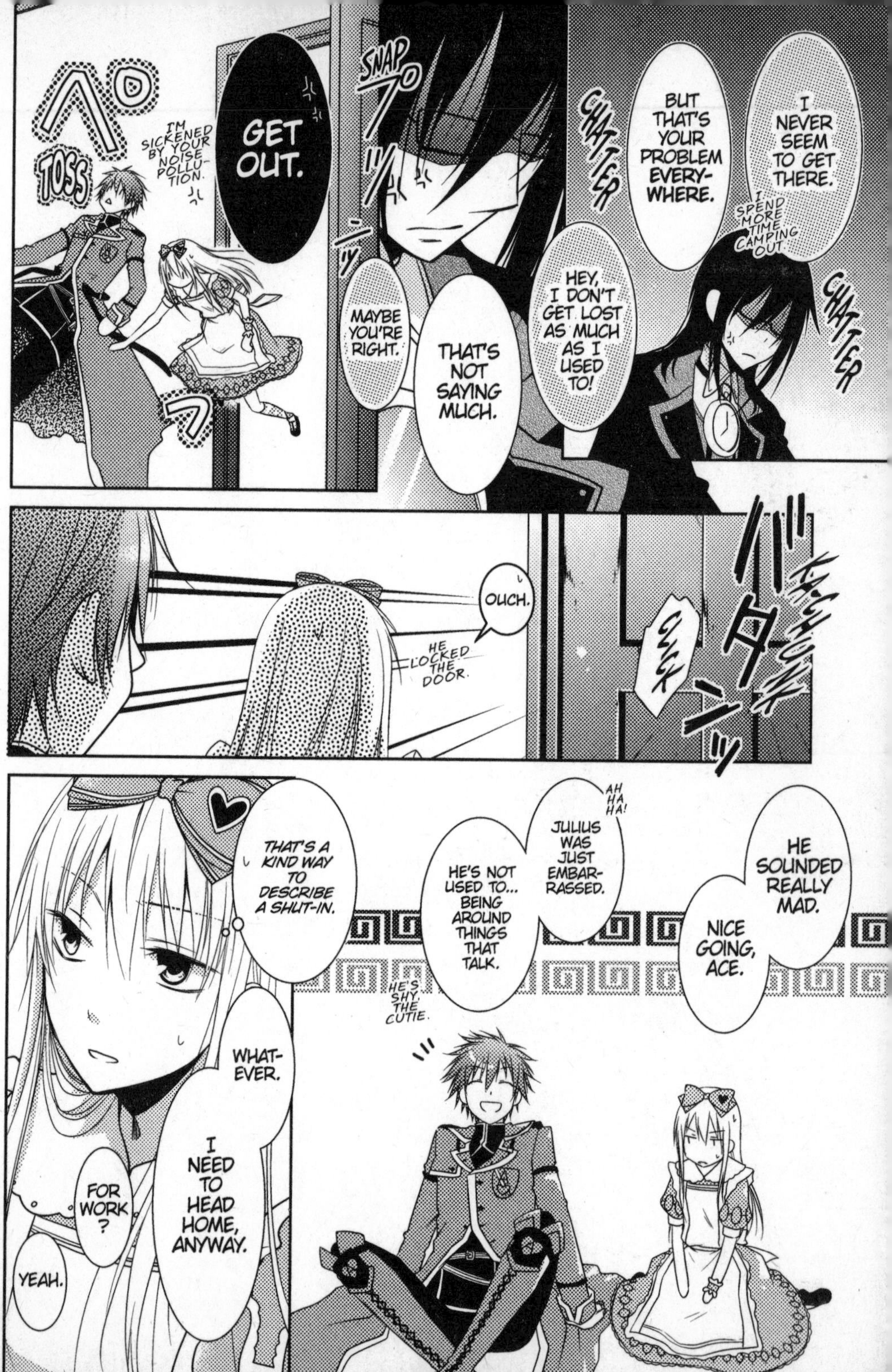
I NEVER SEEM TO GET THERE.
I SPEND MORE TIME CAMPING OUT.
BUT THAT'S YOUR PROBLEM EVERYWHERE.
CHATTER
CHATTER
HEY, I DON'T GET LOST AS MUCH AS I USED TO!
THAT'S NOT SAYING MUCH.
MAYBE YOU'RE RIGHT.
SNAP
GET OUT.
I'M SICKENED BY YOUR NOISE POLLUTION.
TOSS
KACHUNK
CLICK
OUCH.
HE LOCKED THE DOOR.
HE SOUNDED REALLY MAD.
NICE GOING, ACE.
AH HA HA!
JULIUS WAS JUST EMBARRASSED.
HE'S NOT USED TO... BEING AROUND THINGS THAT TALK.
HE'S SHY, THE CUTIE.
THAT'S A KIND WAY TO DESCRIBE A SHUT-IN.
WHATEVER.
I NEED TO HEAD HOME, ANYWAY.
FOR WORK?
YEAH.

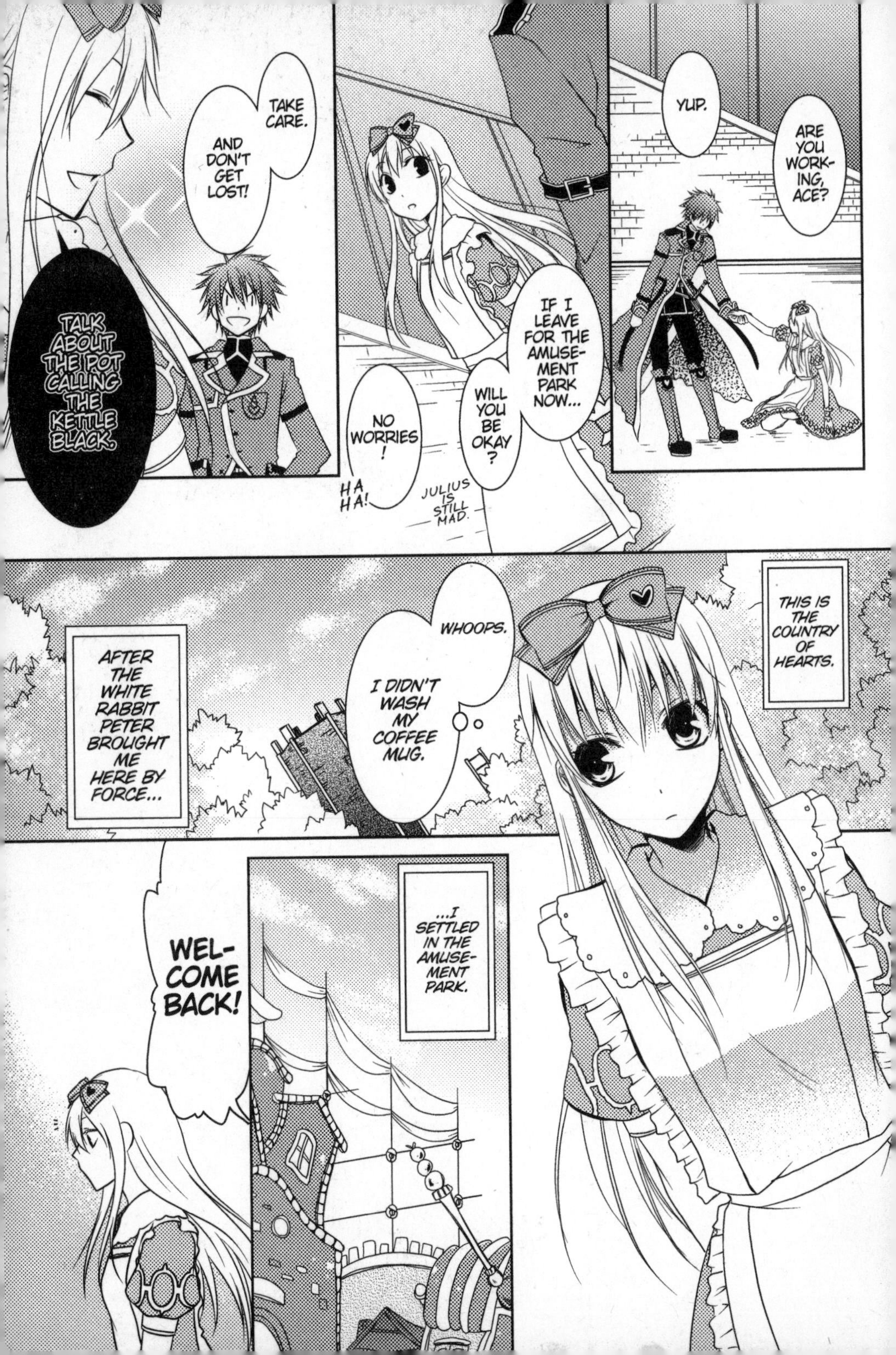
ARE YOU WORKING, ACE?
YUP.
IF I LEAVE FOR THE AMUSEMENT PARK NOW...
WILL YOU BE OKAY?
NO WORRIES!
HA HA!
JULIUS IS STILL MAD.
TAKE CARE.
AND DON'T GET LOST!
TALK ABOUT THE POT CALLING THE KETTLE BLACK.
THIS IS THE COUNTRY OF HEARTS.
WHOOPS.
I DIDN'T WASH MY COFFEE MUG.
AFTER THE WHITE RABBIT PETER BROUGHT ME HERE BY FORCE...
...I SETTLED IN THE AMUSEMENT PARK.
WELCOME BACK!

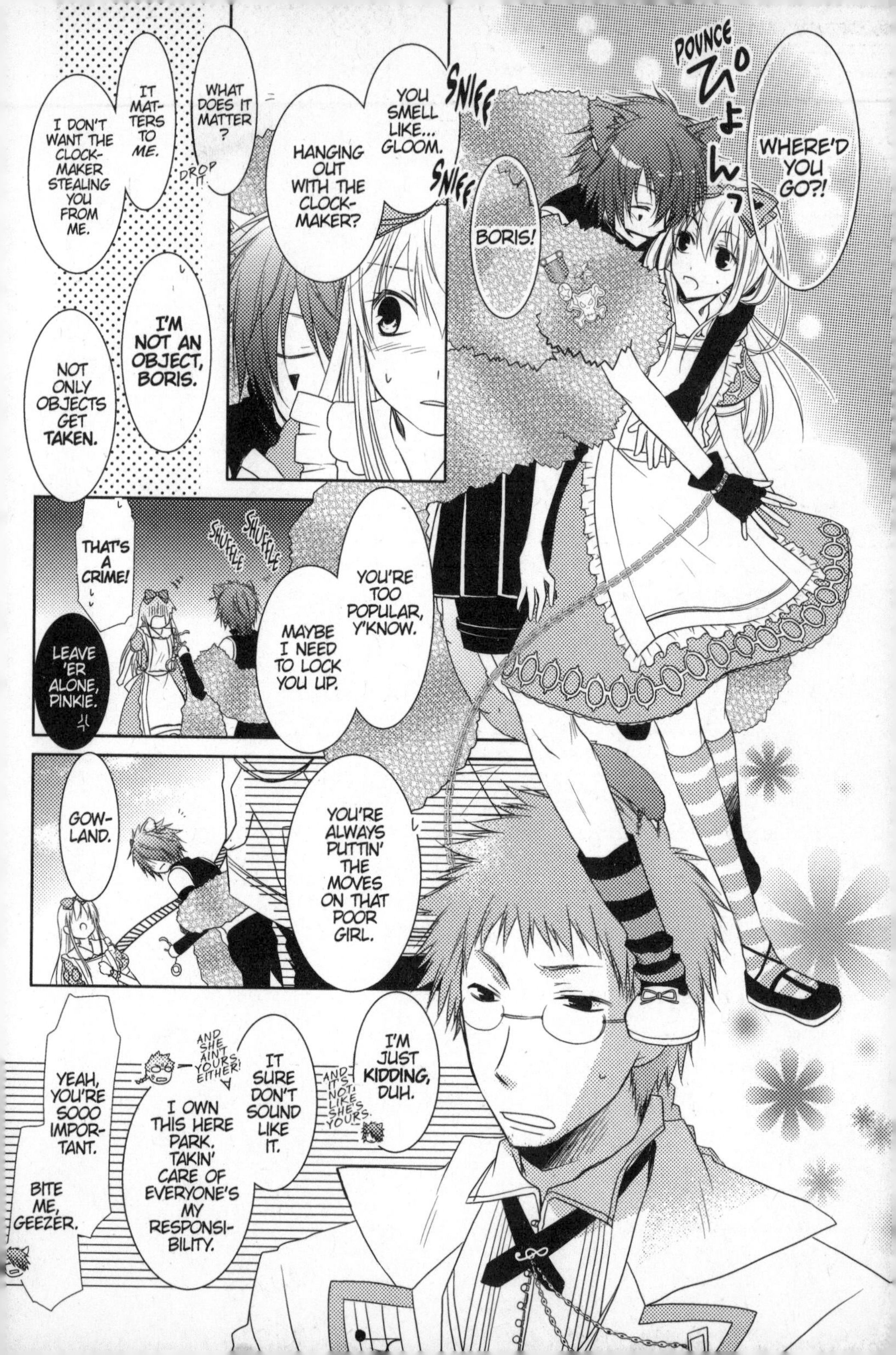
POUNCE
ぴょんっ
WHERE'D YOU GO?!
BORIS!
SNIFF
SNIFF
YOU SMELL LIKE... GLOOM.
HANGING OUT WITH THE CLOCK-MAKER?
WHAT DOES IT MATTER?
DROP IT.
IT MAT-TERS TO ME.
I DON'T WANT THE CLOCK-MAKER STEALING YOU FROM ME.
I'M NOT AN OBJECT, BORIS.
NOT ONLY OBJECTS GET TAKEN.
YOU'RE TOO POPULAR, Y'KNOW.
MAYBE I NEED TO LOCK YOU UP.
SHUFFLE
SHUFFLE
THAT'S A CRIME!
LEAVE 'ER ALONE, PINKIE.
YOU'RE ALWAYS PUTTIN' THE MOVES ON THAT POOR GIRL.
GOW-LAND.
I'M JUST KIDDING, DUH.
AND IT'S NOT LIKE SHE'S YOURS.
IT SURE DON'T SOUND LIKE IT.
I OWN THIS HERE PARK. TAKIN' CARE OF EVERYONE'S MY RESPONSI-BILITY.
AND SHE AINT YOURS, EITHER!
YEAH, YOU'RE SOOO IMPOR-TANT.
BITE ME, GEEZER.

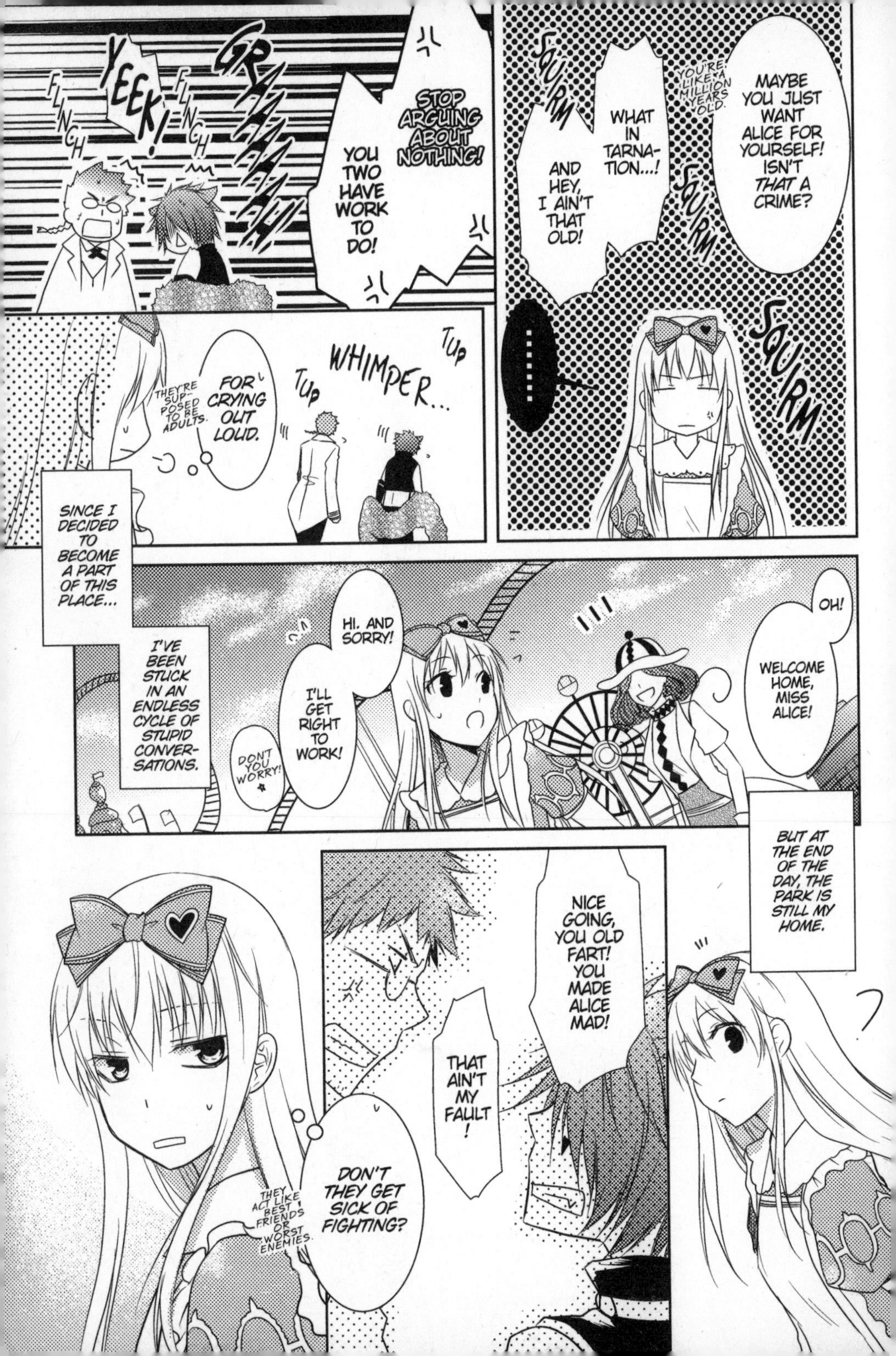
MAYBE YOU JUST WANT ALICE FOR YOURSELF! ISN'T THAT A CRIME?
YOU'RE LIKE A MILLION YEARS OLD.
SQUIRM
SQUIRM
WHAT IN TARNATION...!
AND HEY, I AIN'T THAT OLD!
SQUIRM
......
STOP ARGUING ABOUT NOTHING!
YOU TWO HAVE WORK TO DO!
GRAAAAAAH!
FLINCH
YEEK!
FLINCH
TUP
WHIMPER...
TUP
FOR CRYING OUT LOUD.
THEY'RE SUPPOSED TO BE ADULTS.
SINCE I DECIDED TO BECOME A PART OF THIS PLACE...
OH!
WELCOME HOME, MISS ALICE!
HI. AND SORRY!
I'LL GET RIGHT TO WORK!
DON'T YOU WORRY!
I'VE BEEN STUCK IN AN ENDLESS CYCLE OF STUPID CONVERSATIONS.
BUT AT THE END OF THE DAY, THE PARK IS STILL MY HOME.
NICE GOING, YOU OLD FART! YOU MADE ALICE MAD!
THAT AIN'T MY FAULT!
DON'T THEY GET SICK OF FIGHTING?
THEY ACT LIKE BEST FRIENDS OR WORST ENEMIES.

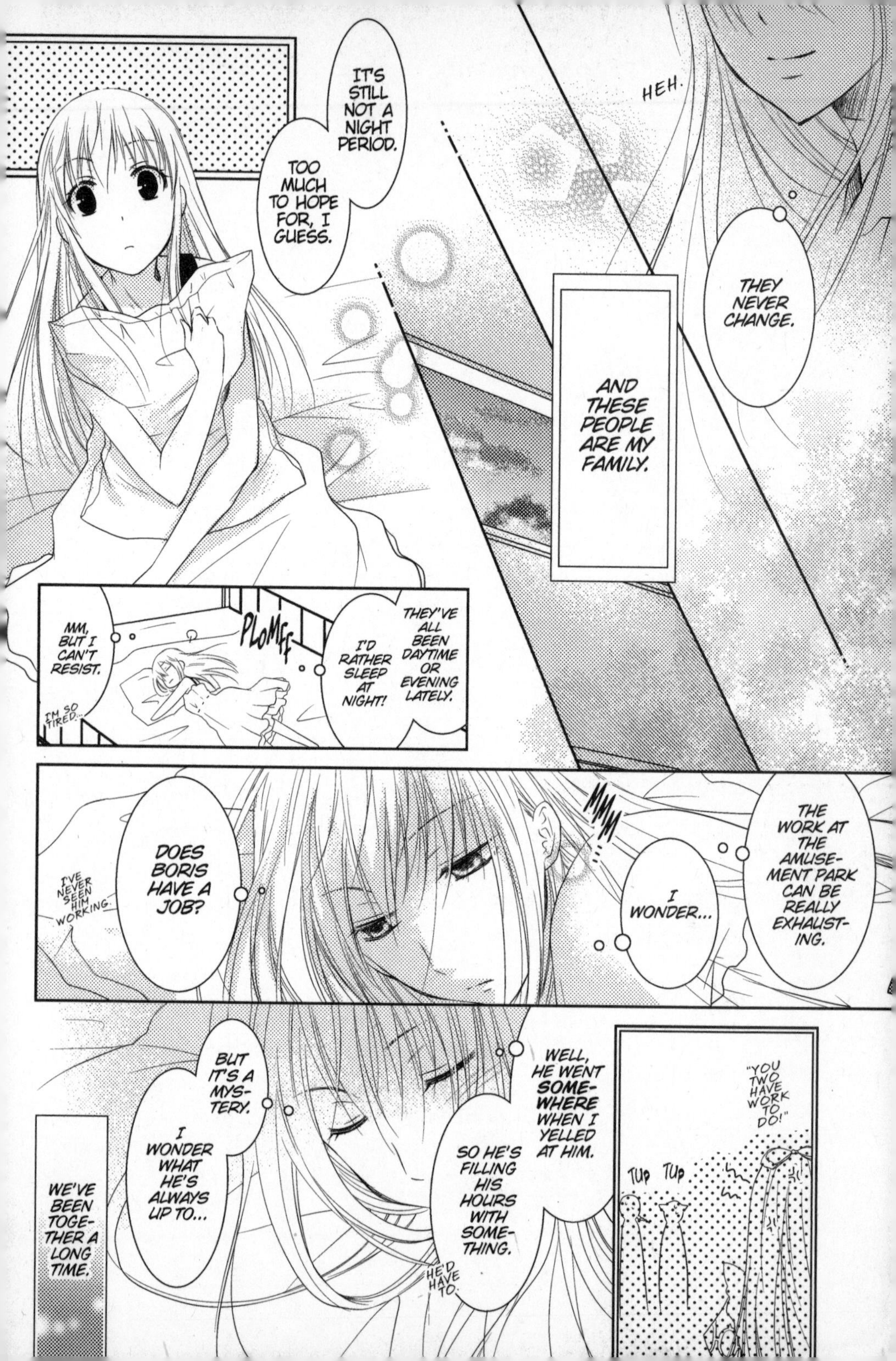
HEH.
THEY NEVER CHANGE.
AND THESE PEOPLE ARE MY FAMILY.
IT'S STILL NOT A NIGHT PERIOD.
TOO MUCH TO HOPE FOR, I GUESS.
THEY'VE ALL BEEN DAYTIME OR EVENING LATELY.
I'D RATHER SLEEP AT NIGHT!
PLOMFF
MM, BUT I CAN'T RESIST.
I'M SO TIRED...
MMM...
THE WORK AT THE AMUSEMENT PARK CAN BE REALLY EXHAUSTING.
I WONDER...
DOES BORIS HAVE A JOB?
I'VE NEVER SEEN HIM WORKING.
"YOU TWO HAVE WORK TO DO!"
TUP TUP
WELL, HE WENT SOMEWHERE WHEN I YELLED AT HIM.
SO HE'S FILLING HIS HOURS WITH SOMETHING.
HE'D HAVE TO.
BUT IT'S A MYSTERY.
I WONDER WHAT HE'S ALWAYS UP TO...
WE'VE BEEN TOGETHER A LONG TIME.

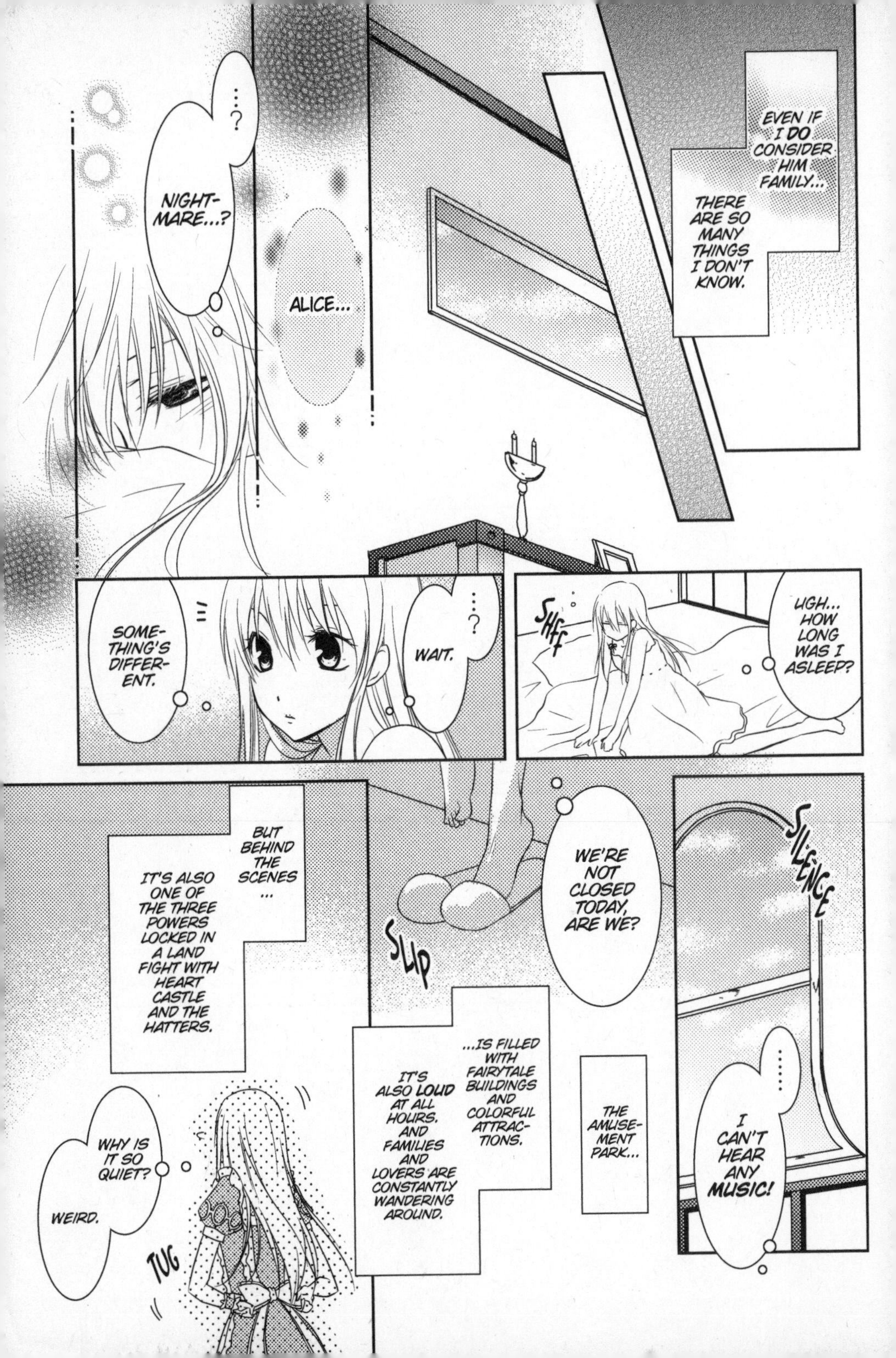
EVEN IF I DO CONSIDER HIM FAMILY...
THERE ARE SO MANY THINGS I DON'T KNOW.
ALICE...
...?
NIGHT-MARE...?
SHFF
UGH... HOW LONG WAS I ASLEEP?
...?
WAIT.
SOME-THING'S DIFFER-ENT.
SILENCE
......
I CAN'T HEAR ANY MUSIC!
WE'RE NOT CLOSED TODAY, ARE WE?
SLIP
THE AMUSE-MENT PARK...
...IS FILLED WITH FAIRYTALE BUILDINGS AND COLORFUL ATTRAC-TIONS.
IT'S ALSO LOUD AT ALL HOURS. AND FAMILIES AND LOVERS ARE CONSTANTLY WANDERING AROUND.
BUT BEHIND THE SCENES...
IT'S ALSO ONE OF THE THREE POWERS LOCKED IN A LAND FIGHT WITH HEART CASTLE AND THE HATTERS.
WHY IS IT SO QUIET?
WEIRD.
TUG

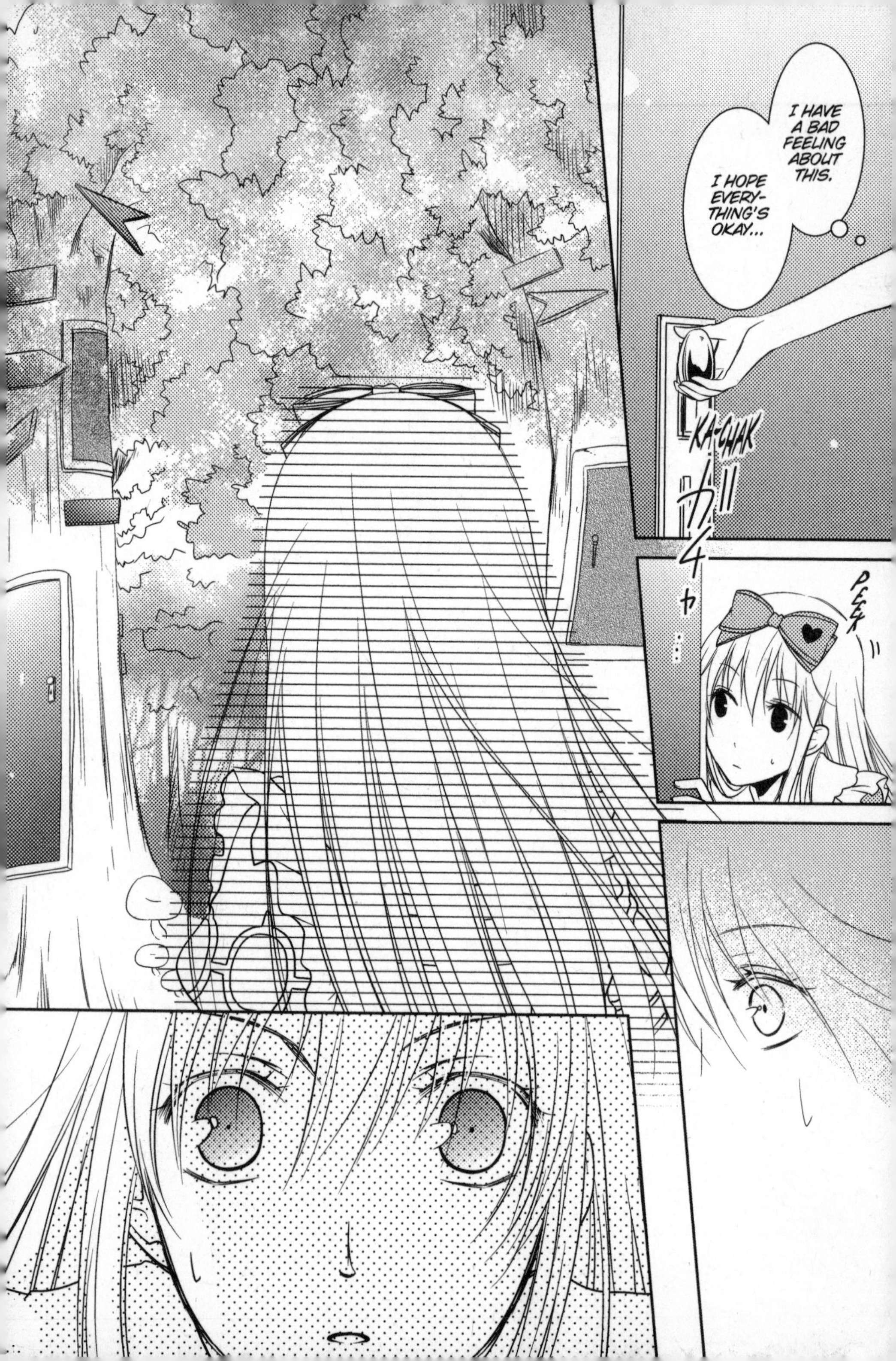
I HAVE A BAD FEELING ABOUT THIS.
I HOPE EVERY-THING'S OKAY...
KA-CHAK
PEEK

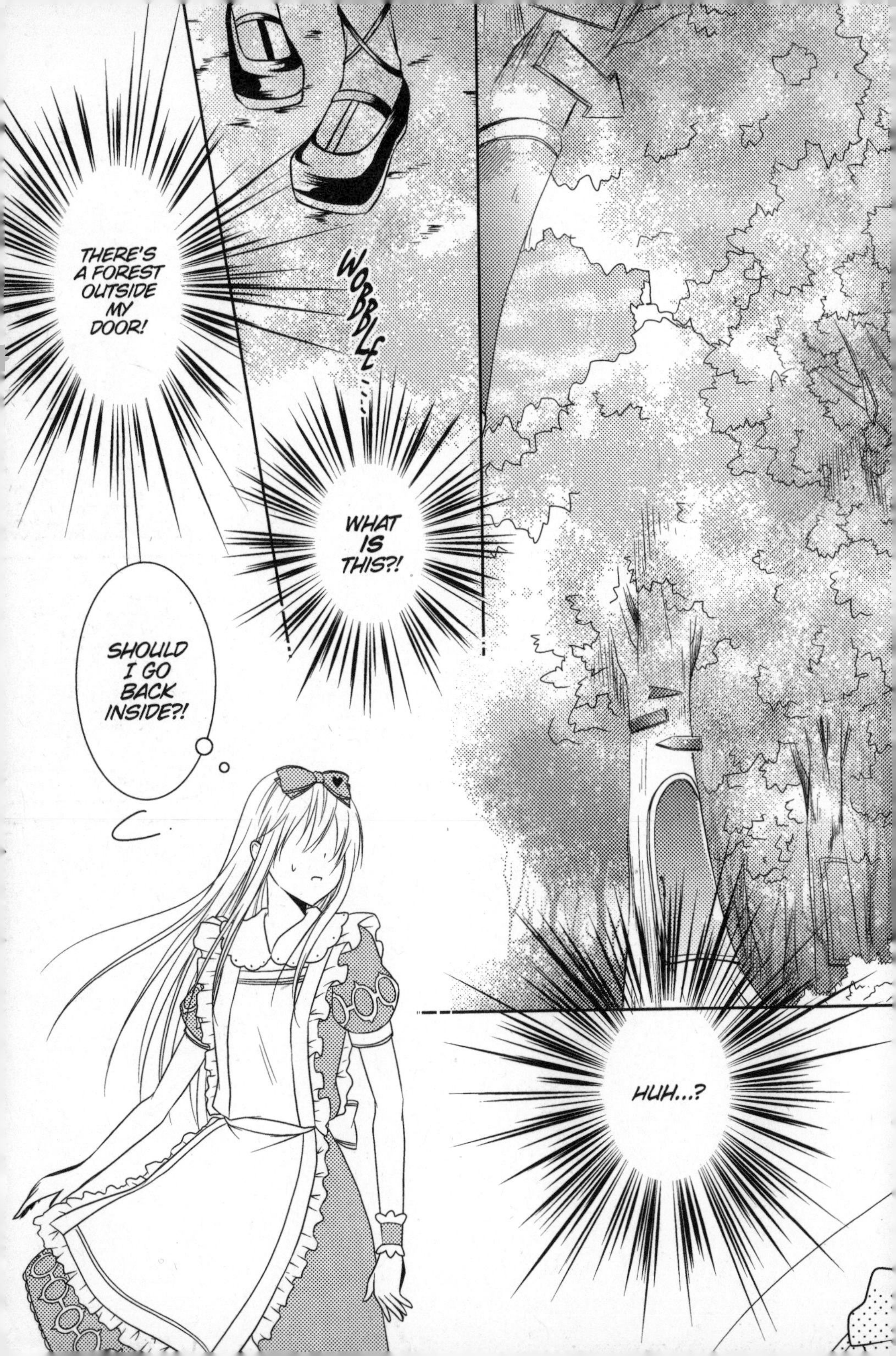
WOBBLE...
WHAT IS THIS?!
THERE'S A FOREST OUTSIDE MY DOOR!
HUH...?
SHOULD I GO BACK INSIDE?!

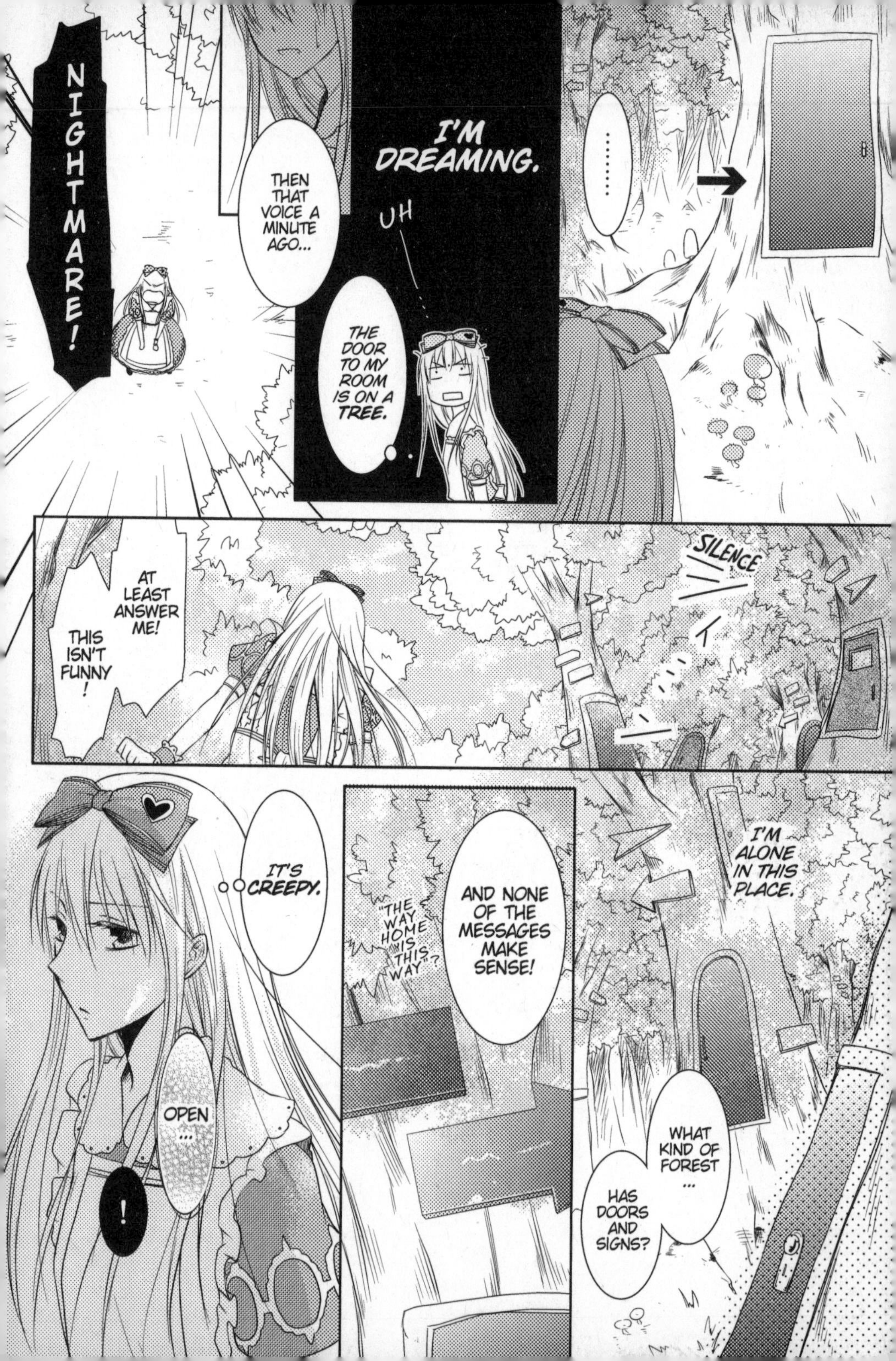

……
THEN THAT VOICE A MINUTE AGO...
I'M DREAMING.
UH
THE DOOR TO MY ROOM IS ON A TREE.
NIGHTMARE!
SILENCE
AT LEAST ANSWER ME!
THIS ISN'T FUNNY!
I'M ALONE IN THIS PLACE.
WHAT KIND OF FOREST...
HAS DOORS AND SIGNS?
AND NONE OF THE MESSAGES MAKE SENSE!
"THE WAY HOME IS THIS WAY"?
IT'S CREEPY.
OPEN...
!

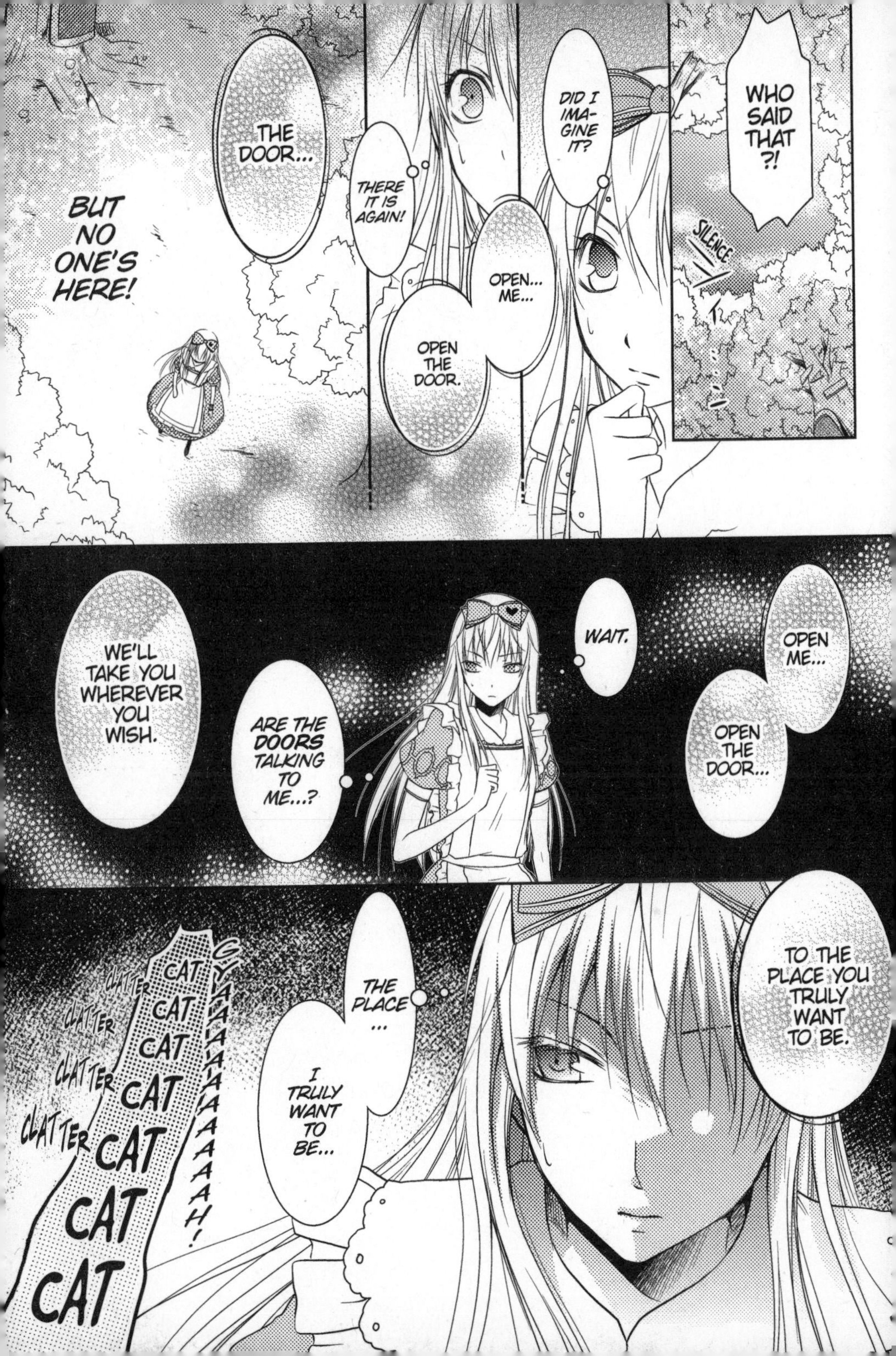
WHO SAID THAT?!
SILENCE
...
DID I IMA-GINE IT?
OPEN... ME...
OPEN THE DOOR.
THERE IT IS AGAIN!
THE DOOR...
BUT NO ONE'S HERE!
OPEN ME...
OPEN THE DOOR...
WAIT.
ARE THE DOORS TALKING TO ME...?
WE'LL TAKE YOU WHEREVER YOU WISH.
TO THE PLACE YOU TRULY WANT TO BE.
THE PLACE...
I TRULY WANT TO BE...
GYAAAAAAAAAAAAAH!
CLATTER CLATTER CLATTER CLATTER
CAT CAT CAT CAT CAT CAT CAT

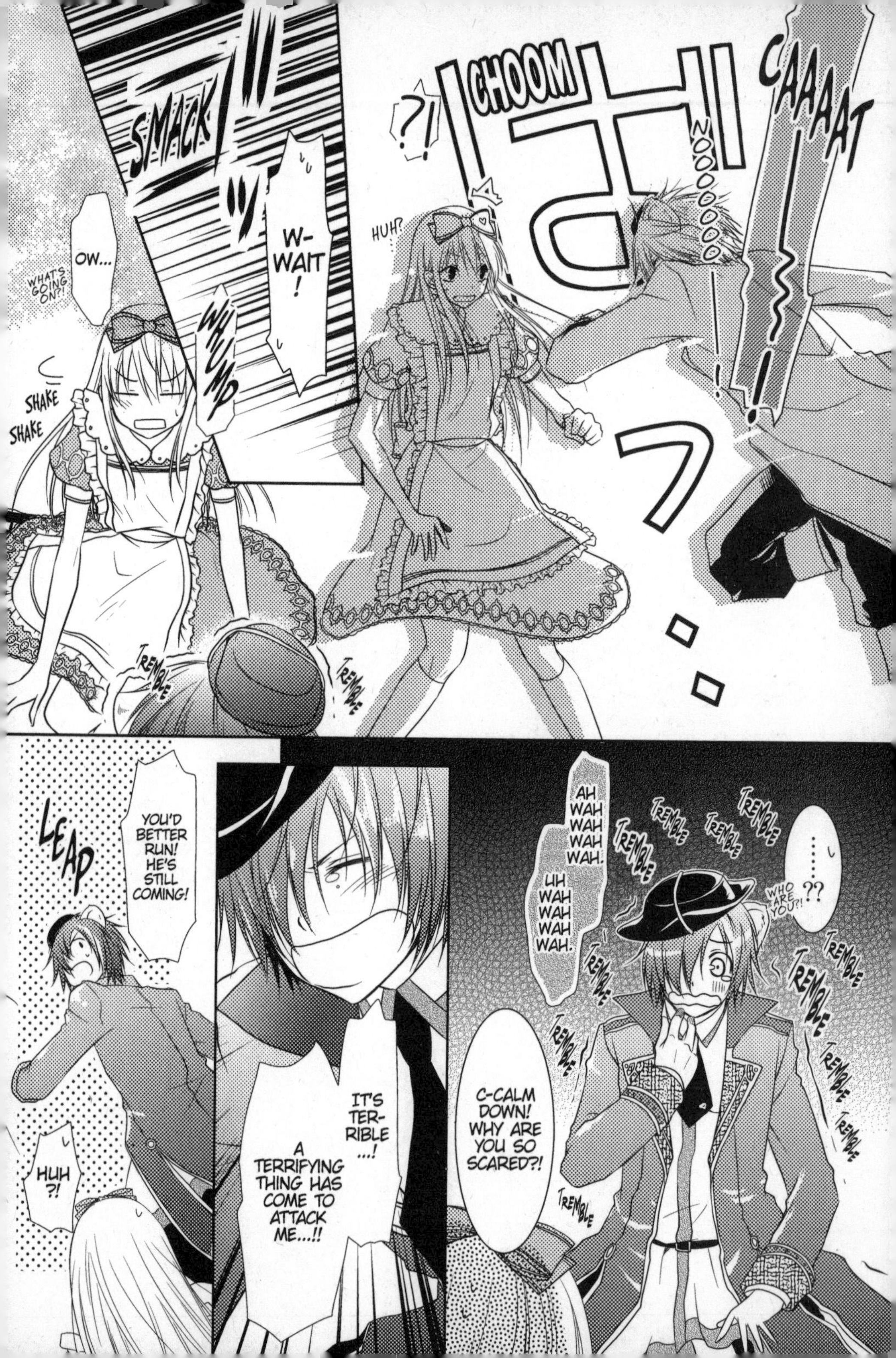
CAAAAT!!
NOOOOOOOO!!
CHOOM
?!
HUH?
W-WAIT!
SMACK!!
WHUMP
OW...
WHAT'S GOING ON?!
SHAKE SHAKE
TREMBLE
TREMBLE
TREMBLE TREMBLE TREMBLE TREMBLE
......??
WHO ARE YOU?!
AH WAH WAH WAH WAH.
UH WAH WAH WAH WAH.
TREMBLE TREMBLE TREMBLE TREMBLE TREMBLE
C-CALM DOWN! WHY ARE YOU SO SCARED?!
IT'S TERRIBLE...!
A TERRIFYING THING HAS COME TO ATTACK ME...!!
YOU'D BETTER RUN! HE'S STILL COMING!
LEAP
HUH?!

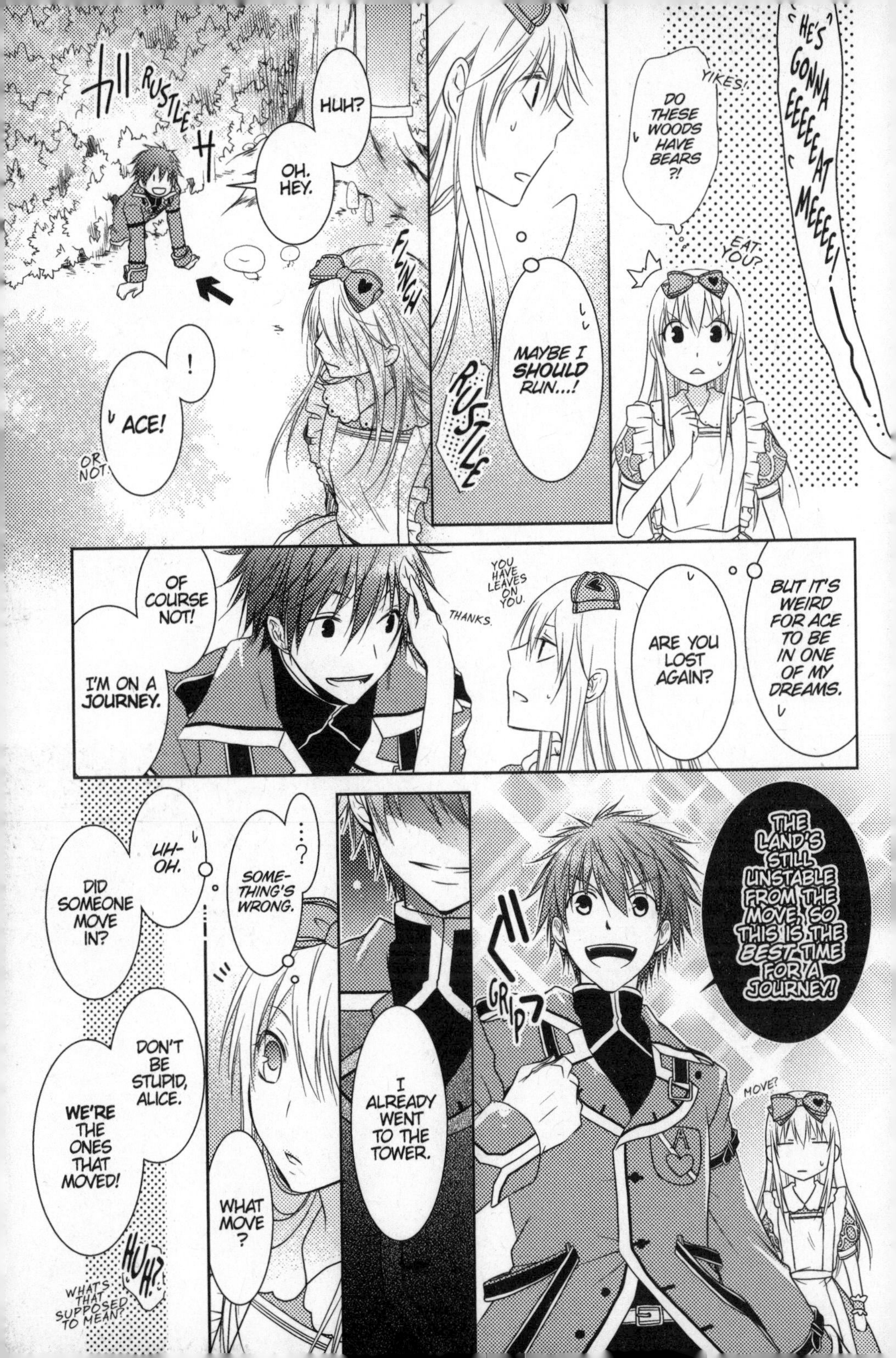
"HE'S GONNA EEEEEAT MEEEEE!"
YIKES!
DO THESE WOODS HAVE BEARS?!
EAT YOU?
MAYBE I SHOULD RUN...!
RUSTLE
HUH?
OH. HEY.
RUSTLE
FLINCH
!
ACE!
OR NOT.
BUT IT'S WEIRD FOR ACE TO BE IN ONE OF MY DREAMS.
ARE YOU LOST AGAIN?
YOU HAVE LEAVES ON YOU.
THANKS.
OF COURSE NOT!
I'M ON A JOURNEY.
THE LAND'S STILL UNSTABLE FROM THE MOVE, SO THIS IS THE BEST TIME FOR A JOURNEY!
GRIP
MOVE?
I ALREADY WENT TO THE TOWER.
...?
SOME-THING'S WRONG.
UH-OH.
DID SOMEONE MOVE IN?
WHAT MOVE?
DON'T BE STUPID, ALICE.
WE'RE THE ONES THAT MOVED!
HUH?
WHAT'S THAT SUPPOSED TO MEAN?

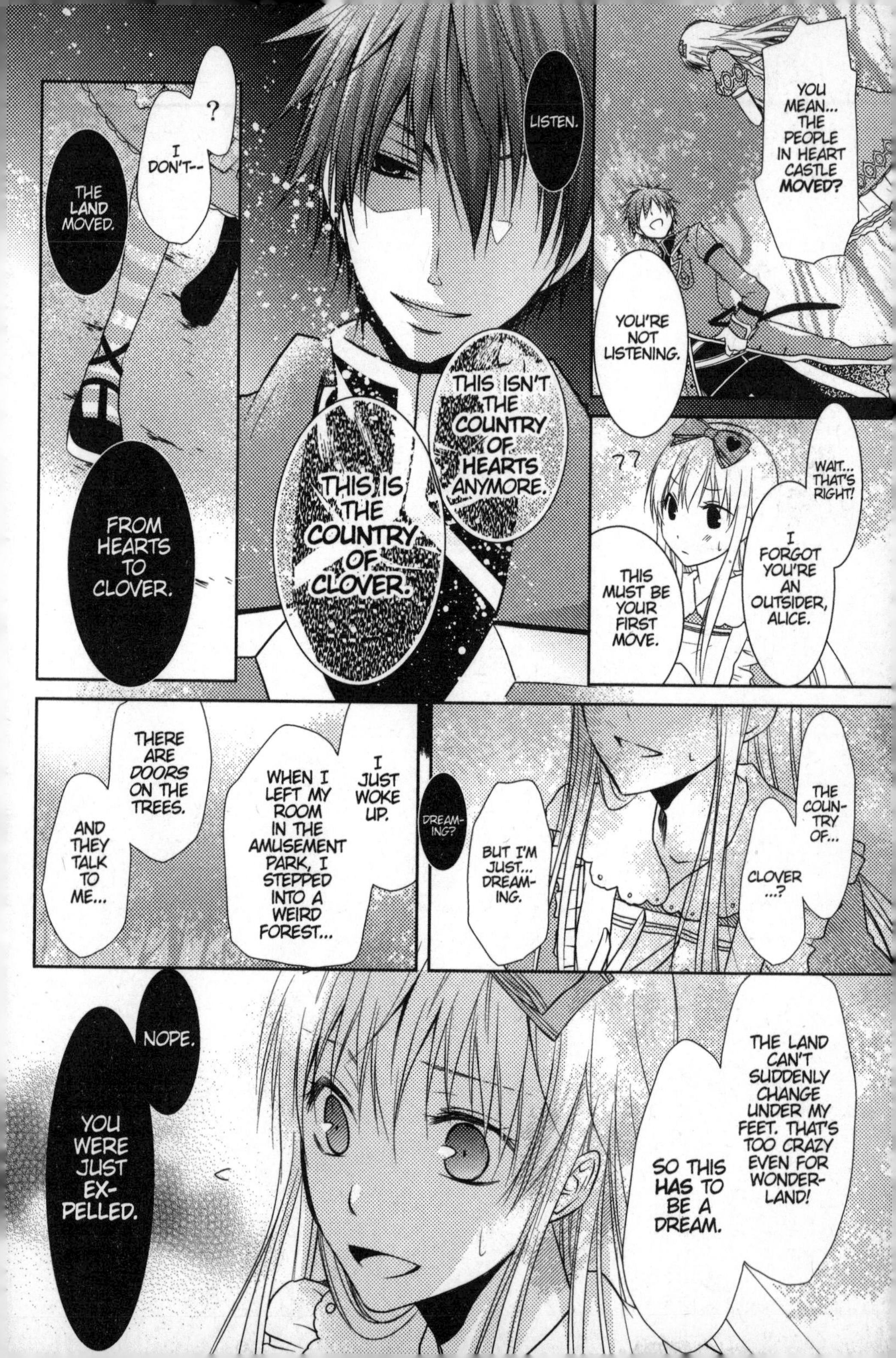
YOU MEAN... THE PEOPLE IN HEART CASTLE MOVED?
YOU'RE NOT LISTENING.
WAIT... THAT'S RIGHT!
I FORGOT YOU'RE AN OUTSIDER, ALICE.
??
THIS MUST BE YOUR FIRST MOVE.
LISTEN.
THIS ISN'T THE COUNTRY OF HEARTS ANYMORE.
THIS IS THE COUNTRY OF CLOVER.
?
I DON'T--
THE LAND MOVED.
FROM HEARTS TO CLOVER.
THE COUNTRY OF... CLOVER...?
BUT I'M JUST... DREAMING.
DREAMING?
I JUST WOKE UP.
WHEN I LEFT MY ROOM IN THE AMUSEMENT PARK, I STEPPED INTO A WEIRD FOREST...
THERE ARE DOORS ON THE TREES.
AND THEY TALK TO ME...
THE LAND CAN'T SUDDENLY CHANGE UNDER MY FEET. THAT'S TOO CRAZY EVEN FOR WONDERLAND!
SO THIS HAS TO BE A DREAM.
NOPE.
YOU WERE JUST EXPELLED.

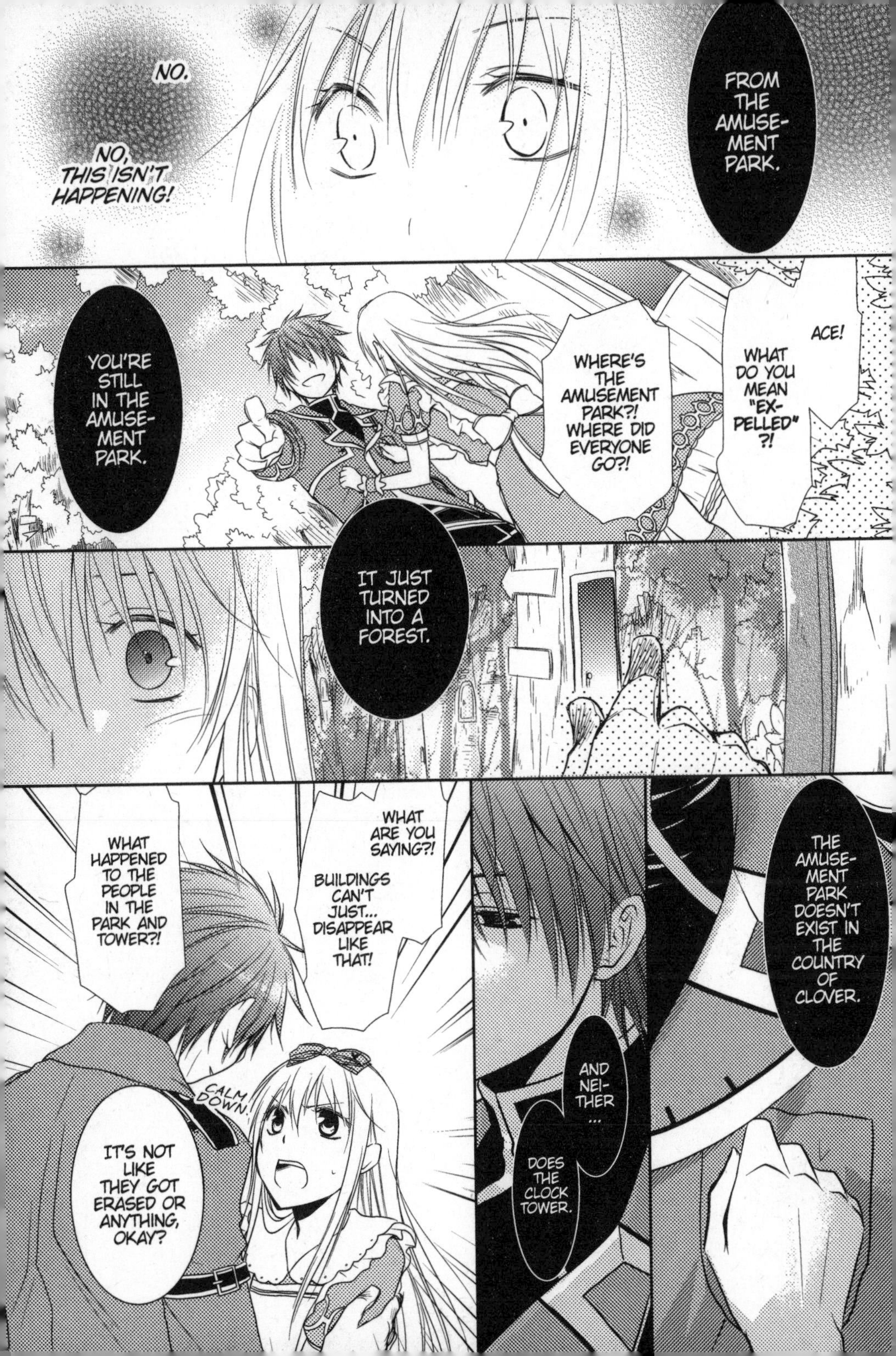
FROM THE AMUSEMENT PARK.
NO.
NO, THIS ISN'T HAPPENING!
ACE!
WHAT DO YOU MEAN "EXPELLED"?!
WHERE'S THE AMUSEMENT PARK?! WHERE DID EVERYONE GO?!
YOU'RE STILL IN THE AMUSEMENT PARK.
IT JUST TURNED INTO A FOREST.
THE AMUSEMENT PARK DOESN'T EXIST IN THE COUNTRY OF CLOVER.
AND NEITHER...
DOES THE CLOCK TOWER.
WHAT ARE YOU SAYING?!
BUILDINGS CAN'T JUST... DISAPPEAR LIKE THAT!
WHAT HAPPENED TO THE PEOPLE IN THE PARK AND TOWER?!
CALM DOWN.
IT'S NOT LIKE THEY GOT ERASED OR ANYTHING, OKAY?

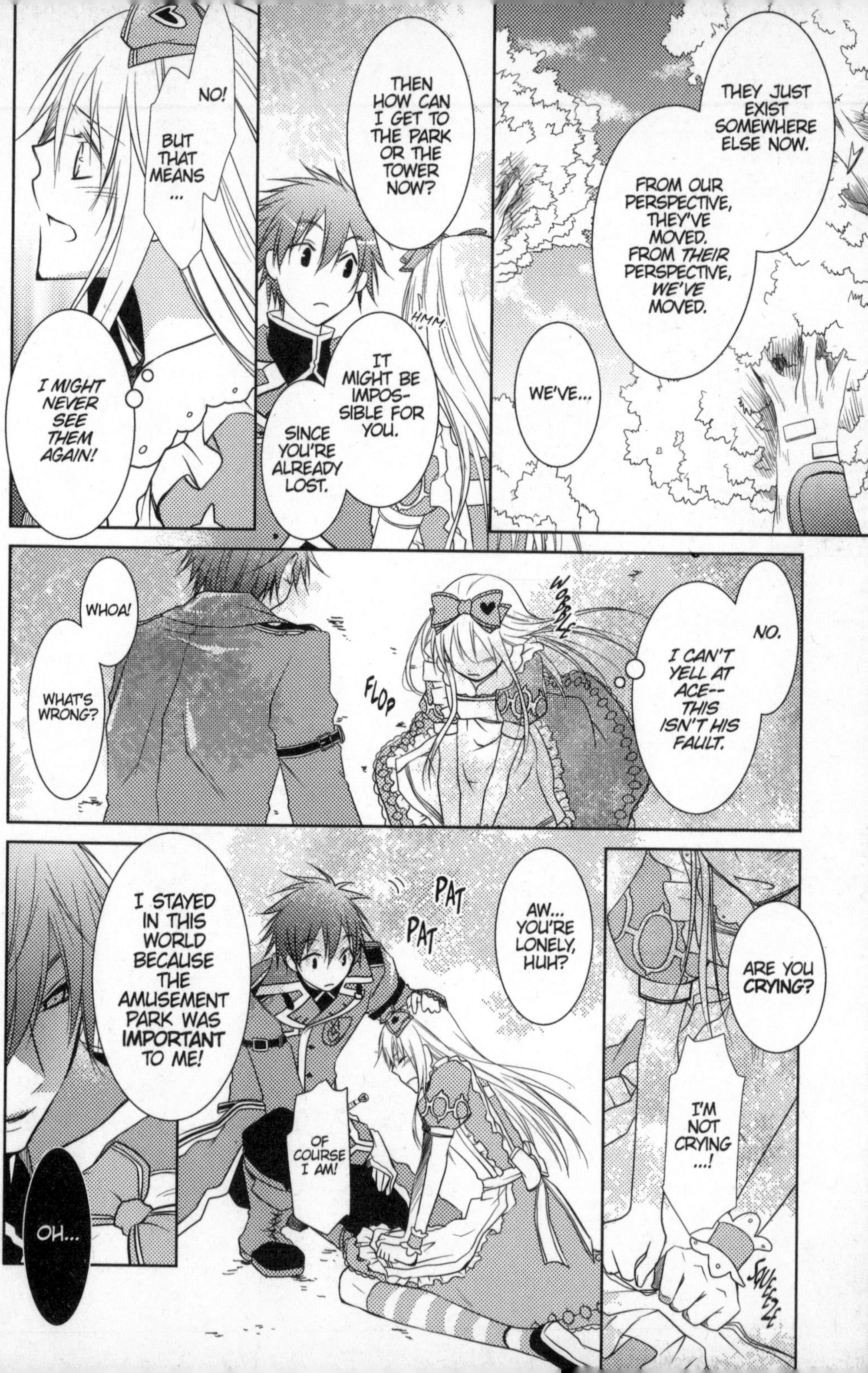
THEY JUST EXIST SOMEWHERE ELSE NOW.
FROM OUR PERSPECTIVE, THEY'VE MOVED. FROM *THEIR* PERSPECTIVE, *WE'VE* MOVED.
WE'VE...
THEN HOW CAN I GET TO THE PARK OR THE TOWER NOW?
HMM.
IT MIGHT BE IMPOS-SIBLE FOR YOU.
SINCE YOU'RE ALREADY LOST.
NO!
BUT THAT MEANS...
I MIGHT NEVER SEE THEM AGAIN!
WOBBLE
NO.
I CAN'T YELL AT ACE-- THIS ISN'T HIS FAULT.
FLOP
WHOA!
WHAT'S WRONG?
ARE YOU CRYING?
I'M NOT CRYING...!
SQUEEZE
AW... YOU'RE LONELY, HUH?
PAT
PAT
I STAYED IN THIS WORLD BECAUSE THE AMUSEMENT PARK WAS IMPORTANT TO ME!
OF COURSE I AM!
OH...

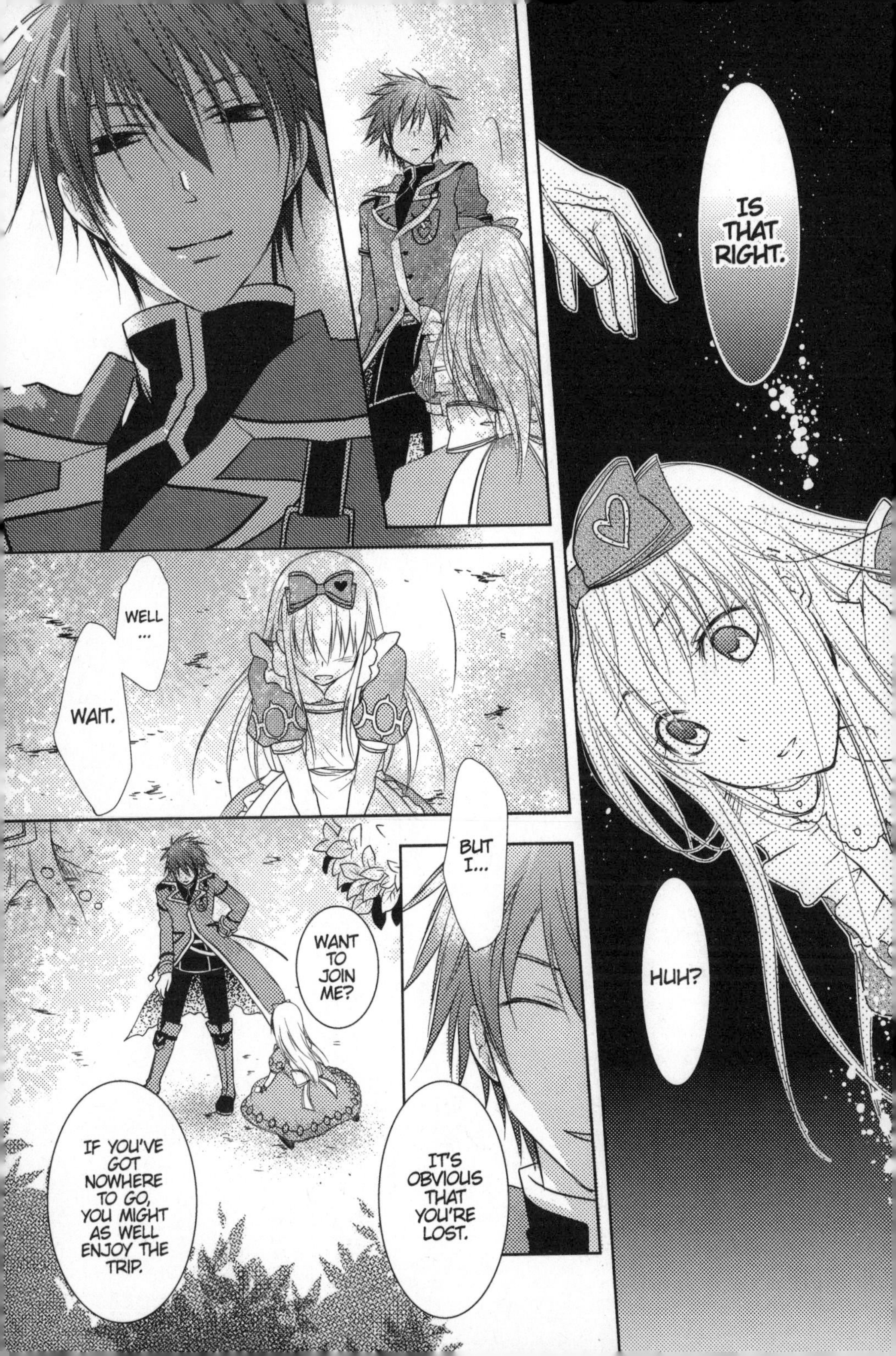

IS THAT RIGHT.
HUH?
WELL ...
WAIT.
BUT I...
IT'S OBVIOUS THAT YOU'RE LOST.
WANT TO JOIN ME?
IF YOU'VE GOT NOWHERE TO GO, YOU MIGHT AS WELL ENJOY THE TRIP.

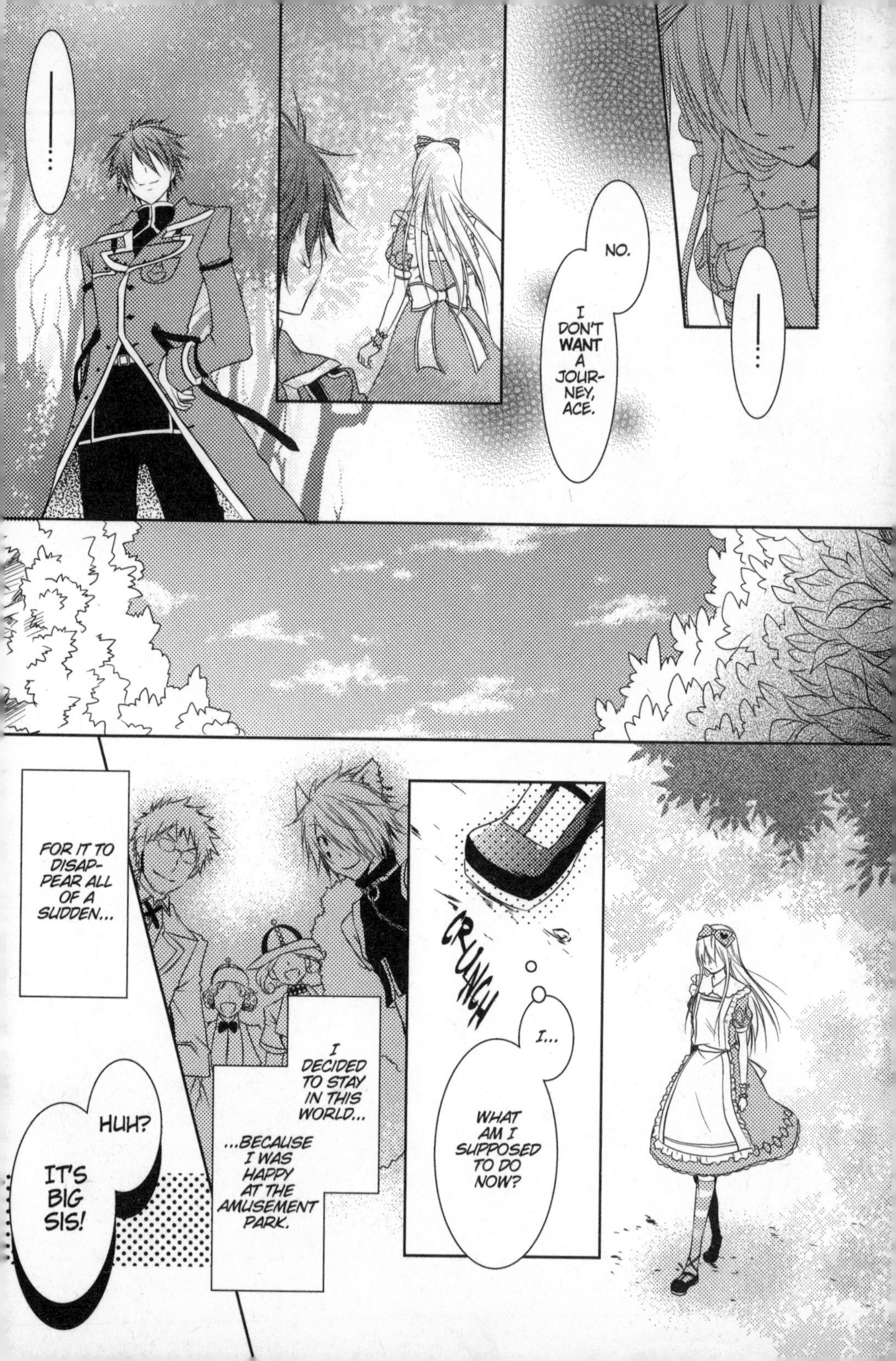
—…
NO.
I DON'T WANT A JOURNEY, ACE.
—…
I…
WHAT AM I SUPPOSED TO DO NOW?
CRUNCH
I DECIDED TO STAY IN THIS WORLD…
…BECAUSE I WAS HAPPY AT THE AMUSEMENT PARK.
FOR IT TO DISAPPEAR ALL OF A SUDDEN…
HUH?
IT'S BIG SIS!

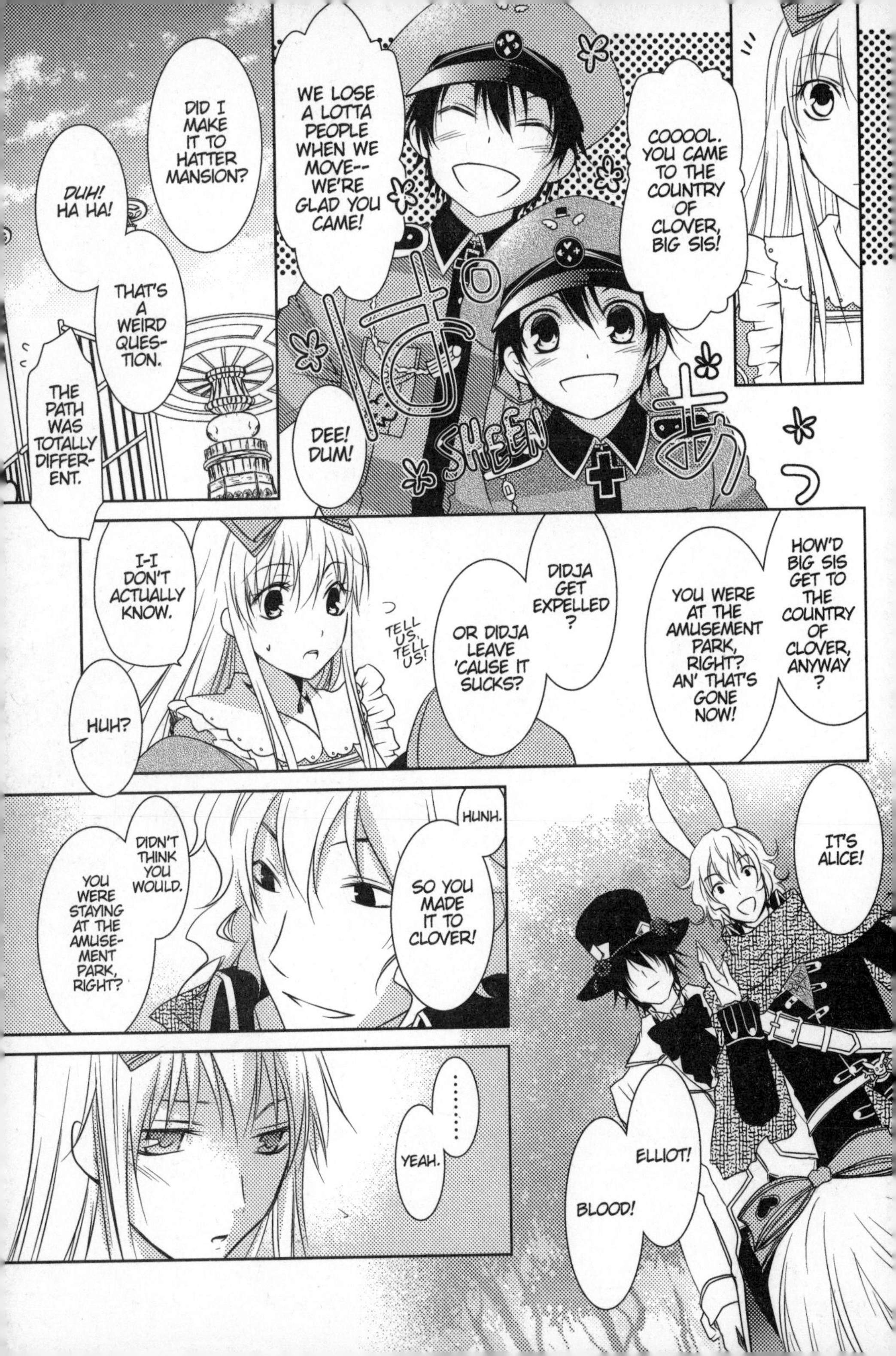
COOOOL. YOU CAME TO THE COUNTRY OF CLOVER, BIG SIS!
WE LOSE A LOTTA PEOPLE WHEN WE MOVE-- WE'RE GLAD YOU CAME!
SHEEN
DEE! DUM!
DID I MAKE IT TO HATTER MANSION?
DUH! HA HA!
THAT'S A WEIRD QUES-TION.
THE PATH WAS TOTALLY DIFFER-ENT.
HOW'D BIG SIS GET TO THE COUNTRY OF CLOVER, ANYWAY?
YOU WERE AT THE AMUSEMENT PARK, RIGHT? AN' THAT'S GONE NOW!
DIDJA GET EXPELLED?
OR DIDJA LEAVE 'CAUSE IT SUCKS?
TELL US, TELL US!
I-I DON'T ACTUALLY KNOW.
HUH?
IT'S ALICE!
ELLIOT!
BLOOD!
HUNH.
SO YOU MADE IT TO CLOVER!
DIDN'T THINK YOU WOULD.
YOU WERE STAYING AT THE AMUSE-MENT PARK, RIGHT?
......
YEAH.

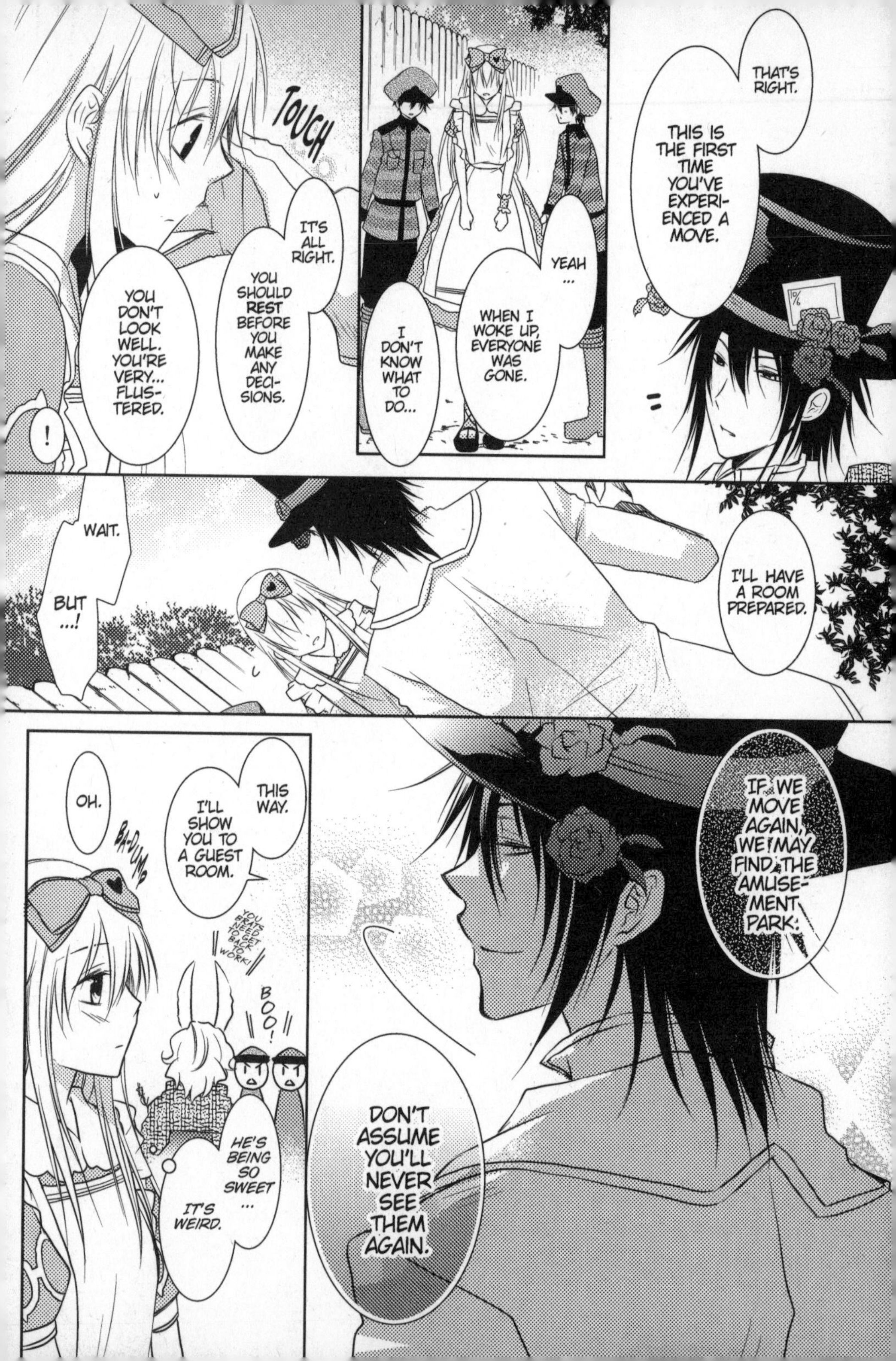
THAT'S RIGHT.
THIS IS THE FIRST TIME YOU'VE EXPERIENCED A MOVE.
YEAH ...
WHEN I WOKE UP, EVERYONE WAS GONE.
I DON'T KNOW WHAT TO DO...
TOUCH
IT'S ALL RIGHT.
YOU SHOULD REST BEFORE YOU MAKE ANY DECISIONS.
YOU DON'T LOOK WELL. YOU'RE VERY... FLUSTERED.
!
I'LL HAVE A ROOM PREPARED.
WAIT.
BUT ...!
IF WE MOVE AGAIN, WE MAY FIND THE AMUSEMENT PARK.
DON'T ASSUME YOU'LL NEVER SEE THEM AGAIN.
THIS WAY.
I'LL SHOW YOU TO A GUEST ROOM.
OH.
BA-DUMP
YOU BRATS NEED TO GET BACK TO WORK!
BOO!
HE'S BEING SO SWEET ...
IT'S WEIRD.

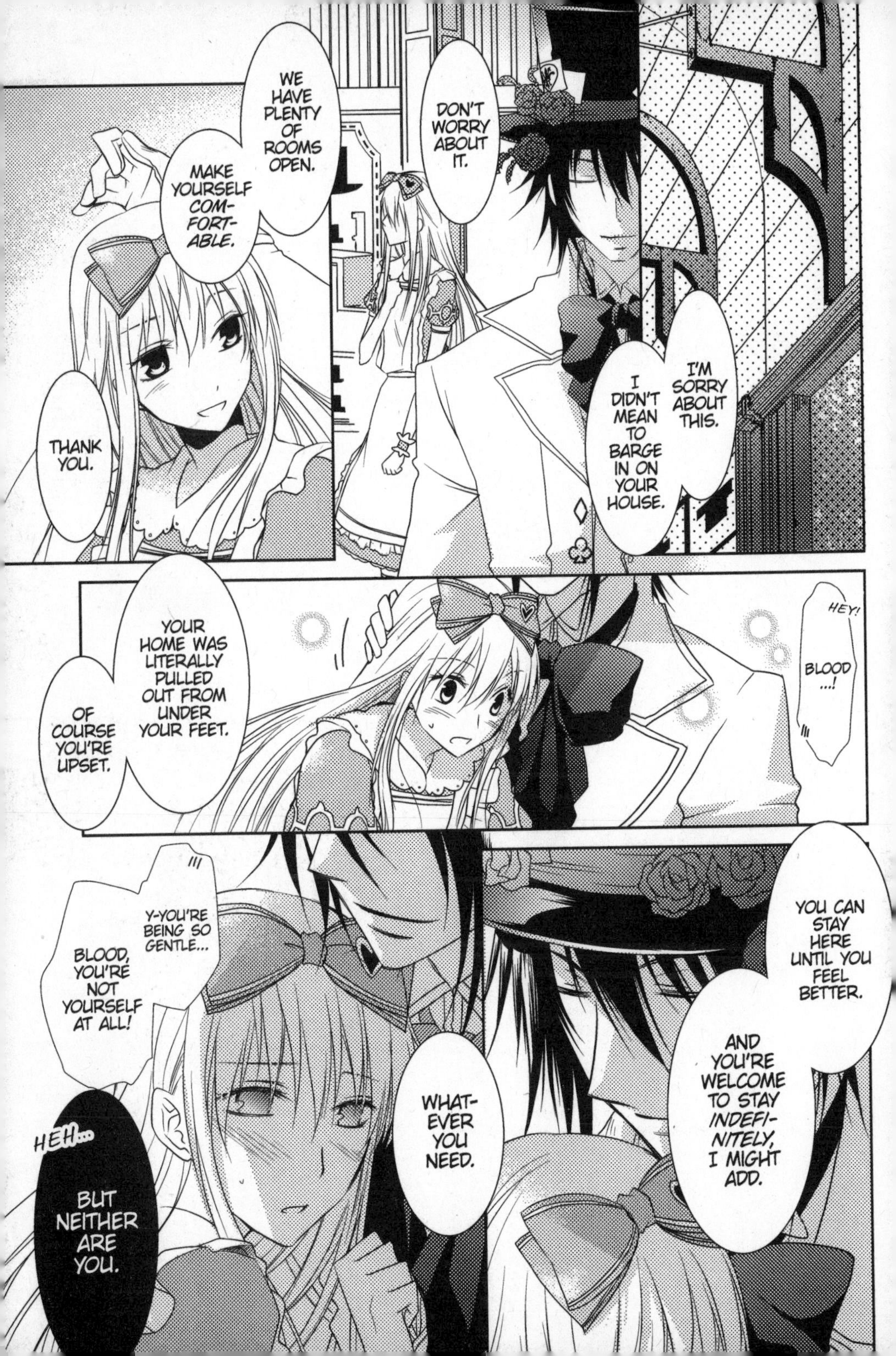
I'M SORRY ABOUT THIS.
I DIDN'T MEAN TO BARGE IN ON YOUR HOUSE.
DON'T WORRY ABOUT IT.
WE HAVE PLENTY OF ROOMS OPEN.
MAKE YOURSELF COMFORTABLE.
THANK YOU.
HEY!
BLOOD...!
YOUR HOME WAS LITERALLY PULLED OUT FROM UNDER YOUR FEET.
OF COURSE YOU'RE UPSET.
YOU CAN STAY HERE UNTIL YOU FEEL BETTER.
AND YOU'RE WELCOME TO STAY *INDEFINITELY*, I MIGHT ADD.
WHATEVER YOU NEED.
Y-YOU'RE BEING SO GENTLE...
BLOOD, YOU'RE NOT YOURSELF AT ALL!
HEH...
BUT NEITHER ARE YOU.

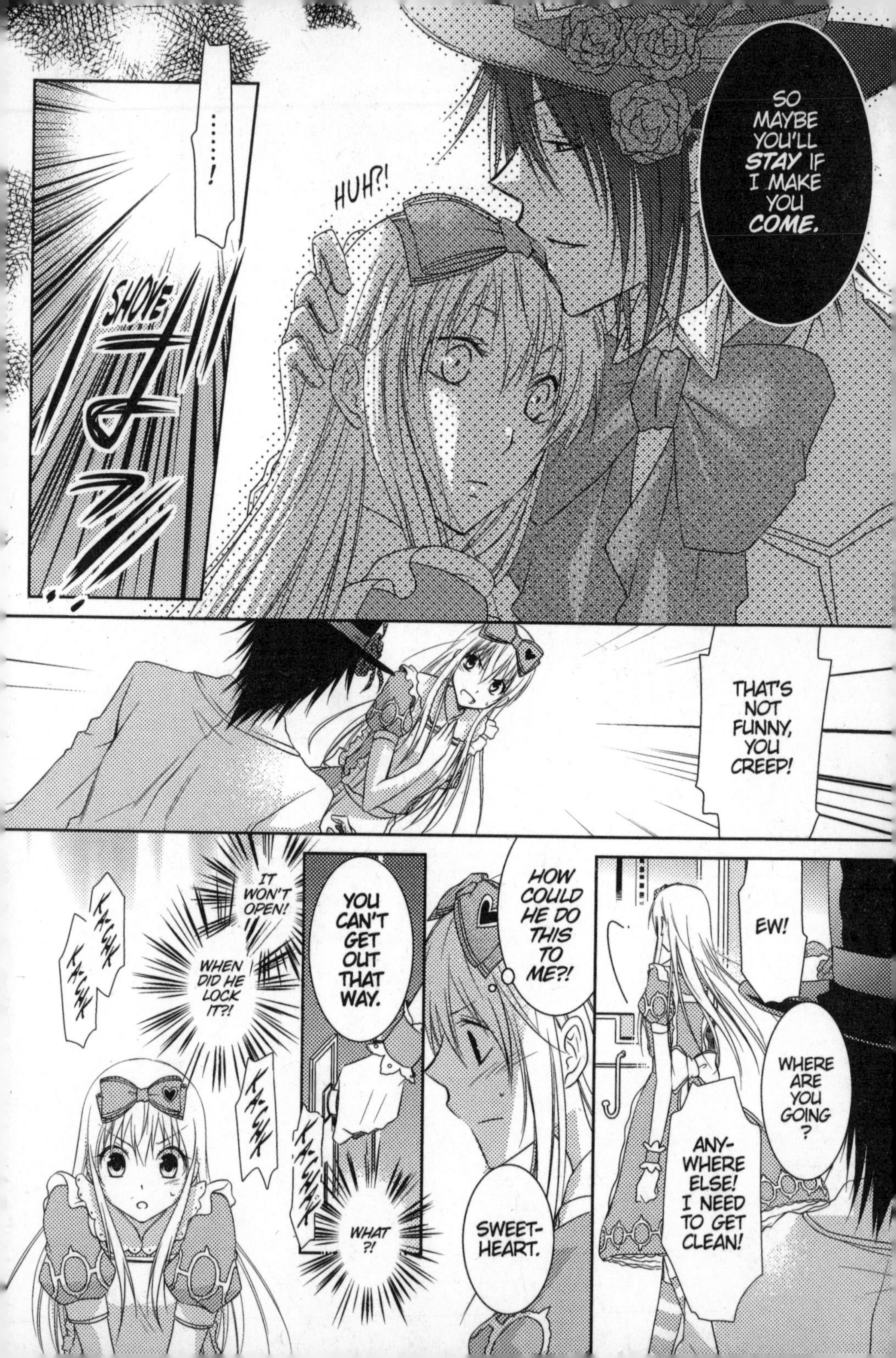
SO MAYBE YOU'LL STAY IF I MAKE YOU COME.
HUH?!
......!
SHOVE
THAT'S NOT FUNNY, YOU CREEP!
EW!
WHERE ARE YOU GOING?
ANY-WHERE ELSE! I NEED TO GET CLEAN!
HOW COULD HE DO THIS TO ME?!
SWEET-HEART.
YOU CAN'T GET OUT THAT WAY.
KA-CHAK
KA-CHAK
WHAT?!
IT WON'T OPEN!
WHEN DID HE LOCK IT?!
KA-CHAK
KA-CHAK

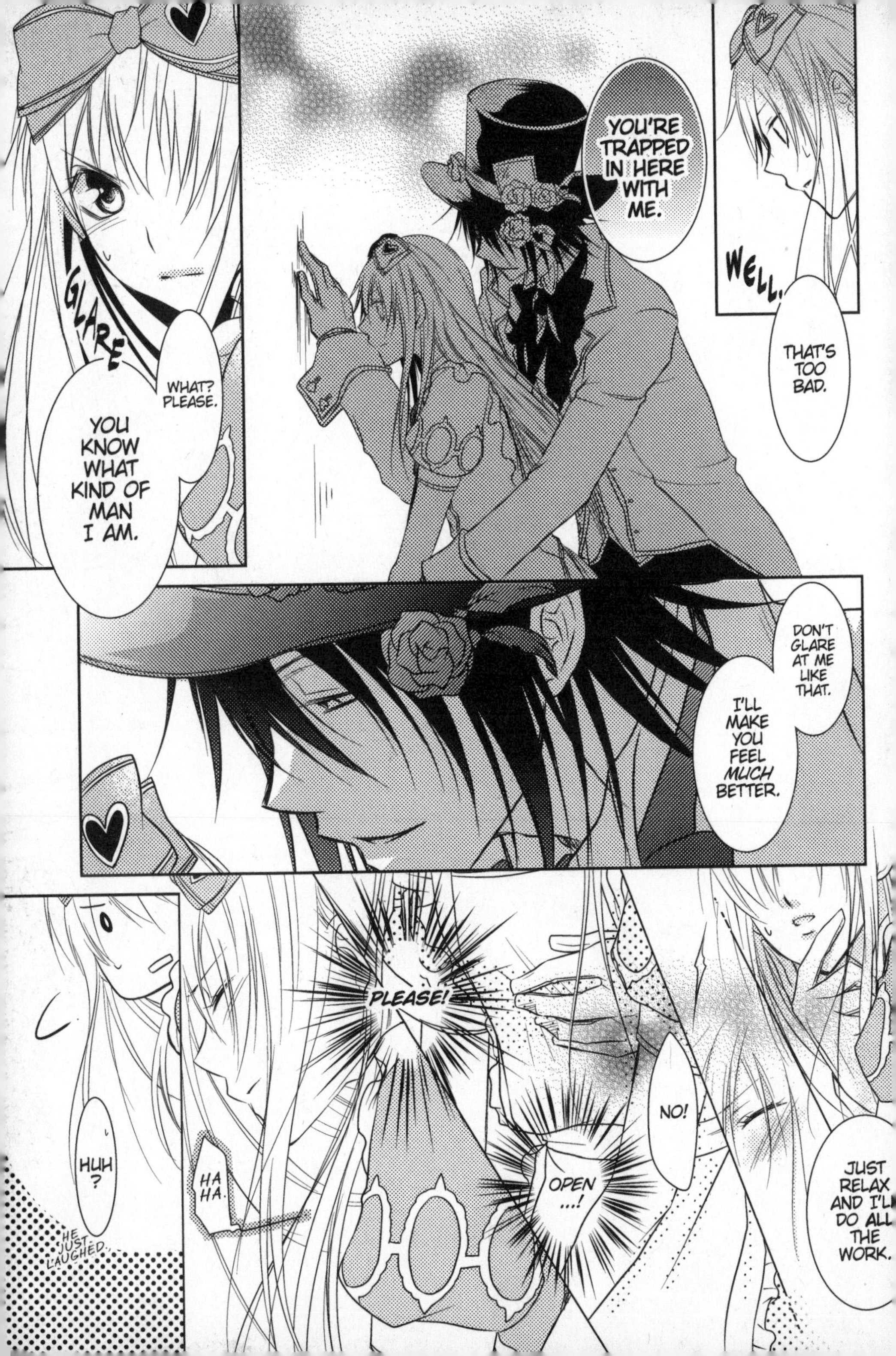
WELL...
THAT'S TOO BAD.
YOU'RE TRAPPED IN HERE WITH ME.
GLARE
WHAT? PLEASE.
YOU KNOW WHAT KIND OF MAN I AM.
DON'T GLARE AT ME LIKE THAT.
I'LL MAKE YOU FEEL *MUCH* BETTER.
JUST RELAX AND I'LL DO ALL THE WORK.
NO!
PLEASE!
OPEN ...!
HA HA.
HUH?
HE JUST LAUGHED...

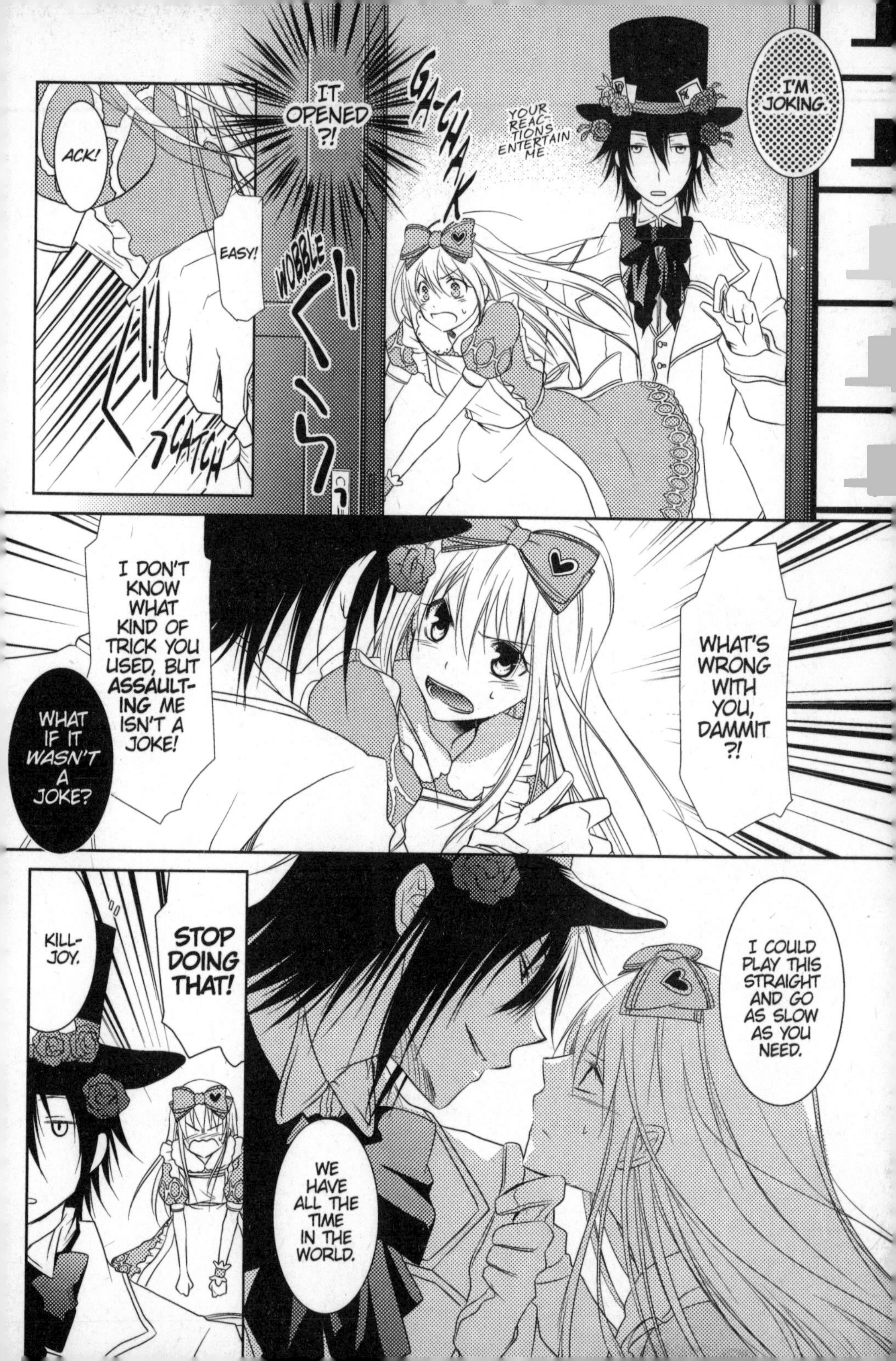
I'M JOKING.
YOUR REACTIONS ENTERTAIN ME.
GA-CHAK
IT OPENED?!
WOBBLE
ACK!
EASY!
CATCH
WHAT'S WRONG WITH YOU, DAMMIT?!
I DON'T KNOW WHAT KIND OF TRICK YOU USED, BUT ASSAULTING ME ISN'T A JOKE!
WHAT IF IT WASN'T A JOKE?
I COULD PLAY THIS STRAIGHT AND GO AS SLOW AS YOU NEED.
WE HAVE ALL THE TIME IN THE WORLD.
STOP DOING THAT!
KILL-JOY.

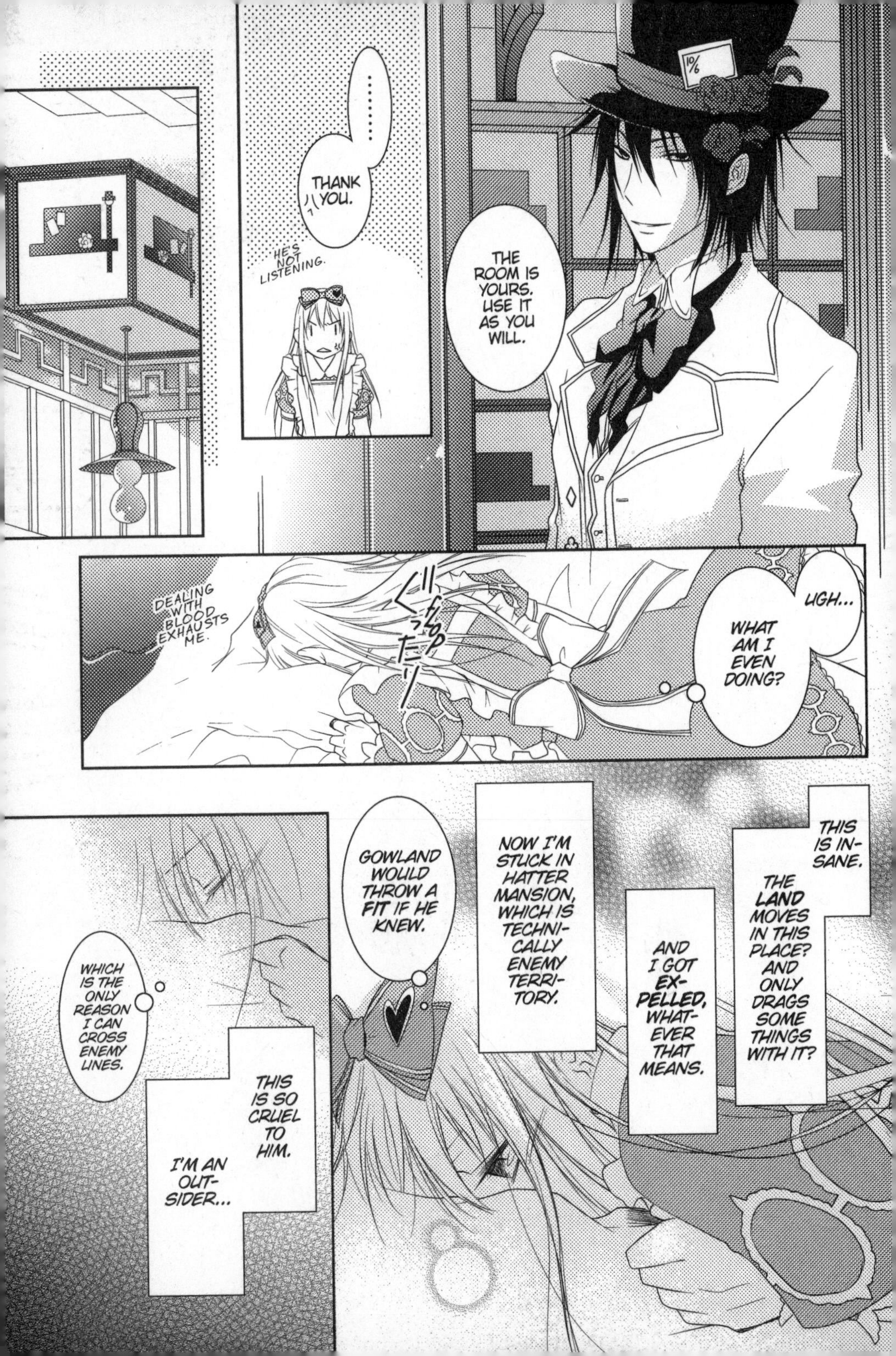
THE ROOM IS YOURS. USE IT AS YOU WILL.
......
THANK YOU.
HE'S NOT LISTENING.
UGH... WHAT AM I EVEN DOING?
FLOP
DEALING WITH BLOOD EXHAUSTS ME.
THIS IS IN-SANE.
THE LAND MOVES IN THIS PLACE? AND ONLY DRAGS SOME THINGS WITH IT?
AND I GOT EX-PELLED, WHAT-EVER THAT MEANS.
NOW I'M STUCK IN HATTER MANSION, WHICH IS TECHNI-CALLY ENEMY TERRI-TORY.
GOWLAND WOULD THROW A FIT IF HE KNEW.
THIS IS SO CRUEL TO HIM.
I'M AN OUT-SIDER...
WHICH IS THE ONLY REASON I CAN CROSS ENEMY LINES.

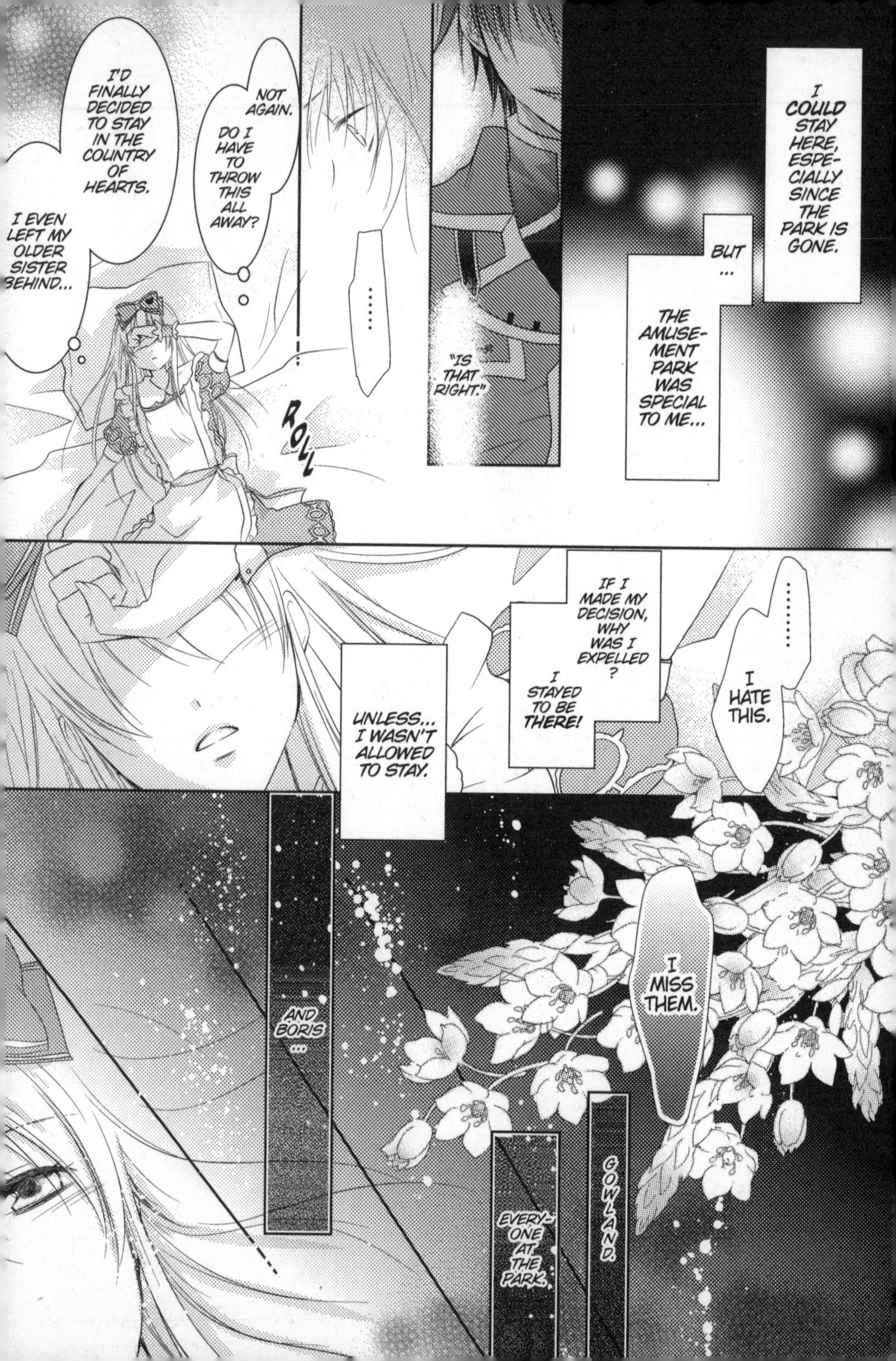
I COULD STAY HERE, ESPECIALLY SINCE THE PARK IS GONE.
BUT ...
THE AMUSEMENT PARK WAS SPECIAL TO ME...
"IS THAT RIGHT."
......
NOT AGAIN. DO I HAVE TO THROW THIS ALL AWAY?
I'D FINALLY DECIDED TO STAY IN THE COUNTRY OF HEARTS.
I EVEN LEFT MY OLDER SISTER BEHIND...
ROLL
......
I HATE THIS.
IF I MADE MY DECISION, WHY WAS I EXPELLED?
I STAYED TO BE THERE!
UNLESS... I WASN'T ALLOWED TO STAY.
I MISS THEM.
GOWLAND.
EVERYONE AT THE PARK.
AND BORIS ...

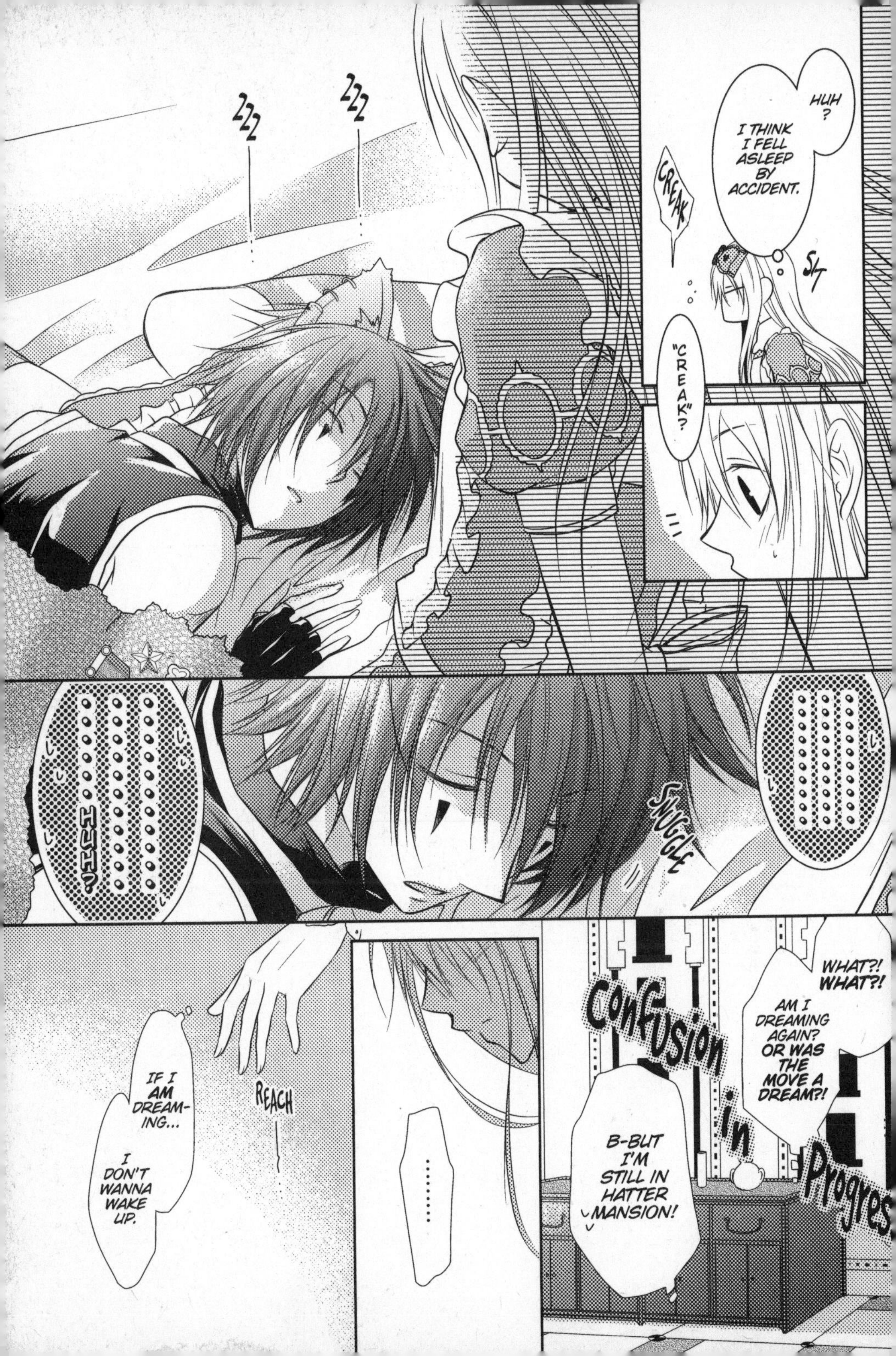
HUH? I THINK I FELL ASLEEP BY ACCIDENT.
CREAK
"CREAK"?
ZZZ...
ZZZ...
SNUGGLE
.... HUH?
WHAT?! WHAT?!
AM I DREAMING AGAIN? OR WAS THE MOVE A DREAM?!
B-BUT I'M STILL IN HATTER MANSION!
Confusion in Progres
....
REACH
IF I AM DREAMING...
I DON'T WANNA WAKE UP.

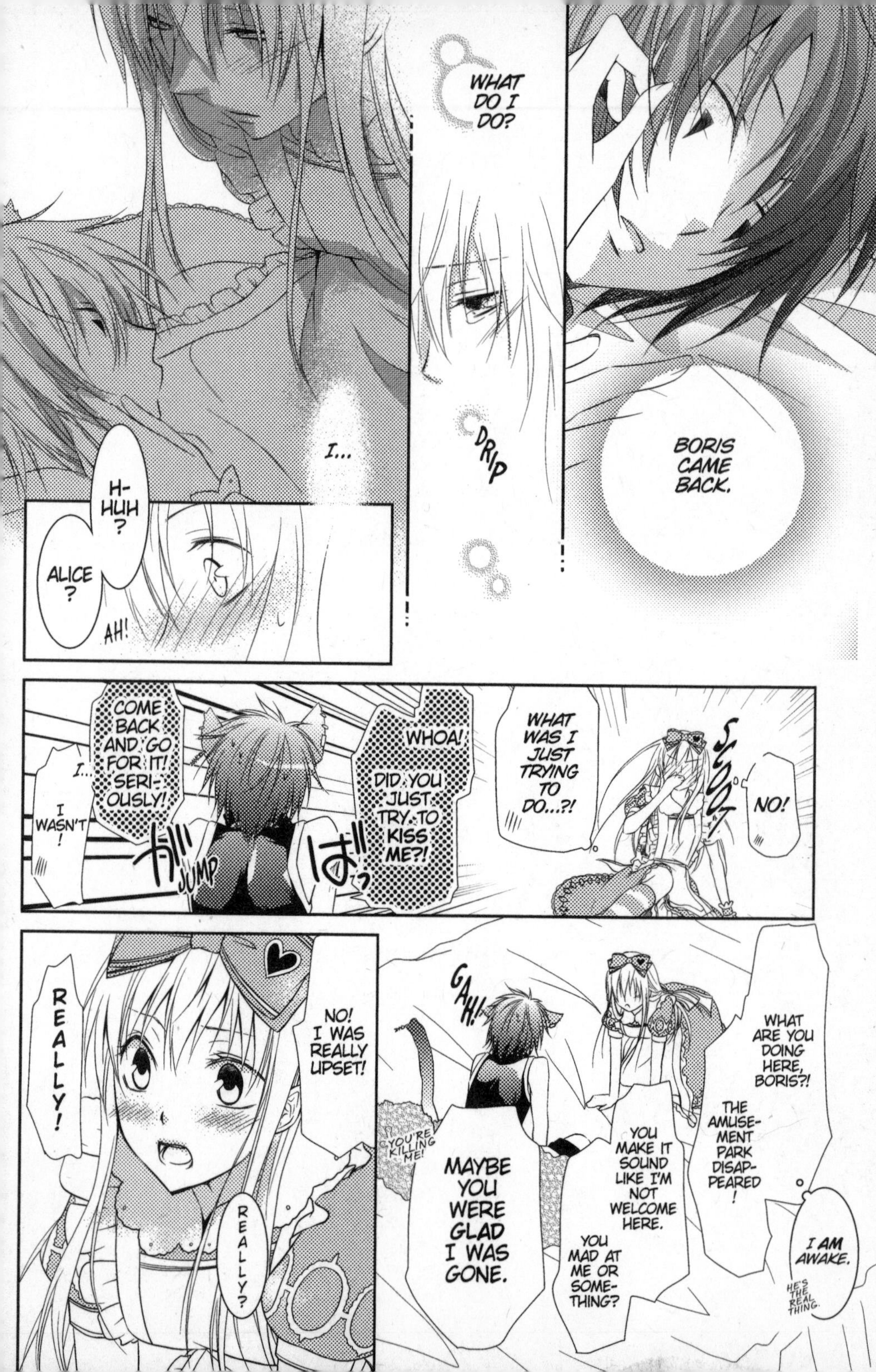
BORIS CAME BACK.
WHAT DO I DO?
DRIP
I...
AH!
H-HUH?
ALICE?
NO!
SCOOT
WHAT WAS I JUST TRYING TO DO...?!
WHOA!
DID YOU JUST TRY TO KISS ME?!
COME BACK AND GO FOR IT! SERIOUSLY!
I...
I WASN'T!
JUMP
I AM AWAKE.
HE'S THE REAL THING.
WHAT ARE YOU DOING HERE, BORIS?!
THE AMUSEMENT PARK DISAPPEARED!
YOU MAKE IT SOUND LIKE I'M NOT WELCOME HERE.
YOU MAD AT ME OR SOMETHING?
GAH!
MAYBE YOU WERE GLAD I WAS GONE.
YOU'RE KILLING ME!
NO! I WAS REALLY UPSET!
REALLY!
REALLY?

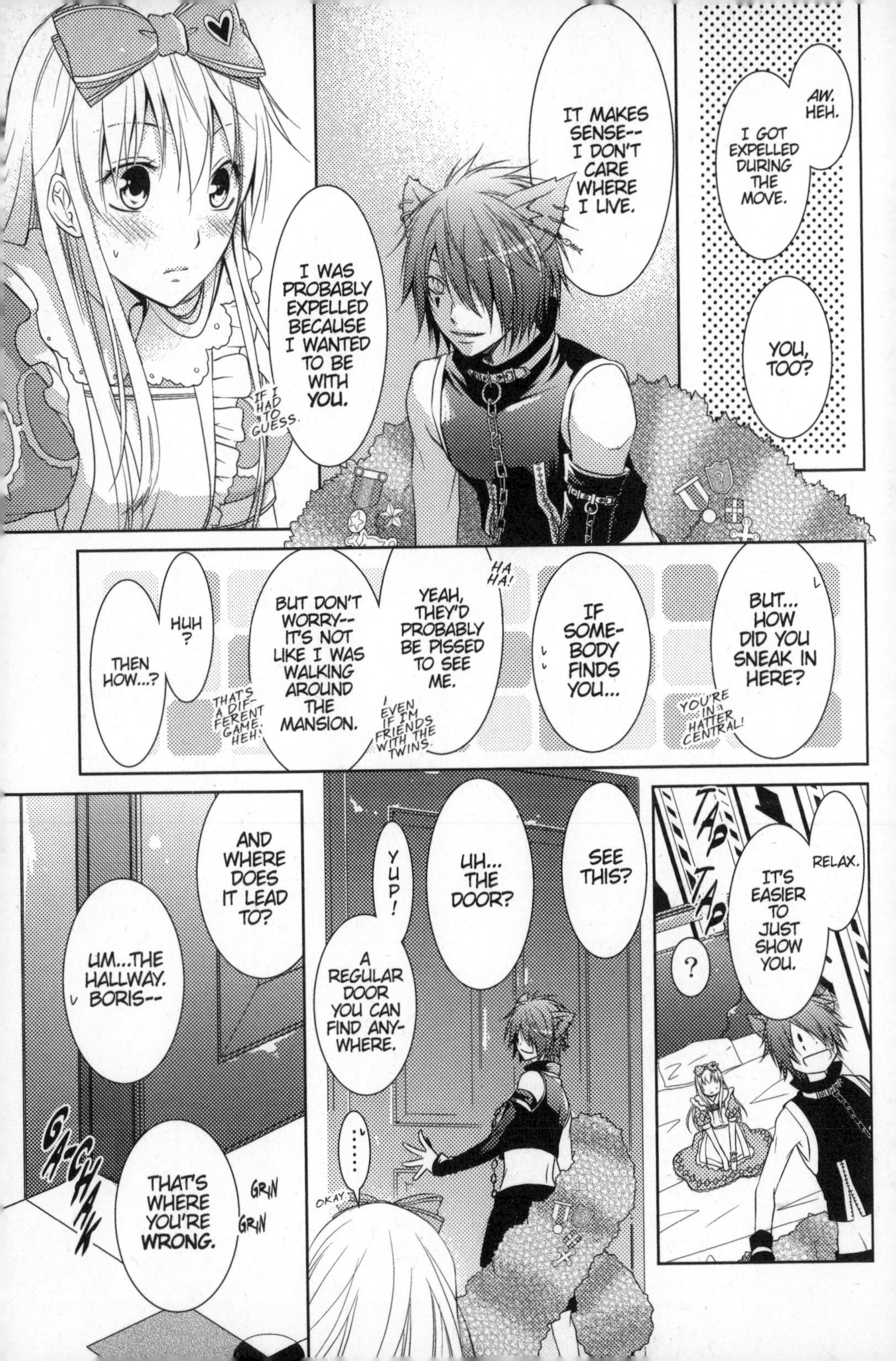
AW. HEH.
I GOT EXPELLED DURING THE MOVE.
YOU, TOO?
IT MAKES SENSE-- I DON'T CARE WHERE I LIVE.
I WAS PROBABLY EXPELLED BECAUSE I WANTED TO BE WITH YOU.
IF I HAD TO GUESS.
BUT... HOW DID YOU SNEAK IN HERE?
YOU'RE IN HATTER CENTRAL!
IF SOMEBODY FINDS YOU...
HA HA!
YEAH, THEY'D PROBABLY BE PISSED TO SEE ME.
EVEN IF I'M FRIENDS WITH THE TWINS.
BUT DON'T WORRY-- IT'S NOT LIKE I WAS WALKING AROUND THE MANSION.
THAT'S A DIFFERENT GAME. HEH.
HUH?
THEN HOW...?
TAP TAP
RELAX.
IT'S EASIER TO JUST SHOW YOU.
?
SEE THIS?
UH... THE DOOR?
YUP!
A REGULAR DOOR YOU CAN FIND ANYWHERE.
......
OKAY.
AND WHERE DOES IT LEAD TO?
UM...THE HALLWAY. BORIS--
GA-CHAK
GRIN GRIN
THAT'S WHERE YOU'RE WRONG.

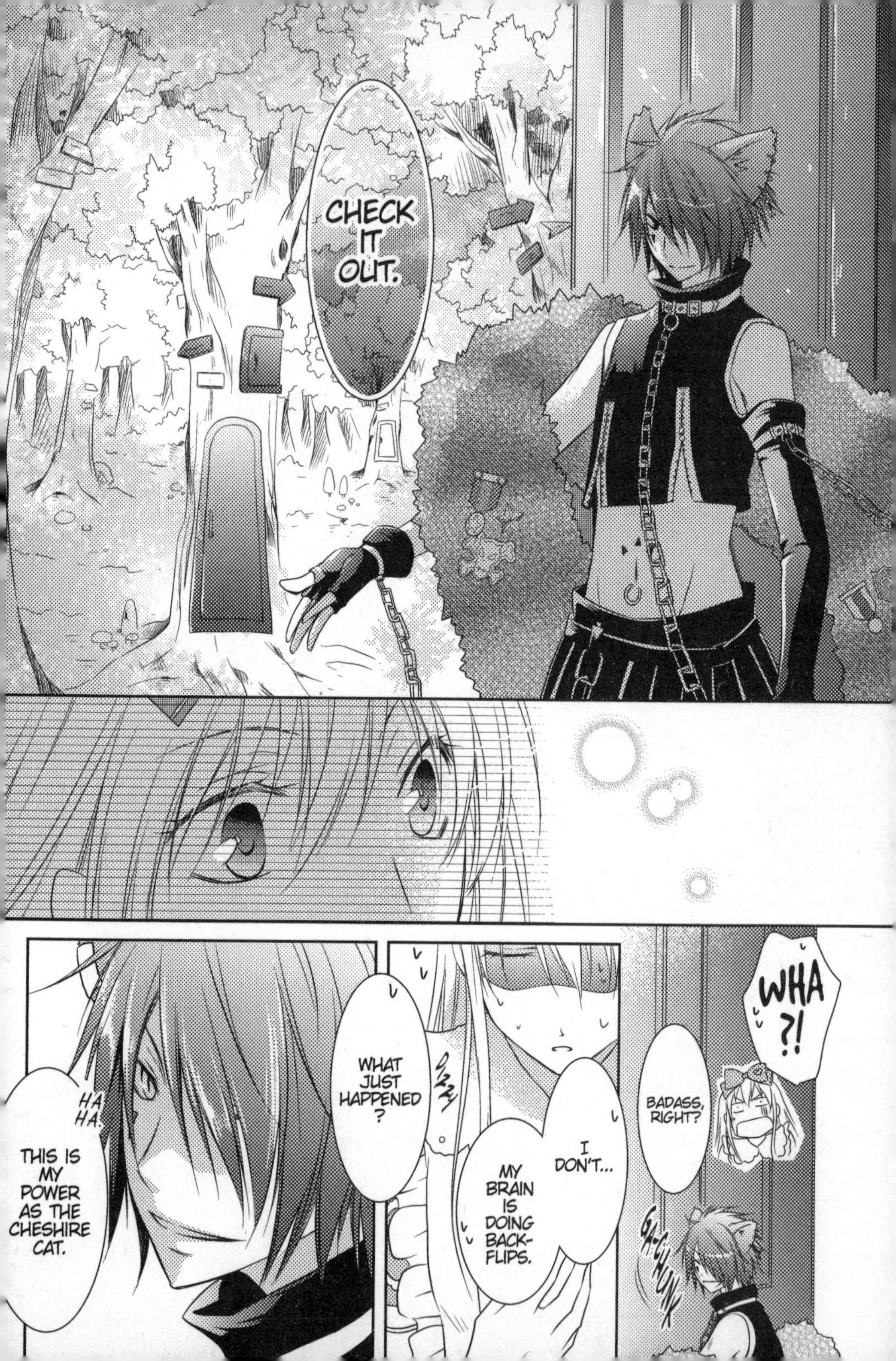
CHECK IT OUT.
WHA ?!
BADASS, RIGHT?
GA-CHUNK
WHAT JUST HAPPENED ?
DIZZY
I DON'T...
MY BRAIN IS DOING BACK-FLIPS.
HA HA.
THIS IS MY POWER AS THE CHESHIRE CAT.

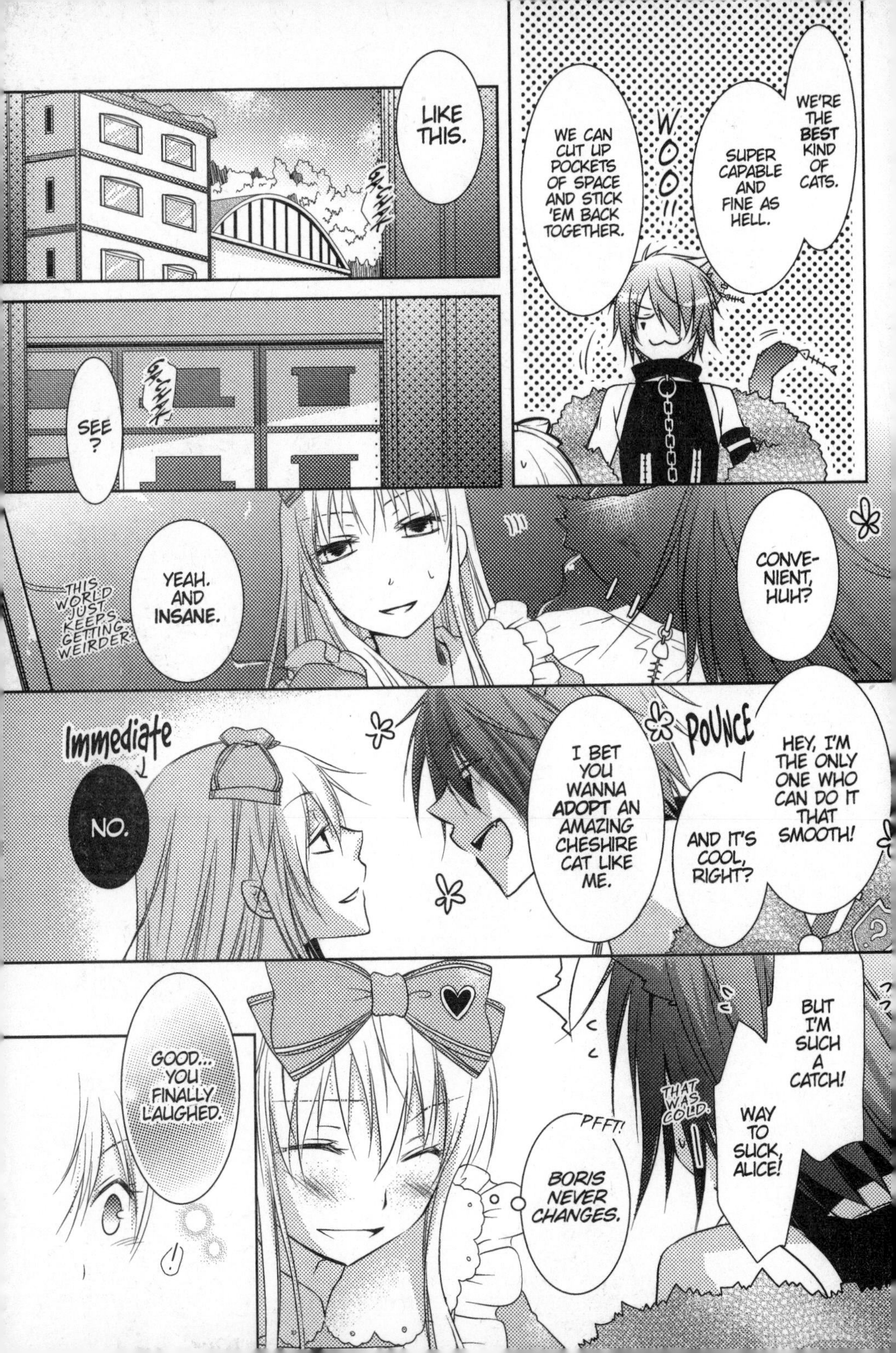

WE'RE THE BEST KIND OF CATS.
SUPER CAPABLE AND FINE AS HELL.
WOO!!
WE CAN CUT UP POCKETS OF SPACE AND STICK 'EM BACK TOGETHER.
LIKE THIS.
SEE?
CONVE-NIENT, HUH?
YEAH. AND INSANE.
THIS WORLD JUST KEEPS GETTING WEIRDER.
POUNCE
HEY, I'M THE ONLY ONE WHO CAN DO IT THAT SMOOTH!
AND IT'S COOL, RIGHT?
I BET YOU WANNA ADOPT AN AMAZING CHESHIRE CAT LIKE ME.
Immediate
NO.
BUT I'M SUCH A CATCH!
WAY TO SUCK, ALICE!
THAT WAS COLD.
PFFT!
BORIS NEVER CHANGES.
GOOD... YOU FINALLY LAUGHED.

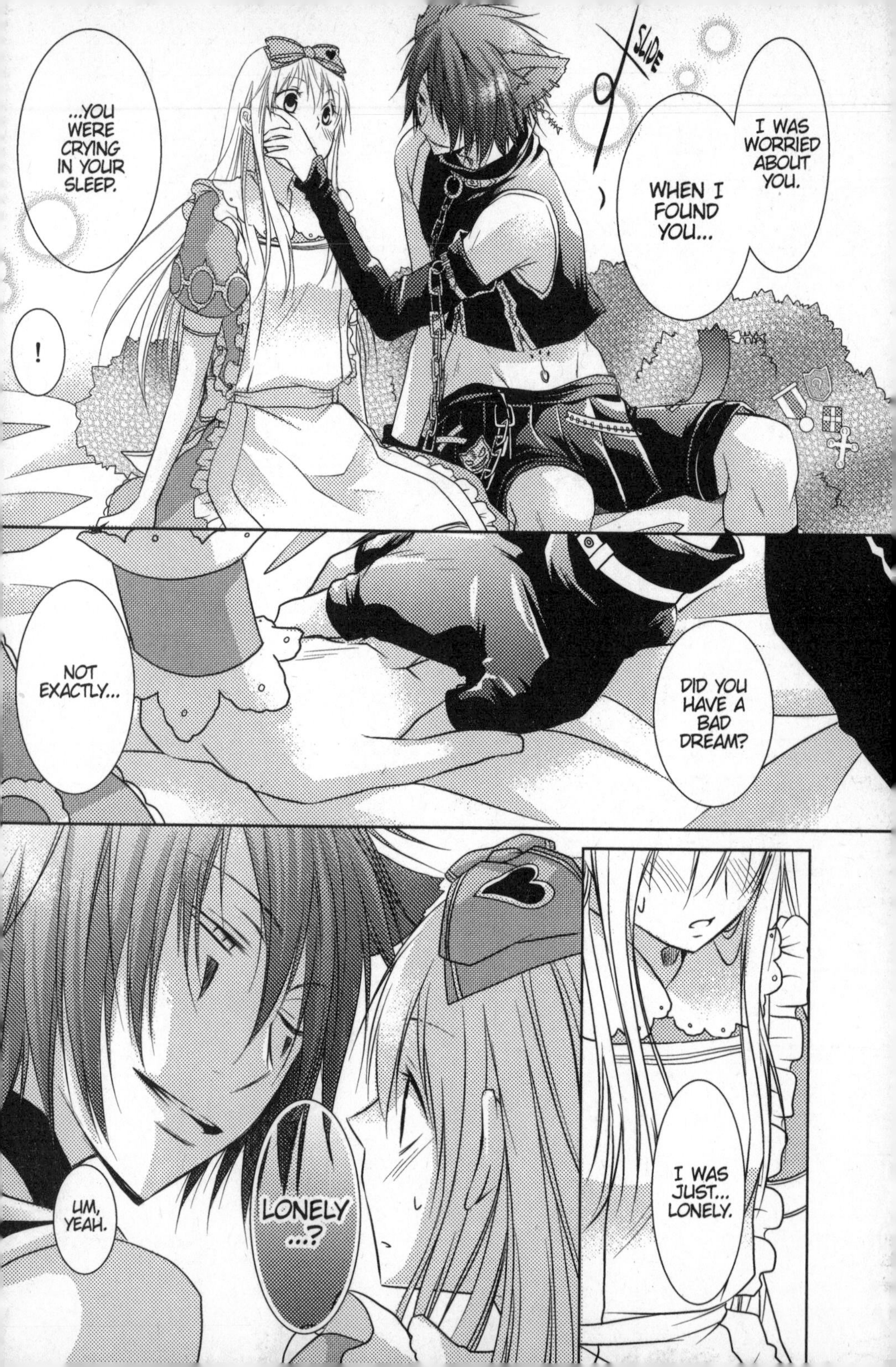
SLIDE
I WAS WORRIED ABOUT YOU.
WHEN I FOUND YOU...
...YOU WERE CRYING IN YOUR SLEEP.
!
DID YOU HAVE A BAD DREAM?
NOT EXACTLY...
I WAS JUST... LONELY.
LONELY ...?
UM, YEAH.

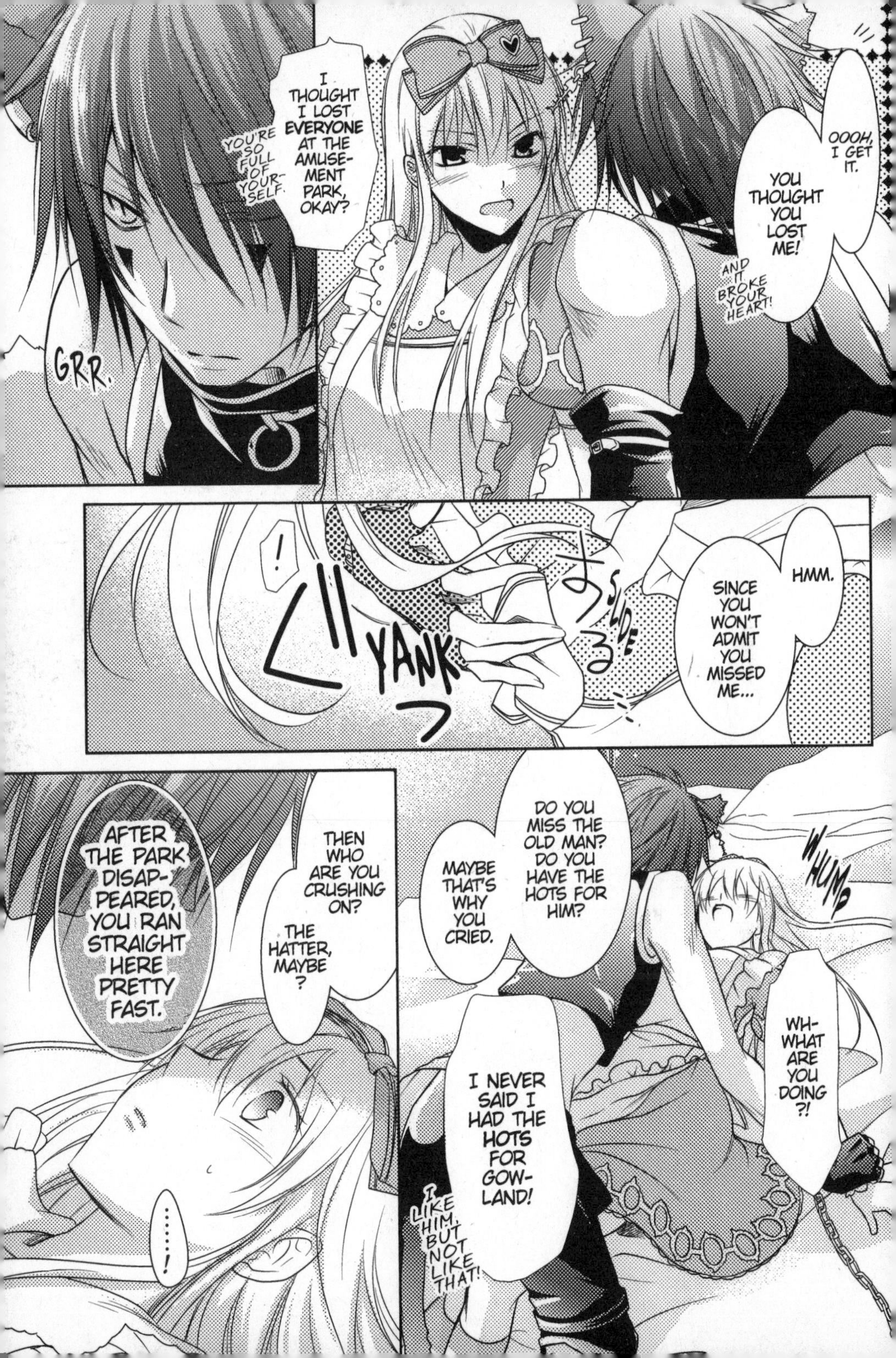
OOOH, I GET IT.
YOU THOUGHT YOU LOST ME!
AND IT BROKE YOUR HEART!
I THOUGHT I LOST EVERYONE AT THE AMUSEMENT PARK, OKAY?
YOU'RE SO FULL OF YOURSELF.
GRR.
HMM.
SINCE YOU WON'T ADMIT YOU MISSED ME...
SLIDE
YANK
!
WHUMP
WH-WHAT ARE YOU DOING?!
DO YOU MISS THE OLD MAN? DO YOU HAVE THE HOTS FOR HIM?
MAYBE THAT'S WHY YOU CRIED.
I NEVER SAID I HAD THE HOTS FOR GOWLAND!
I LIKE HIM, BUT NOT LIKE THAT!
THEN WHO ARE YOU CRUSHING ON?
THE HATTER, MAYBE?
AFTER THE PARK DISAPPEARED, YOU RAN STRAIGHT HERE PRETTY FAST.
......!

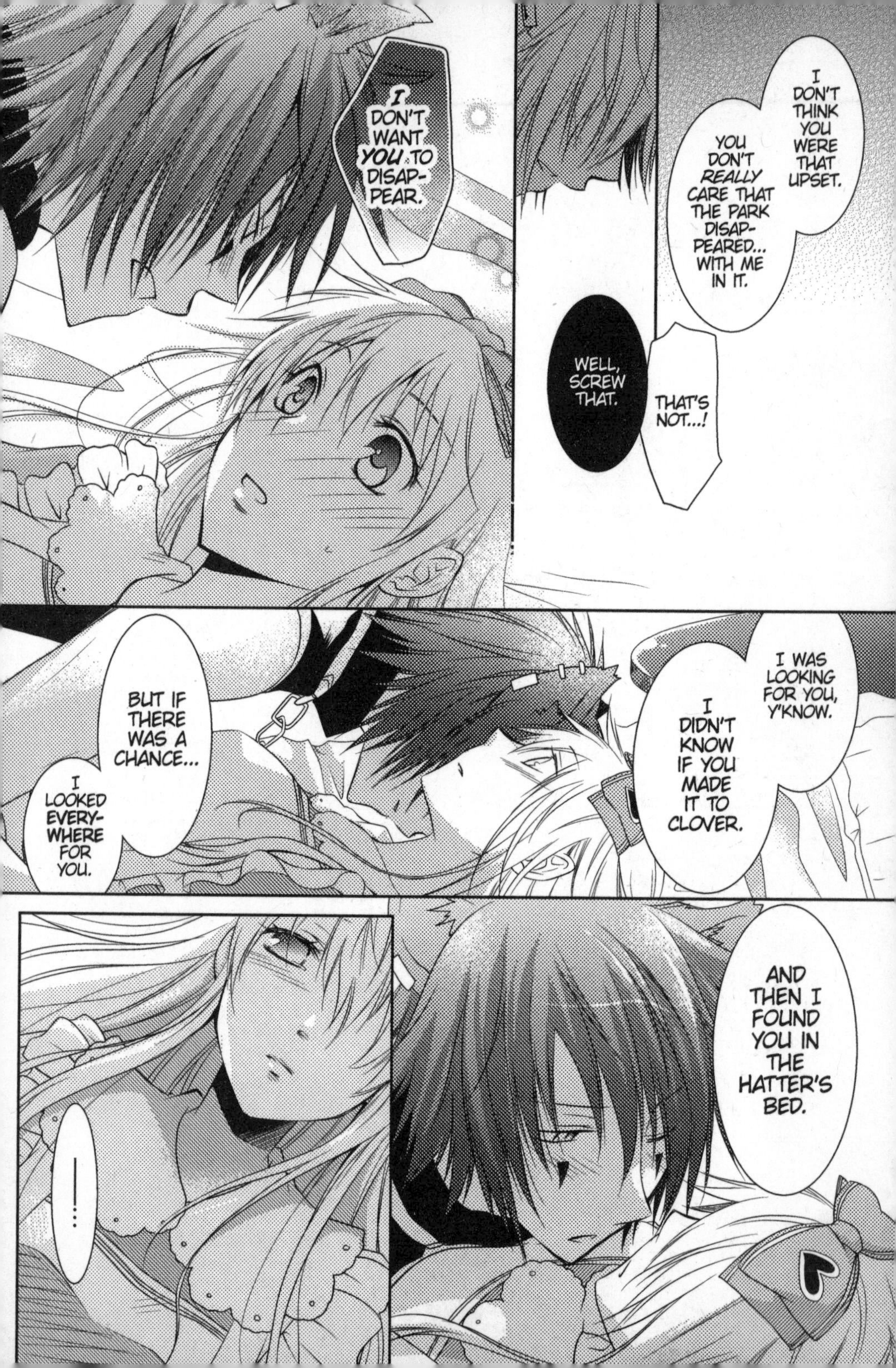
I DON'T THINK YOU WERE THAT UPSET.
YOU DON'T *REALLY* CARE THAT THE PARK DISAPPEARED... WITH ME IN IT.
THAT'S NOT...!
WELL, SCREW THAT.
I DON'T WANT *YOU* TO DISAPPEAR.
I WAS LOOKING FOR YOU, Y'KNOW.
I DIDN'T KNOW IF YOU MADE IT TO CLOVER.
BUT IF THERE WAS A CHANCE...
I LOOKED EVERYWHERE FOR YOU.
AND THEN I FOUND YOU IN THE HATTER'S BED.
......!

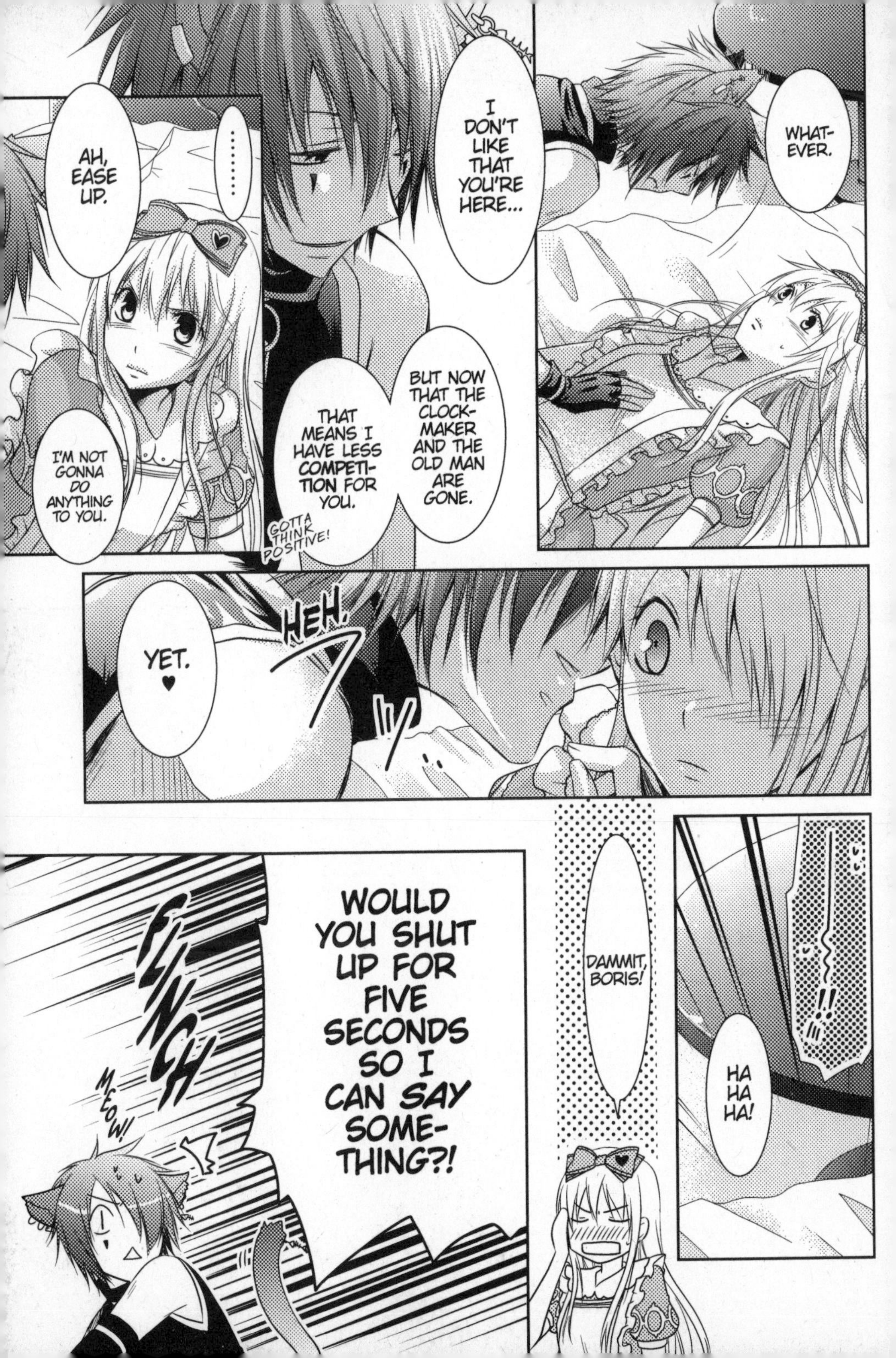
WHAT-EVER.
I DON'T LIKE THAT YOU'RE HERE...
BUT NOW THAT THE CLOCK-MAKER AND THE OLD MAN ARE GONE.
THAT MEANS I HAVE LESS COMPETI-TION FOR YOU.
GOTTA THINK POSITIVE!
......
AH, EASE UP.
I'M NOT GONNA DO ANYTHING TO YOU.
YET. ♥
HEH.
HA HA HA!
DAMMIT, BORIS!
WOULD YOU SHUT UP FOR FIVE SECONDS SO I CAN *SAY* SOME-THING?!
FLINCH
MEOW!

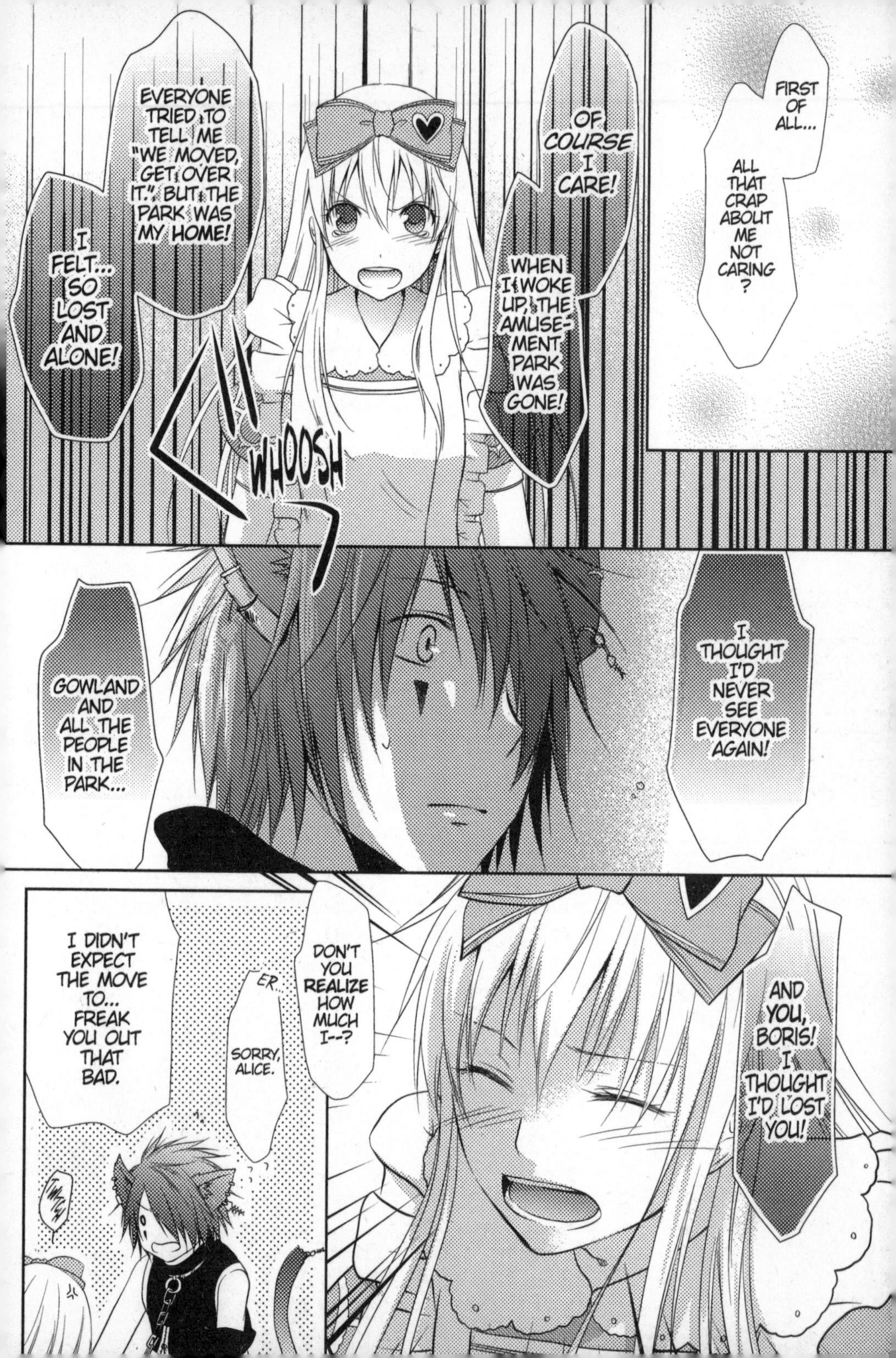
FIRST OF ALL...
ALL THAT CRAP ABOUT ME NOT CARING?
OF COURSE I CARE!
WHEN I WOKE UP, THE AMUSEMENT PARK WAS GONE!
EVERYONE TRIED TO TELL ME "WE MOVED, GET OVER IT." BUT THE PARK WAS MY HOME!
I FELT... SO LOST AND ALONE!
WHOOSH
I THOUGHT I'D NEVER SEE EVERYONE AGAIN!
GOWLAND AND ALL THE PEOPLE IN THE PARK...
AND YOU, BORIS! I THOUGHT I'D LOST YOU!
DON'T YOU REALIZE HOW MUCH I--?
ER...
SORRY, ALICE.
I DIDN'T EXPECT THE MOVE TO... FREAK YOU OUT THAT BAD.

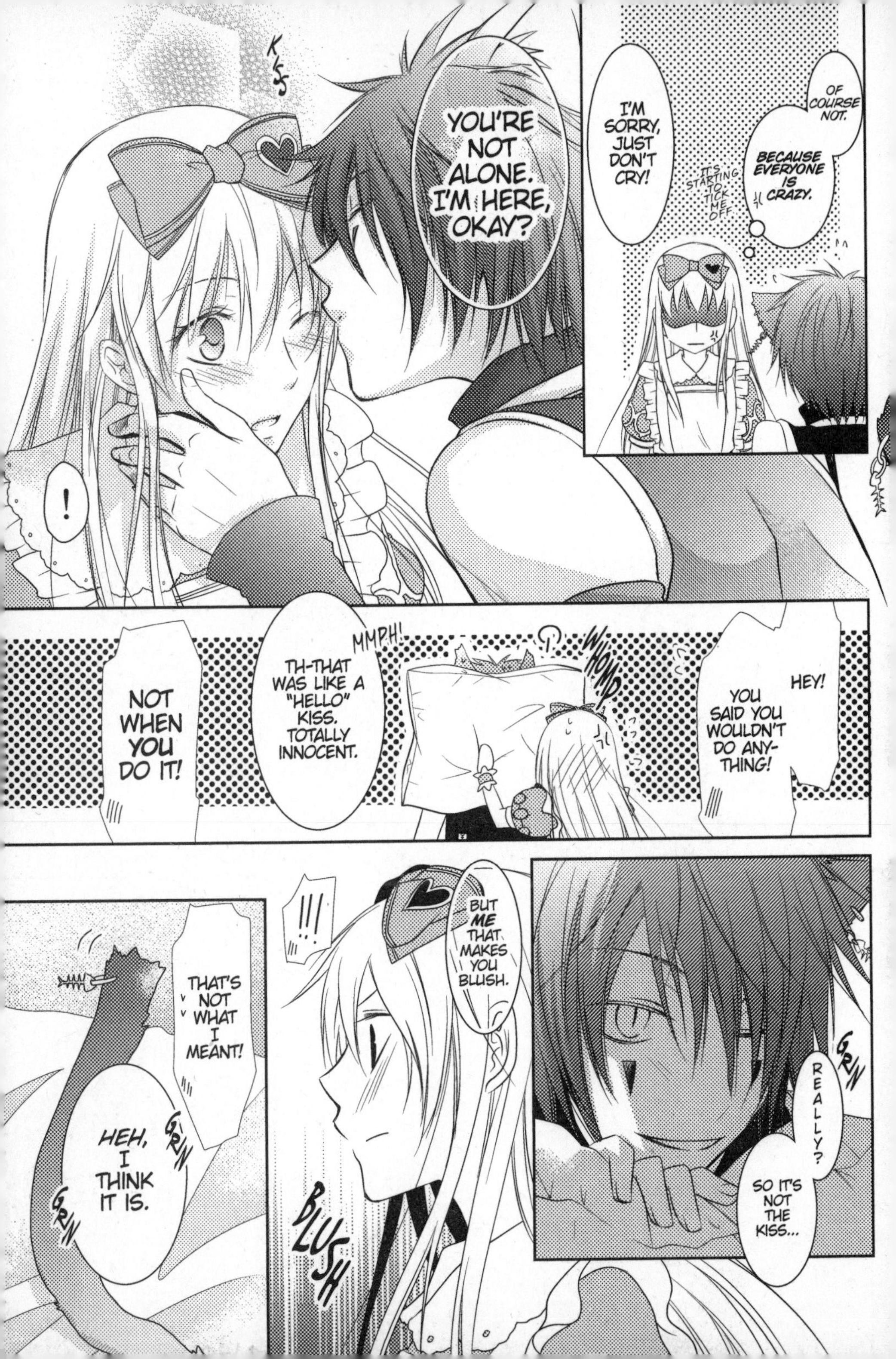
OF COURSE NOT.
BECAUSE EVERYONE IS CRAZY.
IT'S STARTING TO TICK ME OFF.
I'M SORRY, JUST DON'T CRY!
YOU'RE NOT ALONE. I'M HERE, OKAY?
KISS
!
HEY!
YOU SAID YOU WOULDN'T DO ANY-THING!
WHOMP
MMPH!
TH-THAT WAS LIKE A "HELLO" KISS. TOTALLY INNOCENT.
NOT WHEN YOU DO IT!
GRIN
REALLY?
SO IT'S NOT THE KISS...
BUT ME THAT MAKES YOU BLUSH.
!!!
BLUSH
THAT'S NOT WHAT I MEANT!
GRIN
HEH, I THINK IT IS.
GRIN

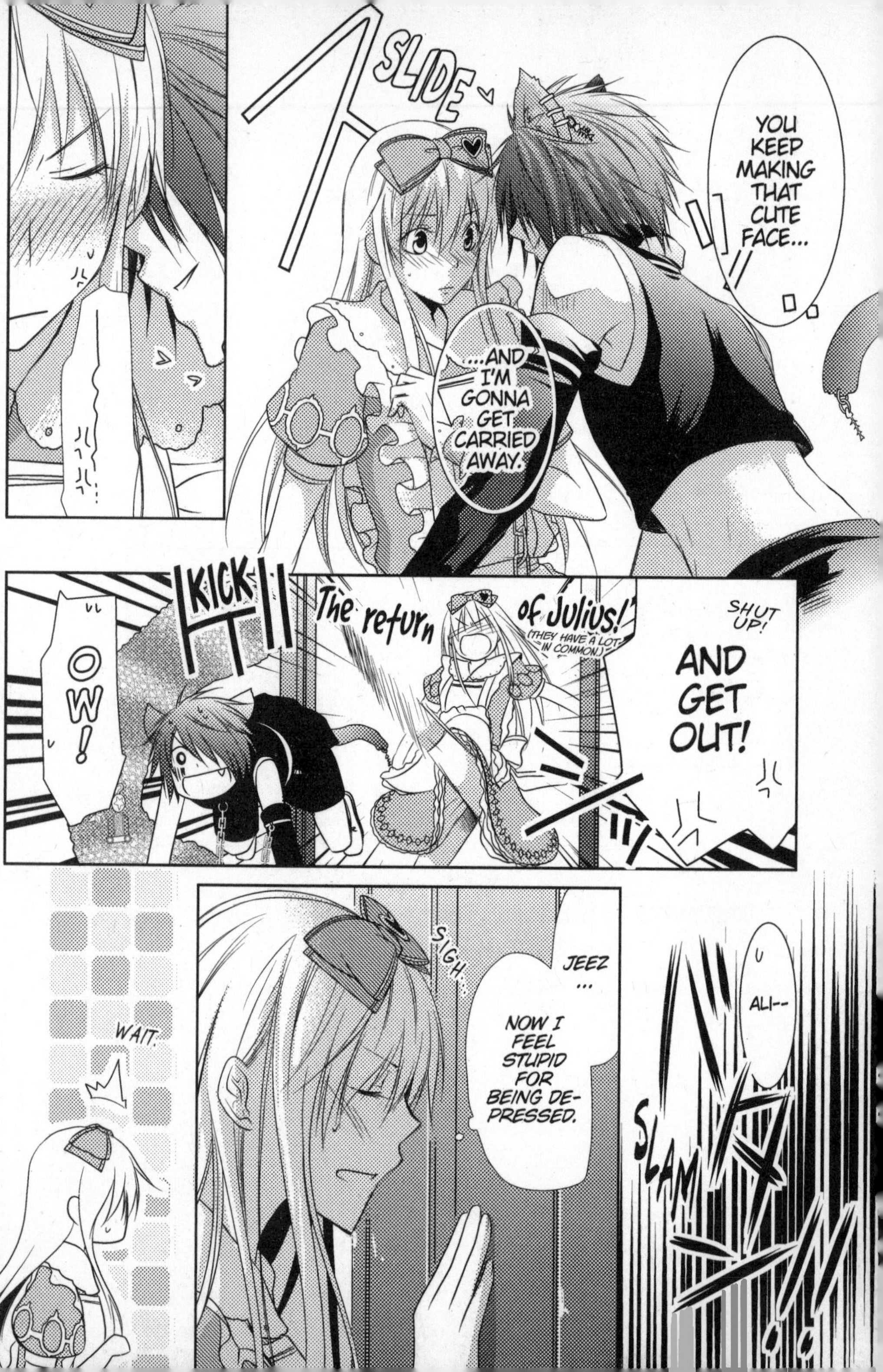
SLIDE
YOU KEEP MAKING THAT CUTE FACE...
...AND I'M GONNA GET CARRIED AWAY.
SHUT UP!
AND GET OUT!
The return of Julius!
(THEY HAVE A LOT IN COMMON.)
KICK
OW!
ALI--
SLAM
SIGH...
JEEZ...
NOW I FEEL STUPID FOR BEING DE-PRESSED.
WAIT.

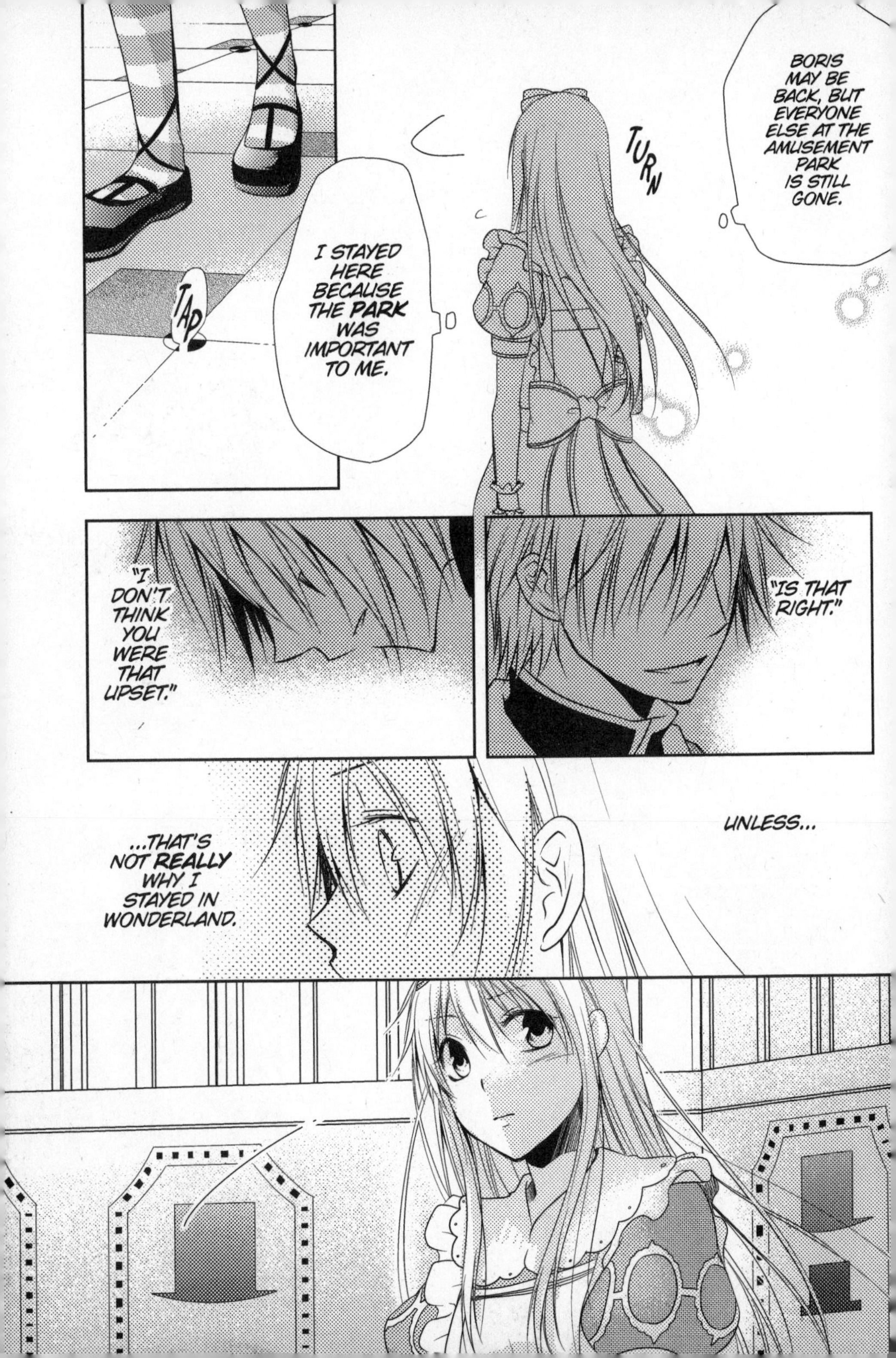
BORIS MAY BE BACK, BUT EVERYONE ELSE AT THE AMUSEMENT PARK IS STILL GONE.
TURN
I STAYED HERE BECAUSE THE PARK WAS IMPORTANT TO ME.
TAP
"IS THAT RIGHT."
"I DON'T THINK YOU WERE THAT UPSET."
UNLESS...
...THAT'S NOT REALLY WHY I STAYED IN WONDERLAND.

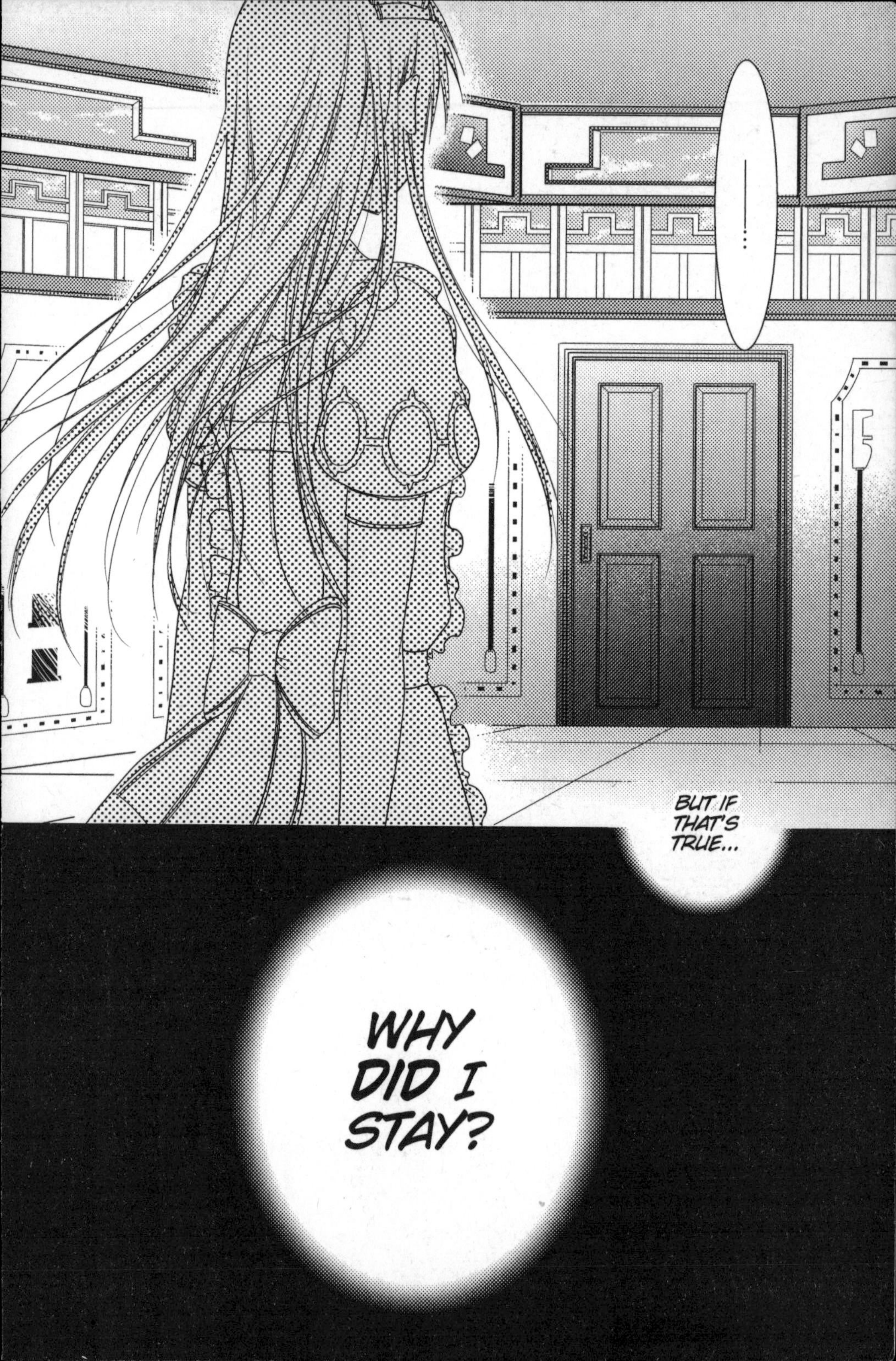
......
BUT IF THAT'S TRUE...
WHY DID I STAY?

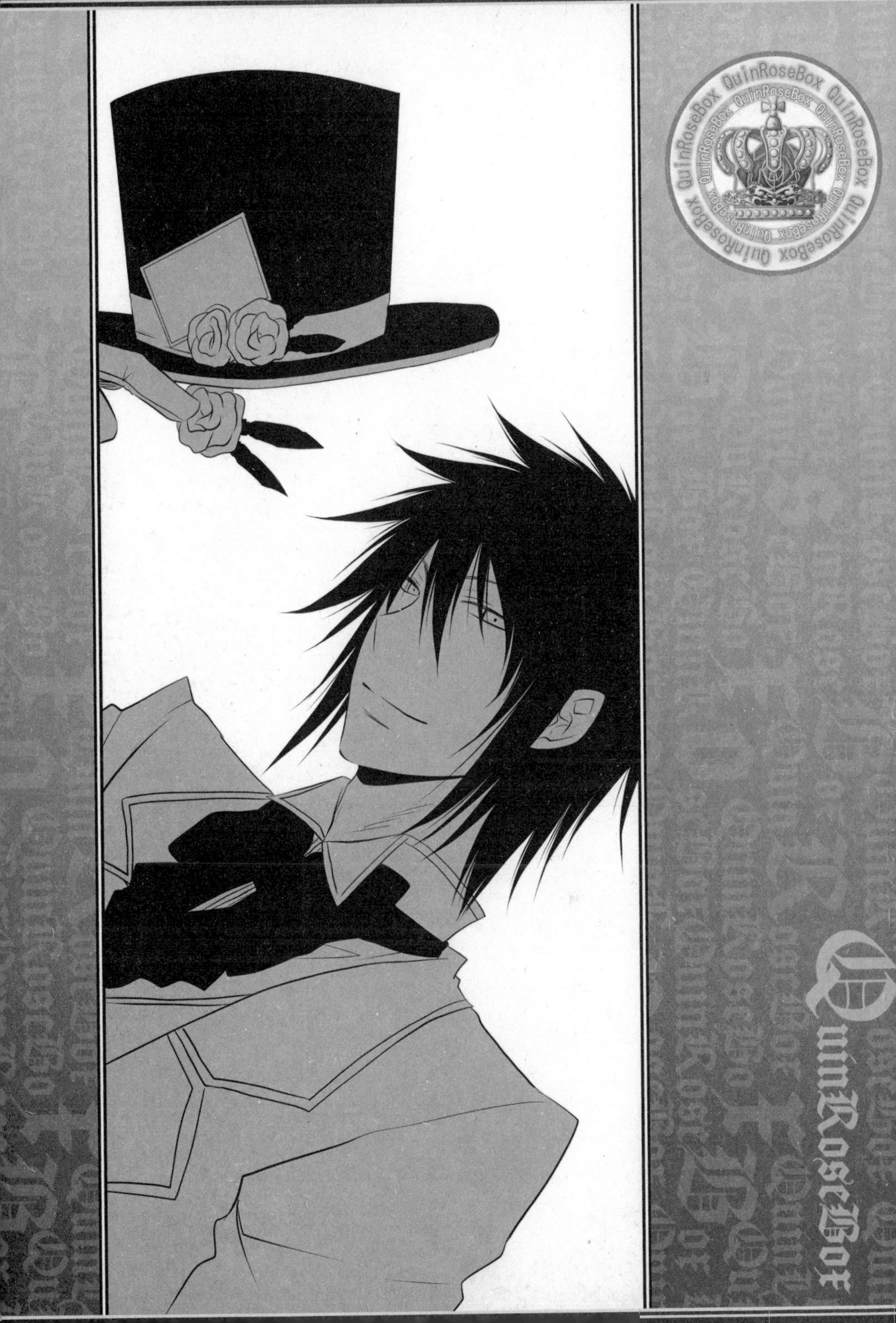
QuinRoseBox
QuinRoseBox

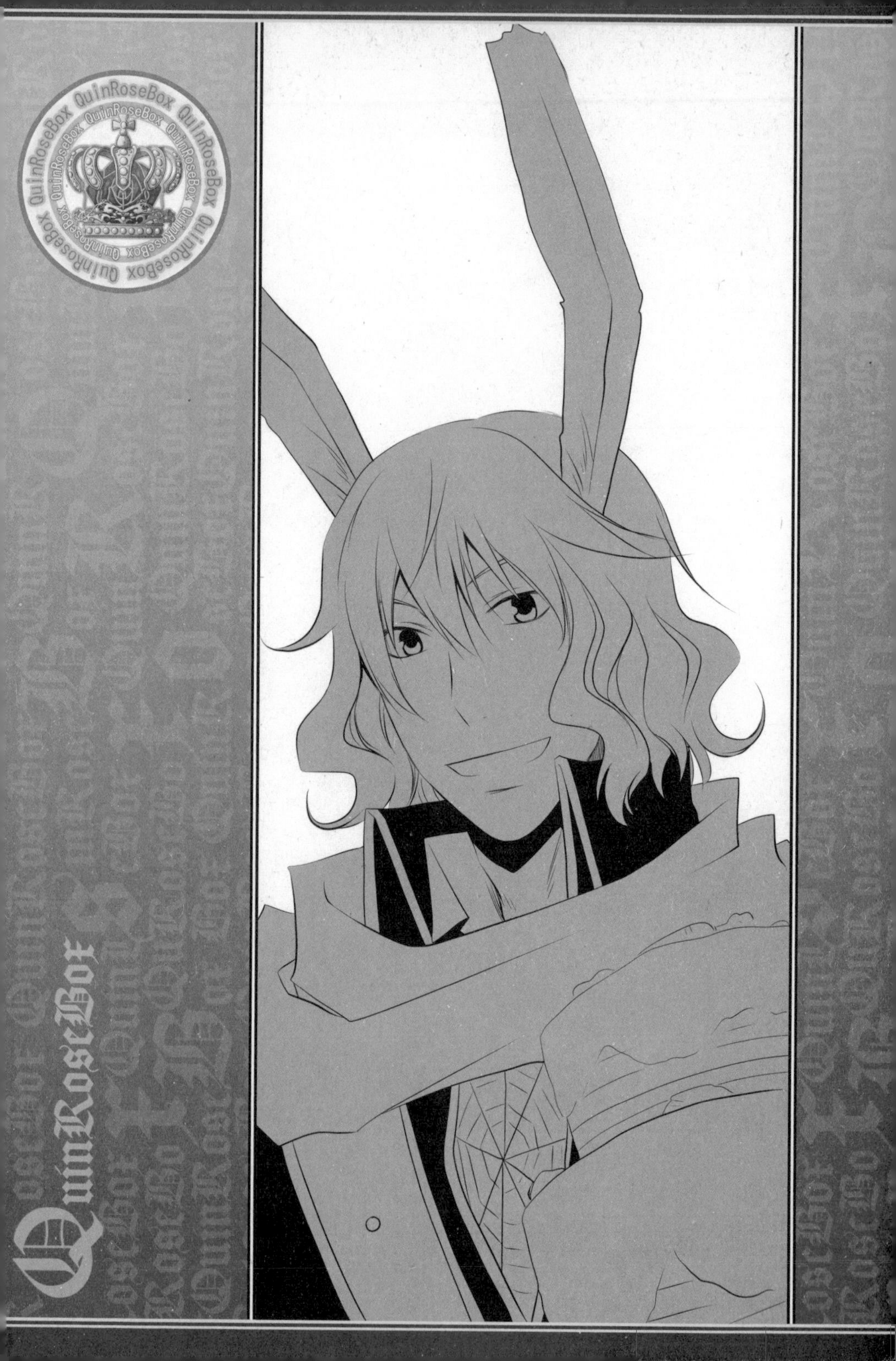

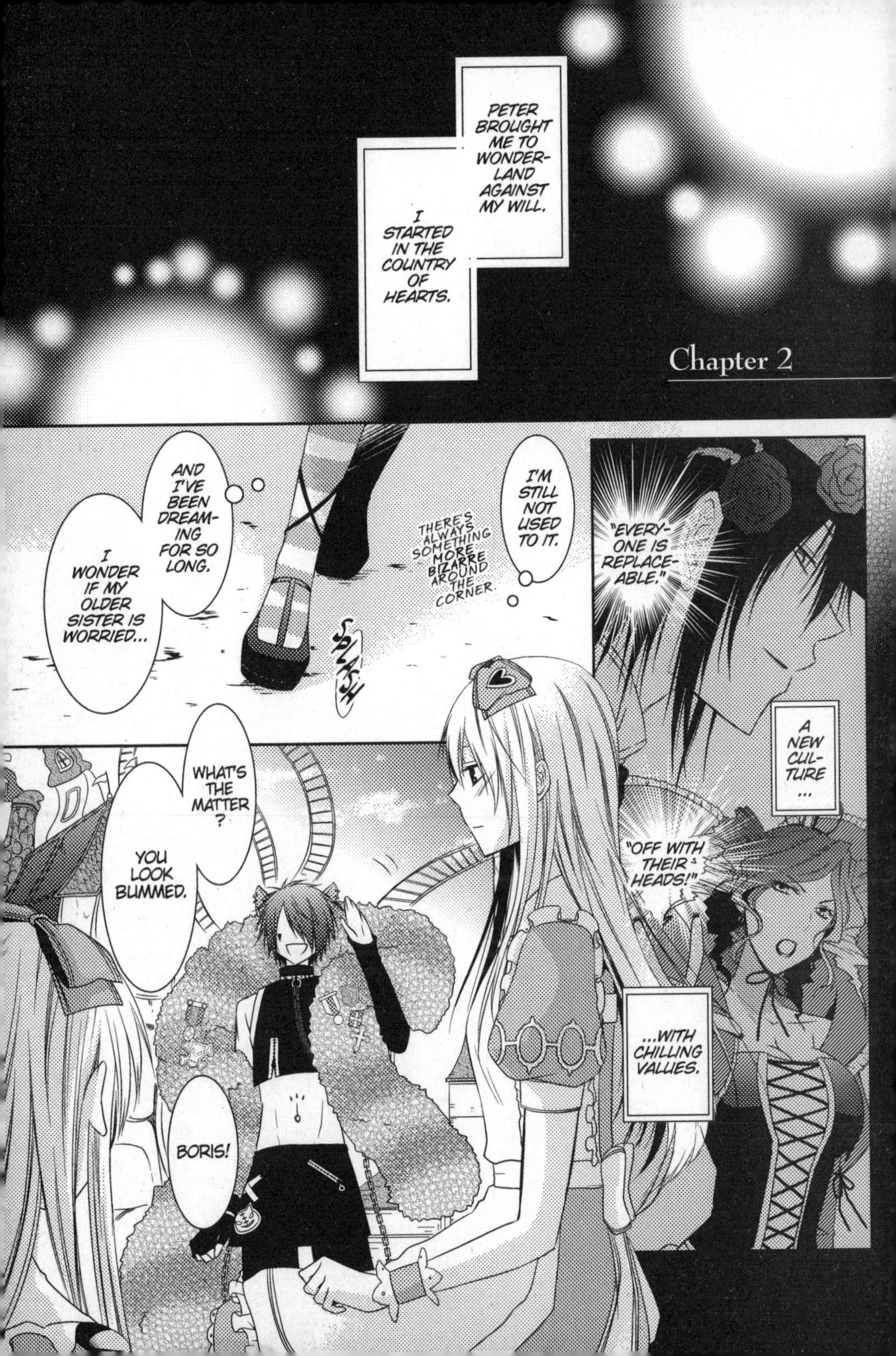
PETER BROUGHT ME TO WONDER-LAND AGAINST MY WILL.
I STARTED IN THE COUNTRY OF HEARTS.
Chapter 2
"EVERY-ONE IS REPLACE-ABLE."
A NEW CUL-TURE ...
"OFF WITH THEIR HEADS!"
...WITH CHILLING VALUES.
I'M STILL NOT USED TO IT.
THERE'S ALWAYS SOMETHING MORE BIZARRE AROUND THE CORNER.
AND I'VE BEEN DREAM-ING FOR SO LONG.
I WONDER IF MY OLDER SISTER IS WORRIED...
SPLASH
WHAT'S THE MATTER?
YOU LOOK BUMMED.
BORIS!

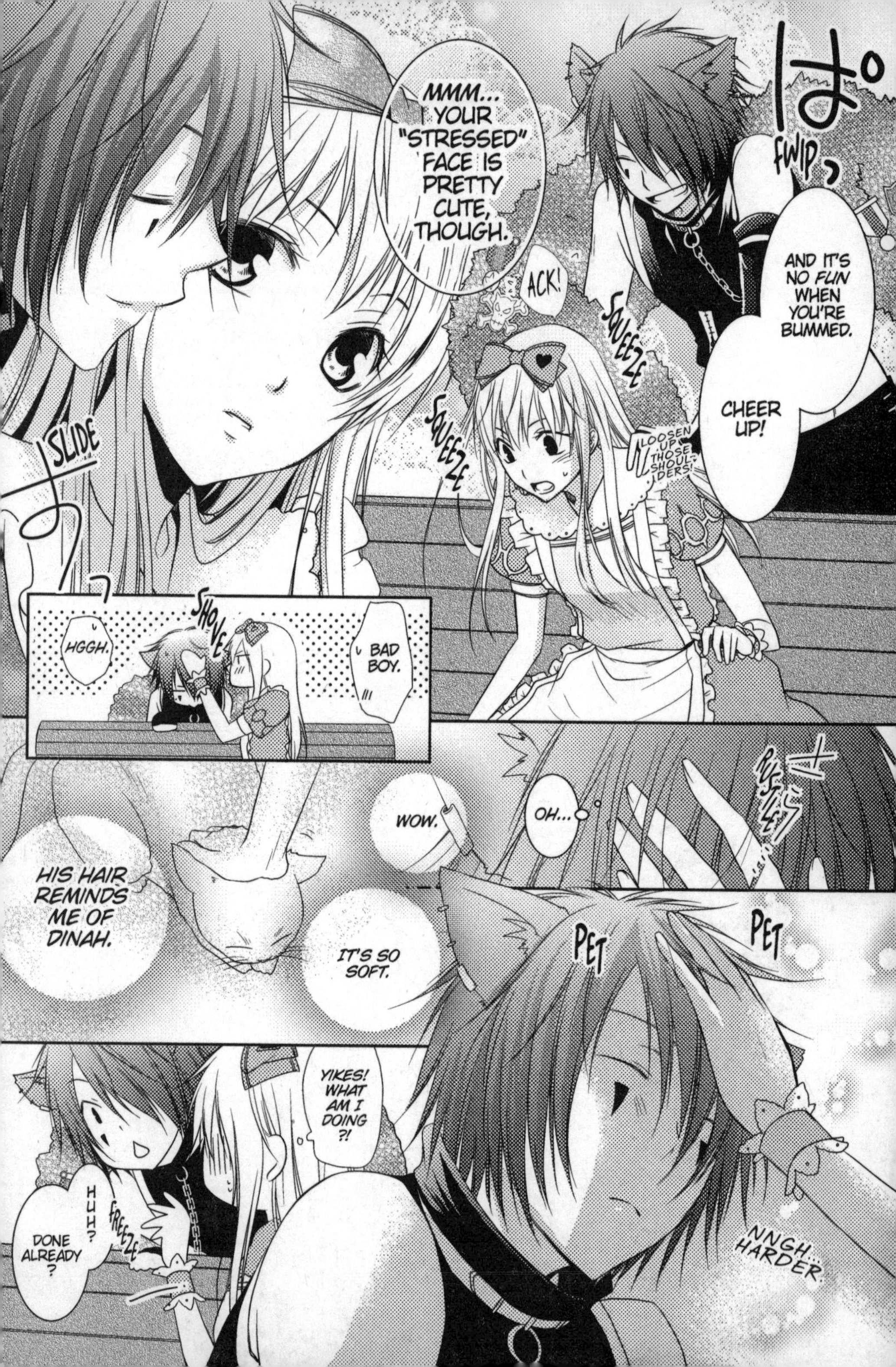
ぱ
FWIP,
AND IT'S NO FUN WHEN YOU'RE BUMMED.
CHEER UP!
LOOSEN UP THOSE SHOULDERS!
SQUEEZE
SQUEEZE
ACK!
MMM... YOUR "STRESSED" FACE IS PRETTY CUTE, THOUGH.
SLIDE
BAD BOY.
SHOVE
HGGH.
RUSTLE
OH...
WOW.
HIS HAIR REMINDS ME OF DINAH.
IT'S SO SOFT.
PET
PET
NNGH... HARDER.
YIKES! WHAT AM I DOING?!
FREEZE
HUH?
DONE ALREADY?

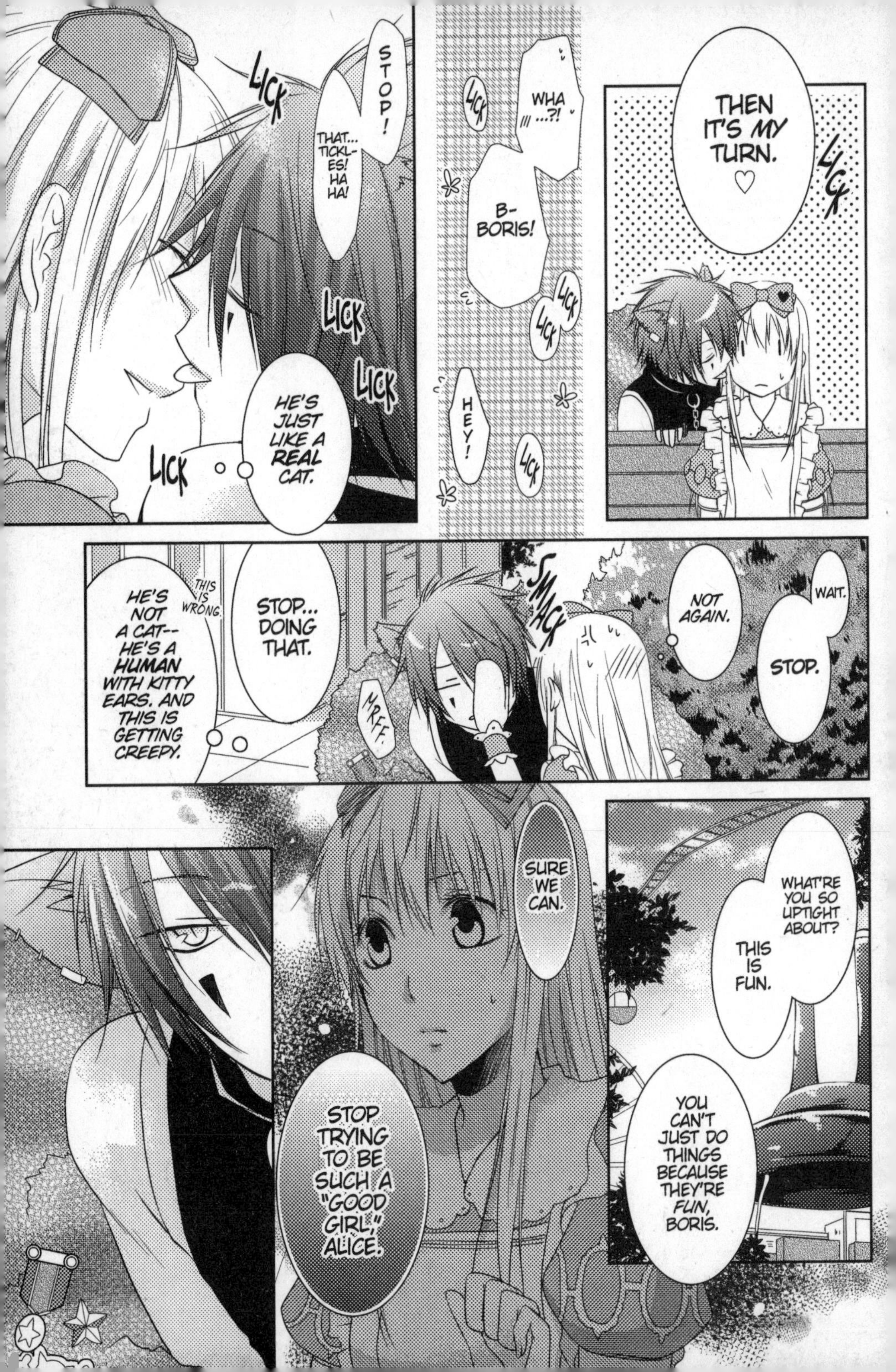
THEN IT'S *MY* TURN. ♡
LICK
WHA ...?!
LICK
B- BORIS!
LICK
LICK
HEY!
LICK
STOP!
THAT... TICKL- ES! HA HA!
LICK
LICK
LICK
HE'S JUST LIKE A **REAL** CAT.
LICK
WAIT.
STOP.
NOT AGAIN.
SMACK
MRFF.
STOP... DOING THAT.
THIS IS WRONG.
HE'S NOT A CAT-- HE'S A **HUMAN** WITH KITTY EARS. AND THIS IS GETTING CREEPY.
WHAT'RE YOU SO UPTIGHT ABOUT?
THIS IS FUN.
YOU CAN'T JUST DO THINGS BECAUSE THEY'RE *FUN*, BORIS.
SURE WE CAN.
STOP TRYING TO BE SUCH A "GOOD GIRL," ALICE.

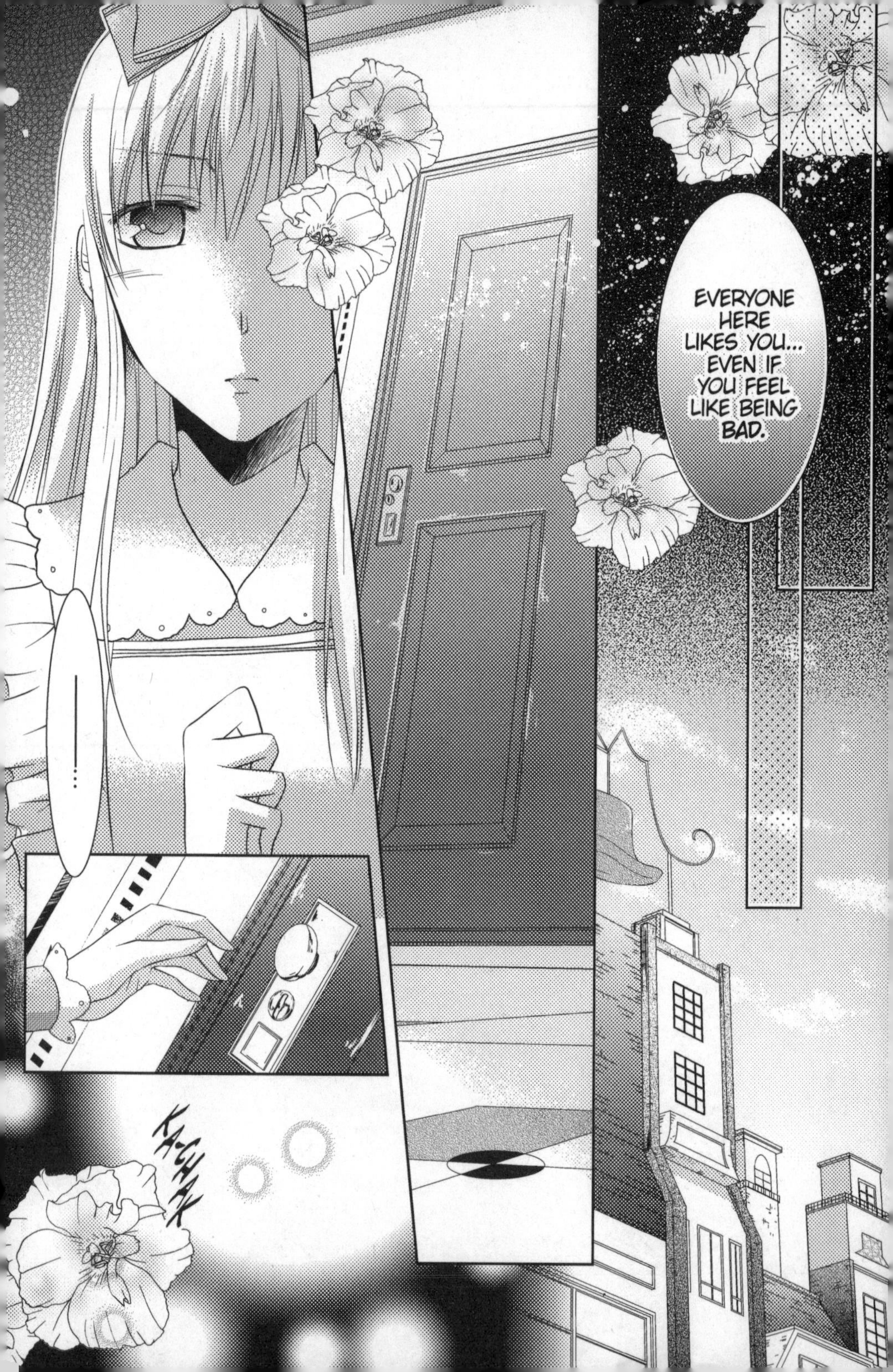

EVERYONE HERE LIKES YOU... EVEN IF YOU FEEL LIKE BEING BAD.
......
KA-CHAK

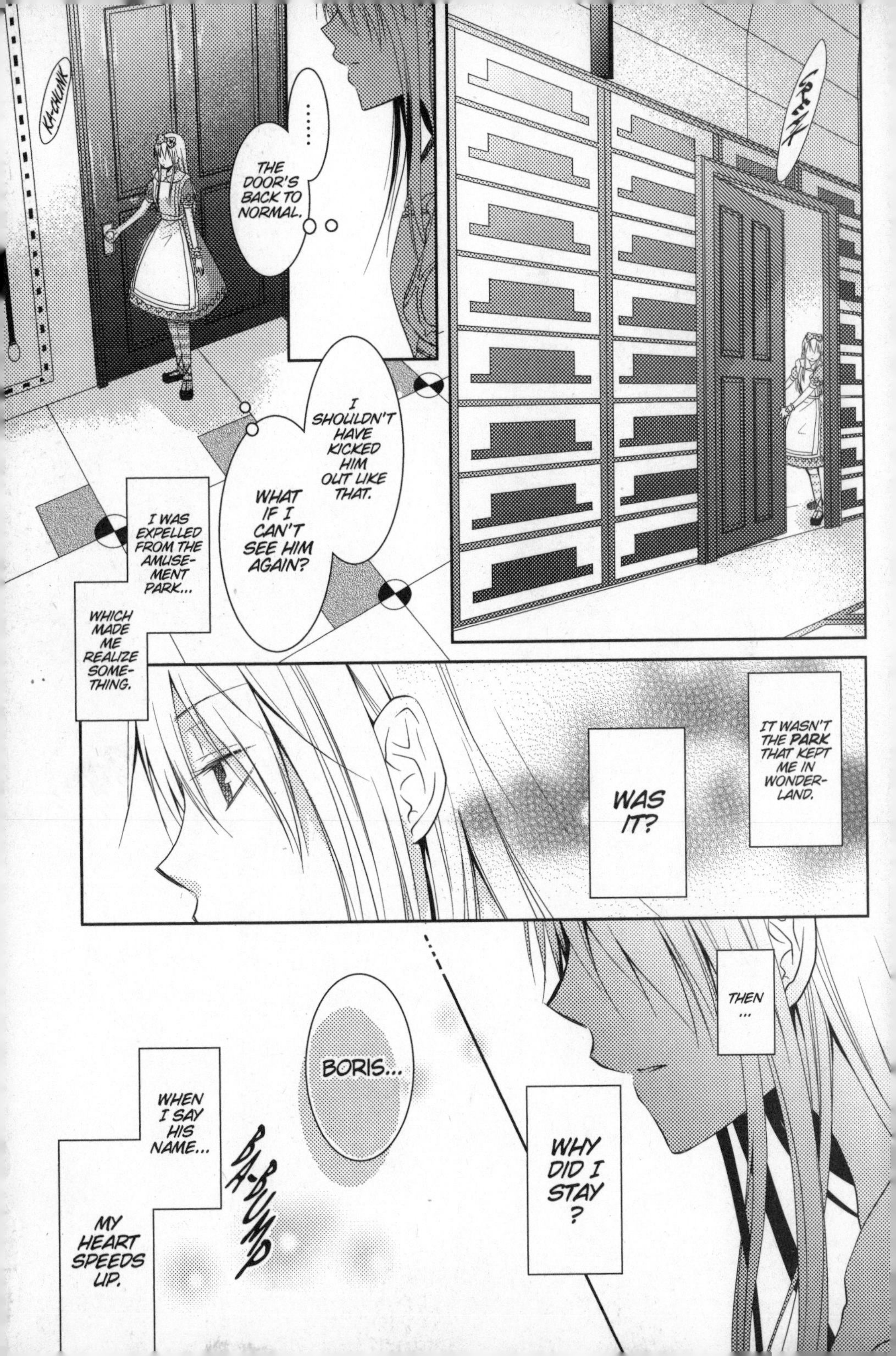
CREAK
......
THE DOOR'S BACK TO NORMAL.
KA-CHUNK
I SHOULDN'T HAVE KICKED HIM OUT LIKE THAT.
WHAT IF I CAN'T SEE HIM AGAIN?
I WAS EXPELLED FROM THE AMUSEMENT PARK...
WHICH MADE ME REALIZE SOMETHING.
IT WASN'T THE PARK THAT KEPT ME IN WONDERLAND.
WAS IT?
THEN...
WHY DID I STAY?
BORIS...
WHEN I SAY HIS NAME...
BA-BUMP
MY HEART SPEEDS UP.

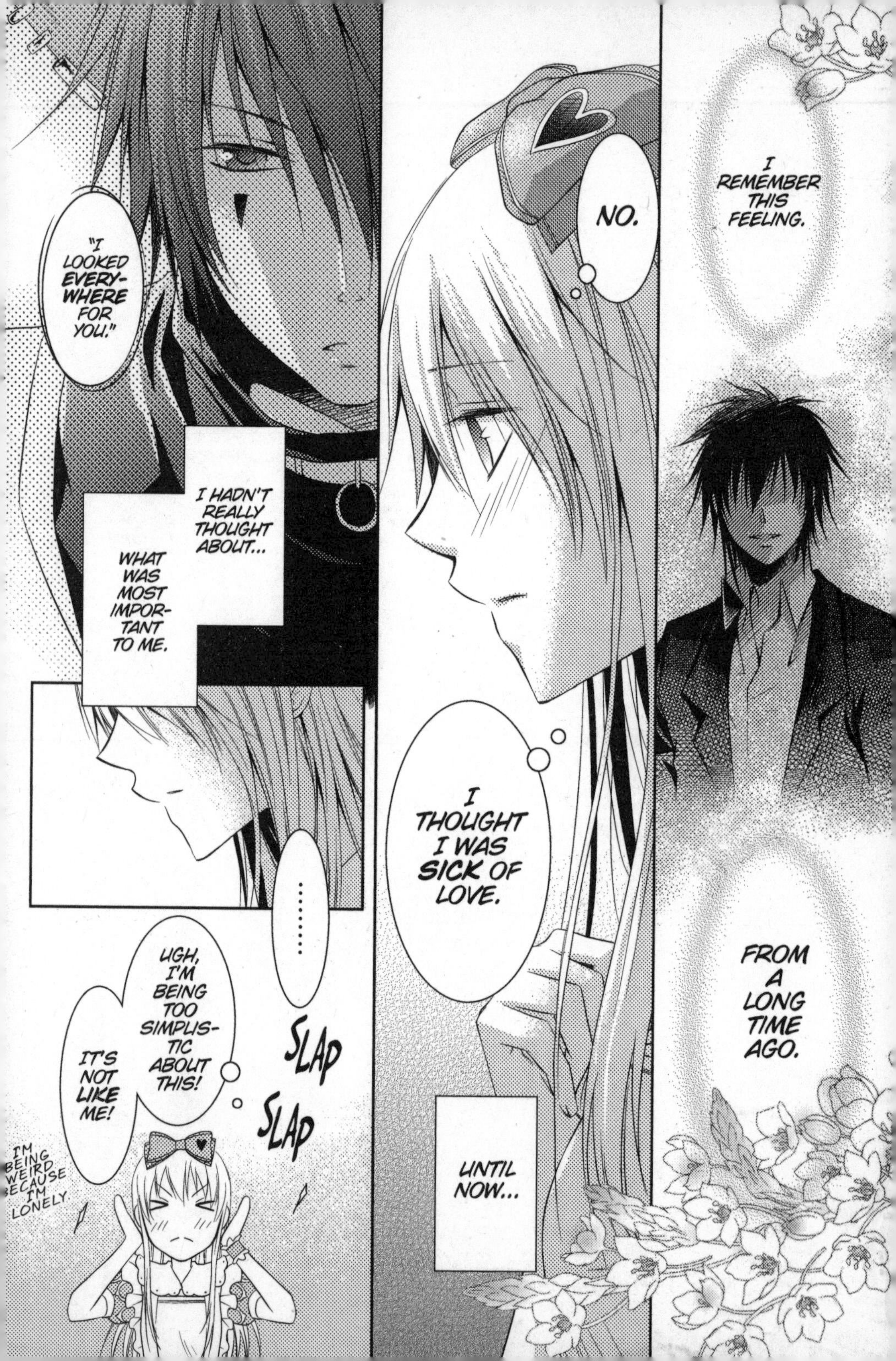
I REMEMBER THIS FEELING.
FROM A LONG TIME AGO.
NO.
I THOUGHT I WAS SICK OF LOVE.
UNTIL NOW...
"I LOOKED EVERY-WHERE FOR YOU."
I HADN'T REALLY THOUGHT ABOUT...
WHAT WAS MOST IMPOR-TANT TO ME.
......
UGH, I'M BEING TOO SIMPLIS-TIC ABOUT THIS!
IT'S NOT LIKE ME!
SLAP
SLAP
I'M BEING WEIRD BECAUSE I'M LONELY

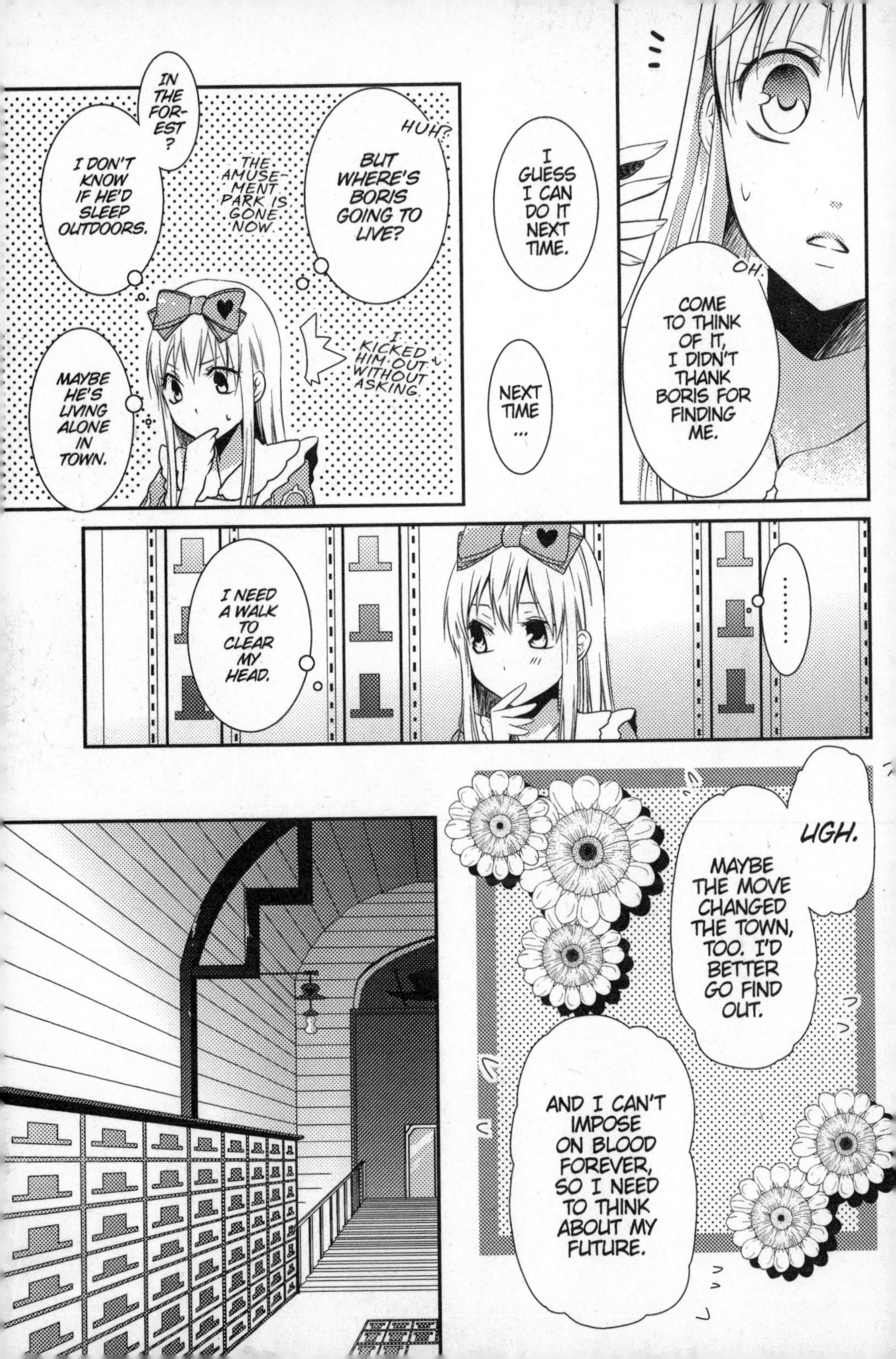
OH.
COME TO THINK OF IT, I DIDN'T THANK BORIS FOR FINDING ME.
I GUESS I CAN DO IT NEXT TIME.
NEXT TIME...
HUH?
BUT WHERE'S BORIS GOING TO LIVE?
THE AMUSEMENT PARK IS GONE NOW.
IN THE FOR-EST?
I DON'T KNOW IF HE'D SLEEP OUTDOORS.
I KICKED HIM OUT WITHOUT ASKING.
MAYBE HE'S LIVING ALONE IN TOWN.
......
I NEED A WALK TO CLEAR MY HEAD.
UGH.
MAYBE THE MOVE CHANGED THE TOWN, TOO. I'D BETTER GO FIND OUT.
AND I CAN'T IMPOSE ON BLOOD FOREVER, SO I NEED TO THINK ABOUT MY FUTURE.

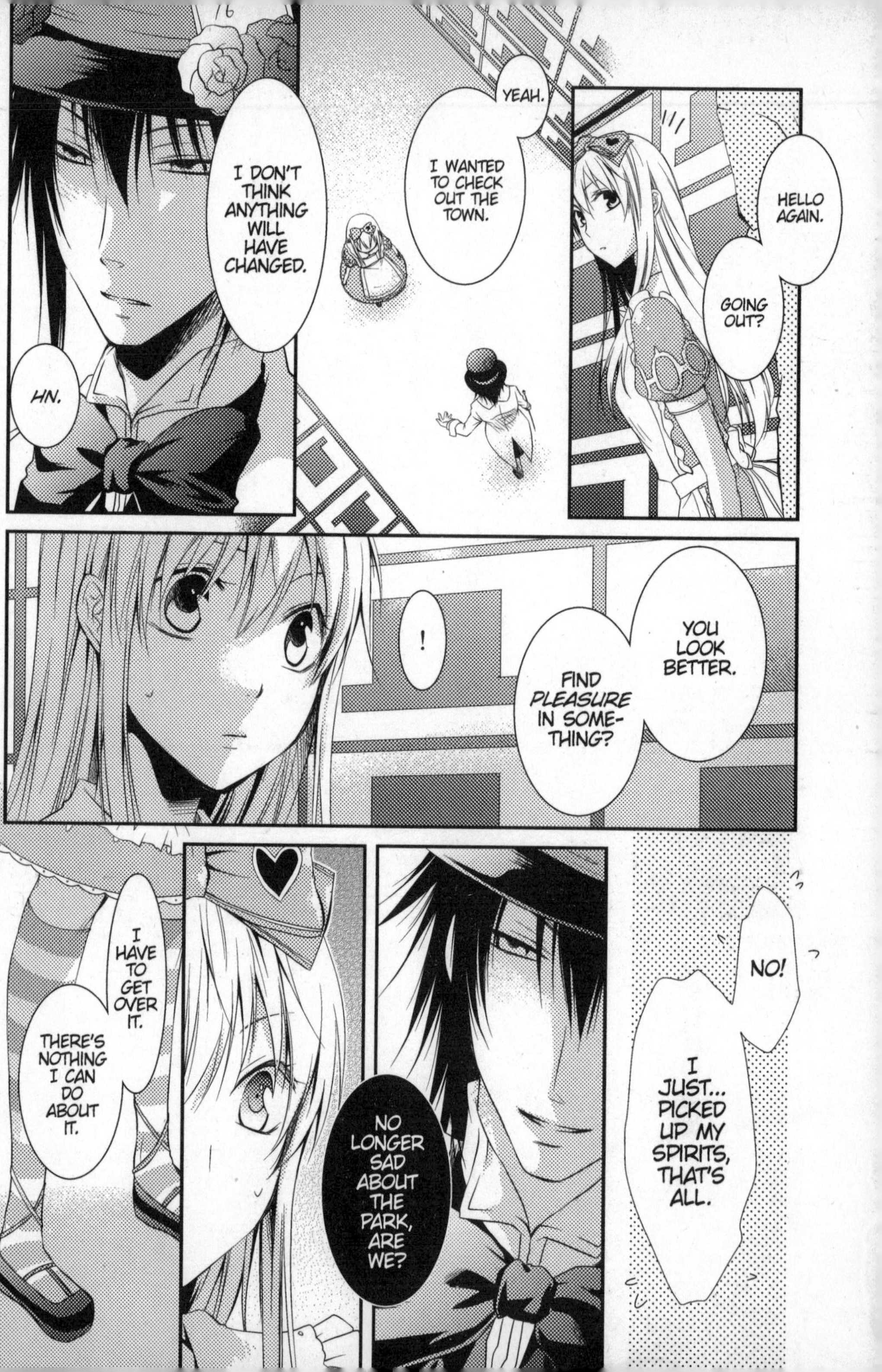
HELLO AGAIN.
GOING OUT?
YEAH.
I WANTED TO CHECK OUT THE TOWN.
I DON'T THINK ANYTHING WILL HAVE CHANGED.
HN.
YOU LOOK BETTER.
FIND *PLEASURE* IN SOME-THING?
!
NO!
I JUST... PICKED UP MY SPIRITS, THAT'S ALL.
NO LONGER SAD ABOUT THE PARK, ARE WE?
I HAVE TO GET OVER IT.
THERE'S NOTHING I CAN DO ABOUT IT.

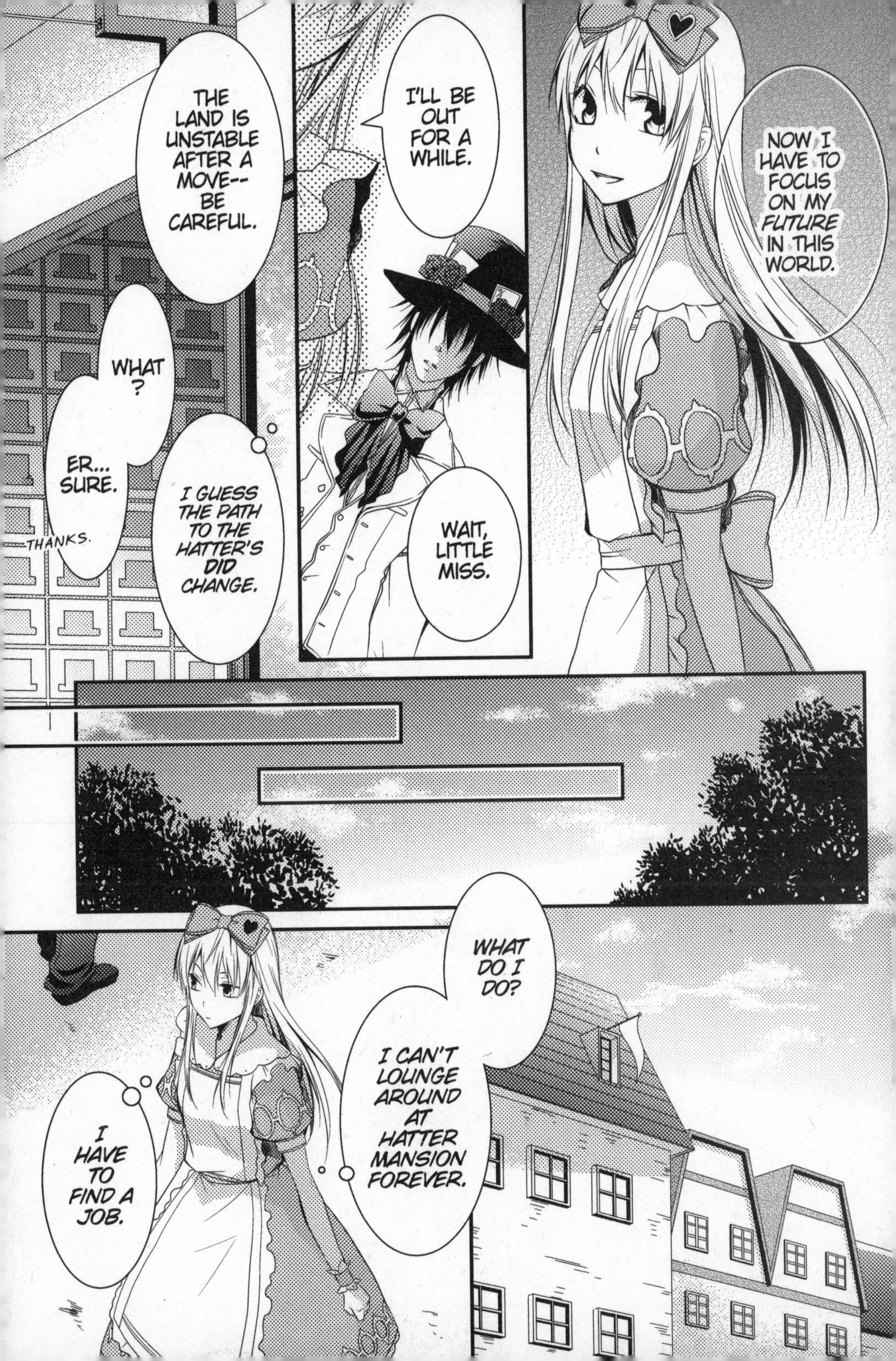
NOW I HAVE TO FOCUS ON MY FUTURE IN THIS WORLD.
I'LL BE OUT FOR A WHILE.
WAIT, LITTLE MISS.
THE LAND IS UNSTABLE AFTER A MOVE--BE CAREFUL.
WHAT?
I GUESS THE PATH TO THE HATTER'S DID CHANGE.
ER... SURE.
THANKS.
WHAT DO I DO?
I CAN'T LOUNGE AROUND AT HATTER MANSION FOREVER.
I HAVE TO FIND A JOB.

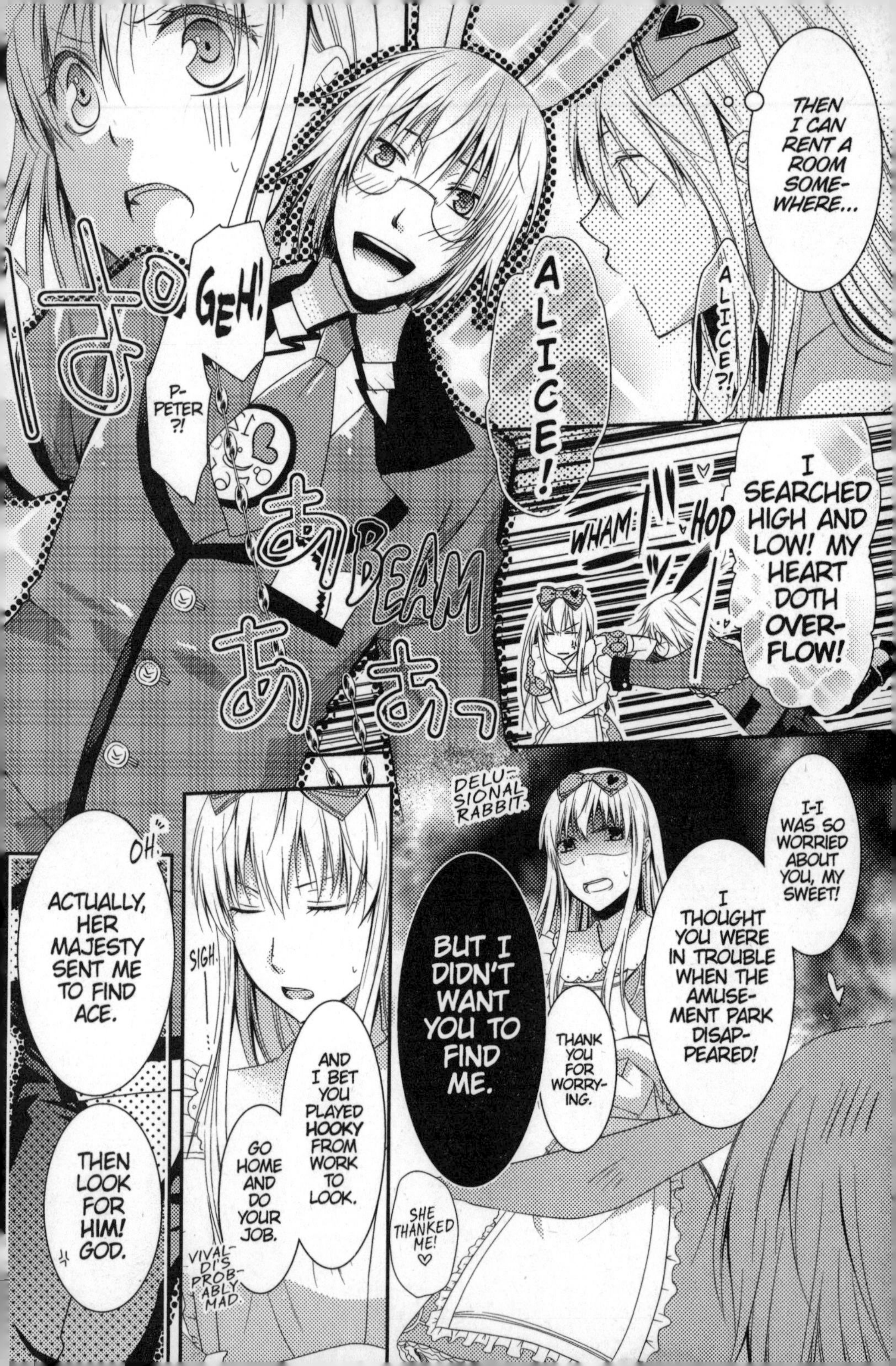
THEN I CAN RENT A ROOM SOME-WHERE...
ALICE?!
ALICE!
WHAM
HOP
I SEARCHED HIGH AND LOW! MY HEART DOTH OVER-FLOW!
GEH!
P-PETER?!
BEAM
あああっ
DELU-SIONAL RABBIT.
I-I WAS SO WORRIED ABOUT YOU, MY SWEET!
I THOUGHT YOU WERE IN TROUBLE WHEN THE AMUSE-MENT PARK DISAP-PEARED!
THANK YOU FOR WORRY-ING.
BUT I DIDN'T WANT YOU TO FIND ME.
SHE THANKED ME!
SIGH.
AND I BET YOU PLAYED HOOKY FROM WORK TO LOOK.
GO HOME AND DO YOUR JOB.
VIVAL-DI'S PROB-ABLY MAD.
OH.
ACTUALLY, HER MAJESTY SENT ME TO FIND ACE.
THEN LOOK FOR HIM! GOD.

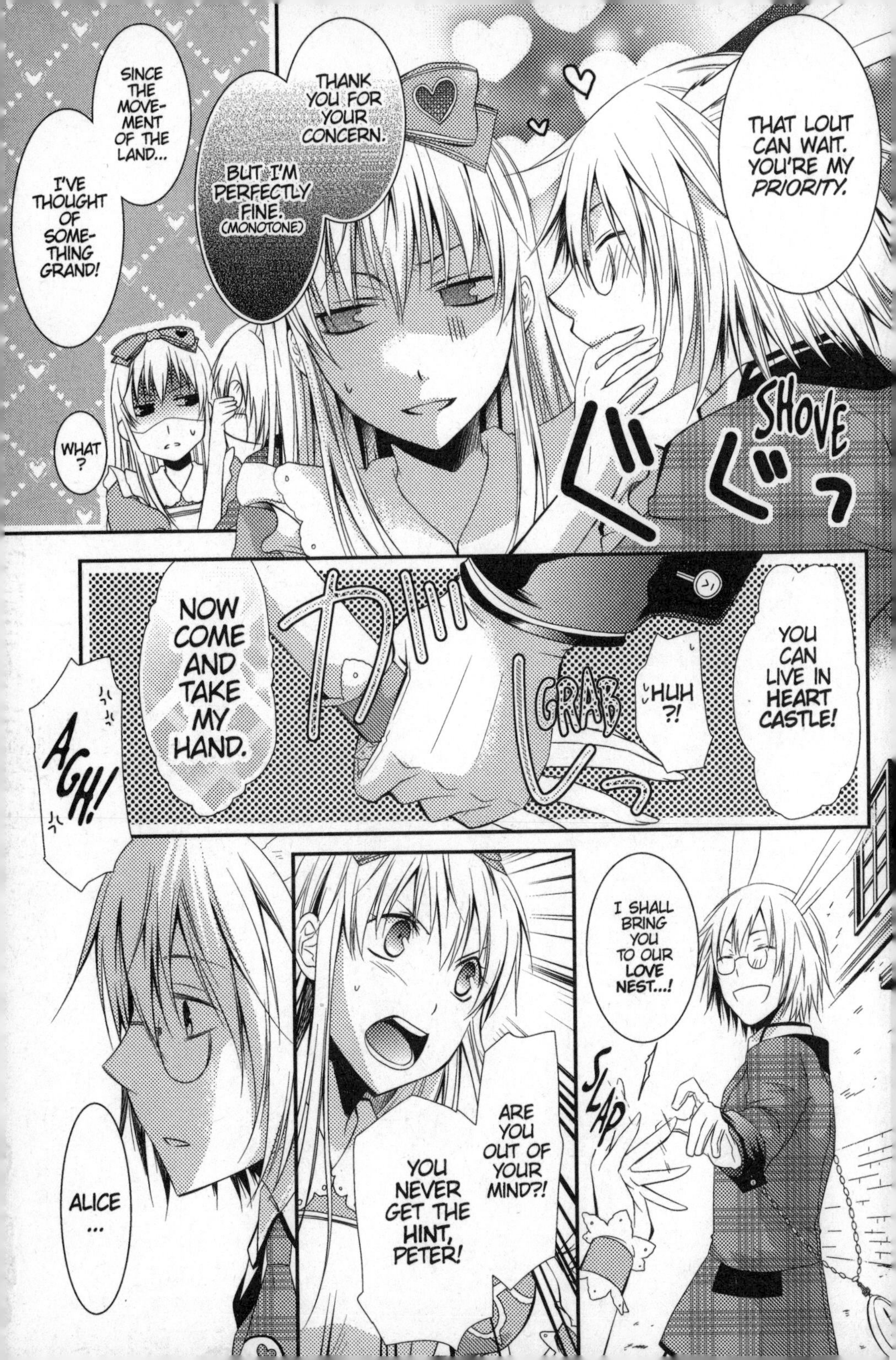
THAT LOUT CAN WAIT. YOU'RE MY *PRIORITY.*
THANK YOU FOR YOUR CONCERN.
BUT I'M PERFECTLY FINE. (MONOTONE)
SHOVE
SINCE THE MOVE-MENT OF THE LAND...
I'VE THOUGHT OF SOME-THING GRAND!
WHAT?
YOU CAN LIVE IN HEART CASTLE!
HUH?!
GRAB
NOW COME AND TAKE MY HAND.
AGH!
I SHALL BRING YOU TO OUR LOVE NEST...!
SLAP
ARE YOU OUT OF YOUR MIND?!
YOU NEVER GET THE HINT, PETER!
ALICE...

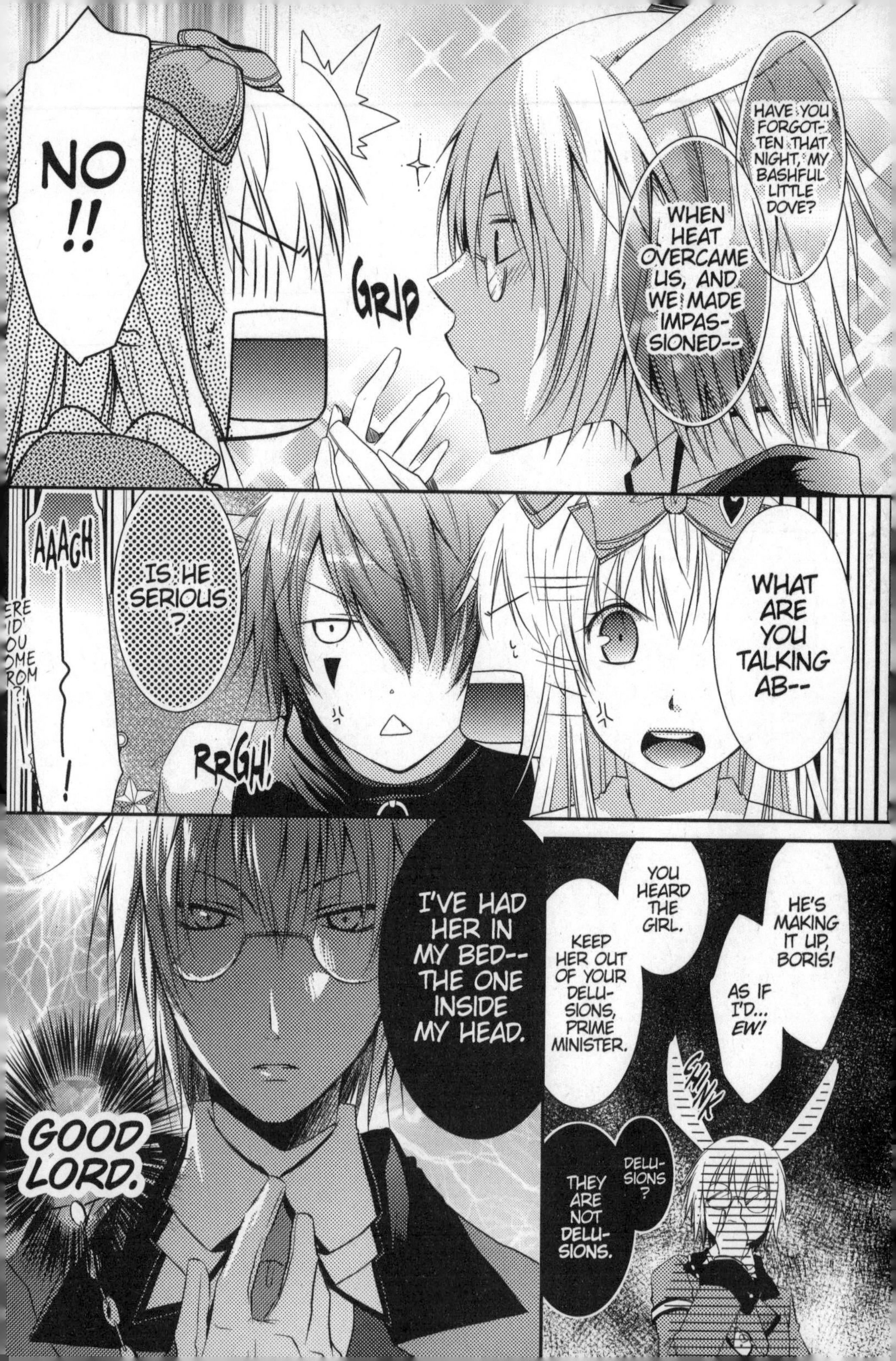
HAVE YOU FORGOTTEN THAT NIGHT, MY BASHFUL LITTLE DOVE?
WHEN HEAT OVERCAME US, AND WE MADE IMPASSIONED--
GRIP
NO !!
WHAT ARE YOU TALKING AB--
IS HE SERIOUS?
RRGH!
AAAGH
HE'S MAKING IT UP, BORIS!
AS IF I'D... *EW!*
YOU HEARD THE GIRL.
KEEP HER OUT OF YOUR DELUSIONS, PRIME MINISTER.
SHINK
DELUSIONS?
THEY ARE NOT DELUSIONS.
I'VE HAD HER IN MY BED-- THE ONE INSIDE MY HEAD.
GOOD LORD.

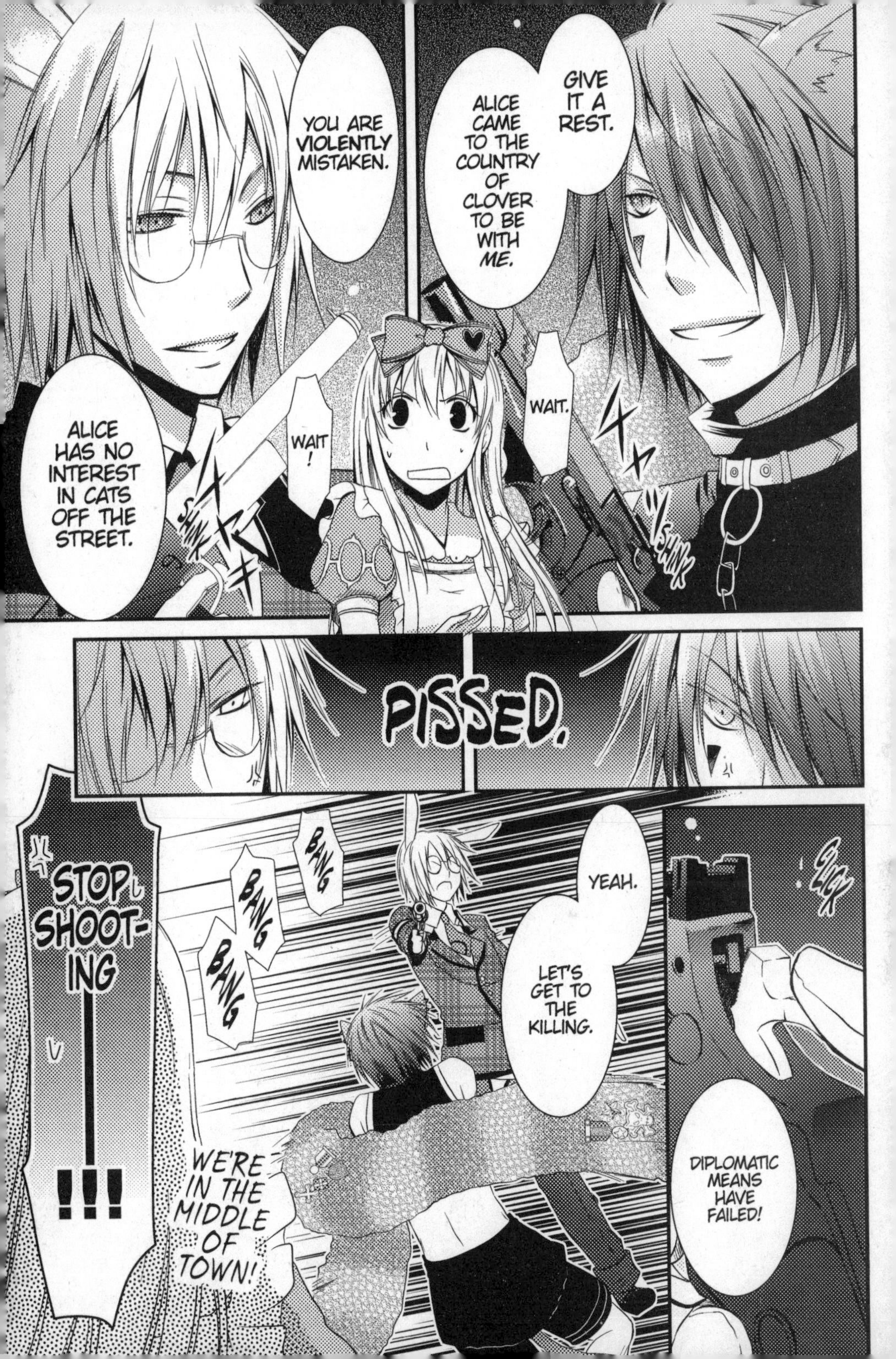
GIVE IT A REST.
ALICE CAME TO THE COUNTRY OF CLOVER TO BE WITH ME.
WAIT.
SHINK
YOU ARE VIOLENTLY MISTAKEN.
WAIT!
ALICE HAS NO INTEREST IN CATS OFF THE STREET.
SHINK
PISSED.
CLICK
DIPLOMATIC MEANS HAVE FAILED!
YEAH.
LET'S GET TO THE KILLING.
BANG
BANG
BANG
WE'RE IN THE MIDDLE OF TOWN!
STOP SHOOTING!!!

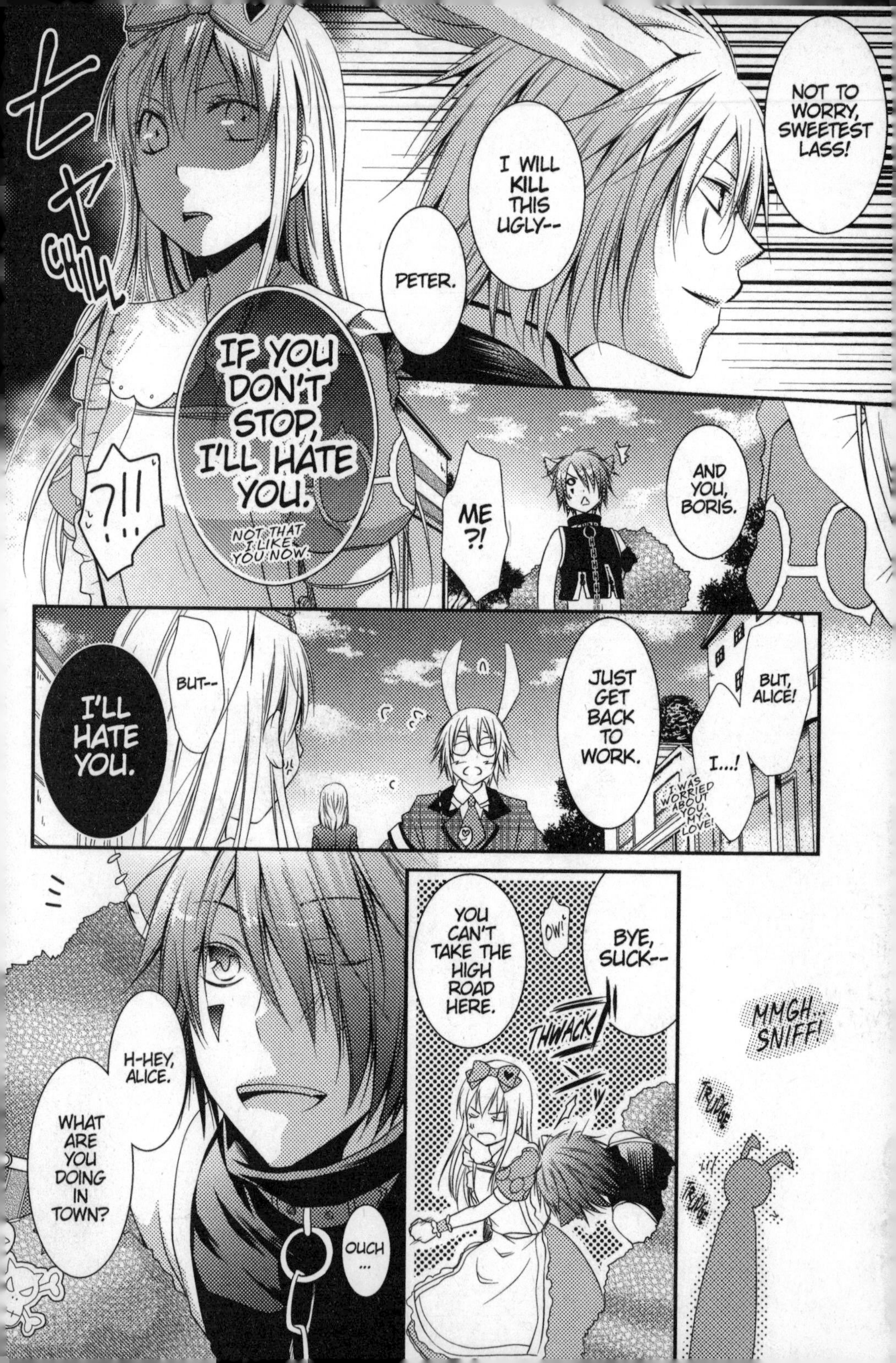
NOT TO WORRY, SWEETEST LASS!
I WILL KILL THIS UGLY--
PETER.
AND YOU, BORIS.
ME ?!
CHILL
IF YOU DON'T STOP, I'LL HATE YOU.
NOT THAT I LIKE YOU NOW.
?!!
BUT, ALICE!
I...!
I WAS WORRIED ABOUT YOU, MY LOVE!
JUST GET BACK TO WORK.
BUT--
I'LL HATE YOU.
MMGH... SNIFF!
TRUDGE
TRUDGE
BYE, SUCK--
OW!
YOU CAN'T TAKE THE HIGH ROAD HERE.
THWACK
H-HEY, ALICE.
WHAT ARE YOU DOING IN TOWN?
OUCH ...

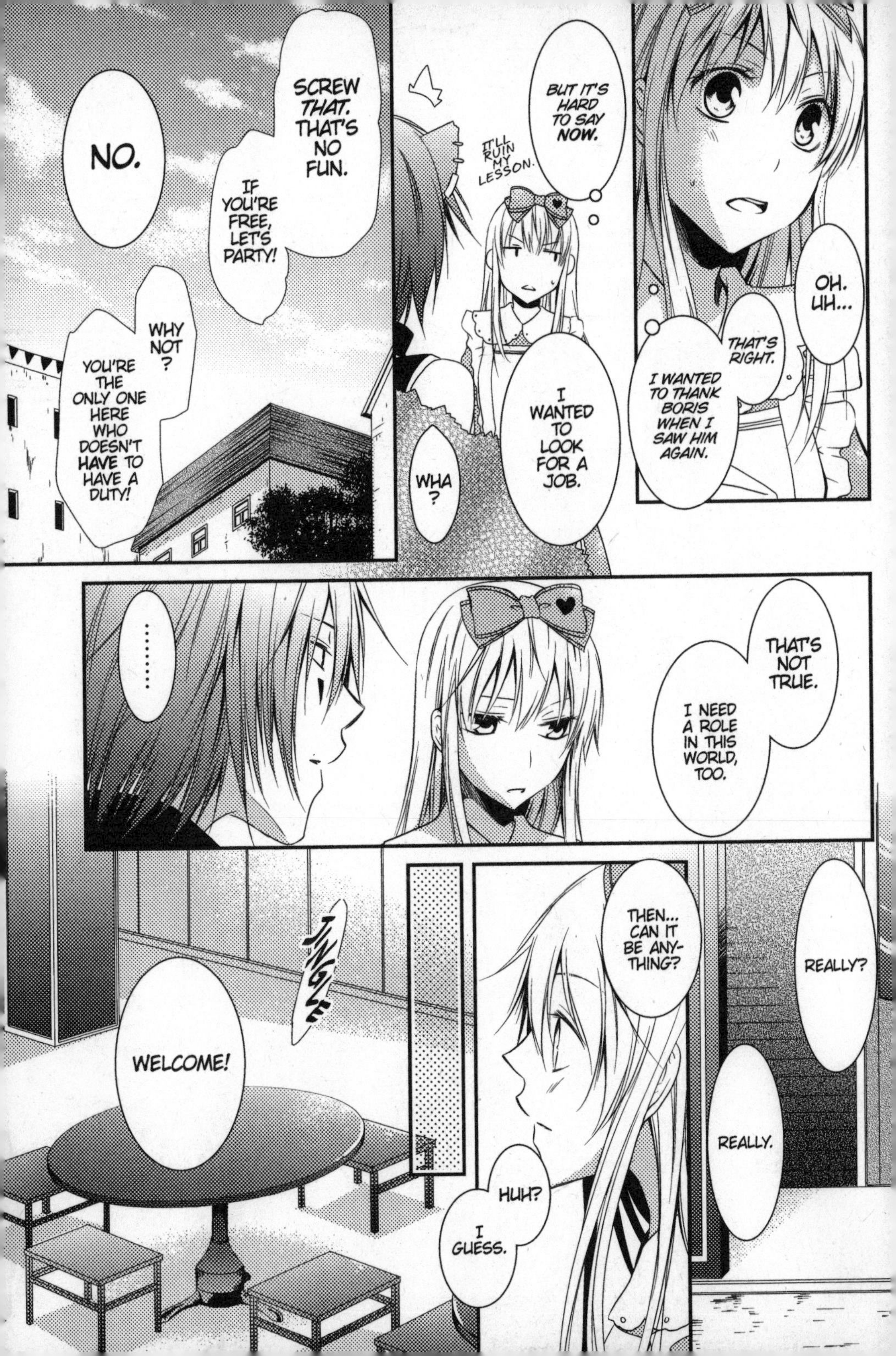
OH. UH...
THAT'S RIGHT.
I WANTED TO THANK BORIS WHEN I SAW HIM AGAIN.
BUT IT'S HARD TO SAY NOW.
IT'LL RUIN MY LESSON.
I WANTED TO LOOK FOR A JOB.
WHA?
SCREW THAT. THAT'S NO FUN.
IF YOU'RE FREE, LET'S PARTY!
NO.
WHY NOT?
YOU'RE THE ONLY ONE HERE WHO DOESN'T HAVE TO HAVE A DUTY!
THAT'S NOT TRUE.
I NEED A ROLE IN THIS WORLD, TOO.
......
REALLY?
THEN... CAN IT BE ANY-THING?
REALLY.
HUH?
I GUESS.
JINGLE
WELCOME!

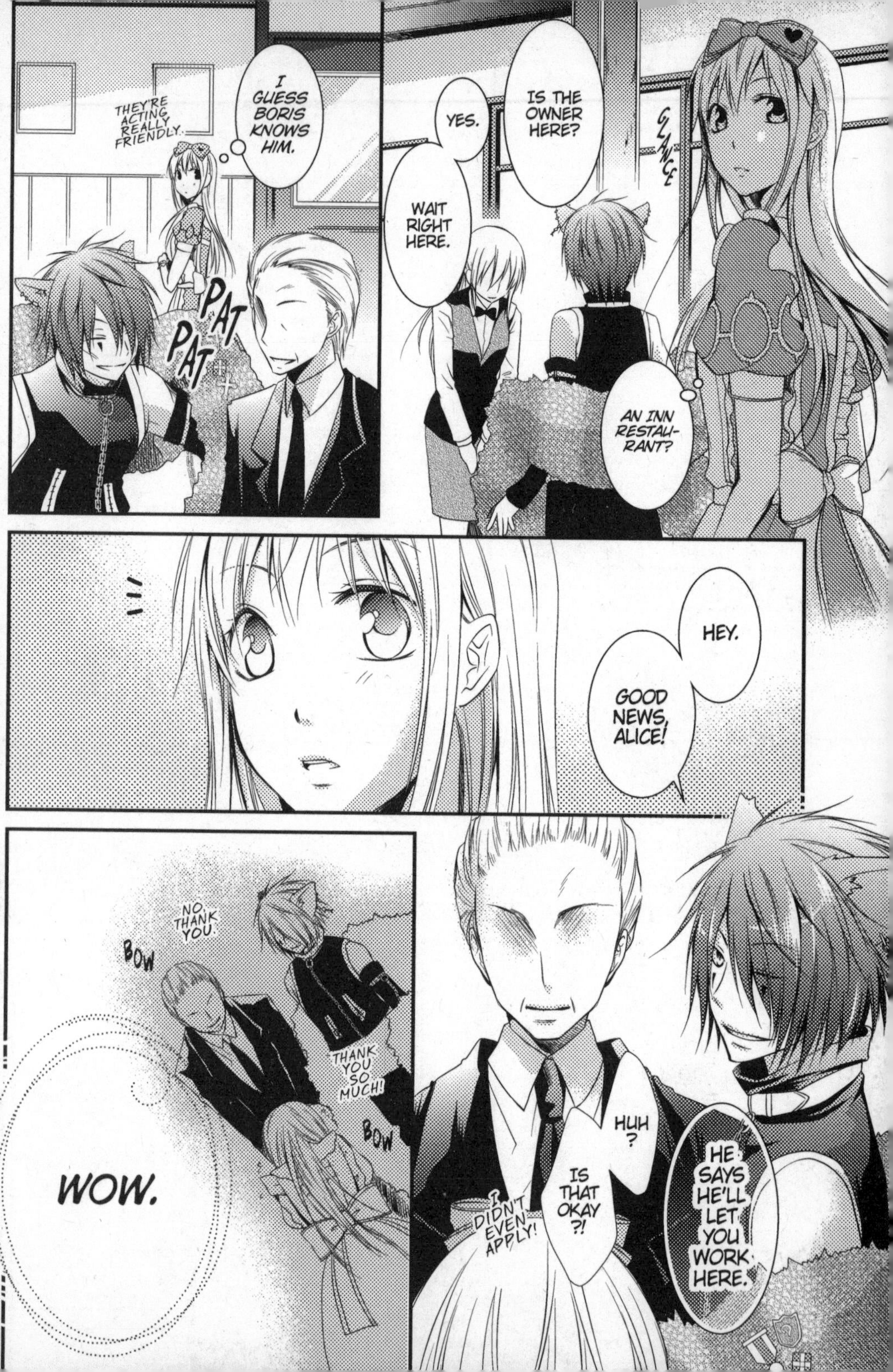
IS THE OWNER HERE?
YES.
WAIT RIGHT HERE.
GLANCE
AN INN RESTAURANT?
I GUESS BORIS KNOWS HIM.
THEY'RE ACTING REALLY FRIENDLY.
PAT PAT
HEY.
GOOD NEWS, ALICE!
HE SAYS HE'LL LET YOU WORK HERE.
HUH?
IS THAT OKAY?!
I DIDN'T EVEN APPLY!
NO THANK YOU.
BOW
THANK YOU SO MUCH!
BOW
WOW.

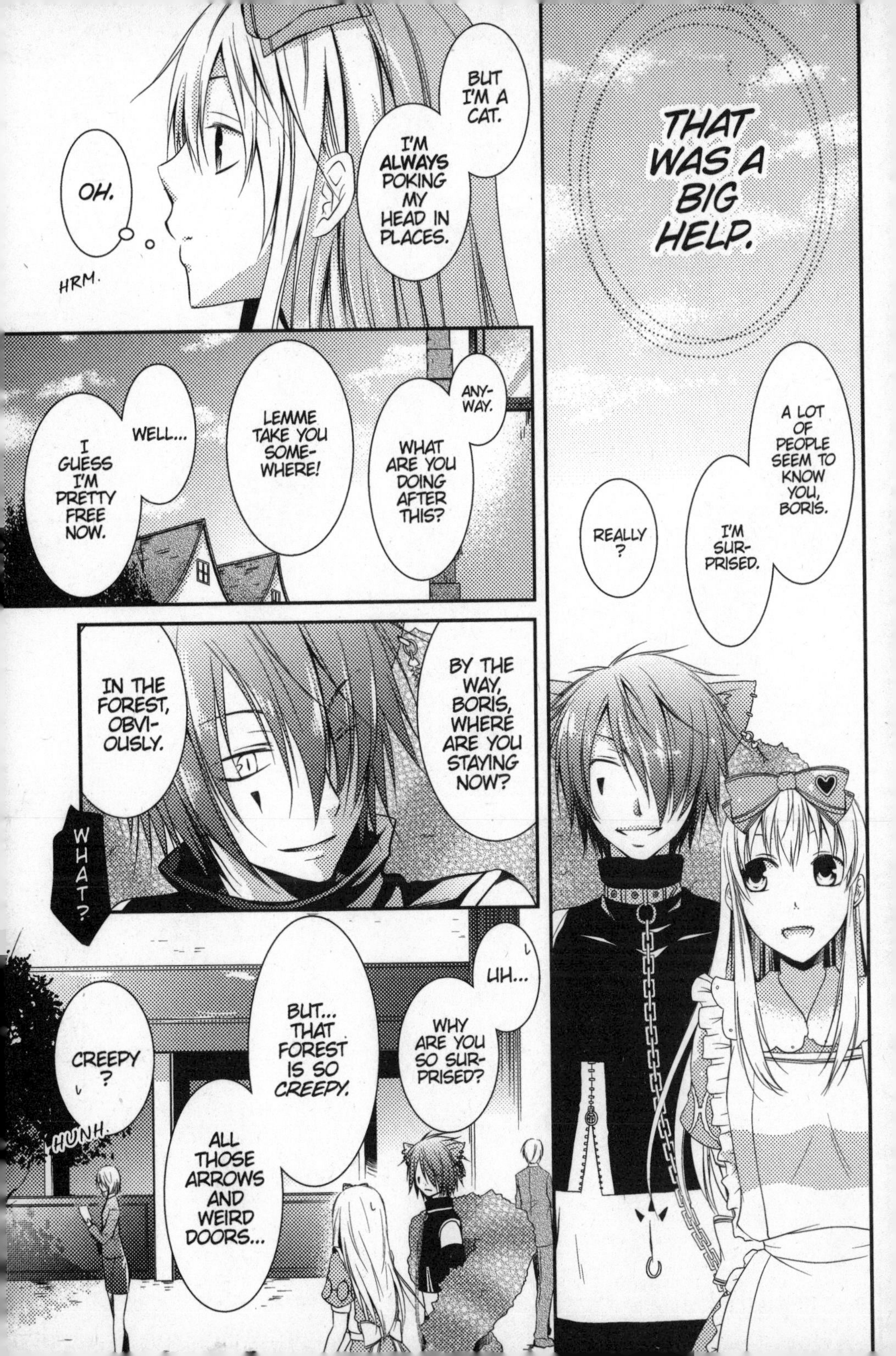
THAT WAS A BIG HELP.
A LOT OF PEOPLE SEEM TO KNOW YOU, BORIS.
I'M SURPRISED.
REALLY?
BUT I'M A CAT.
I'M ALWAYS POKING MY HEAD IN PLACES.
OH.
HRM.
ANY-WAY.
WHAT ARE YOU DOING AFTER THIS?
LEMME TAKE YOU SOME-WHERE!
WELL...
I GUESS I'M PRETTY FREE NOW.
BY THE WAY, BORIS, WHERE ARE YOU STAYING NOW?
IN THE FOREST, OBVI-OUSLY.
WHAT?
UH...
WHY ARE YOU SO SUR-PRISED?
BUT... THAT FOREST IS SO CREEPY.
ALL THOSE ARROWS AND WEIRD DOORS...
CREEPY?
HUNH.

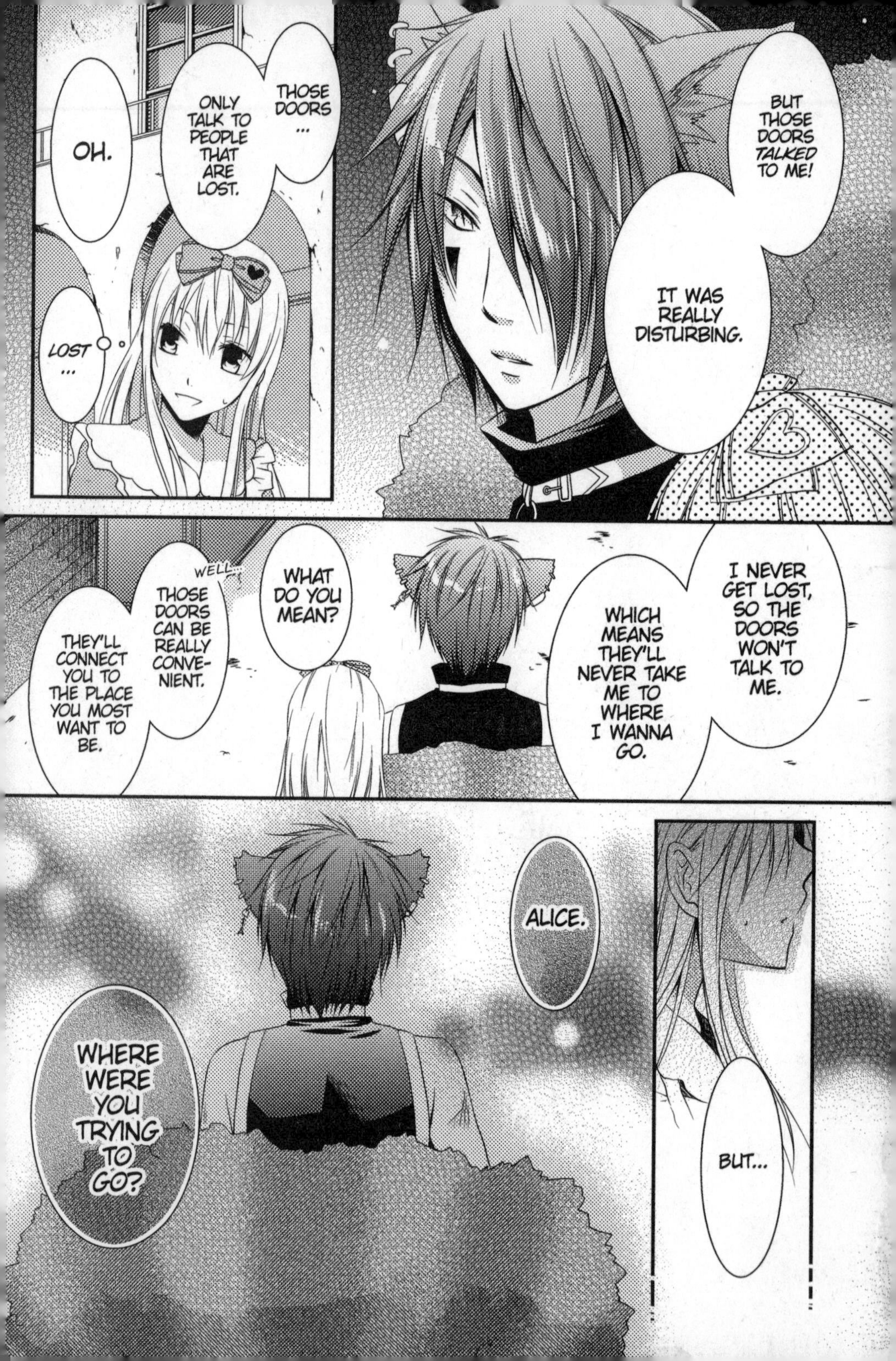
BUT THOSE DOORS *TALKED* TO ME!
IT WAS REALLY DISTURBING.
THOSE DOORS...
ONLY TALK TO PEOPLE THAT ARE LOST.
OH.
LOST...
I NEVER GET LOST, SO THE DOORS WON'T TALK TO ME.
WHICH MEANS THEY'LL NEVER TAKE ME TO WHERE I WANNA GO.
WHAT DO YOU MEAN?
WELL...
THOSE DOORS CAN BE REALLY CONVE-NIENT.
THEY'LL CONNECT YOU TO THE PLACE YOU MOST WANT TO BE.
BUT...
ALICE.
WHERE WERE YOU TRYING TO GO?

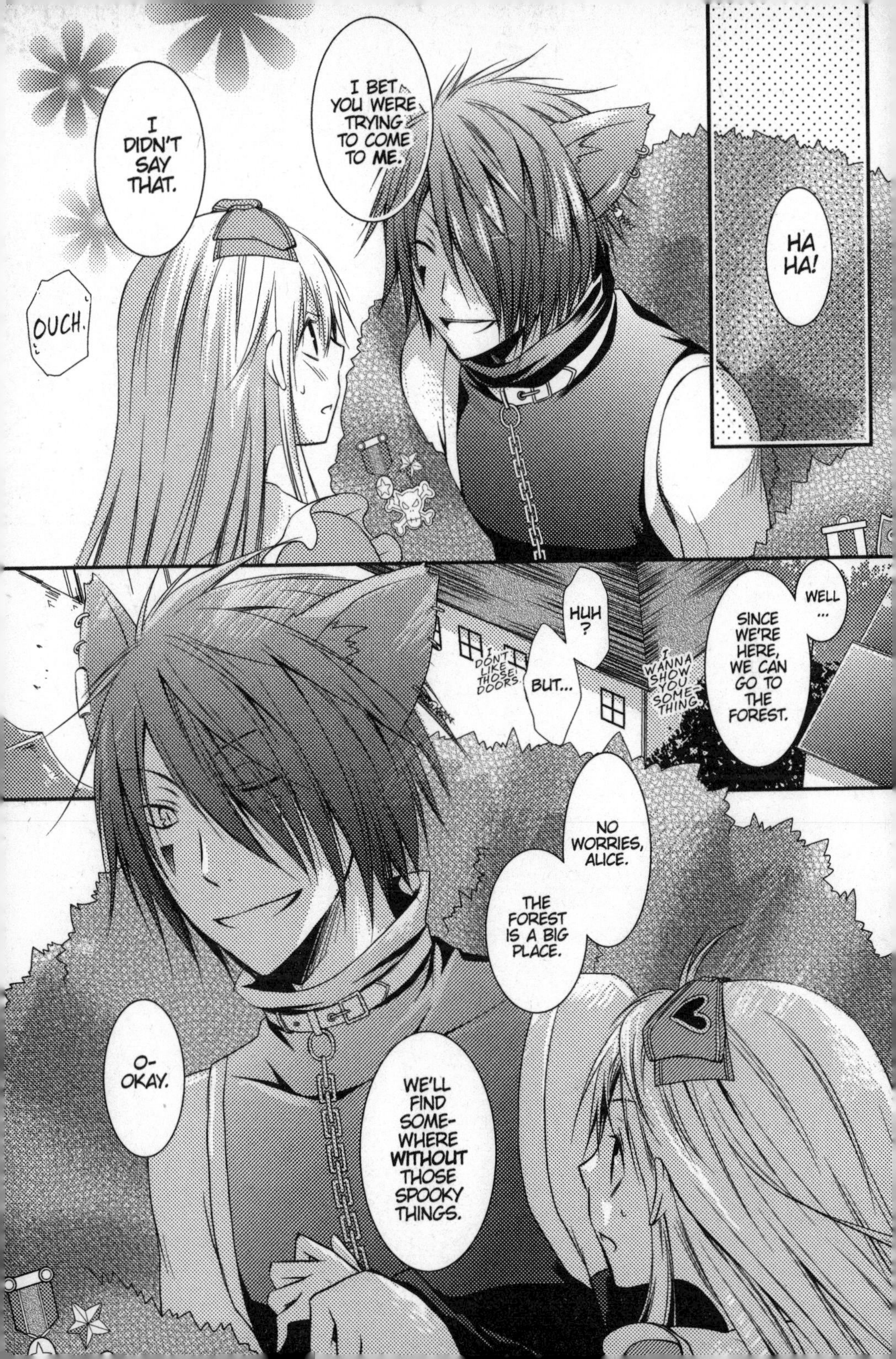
HA HA!
I BET YOU WERE TRYING TO COME TO ME.
I DIDN'T SAY THAT.
OUCH.
WELL ...
SINCE WE'RE HERE, WE CAN GO TO THE FOREST.
I WANNA SHOW YOU SOMETHING.
HUH?
BUT...
I DON'T LIKE THOSE DOORS.
NO WORRIES, ALICE.
THE FOREST IS A BIG PLACE.
WE'LL FIND SOME-WHERE WITHOUT THOSE SPOOKY THINGS.
O-OKAY.

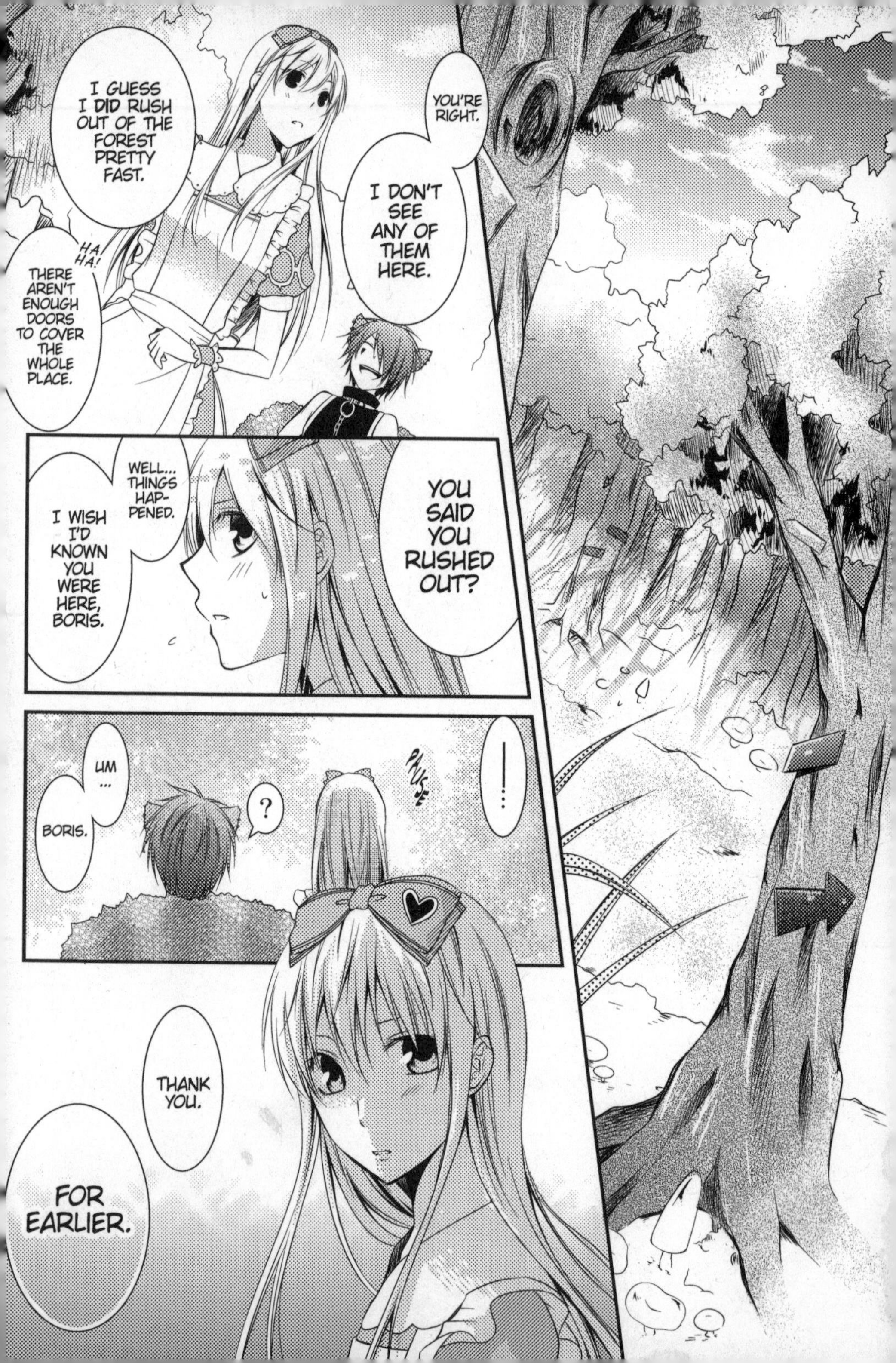
YOU'RE RIGHT.
I DON'T SEE ANY OF THEM HERE.
I GUESS I DID RUSH OUT OF THE FOREST PRETTY FAST.
HA HA!
THERE AREN'T ENOUGH DOORS TO COVER THE WHOLE PLACE.
YOU SAID YOU RUSHED OUT?
WELL... THINGS HAP-PENED.
I WISH I'D KNOWN YOU WERE HERE, BORIS.
!
PAUSE
?
UM ...
BORIS.
THANK YOU.
FOR EARLIER.

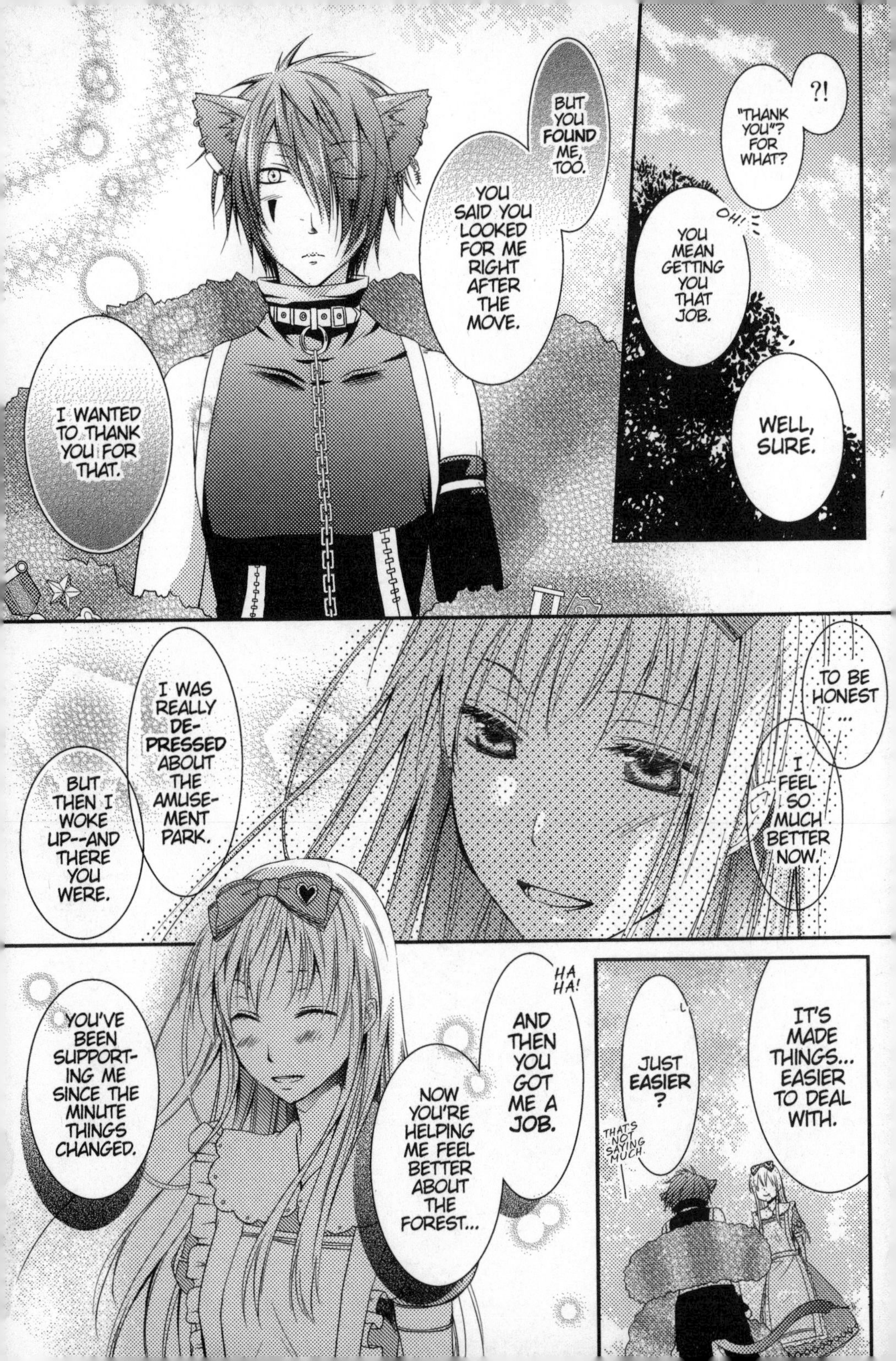
?!
"THANK YOU"? FOR WHAT?
OH!
YOU MEAN GETTING YOU THAT JOB.
WELL, SURE.
BUT YOU FOUND ME, TOO.
YOU SAID YOU LOOKED FOR ME RIGHT AFTER THE MOVE.
I WANTED TO THANK YOU FOR THAT.
TO BE HONEST...
I FEEL SO MUCH BETTER NOW.
I WAS REALLY DE-PRESSED ABOUT THE AMUSE-MENT PARK.
BUT THEN I WOKE UP--AND THERE YOU WERE.
IT'S MADE THINGS... EASIER TO DEAL WITH.
JUST EASIER?
THAT'S NOT SAYING MUCH.
HA HA!
AND THEN YOU GOT ME A JOB.
NOW YOU'RE HELPING ME FEEL BETTER ABOUT THE FOREST...
YOU'VE BEEN SUPPORT-ING ME SINCE THE MINUTE THINGS CHANGED.

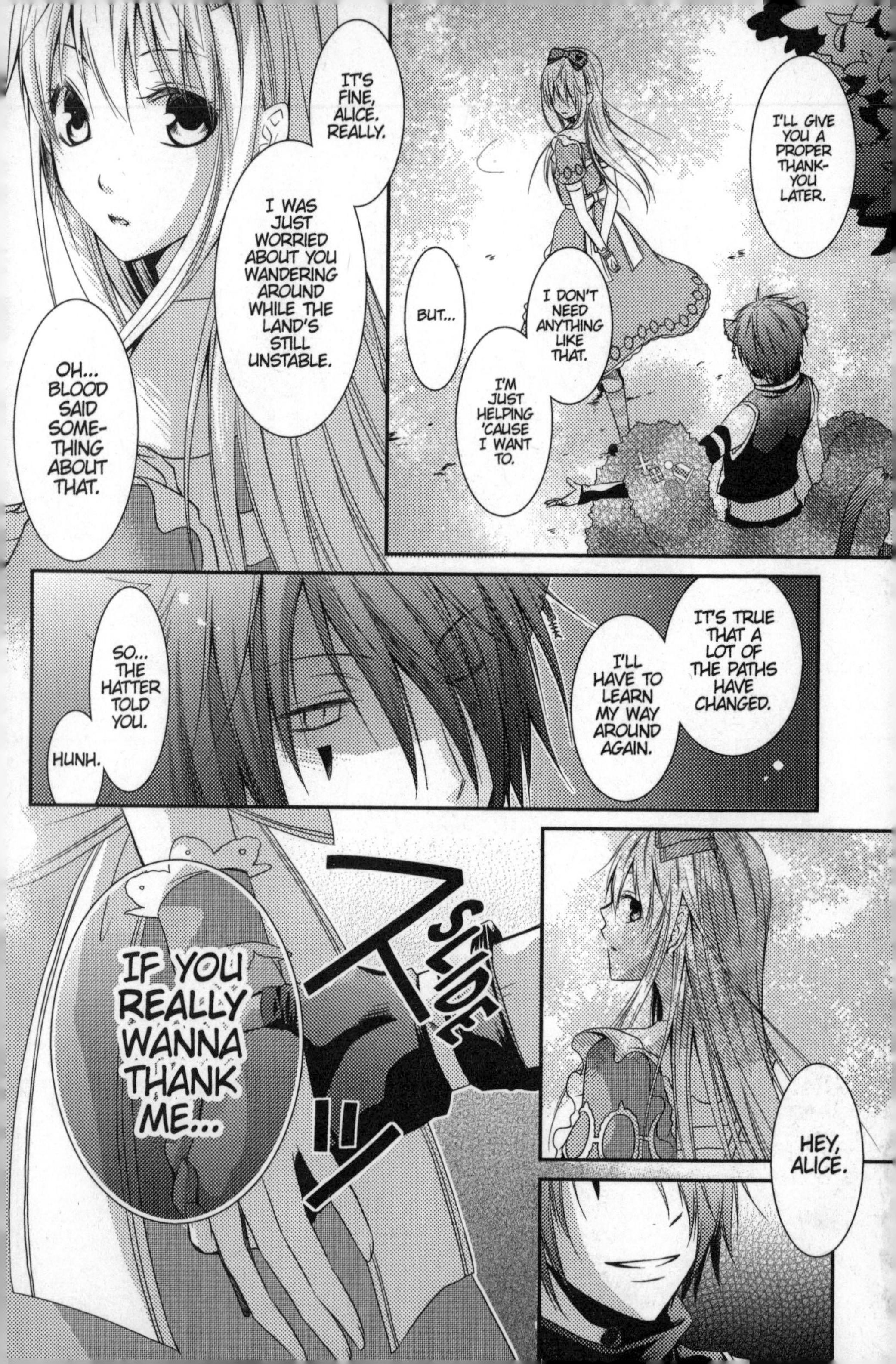
I'LL GIVE YOU A PROPER THANK-YOU LATER.
I DON'T NEED ANYTHING LIKE THAT.
I'M JUST HELPING 'CAUSE I WANT TO.
BUT...
IT'S FINE, ALICE. REALLY.
I WAS JUST WORRIED ABOUT YOU WANDERING AROUND WHILE THE LAND'S STILL UNSTABLE.
OH... BLOOD SAID SOMETHING ABOUT THAT.
IT'S TRUE THAT A LOT OF THE PATHS HAVE CHANGED.
I'LL HAVE TO LEARN MY WAY AROUND AGAIN.
SO... THE HATTER TOLD YOU.
HUNH.
HEY, ALICE.
SLIDE
IF YOU REALLY WANNA THANK ME...

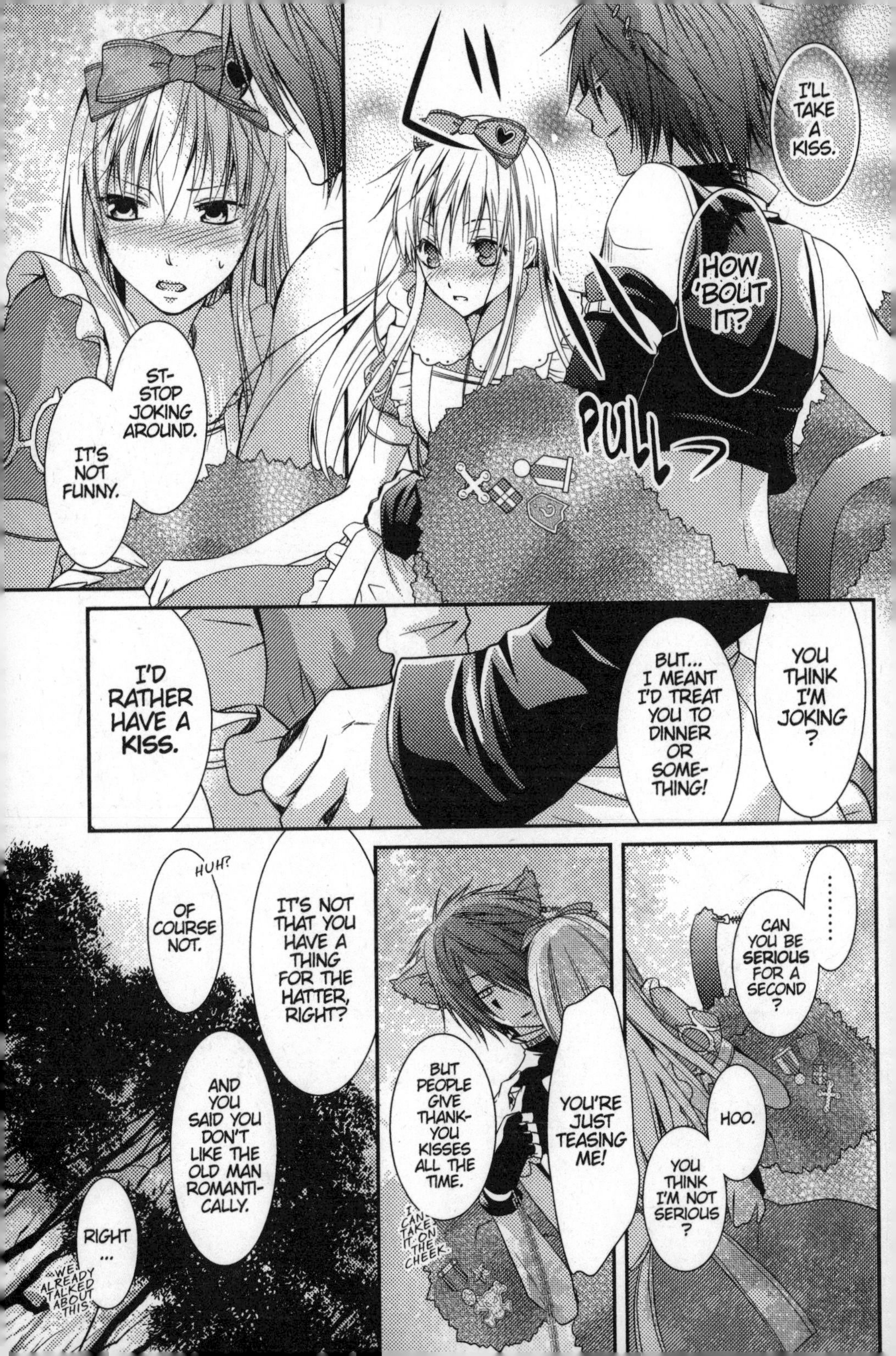
I'LL TAKE A KISS.
HOW 'BOUT IT?
PULL
ST-STOP JOKING AROUND.
IT'S NOT FUNNY.
YOU THINK I'M JOKING?
BUT... I MEANT I'D TREAT YOU TO DINNER OR SOME-THING!
I'D RATHER HAVE A KISS.
......
CAN YOU BE SERIOUS FOR A SECOND?
HOO.
YOU THINK I'M NOT SERIOUS?
YOU'RE JUST TEASING ME!
BUT PEOPLE GIVE THANK-YOU KISSES ALL THE TIME.
I CAN TAKE IT ON THE CHEEK.
IT'S NOT THAT YOU HAVE A THING FOR THE HATTER, RIGHT?
HUH?
OF COURSE NOT.
AND YOU SAID YOU DON'T LIKE THE OLD MAN ROMANTI-CALLY.
RIGHT...
WE ALREADY TALKED ABOUT THIS.

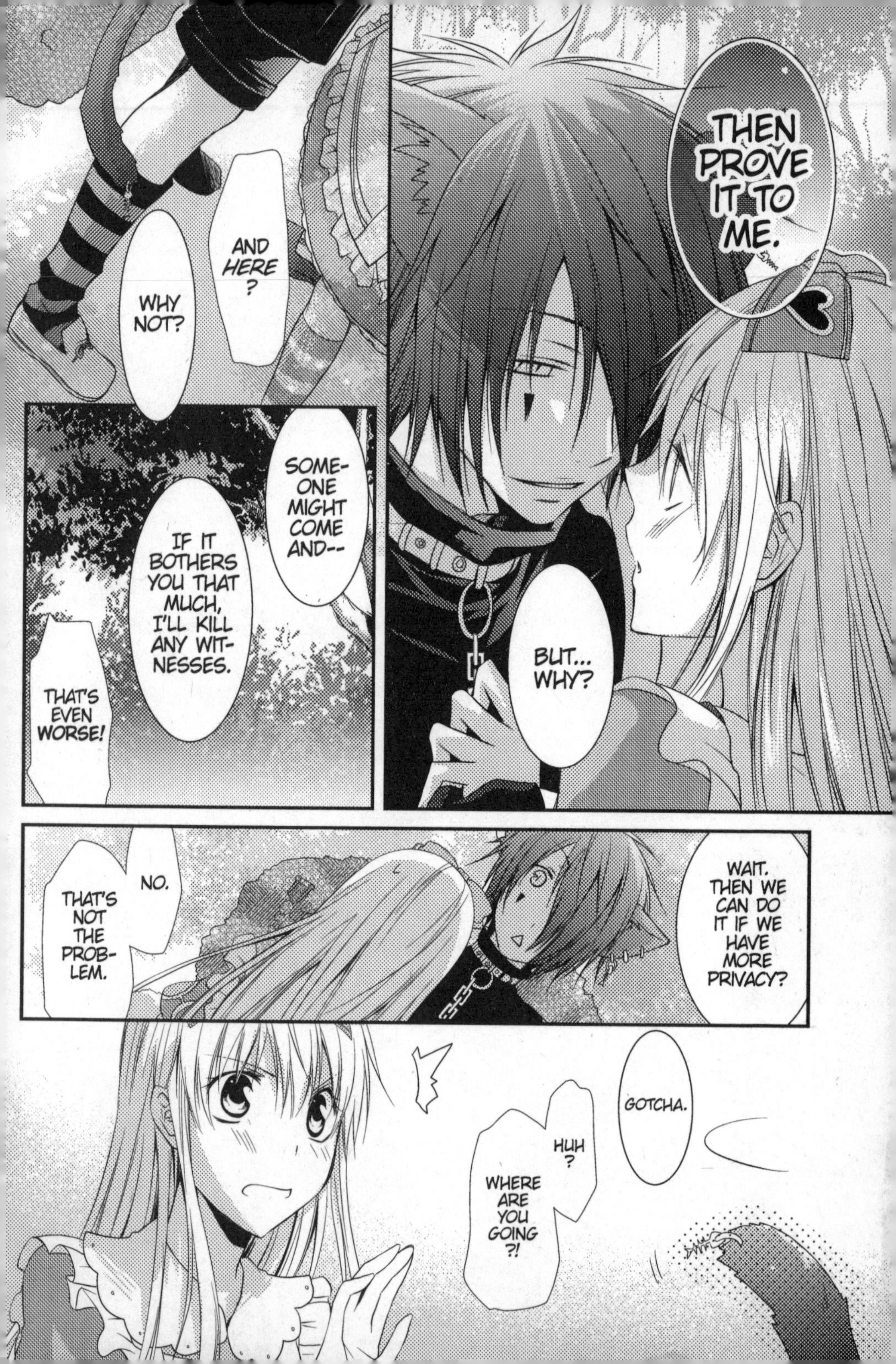
THEN PROVE IT TO ME.
BUT... WHY?
AND HERE?
WHY NOT?
SOME-ONE MIGHT COME AND--
IF IT BOTHERS YOU THAT MUCH, I'LL KILL ANY WIT-NESSES.
THAT'S EVEN WORSE!
WAIT. THEN WE CAN DO IT IF WE HAVE MORE PRIVACY?
NO.
THAT'S NOT THE PROB-LEM.
GOTCHA.
HUH?
WHERE ARE YOU GOING?!

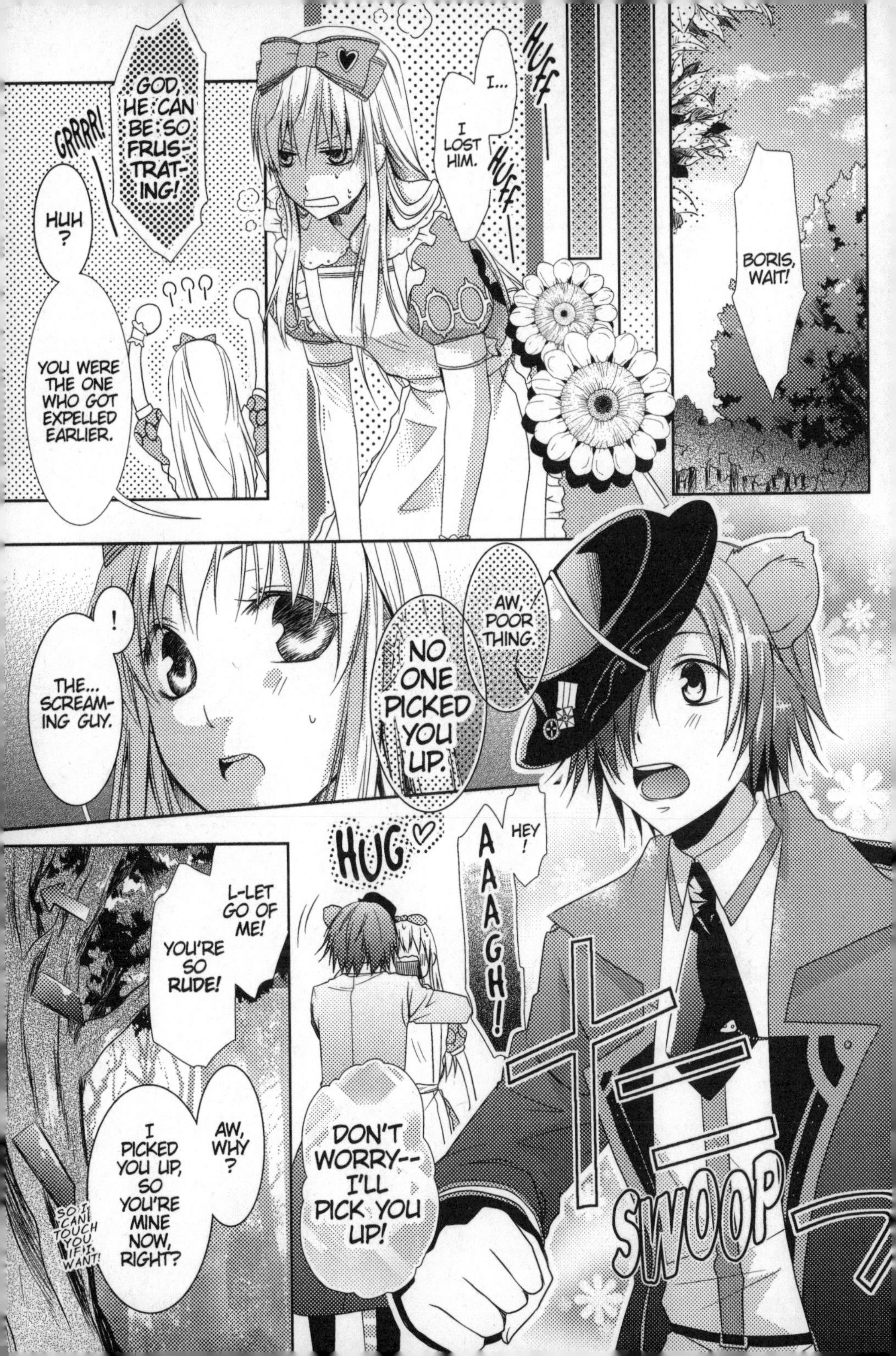
BORIS, WAIT!
HUFF—
HUFF—
I...
I LOST HIM.
GOD, HE CAN BE SO FRUS-TRAT-ING!
GRRRR!
HUH?
YOU WERE THE ONE WHO GOT EXPELLED EARLIER.
AW, POOR THING.
NO ONE PICKED YOU UP.
!
THE... SCREAM-ING GUY.
HEY!
AAAAGH!
HUG
SWOOP
DON'T WORRY-- I'LL PICK YOU UP!
L-LET GO OF ME!
YOU'RE SO RUDE!
AW, WHY?
I PICKED YOU UP, SO YOU'RE MINE NOW, RIGHT?
SO I CAN TOUCH YOU IF I WANT!

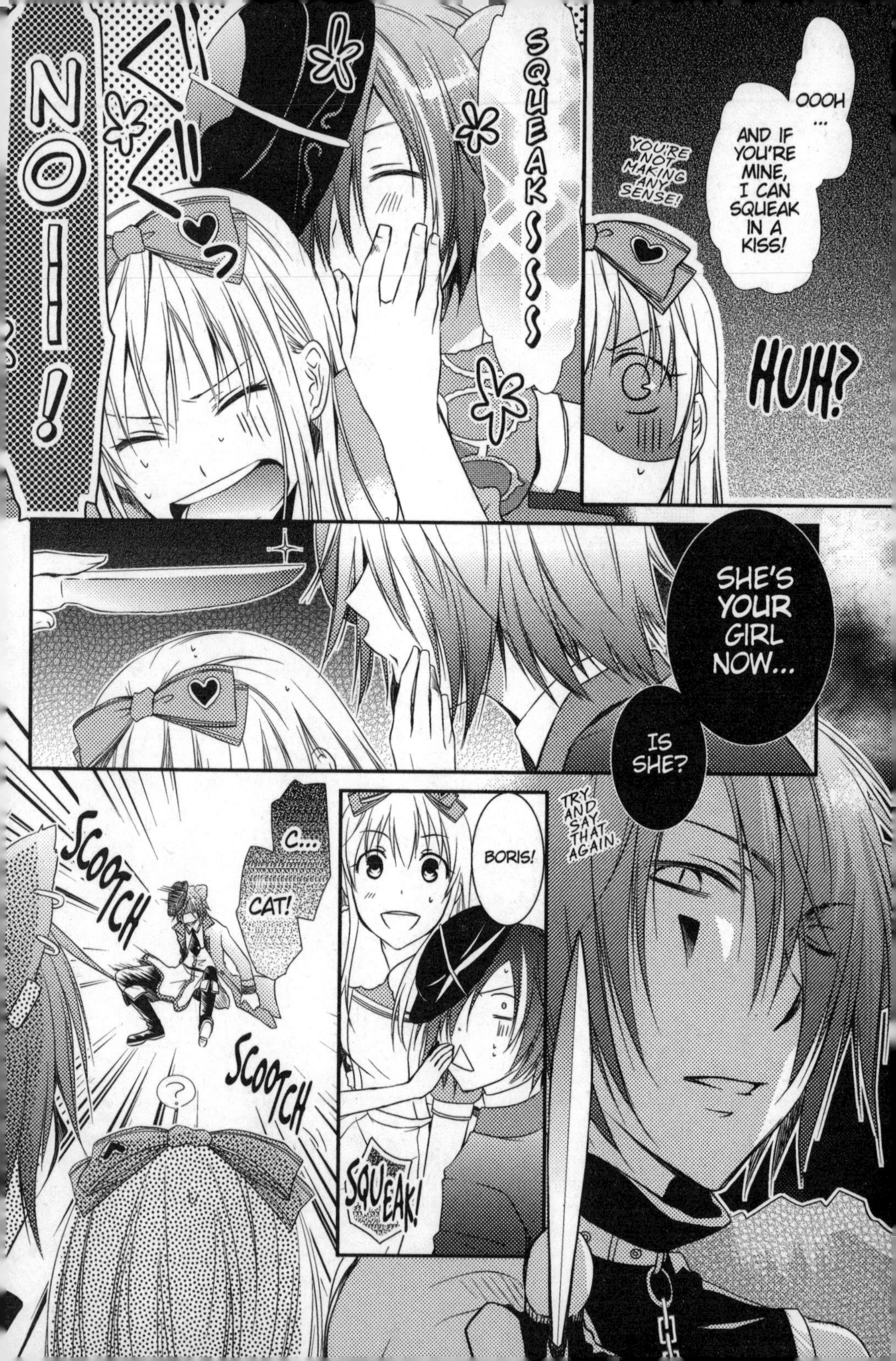
OOOH ... AND IF YOU'RE MINE, I CAN SQUEAK IN A KISS!
YOU'RE NOT MAKING ANY SENSE!
HUH?
SQUEAKSSSS
NO---!
SHE'S YOUR GIRL NOW...
IS SHE?
TRY AND SAY THAT AGAIN.
BORIS!
SQUEAK!
C...
CAT!
SCOOTCH
SCOOTCH
?

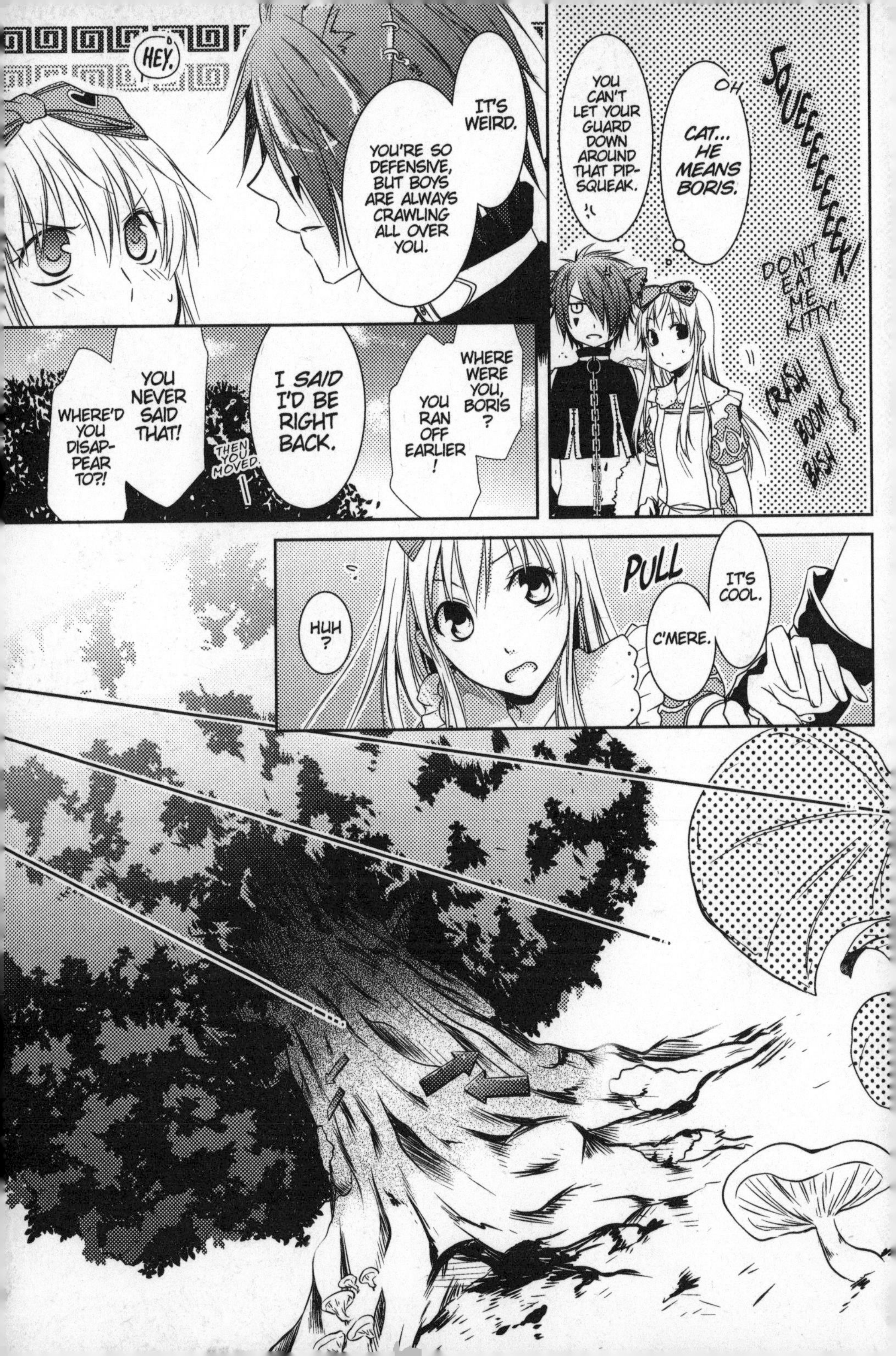
SQUEEEEEEEEEK!
DON'T EAT ME, KITTY!
OH
CAT... HE MEANS BORIS.
YOU CAN'T LET YOUR GUARD DOWN AROUND THAT PIP-SQUEAK.
CRASH BOOM BASH
HEY.
IT'S WEIRD.
YOU'RE SO DEFENSIVE, BUT BOYS ARE ALWAYS CRAWLING ALL OVER YOU.
WHERE WERE YOU, BORIS?
YOU RAN OFF EARLIER!
I SAID I'D BE RIGHT BACK.
THEN YOU MOVED.
YOU NEVER SAID THAT!
WHERE'D YOU DISAPPEAR TO?!
IT'S COOL.
C'MERE.
PULL
HUH?

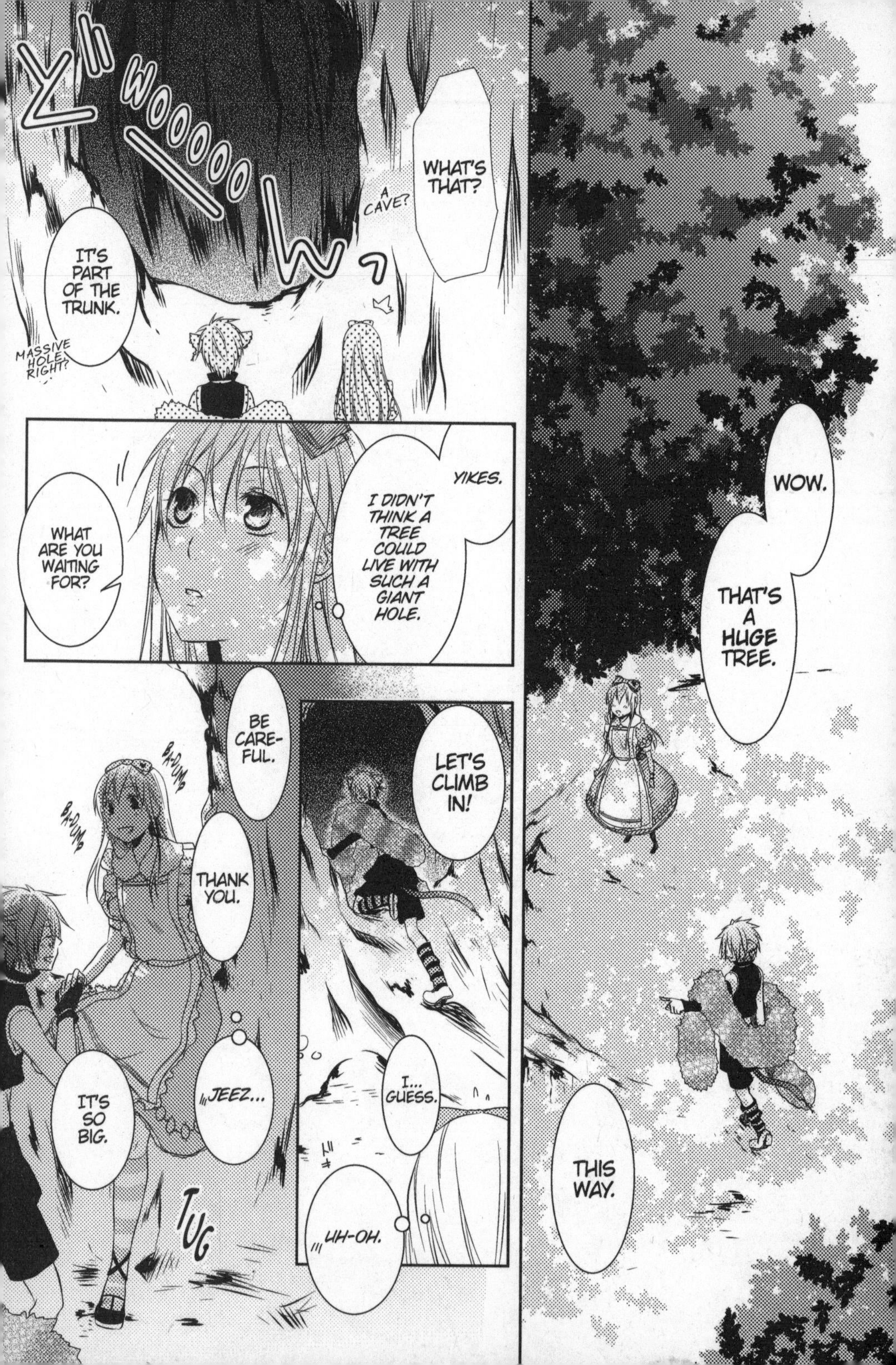
WOW.
THAT'S A HUGE TREE.
THIS WAY.
WHAT'S THAT?
A CAVE?
IT'S PART OF THE TRUNK.
MASSIVE HOLE, RIGHT?
YIKES.
I DIDN'T THINK A TREE COULD LIVE WITH SUCH A GIANT HOLE.
WHAT ARE YOU WAITING FOR?
LET'S CLIMB IN!
I... GUESS.
UH-OH.
BE CAREFUL.
BA-DUMP
BA-DUMP
THANK YOU.
JEEZ...
IT'S SO BIG.
TUG

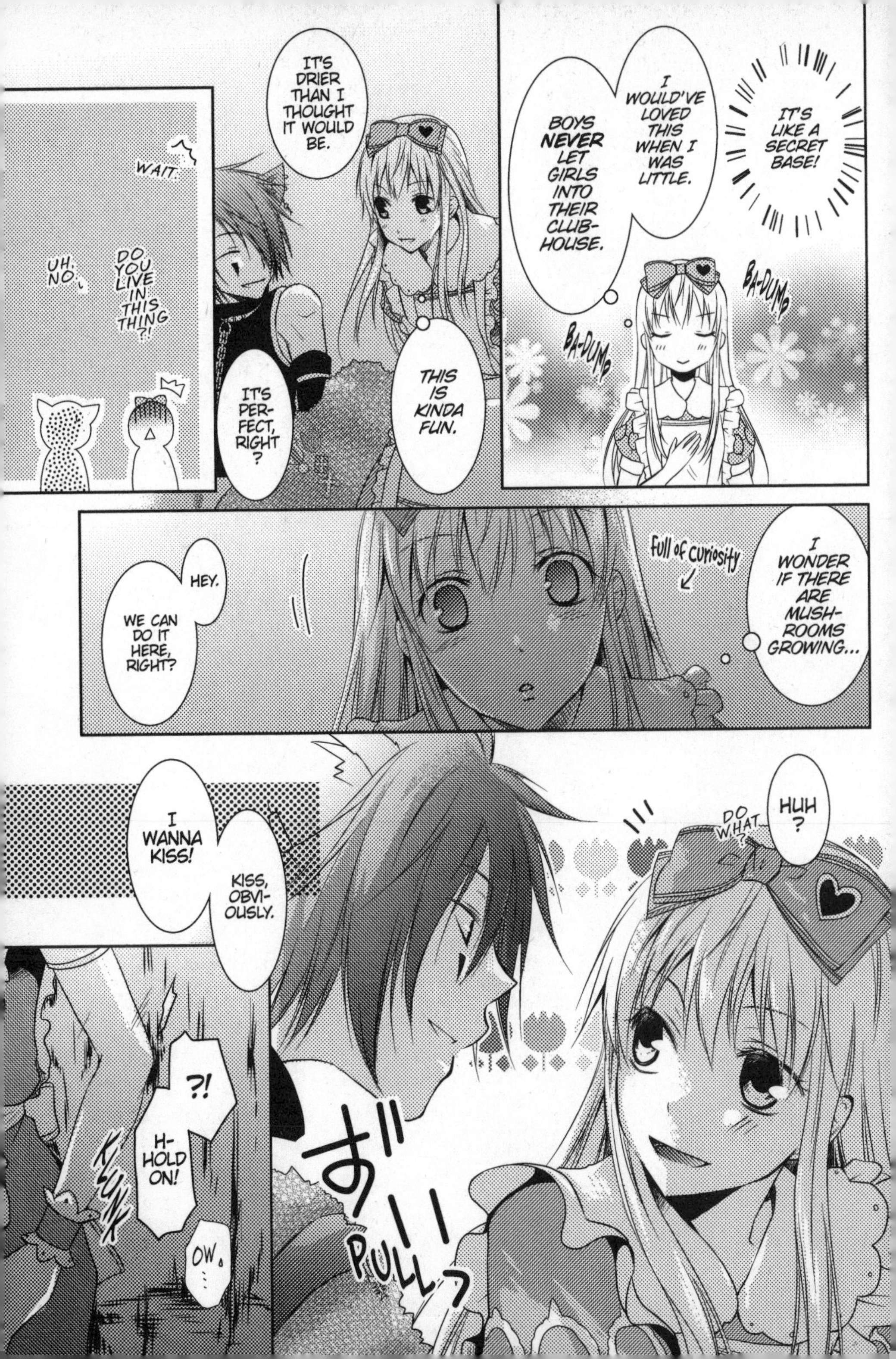
IT'S LIKE A SECRET BASE!
I WOULD'VE LOVED THIS WHEN I WAS LITTLE.
BOYS NEVER LET GIRLS INTO THEIR CLUB-HOUSE.
BA-DUMP
BA-DUMP
IT'S DRIER THAN I THOUGHT IT WOULD BE.
THIS IS KINDA FUN.
IT'S PER-FECT, RIGHT?
WAIT.
DO YOU LIVE IN THIS THING?!
UH, NO.
I WONDER IF THERE ARE MUSH-ROOMS GROWING...
full of curiosity
HEY.
WE CAN DO IT HERE, RIGHT?
HUH?
DO WHAT?
KISS, OBVI-OUSLY.
I WANNA KISS!
PULL
?!
H-HOLD ON!
KLUNK
OW...

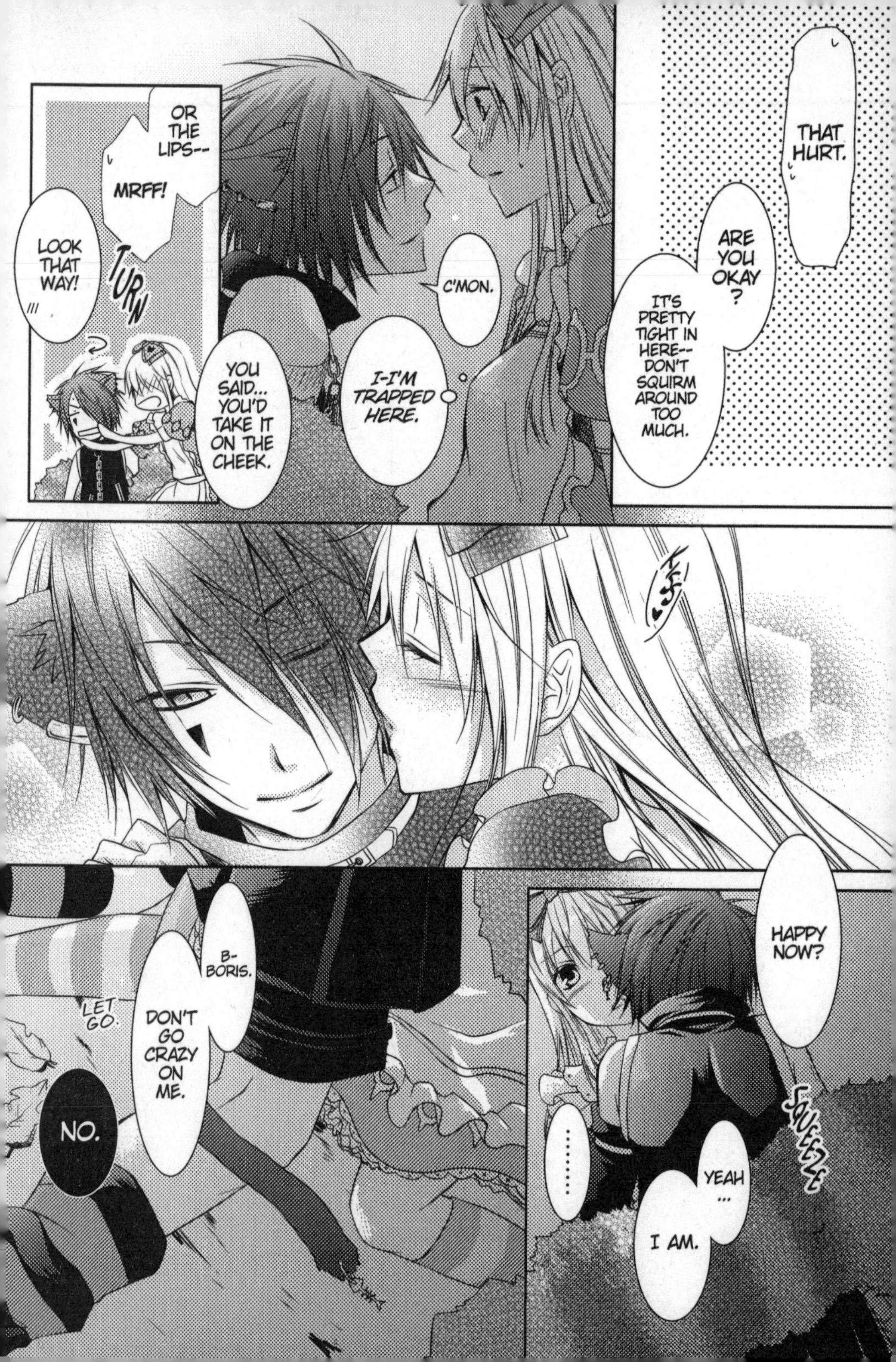
THAT HURT.
ARE YOU OKAY?
IT'S PRETTY TIGHT IN HERE-- DON'T SQUIRM AROUND TOO MUCH.
C'MON.
I-I'M TRAPPED HERE.
YOU SAID... YOU'D TAKE IT ON THE CHEEK.
OR THE LIPS--
MRFF!
TURN
LOOK THAT WAY!
HAPPY NOW?
SQUEEZE
......
YEAH... I AM.
B-BORIS.
DON'T GO CRAZY ON ME.
LET GO.
NO.

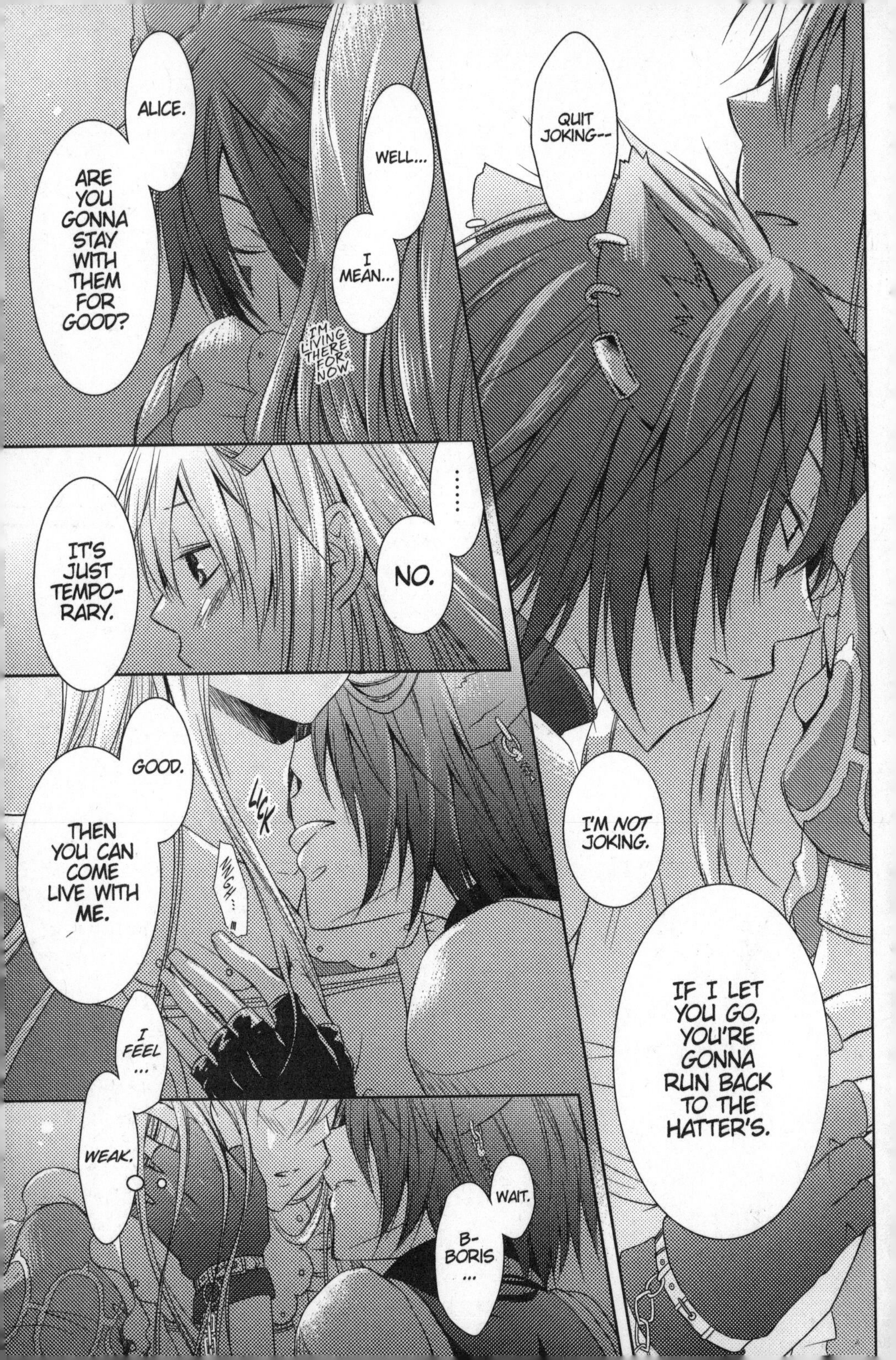
ALICE.
ARE YOU GONNA STAY WITH THEM FOR GOOD?
WELL...
I MEAN...
I'M LIVING THERE FOR NOW.
......
NO.
IT'S JUST TEMPORARY.
GOOD.
THEN YOU CAN COME LIVE WITH ME.
LICK
NNGH...!!
QUIT JOKING--
I'M *NOT* JOKING.
IF I LET YOU GO, YOU'RE GONNA RUN BACK TO THE HATTER'S.
WAIT.
B-BORIS...
I FEEL...
WEAK.

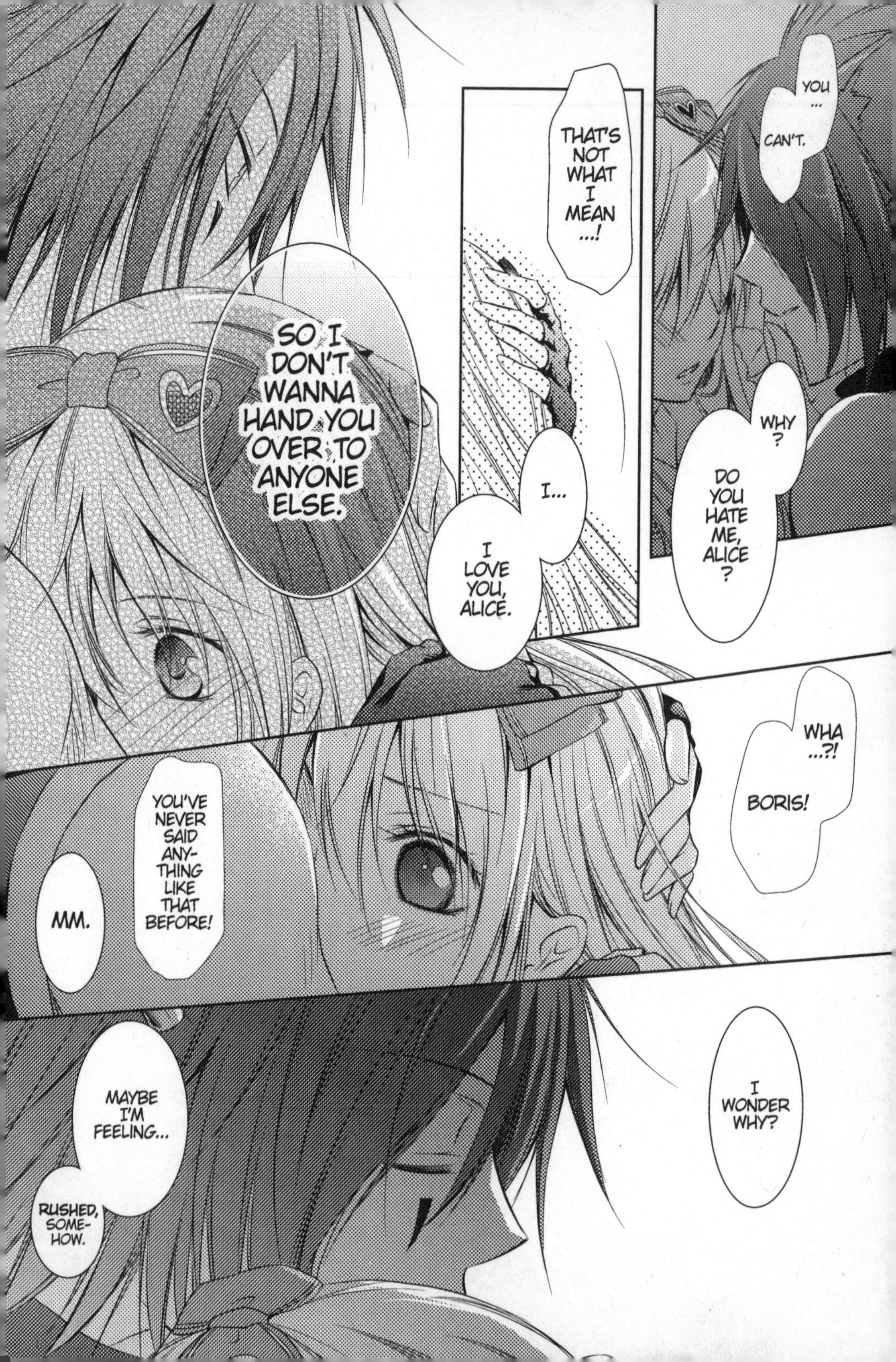
YOU ... CAN'T.
WHY?
DO YOU HATE ME, ALICE?
THAT'S NOT WHAT I MEAN ...!
I...
I LOVE YOU, ALICE.
SO I DON'T WANNA HAND YOU OVER TO ANYONE ELSE.
WHA ...?!
BORIS!
YOU'VE NEVER SAID ANY-THING LIKE THAT BEFORE!
MM.
I WONDER WHY?
MAYBE I'M FEELING...
RUSHED, SOME-HOW.

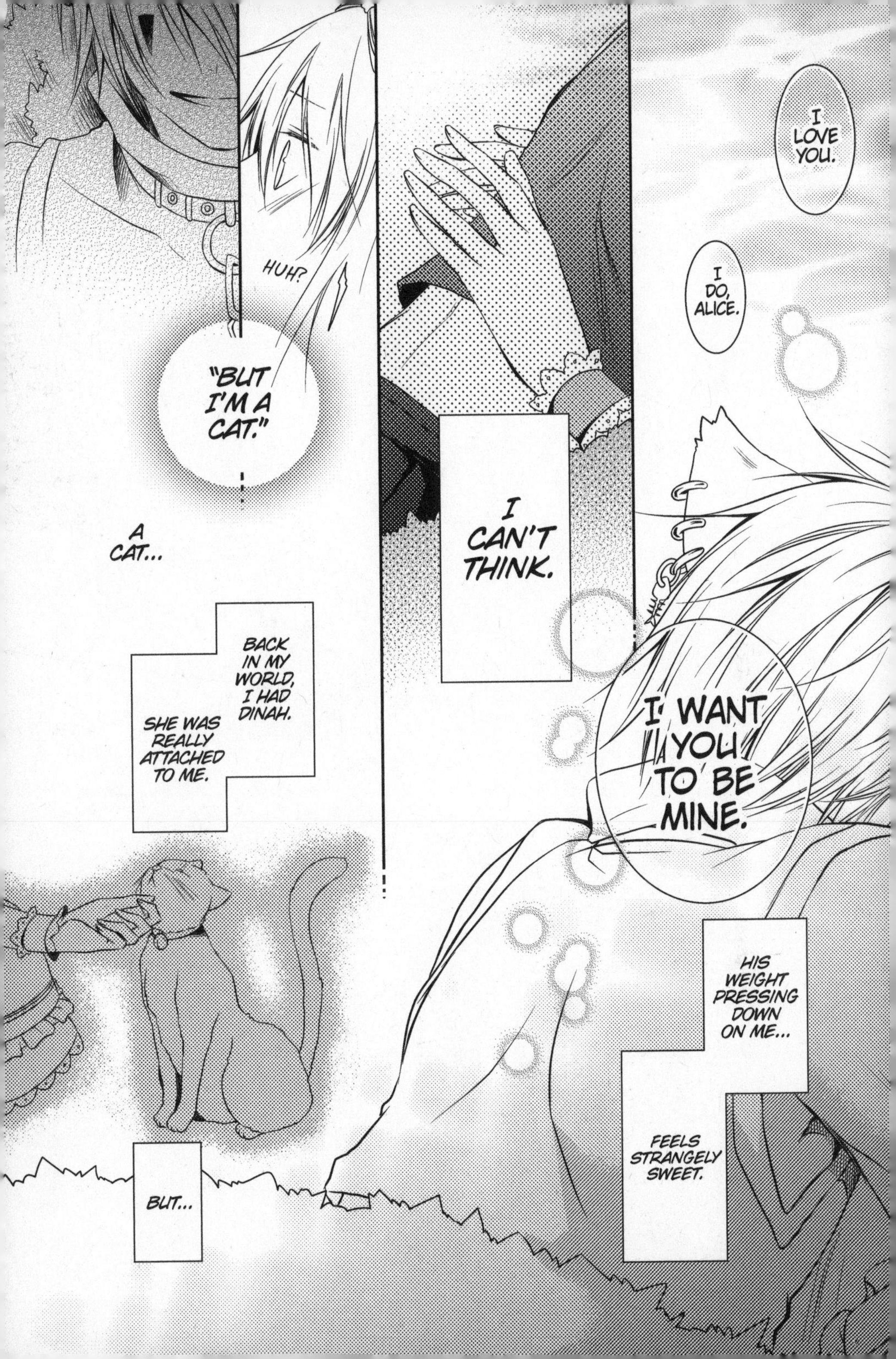
I LOVE YOU.
I DO, ALICE.
I WANT YOU TO BE MINE.
HIS WEIGHT PRESSING DOWN ON ME...
FEELS STRANGELY SWEET.
I CAN'T THINK.
HUH?
"BUT I'M A CAT."
A CAT...
BACK IN MY WORLD, I HAD DINAH.
SHE WAS REALLY ATTACHED TO ME.
BUT...

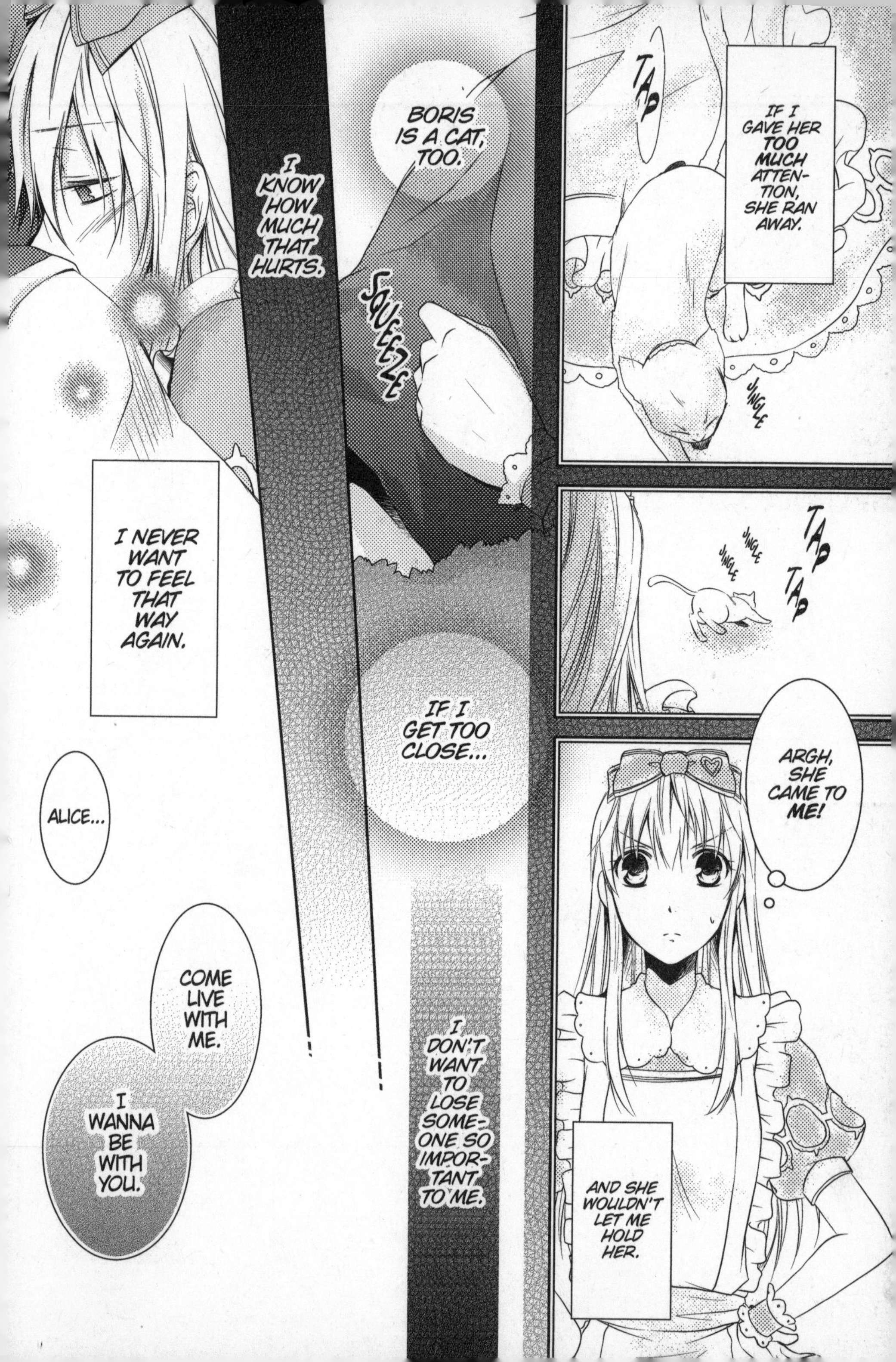
TAP
IF I GAVE HER TOO MUCH ATTENTION, SHE RAN AWAY.
JINGLE
TAP TAP
JINGLE JINGLE
ARGH, SHE CAME TO ME!
AND SHE WOULDN'T LET ME HOLD HER.
BORIS IS A CAT, TOO.
I KNOW HOW MUCH THAT HURTS.
SQUEEZE
IF I GET TOO CLOSE...
I DON'T WANT TO LOSE SOMEONE SO IMPORTANT TO ME.
I NEVER WANT TO FEEL THAT WAY AGAIN.
ALICE...
COME LIVE WITH ME.
I WANNA BE WITH YOU.

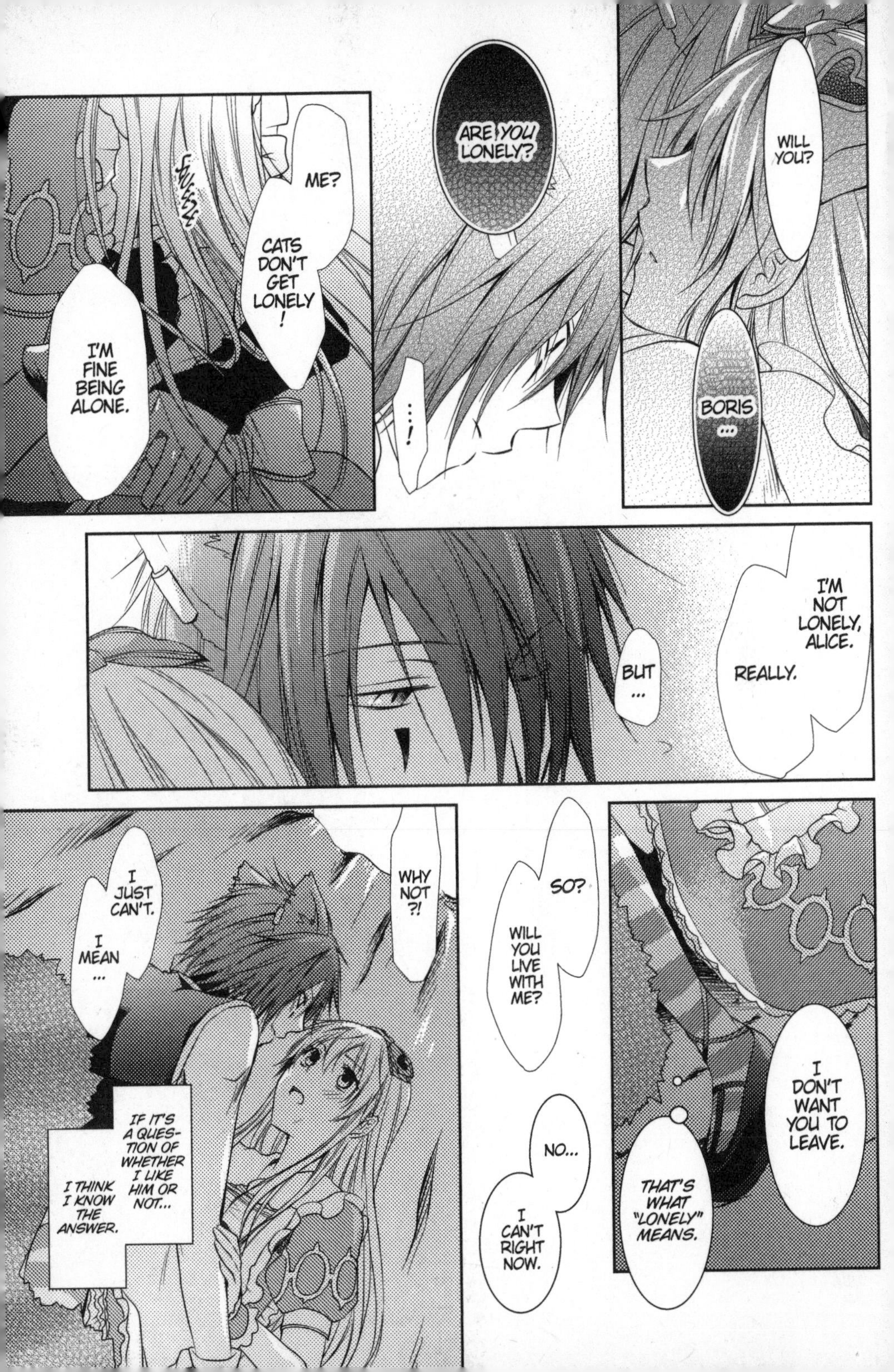
WILL YOU?
BORIS...
ARE YOU LONELY?
...!
SQUEEZE
ME?
CATS DON'T GET LONELY!
I'M FINE BEING ALONE.
I'M NOT LONELY, ALICE.
REALLY.
BUT...
I DON'T WANT YOU TO LEAVE.
THAT'S WHAT "LONELY" MEANS.
SO?
WILL YOU LIVE WITH ME?
NO...
I CAN'T RIGHT NOW.
WHY NOT?!
I JUST CAN'T.
I MEAN...
IF IT'S A QUESTION OF WHETHER I LIKE HIM OR NOT...
I THINK I KNOW THE ANSWER.

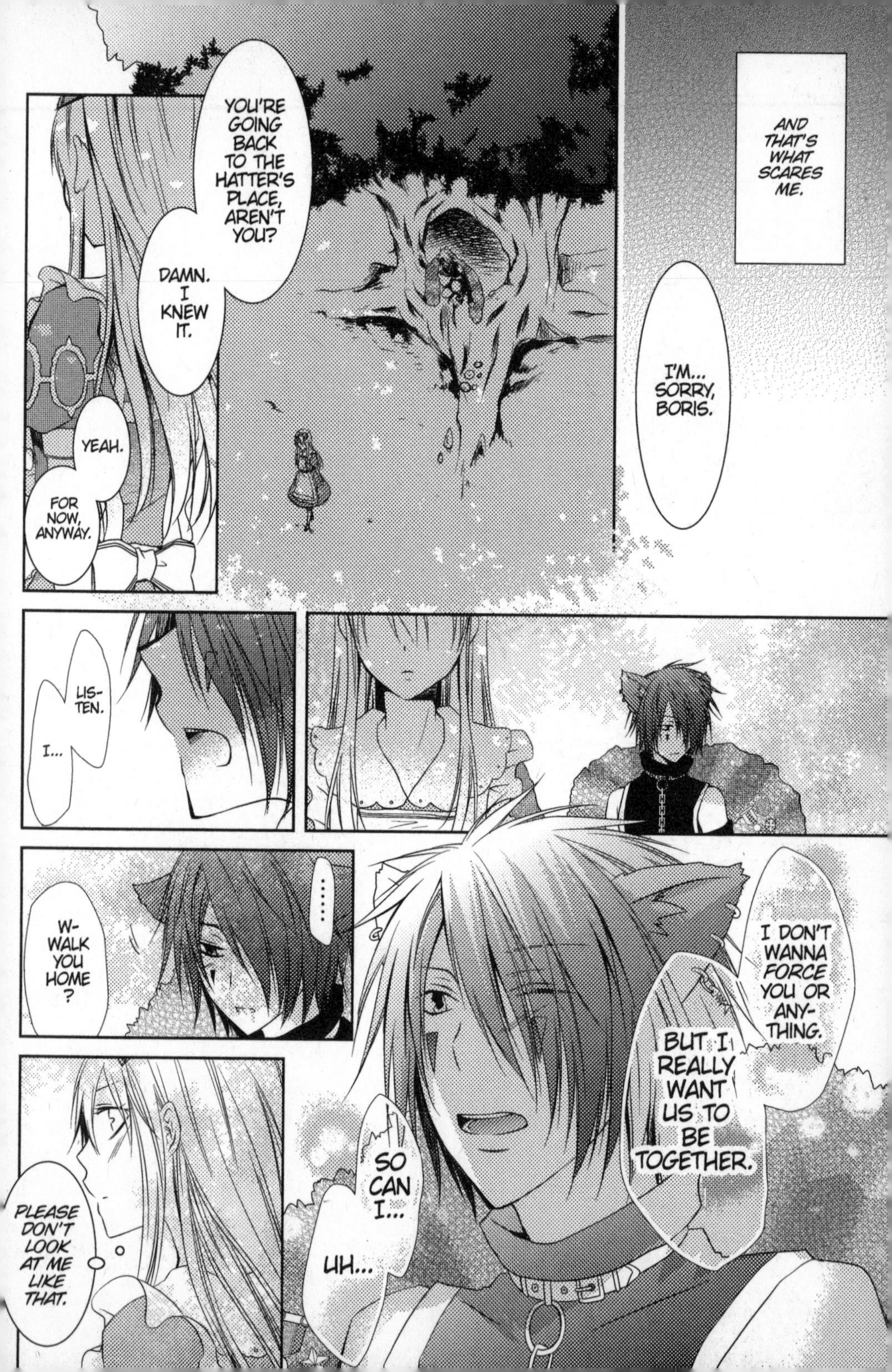
AND THAT'S WHAT SCARES ME.
I'M... SORRY, BORIS.
YOU'RE GOING BACK TO THE HATTER'S PLACE, AREN'T YOU?
DAMN. I KNEW IT.
YEAH.
FOR NOW, ANYWAY.
LIS-TEN.
I...
I DON'T WANNA FORCE YOU OR ANY-THING.
BUT I REALLY WANT US TO BE TOGETHER.
SO CAN I...
UH...
......
W-WALK YOU HOME?
PLEASE DON'T LOOK AT ME LIKE THAT.

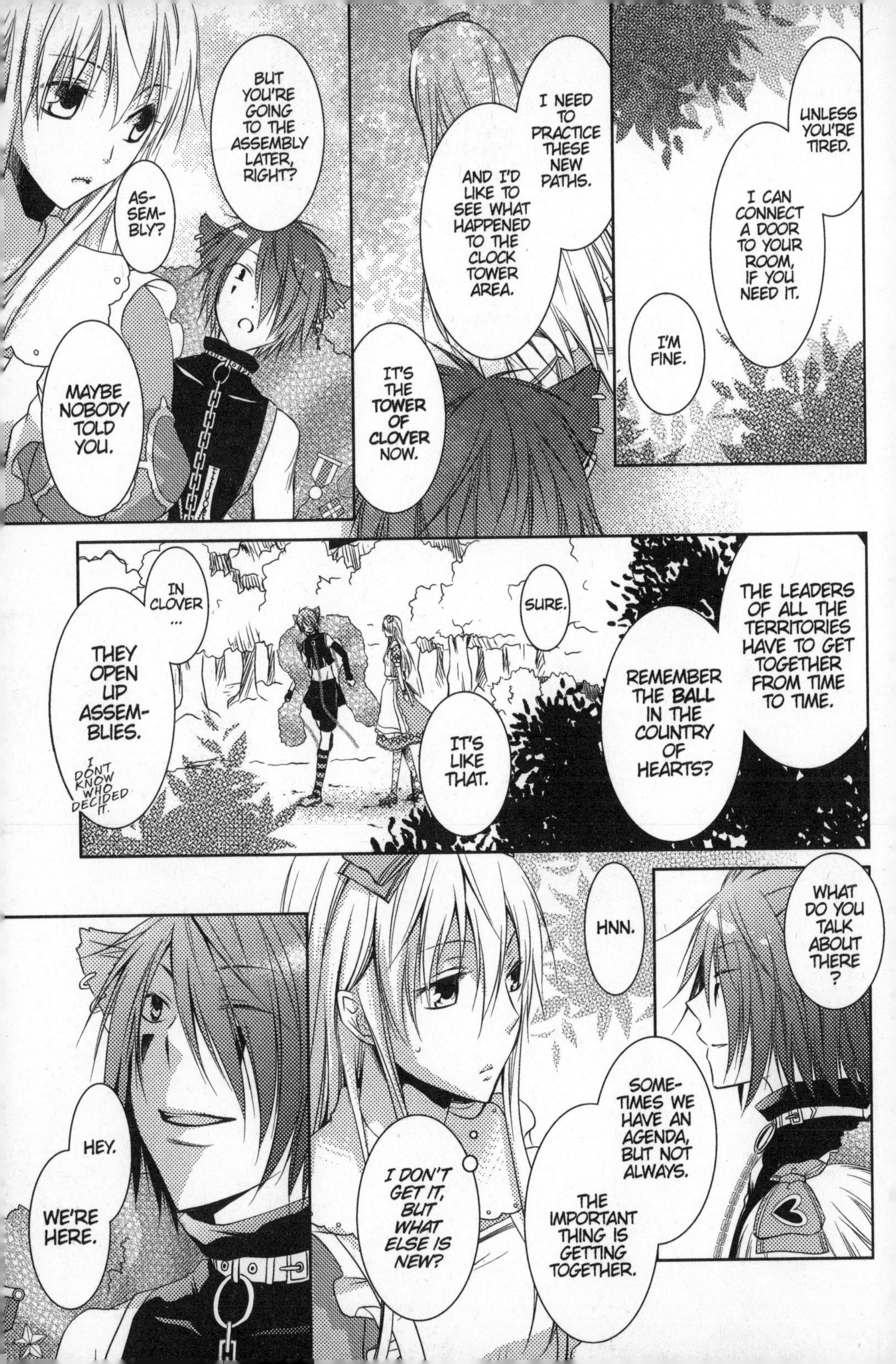
UNLESS YOU'RE TIRED.
I CAN CONNECT A DOOR TO YOUR ROOM, IF YOU NEED IT.
I'M FINE.
I NEED TO PRACTICE THESE NEW PATHS.
AND I'D LIKE TO SEE WHAT HAPPENED TO THE CLOCK TOWER AREA.
IT'S THE TOWER OF CLOVER NOW.
BUT YOU'RE GOING TO THE ASSEMBLY LATER, RIGHT?
AS-SEM-BLY?
MAYBE NOBODY TOLD YOU.
THE LEADERS OF ALL THE TERRITORIES HAVE TO GET TOGETHER FROM TIME TO TIME.
REMEMBER THE BALL IN THE COUNTRY OF HEARTS?
SURE.
IT'S LIKE THAT.
IN CLOVER...
THEY OPEN UP ASSEM-BLIES.
I DON'T KNOW WHO DECIDED IT.
WHAT DO YOU TALK ABOUT THERE?
HNN.
SOME-TIMES WE HAVE AN AGENDA, BUT NOT ALWAYS.
THE IMPORTANT THING IS GETTING TOGETHER.
I DON'T GET IT, BUT WHAT ELSE IS NEW?
HEY.
WE'RE HERE.

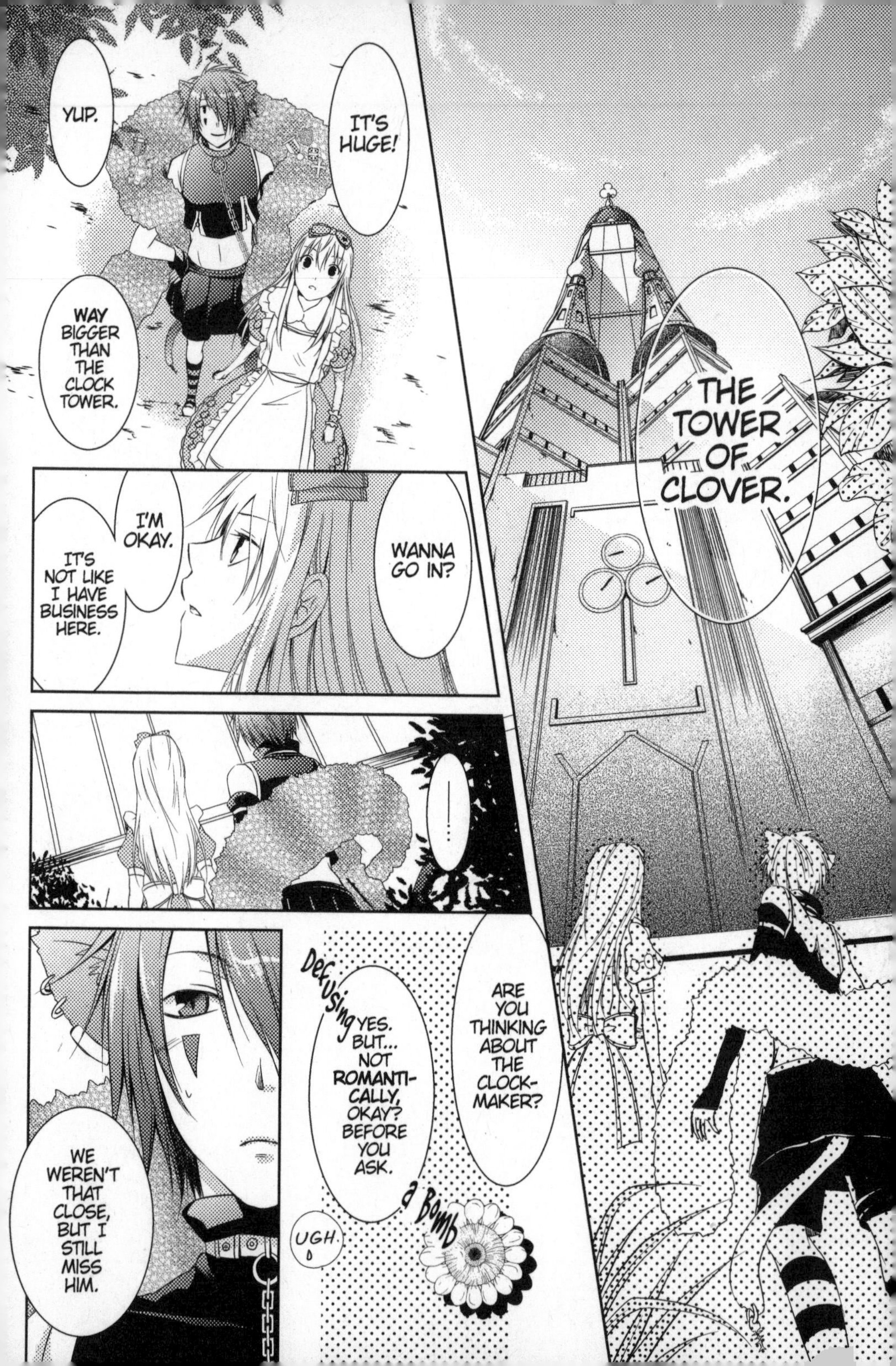
THE TOWER OF CLOVER.
IT'S HUGE!
YUP.
WAY BIGGER THAN THE CLOCK TOWER.
WANNA GO IN?
I'M OKAY.
IT'S NOT LIKE I HAVE BUSINESS HERE.
!
ARE YOU THINKING ABOUT THE CLOCK-MAKER?
YES. BUT... NOT ROMANTI-CALLY, OKAY? BEFORE YOU ASK.
Defusing a Bomb
UGH.
WE WEREN'T THAT CLOSE, BUT I STILL MISS HIM.

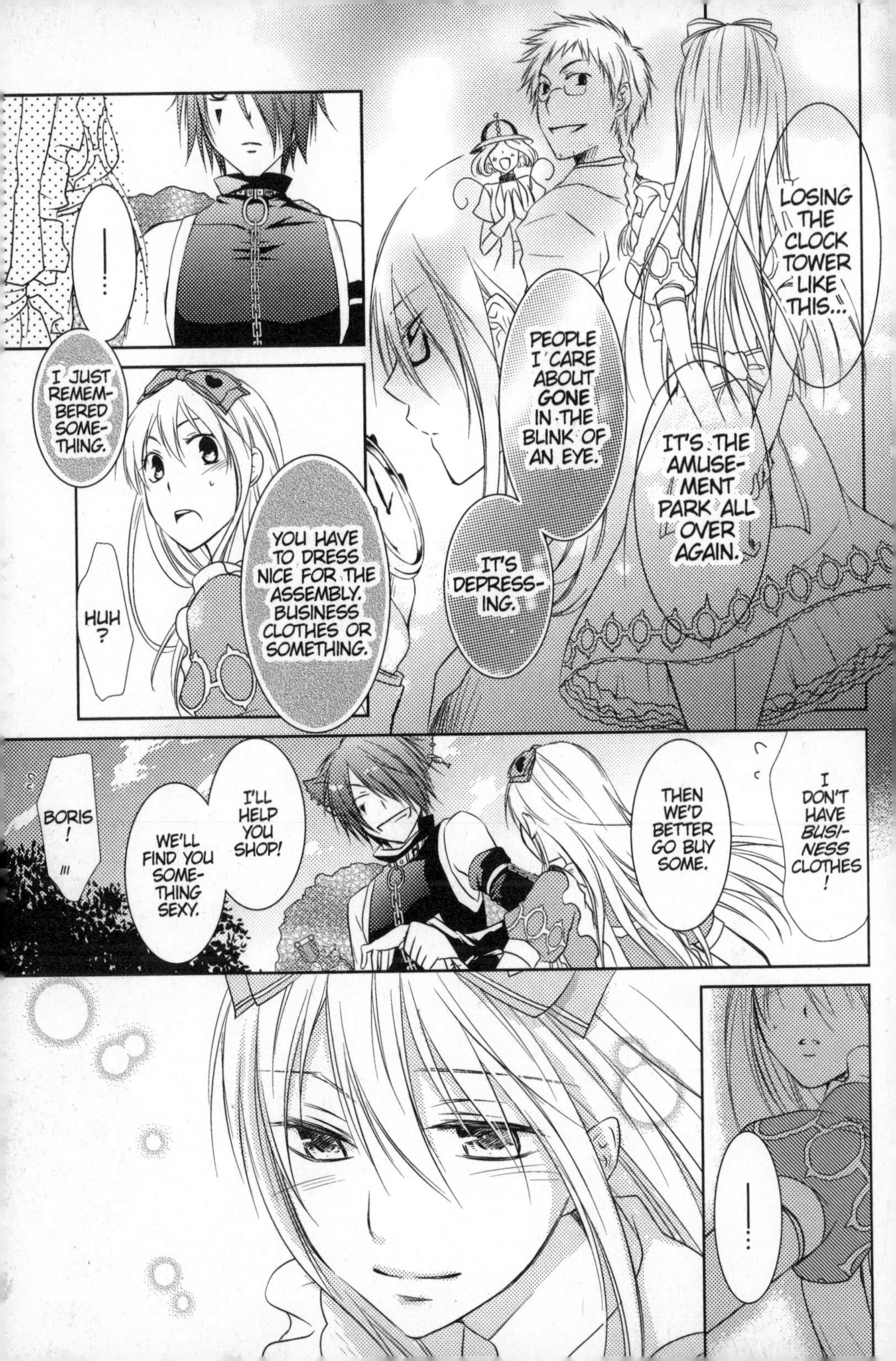
LOSING THE CLOCK TOWER LIKE THIS...
IT'S THE AMUSEMENT PARK ALL OVER AGAIN.
PEOPLE I CARE ABOUT GONE IN THE BLINK OF AN EYE.
IT'S DEPRESSING.
—!...
I JUST REMEMBERED SOMETHING.
YOU HAVE TO DRESS NICE FOR THE ASSEMBLY. BUSINESS CLOTHES OR SOMETHING.
HUH?
I DON'T HAVE BUSINESS CLOTHES!
THEN WE'D BETTER GO BUY SOME.
I'LL HELP YOU SHOP!
WE'LL FIND YOU SOMETHING SEXY.
BORIS!
—!...

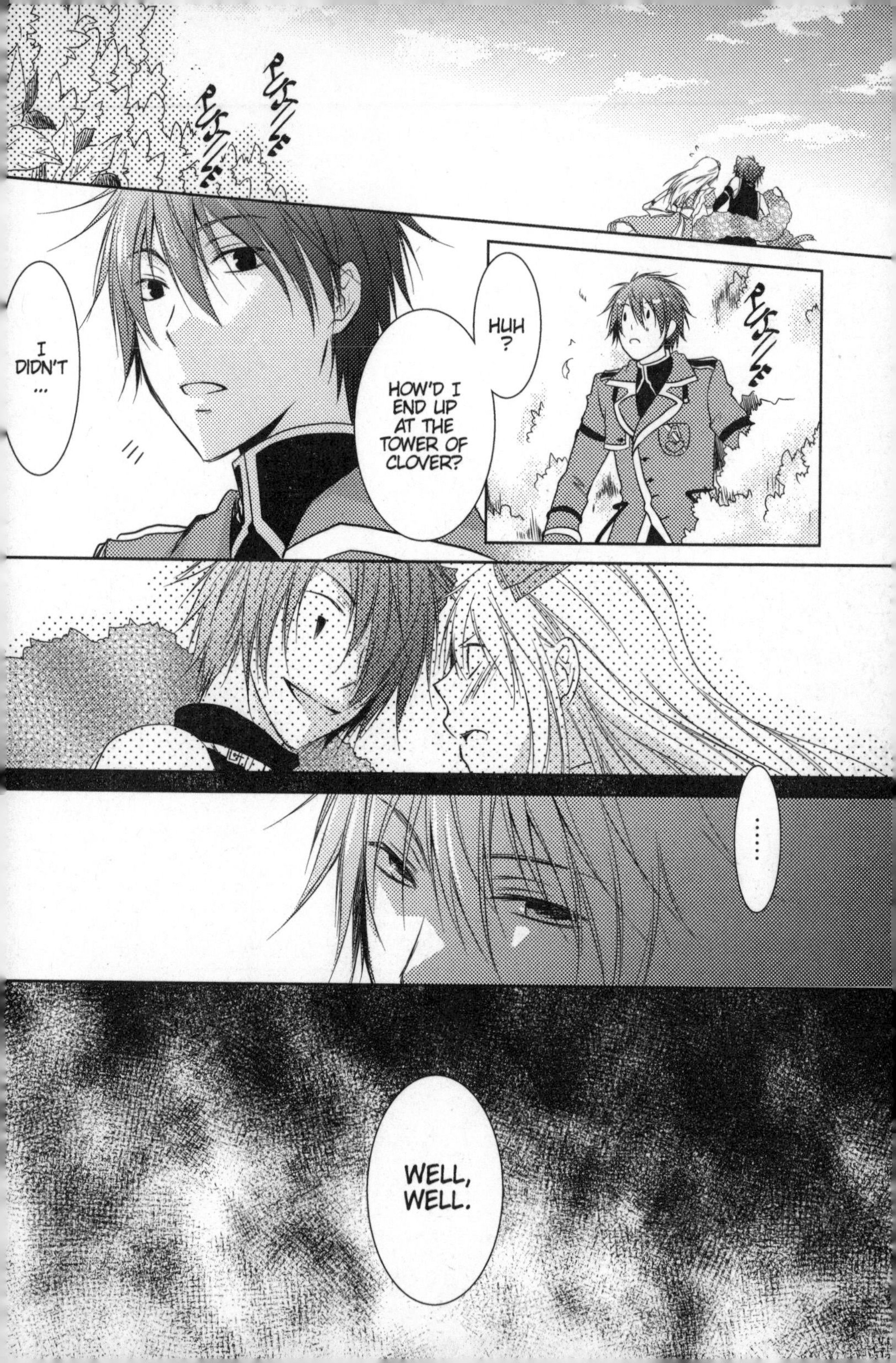
RUSTLE
RUSTLE
RUSTLE
HUH?
HOW'D I END UP AT THE TOWER OF CLOVER?
I DIDN'T ...
......
WELL, WELL.

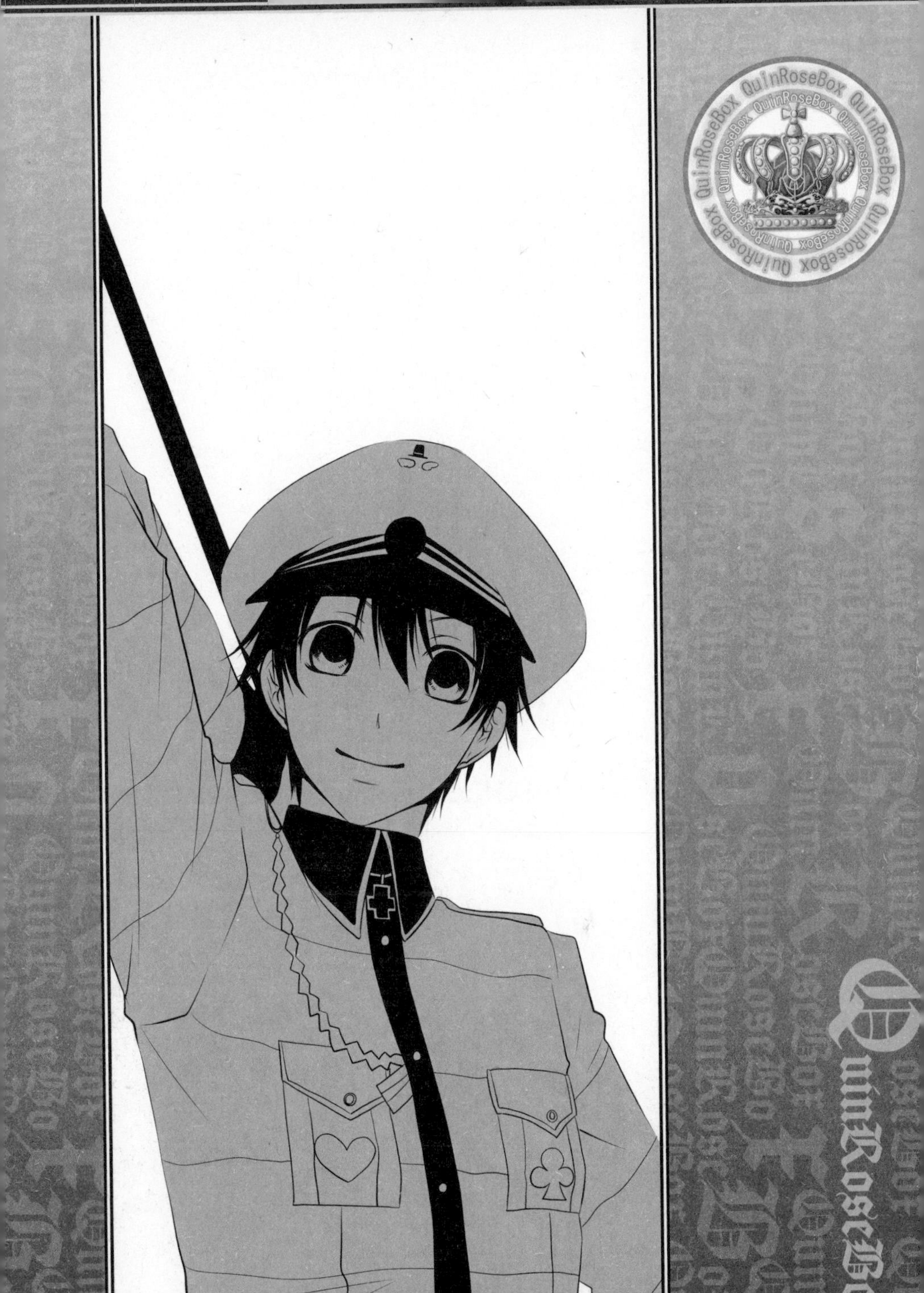
QuinRoseBox

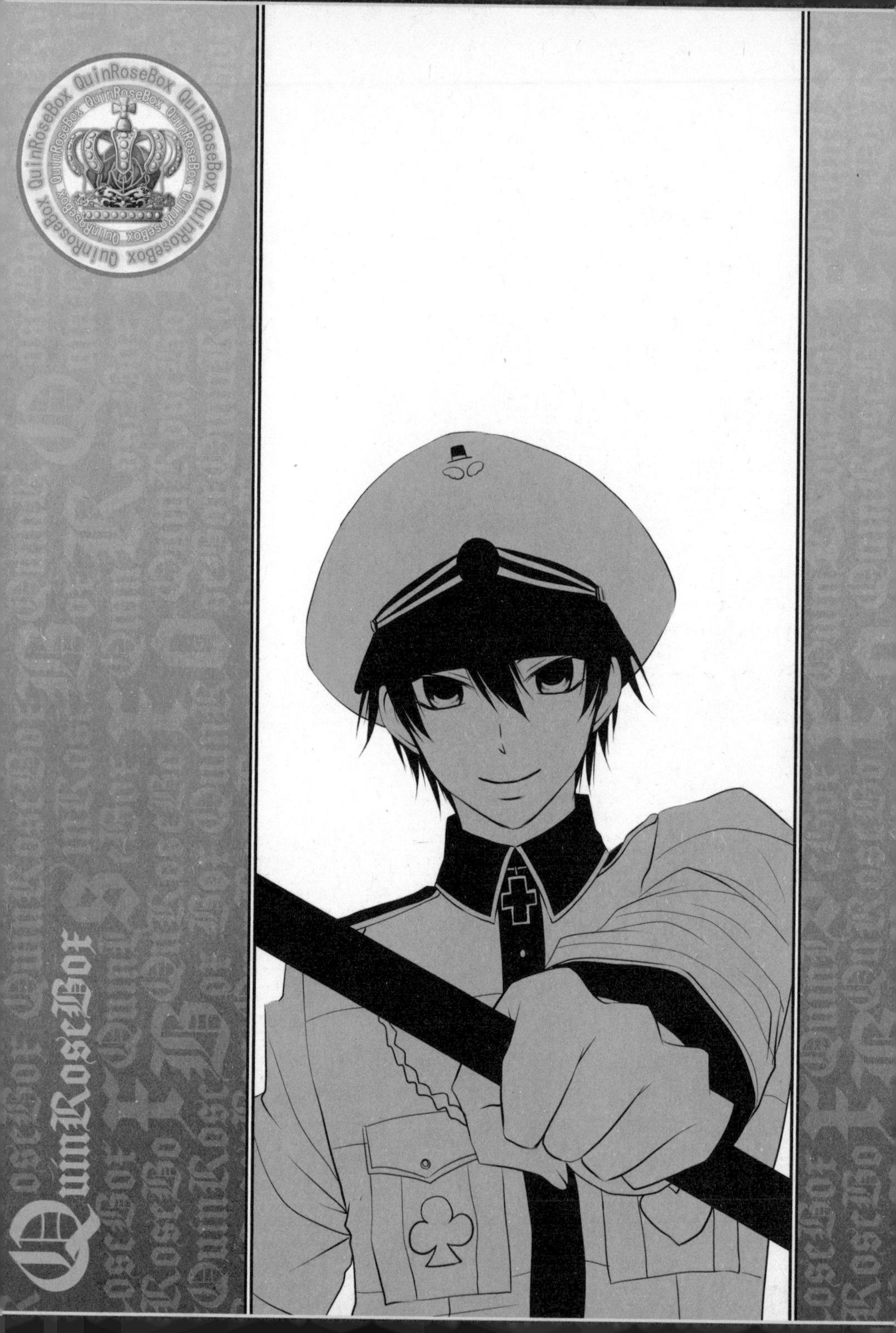
QuinRoseBox

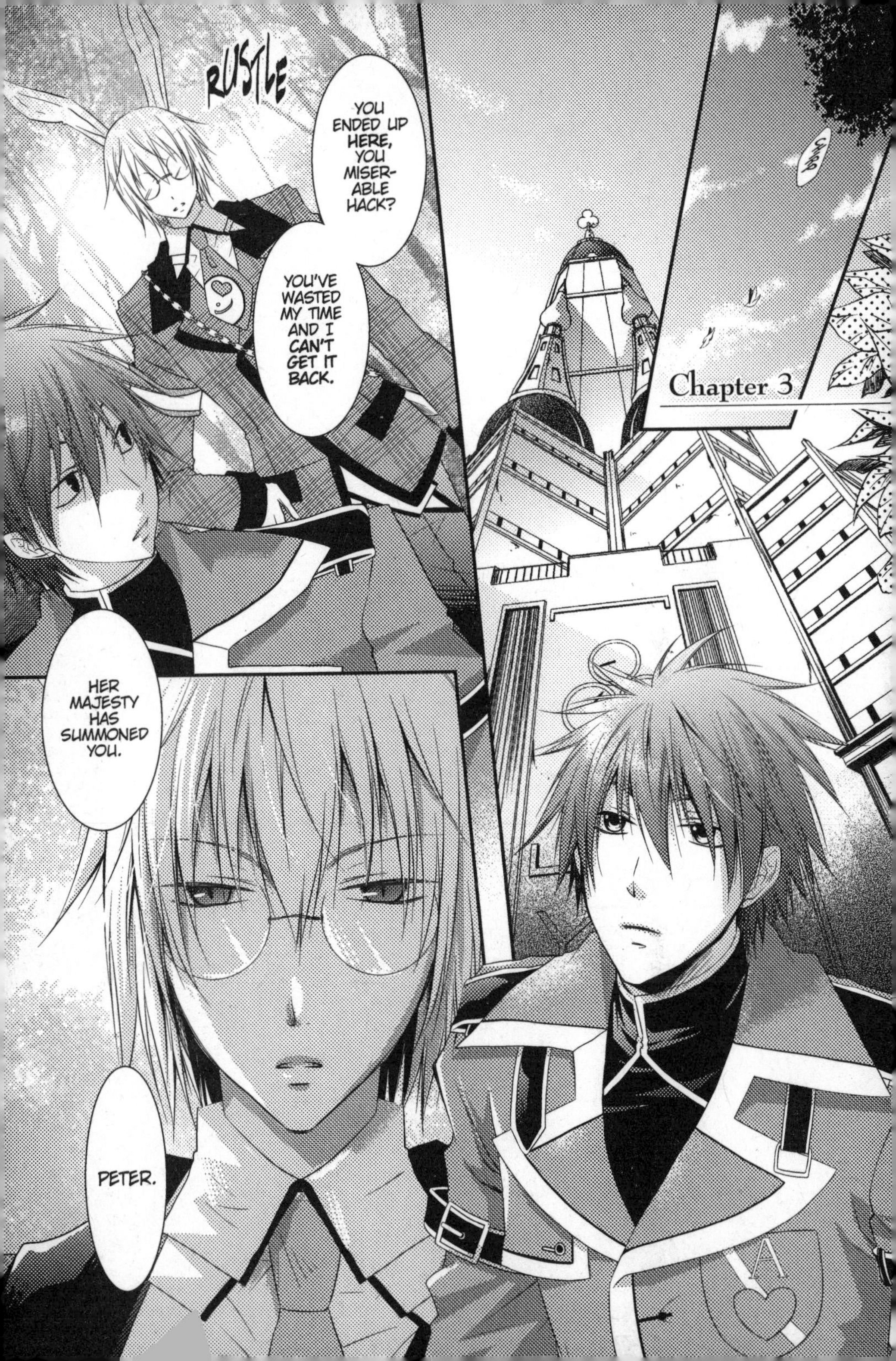
CHIRP
Chapter 3
RUSTLE
YOU ENDED UP HERE, YOU MISERABLE HACK?
YOU'VE WASTED MY TIME AND I CAN'T GET IT BACK.
HER MAJESTY HAS SUMMONED YOU.
PETER.

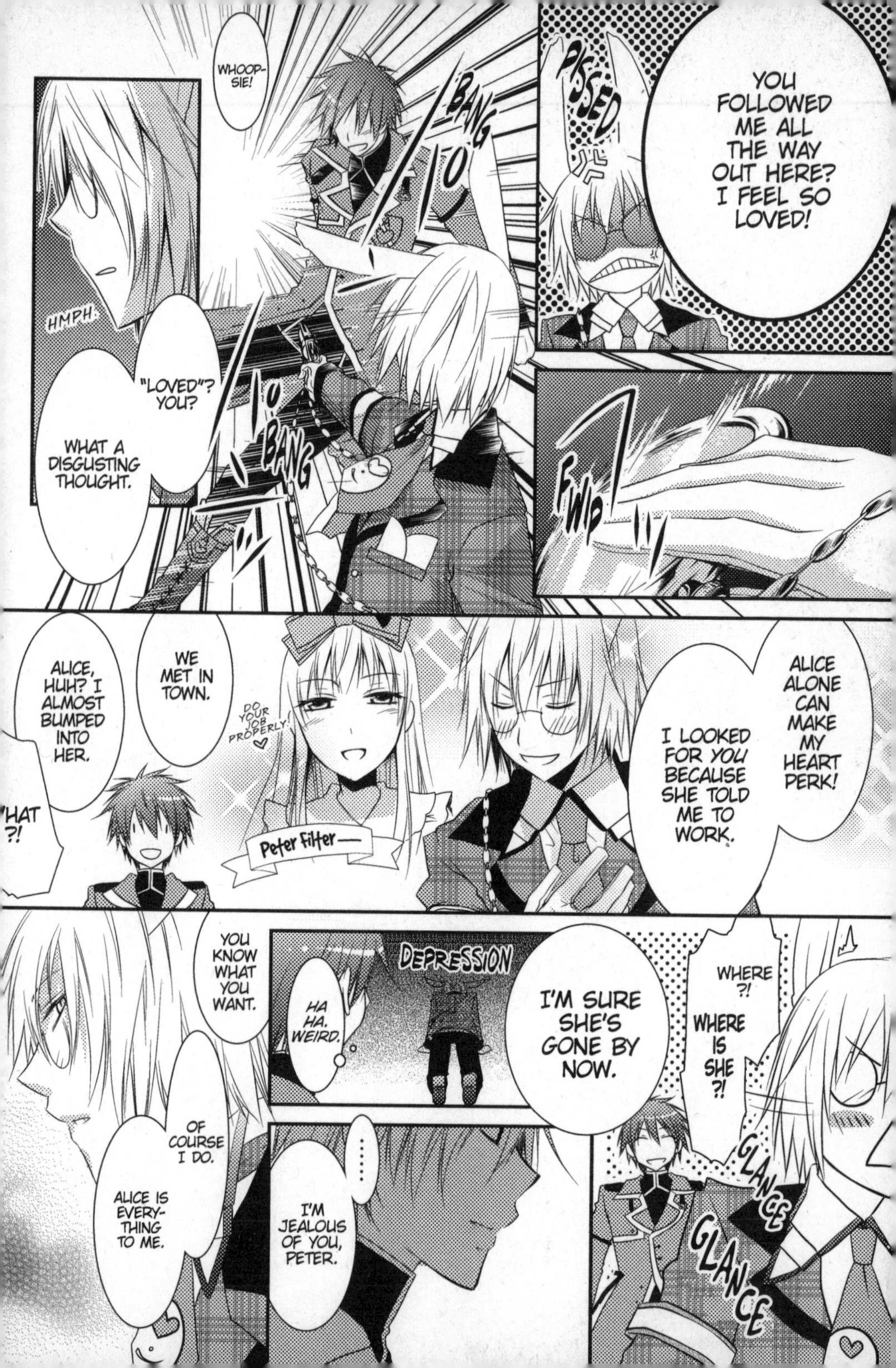
PISSED
YOU FOLLOWED ME ALL THE WAY OUT HERE? I FEEL SO LOVED!
FWIP
WHOOP-SIE!
BANG
BANG
HMPH.
"LOVED"? YOU?
WHAT A DISGUSTING THOUGHT.
ALICE ALONE CAN MAKE MY HEART PERK!
I LOOKED FOR YOU BECAUSE SHE TOLD ME TO WORK.
DO YOUR JOB PROPERLY!
Peter Filter—
WE MET IN TOWN.
ALICE, HUH? I ALMOST BUMPED INTO HER.
HAT ?!
WHERE ?!
WHERE IS SHE ?!
GLANCE
GLANCE
I'M SURE SHE'S GONE BY NOW.
DEPRESSION
HA HA. WEIRD.
YOU KNOW WHAT YOU WANT.
......
I'M JEALOUS OF YOU, PETER.
OF COURSE I DO.
ALICE IS EVERY-THING TO ME.

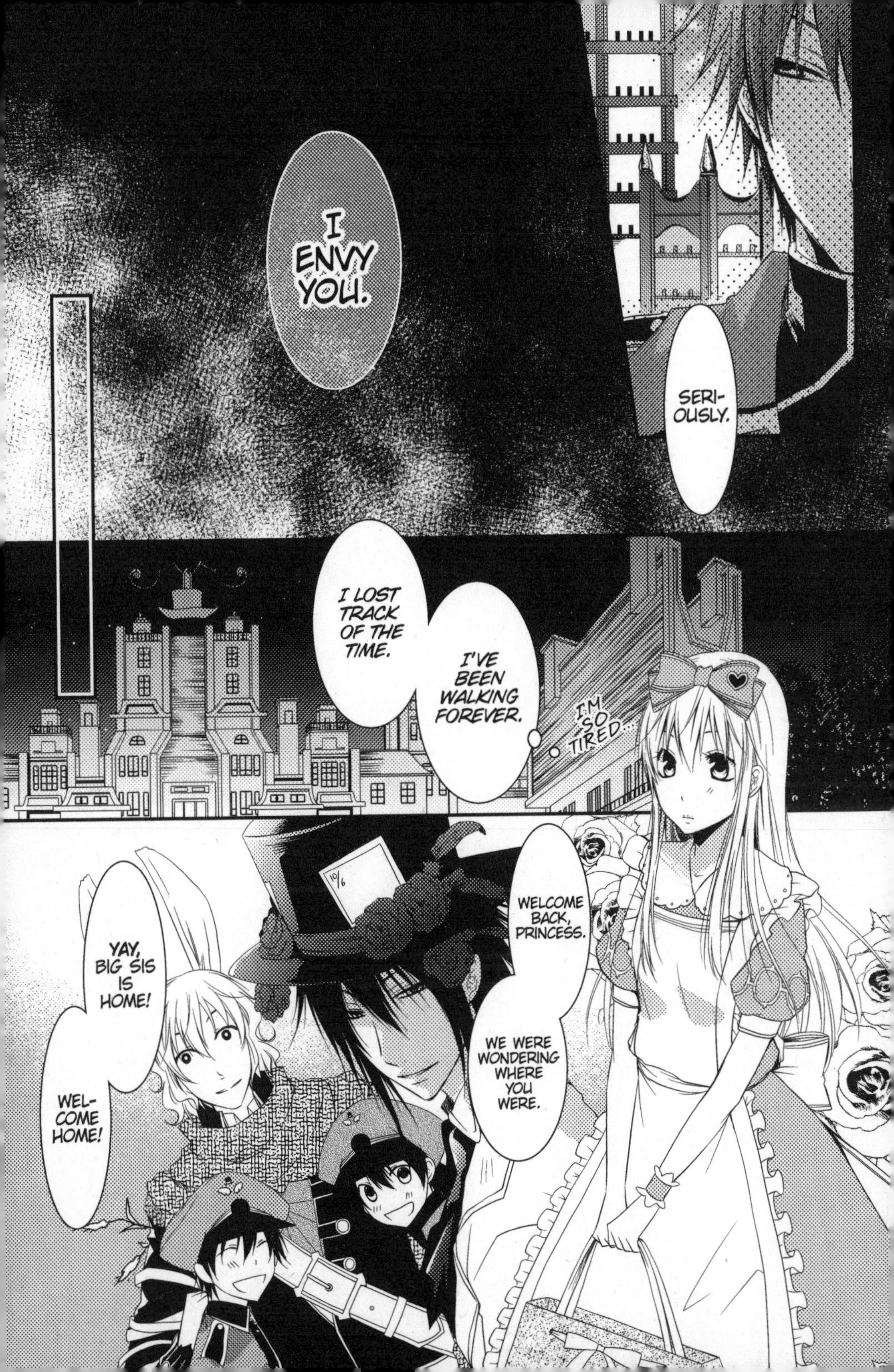
SERI-OUSLY.
I ENVY YOU.
I LOST TRACK OF THE TIME.
I'VE BEEN WALKING FOREVER.
I'M SO TIRED...
WELCOME BACK, PRINCESS.
WE WERE WONDERING WHERE YOU WERE.
YAY, BIG SIS IS HOME!
WEL-COME HOME!

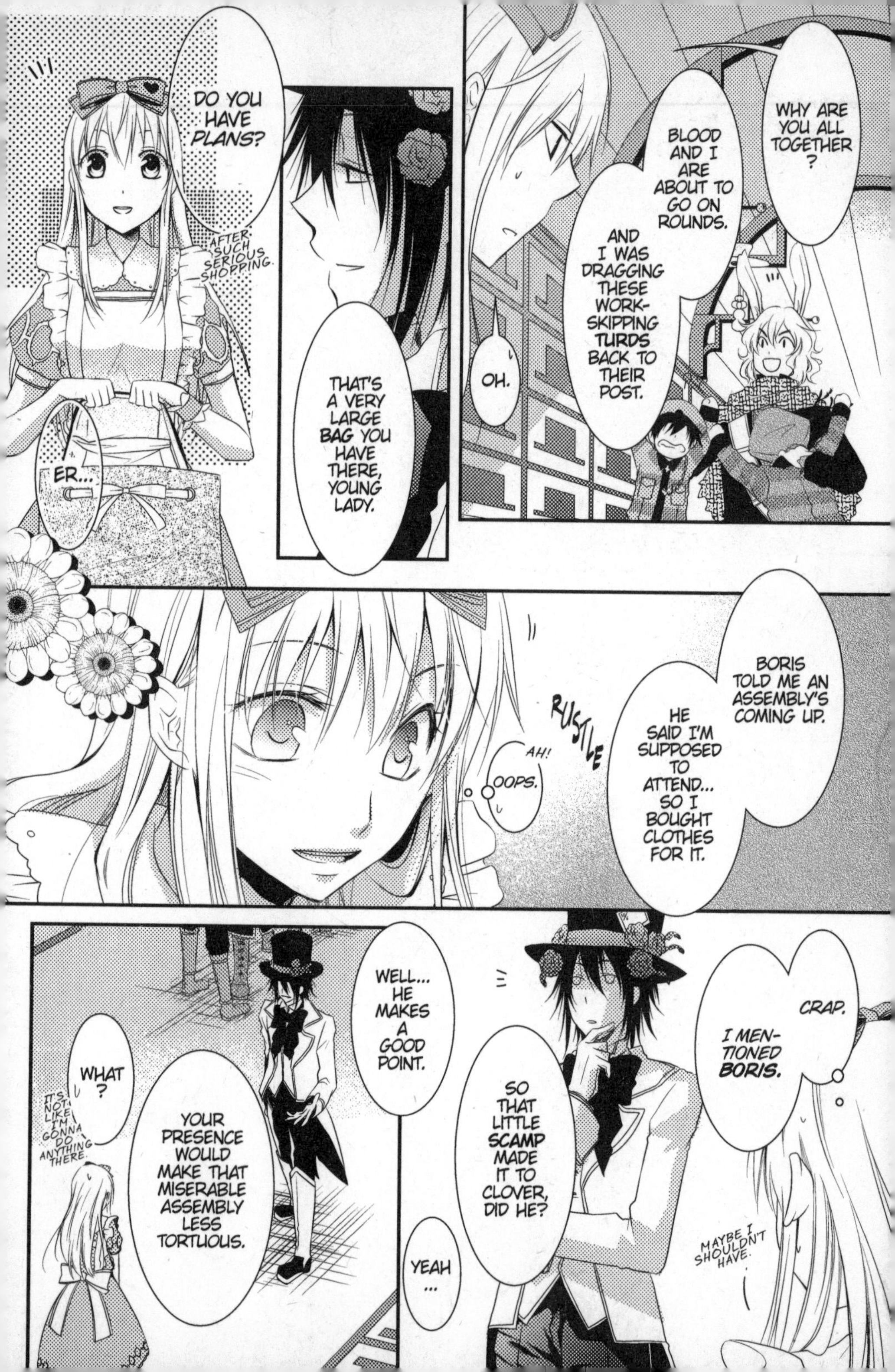
WHY ARE YOU ALL TOGETHER?
BLOOD AND I ARE ABOUT TO GO ON ROUNDS.
AND I WAS DRAGGING THESE WORK-SKIPPING TURDS BACK TO THEIR POST.
OH.
THAT'S A VERY LARGE BAG YOU HAVE THERE, YOUNG LADY.
DO YOU HAVE PLANS?
AFTER SUCH SERIOUS SHOPPING.
ER...
BORIS TOLD ME AN ASSEMBLY'S COMING UP.
HE SAID I'M SUPPOSED TO ATTEND... SO I BOUGHT CLOTHES FOR IT.
RUSTLE
AH!
OOPS.
CRAP.
I MEN-TIONED BORIS.
MAYBE I SHOULDN'T HAVE.
SO THAT LITTLE SCAMP MADE IT TO CLOVER, DID HE?
YEAH...
WELL... HE MAKES A GOOD POINT.
YOUR PRESENCE WOULD MAKE THAT MISERABLE ASSEMBLY LESS TORTUOUS.
WHAT?
IT'S NOT LIKE I'M GONNA DO ANYTHING THERE.

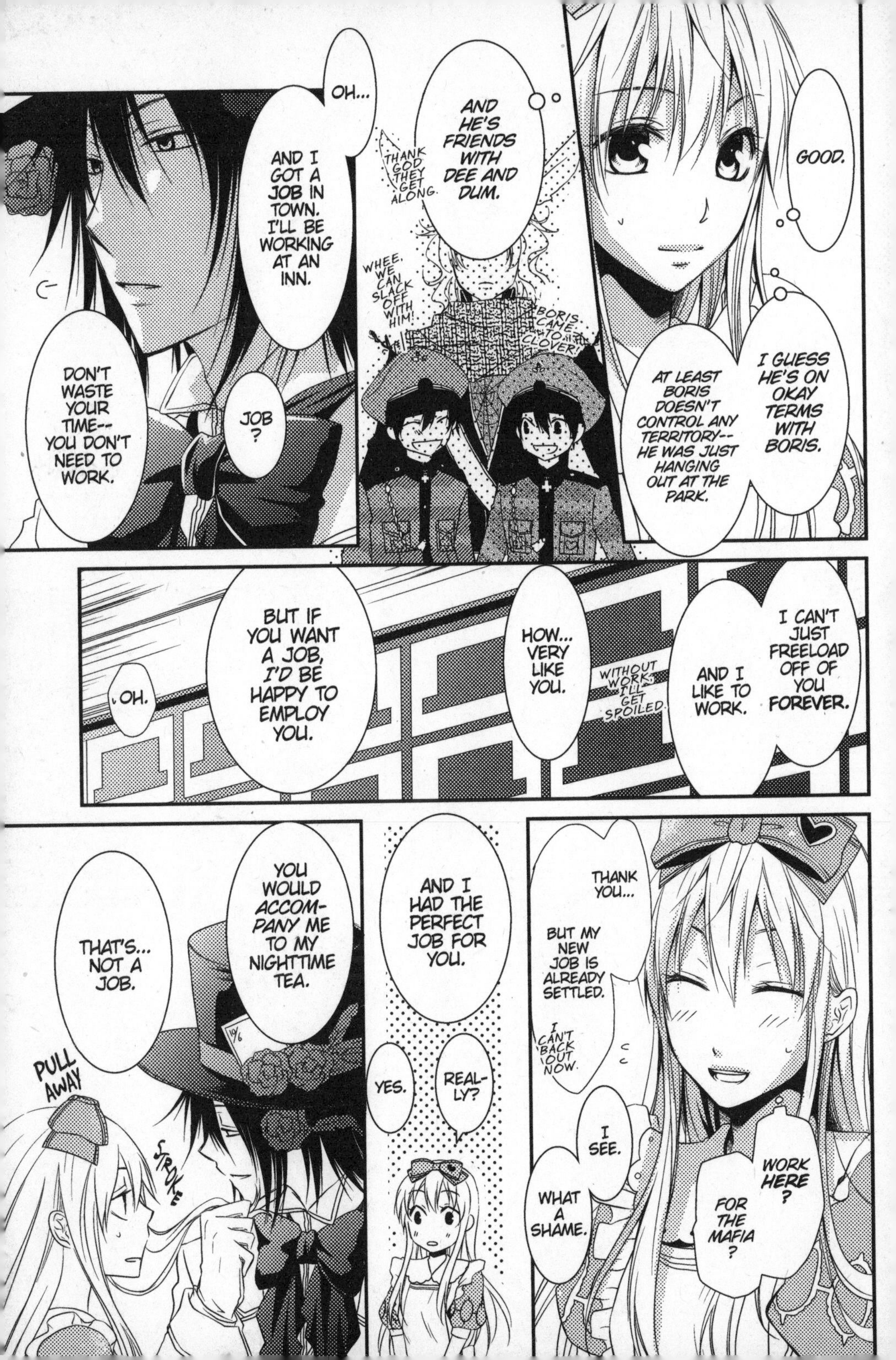
GOOD.
I GUESS HE'S ON OKAY TERMS WITH BORIS.
AT LEAST BORIS DOESN'T CONTROL ANY TERRITORY-- HE WAS JUST HANGING OUT AT THE PARK.
AND HE'S FRIENDS WITH DEE AND DUM.
THANK GOD THEY GET ALONG.
BORIS CAME TO CLOVER!
WHEE, WE CAN SLACK OFF WITH HIM!
OH...
AND I GOT A JOB IN TOWN. I'LL BE WORKING AT AN INN.
JOB?
DON'T WASTE YOUR TIME-- YOU DON'T NEED TO WORK.
I CAN'T JUST FREELOAD OFF OF YOU FOREVER.
AND I LIKE TO WORK.
WITHOUT WORK, I'LL GET SPOILED.
HOW... VERY LIKE YOU.
BUT IF YOU WANT A JOB, I'D BE HAPPY TO EMPLOY YOU.
OH.
WORK HERE?
FOR THE MAFIA?
THANK YOU...
BUT MY NEW JOB IS ALREADY SETTLED.
I CAN'T BACK OUT NOW.
I SEE.
WHAT A SHAME.
AND I HAD THE PERFECT JOB FOR YOU.
REALLY?
YES.
YOU WOULD ACCOMPANY ME TO MY NIGHTTIME TEA.
THAT'S... NOT A JOB.
STROKE
PULL AWAY

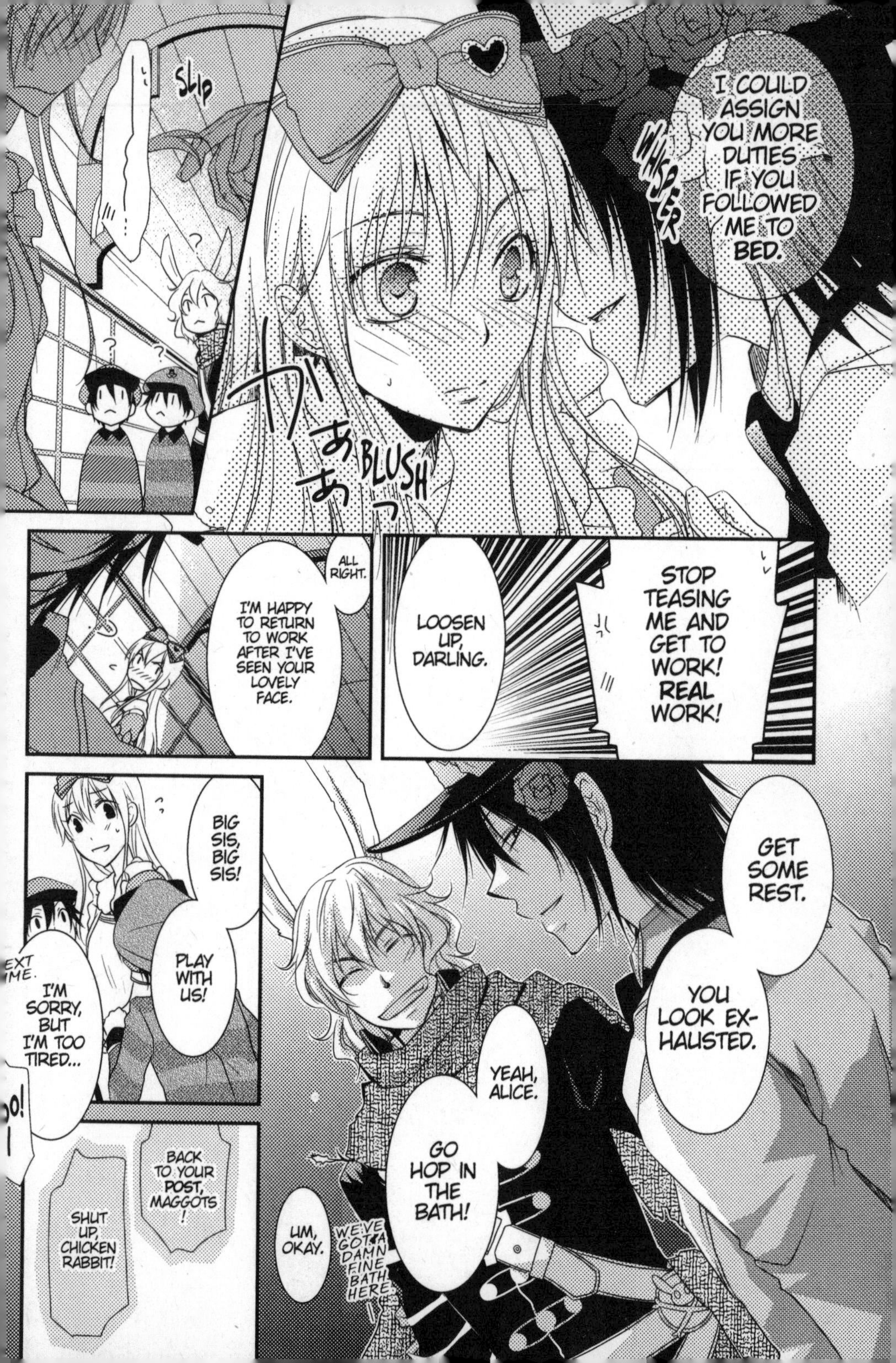
I COULD ASSIGN YOU MORE DUTIES IF YOU FOLLOWED ME TO BED.
WHISPER
BLUSH
SLIP
STOP TEASING ME AND GET TO WORK! REAL WORK!
LOOSEN UP, DARLING.
ALL RIGHT.
I'M HAPPY TO RETURN TO WORK AFTER I'VE SEEN YOUR LOVELY FACE.
GET SOME REST.
YOU LOOK EX- HAUSTED.
YEAH, ALICE.
GO HOP IN THE BATH!
WE'VE GOT A DAMN FINE BATH HERE
UM, OKAY.
BIG SIS, BIG SIS!
PLAY WITH US!
I'M SORRY, BUT I'M TOO TIRED...
BACK TO YOUR POST, MAGGOTS!
SHUT UP, CHICKEN RABBIT!

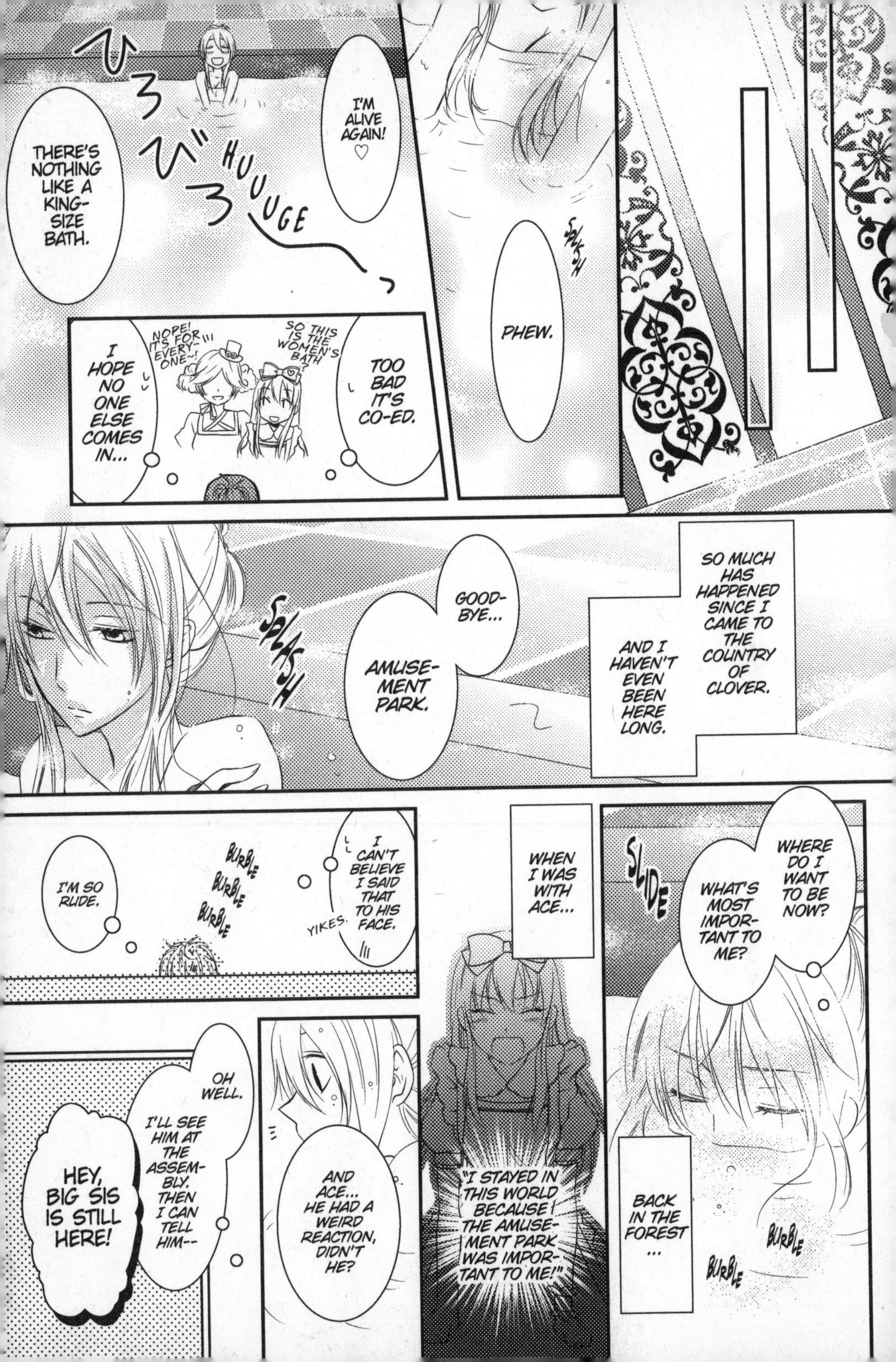
PHEW.
SPLASH
I'M ALIVE AGAIN! ♡
ひろびろ
HUUUGE
THERE'S NOTHING LIKE A KING-SIZE BATH.
TOO BAD IT'S CO-ED.
SO THIS IS THE WOMEN'S BATH?
NOPE! IT'S FOR EVERY-ONE~!
I HOPE NO ONE ELSE COMES IN...
SO MUCH HAS HAPPENED SINCE I CAME TO THE COUNTRY OF CLOVER.
AND I HAVEN'T EVEN BEEN HERE LONG.
GOOD-BYE...
AMUSEMENT PARK.
SPLASH
WHERE DO I WANT TO BE NOW?
WHAT'S MOST IMPORTANT TO ME?
SLIDE
WHEN I WAS WITH ACE...
I CAN'T BELIEVE I SAID THAT TO HIS FACE.
YIKES.
BURBLE BURBLE BURBLE
I'M SO RUDE.
BACK IN THE FOREST...
BURBLE BURBLE
"I STAYED IN THIS WORLD BECAUSE THE AMUSEMENT PARK WAS IMPORTANT TO ME!"
AND ACE... HE HAD A WEIRD REACTION, DIDN'T HE?
OH WELL.
I'LL SEE HIM AT THE ASSEMBLY. THEN I CAN TELL HIM--
HEY, BIG SIS IS STILL HERE!

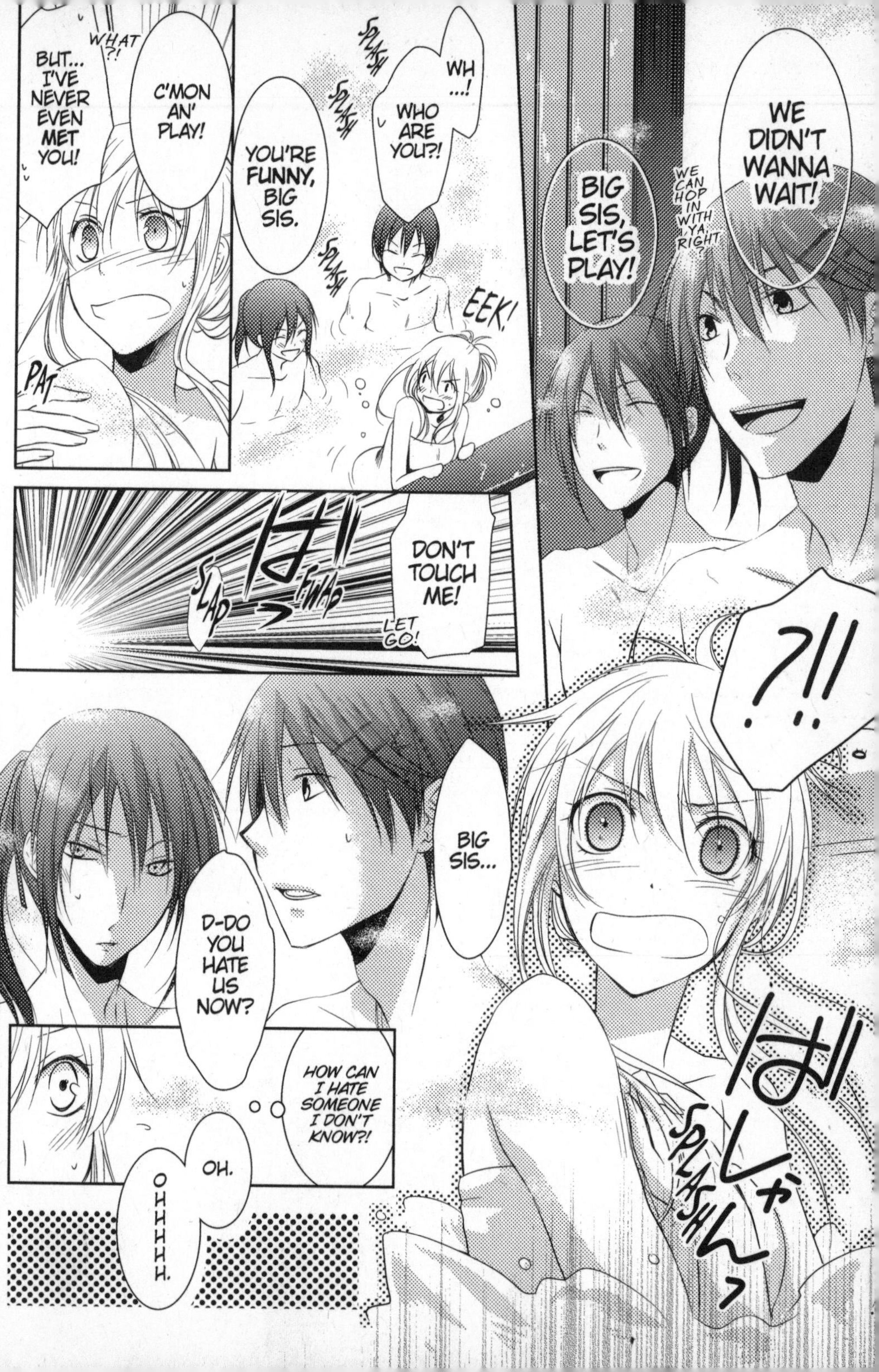

WE DIDN'T WANNA WAIT!
WE CAN HOP IN WITH YA, RIGHT?
BIG SIS, LET'S PLAY!
?!!
WH ...!
WHO ARE YOU?!
SPLASH
SPLASH
YOU'RE FUNNY, BIG SIS.
SPLASH
EEK!
C'MON AN' PLAY!
WHAT ?!
BUT... I'VE NEVER EVEN MET YOU!
PAT
DON'T TOUCH ME!
LET GO!
FWAP
SLAP
SPLASH
BIG SIS...
D-DO YOU HATE US NOW?
HOW CAN I HATE SOMEONE I DON'T KNOW?!
OH.
OHHHHH.

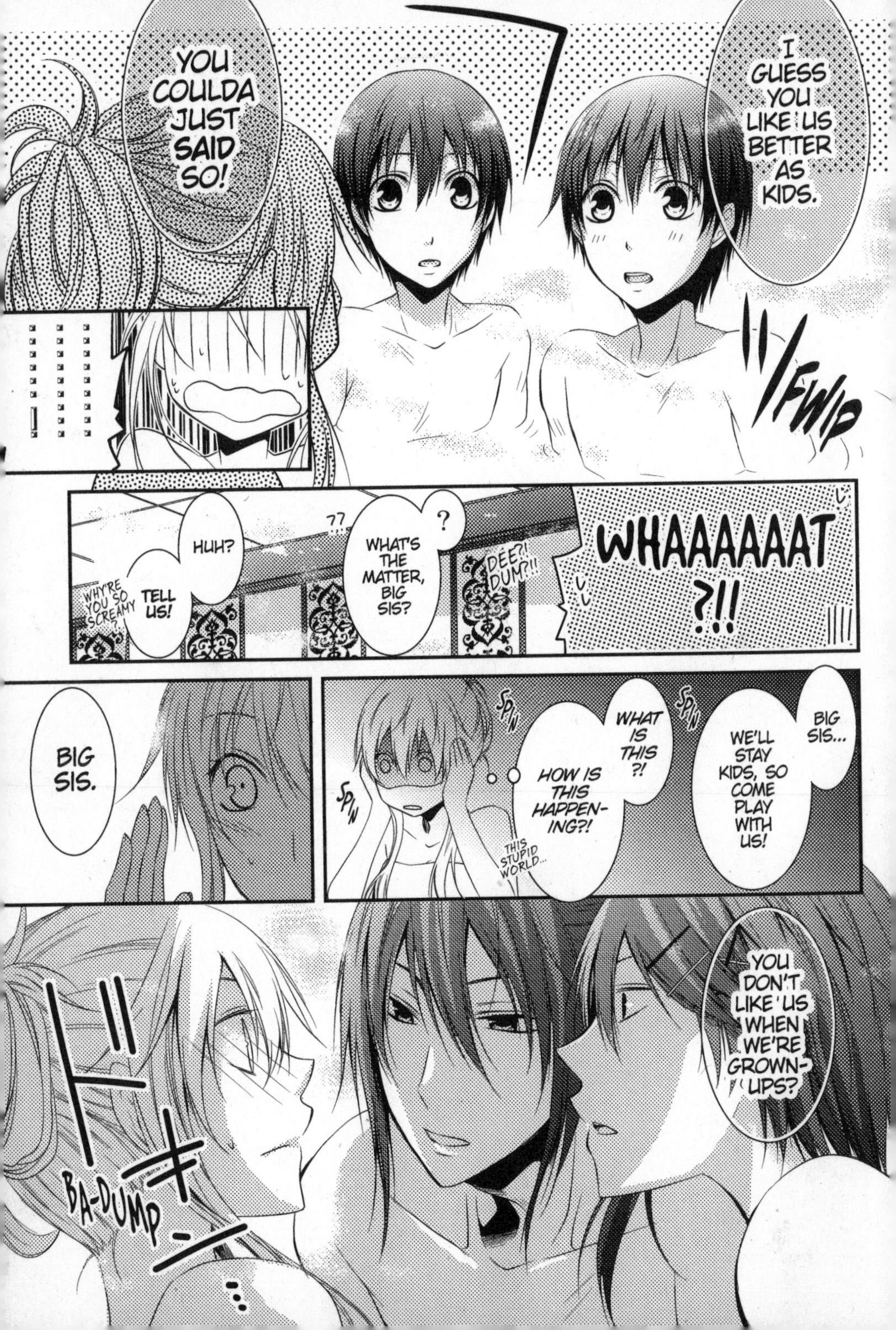
I GUESS YOU LIKE US BETTER AS KIDS.
FWIP
YOU COULDA JUST SAID SO!
......!
WHAAAAAAT ?!!
DEE?! DUM?!!
?
WHAT'S THE MATTER, BIG SIS?
??
HUH?
TELL US!
WHY'RE YOU SO SCREAMY?
BIG SIS...
WE'LL STAY KIDS, SO COME PLAY WITH US!
SPIN
SPIN
WHAT IS THIS?!
HOW IS THIS HAPPENING?!
THIS STUPID WORLD...
SPIN
BIG SIS.
YOU DON'T LIKE US WHEN WE'RE GROWN-UPS?
BA-DUMP
...

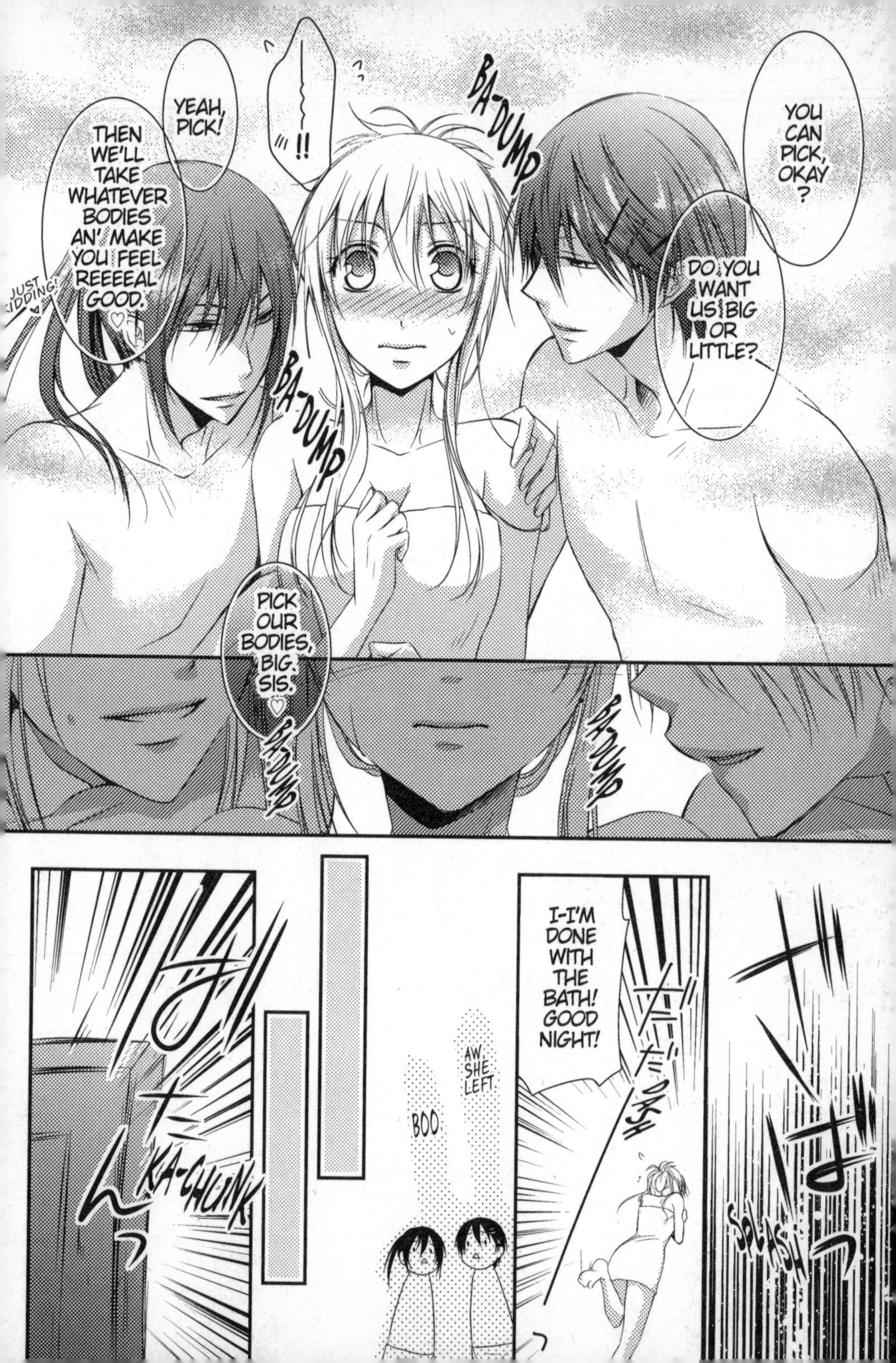
YOU CAN PICK, OKAY?
DO YOU WANT US BIG OR LITTLE?
BA-DUMP
!!
YEAH, PICK!
THEN WE'LL TAKE WHATEVER BODIES AN' MAKE YOU FEEL REEEEAL GOOD.
JUST KIDDING!
BA-DUMP
PICK OUR BODIES, BIG SIS.
BA-DUMP
BA-DUMP
SPLASH
I-I'M DONE WITH THE BATH! GOOD NIGHT!
DASH
AW, SHE LEFT.
BOO
KA-CHUNK

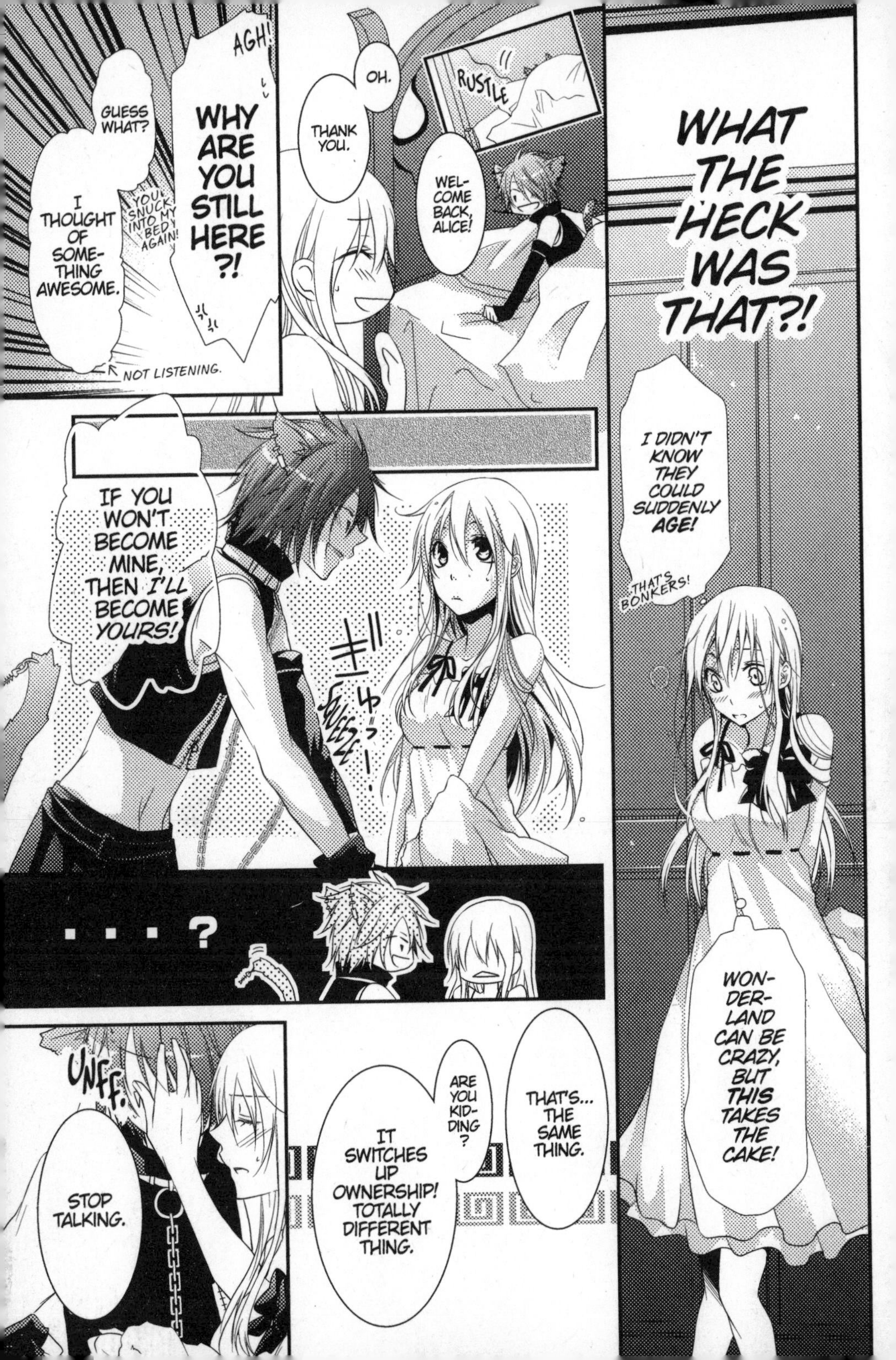
WHAT THE HECK WAS THAT?!
I DIDN'T KNOW THEY COULD SUDDENLY AGE!
THAT'S BONKERS!
WON-DER-LAND CAN BE CRAZY, BUT THIS TAKES THE CAKE!
RUSTLE
OH.
THANK YOU.
WEL-COME BACK, ALICE!
AGH!
WHY ARE YOU STILL HERE?!
YOU SNUCK INTO MY BED AGAIN!
GUESS WHAT?
I THOUGHT OF SOME-THING AWESOME.
NOT LISTENING.
IF YOU WON'T BECOME MINE, THEN I'LL BECOME YOURS!
SQUEEZE
...?
THAT'S... THE SAME THING.
ARE YOU KID-DING?
IT SWITCHES UP OWNERSHIP! TOTALLY DIFFERENT THING.
UNFF.
STOP TALKING.

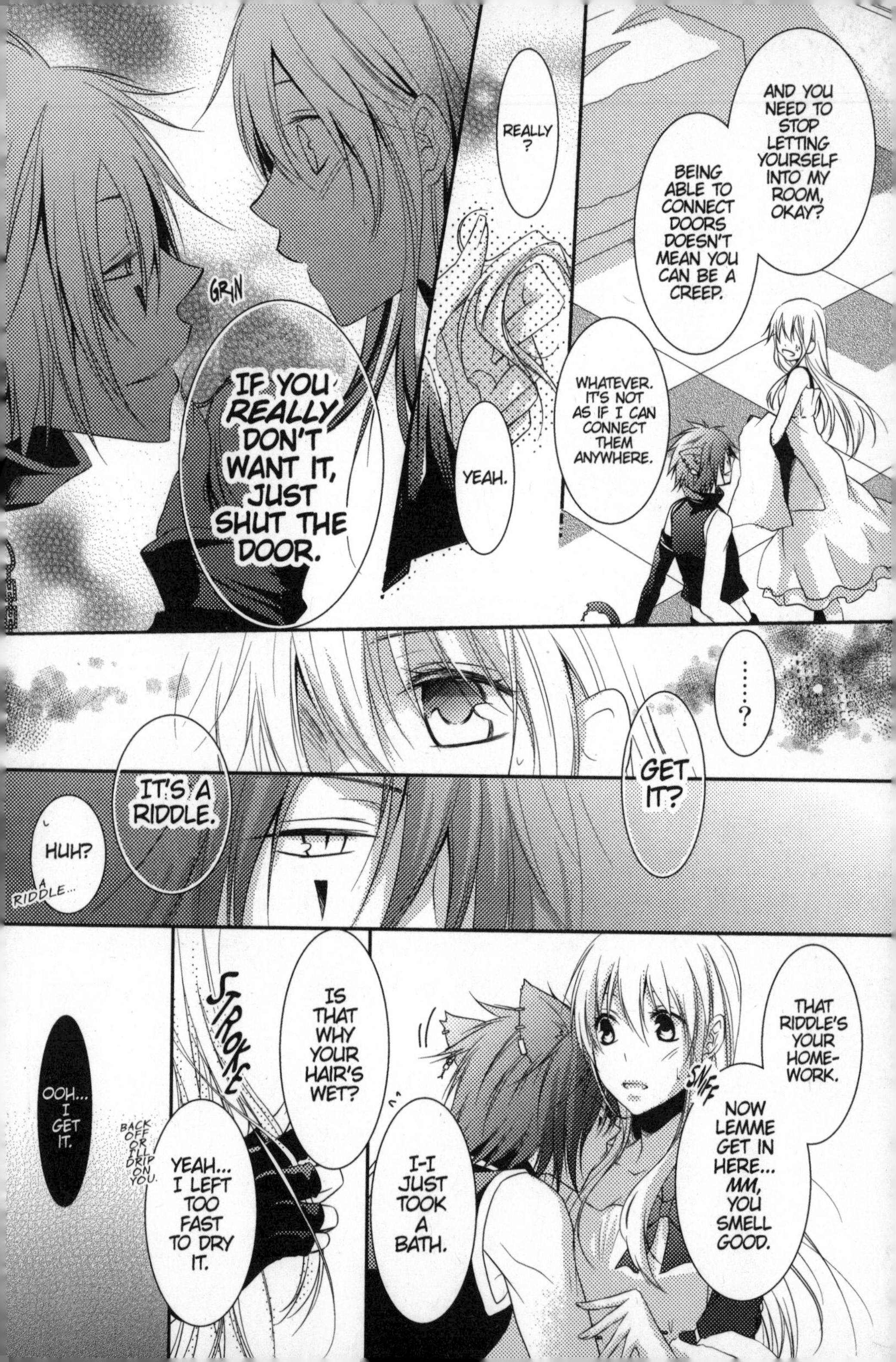
AND YOU NEED TO STOP LETTING YOURSELF INTO MY ROOM, OKAY?
BEING ABLE TO CONNECT DOORS DOESN'T MEAN YOU CAN BE A CREEP.
WHATEVER. IT'S NOT AS IF I CAN CONNECT THEM ANYWHERE.
REALLY?
YEAH.
GRIN
IF YOU REALLY DON'T WANT IT, JUST SHUT THE DOOR.
......?
GET IT?
IT'S A RIDDLE.
HUH?
A RIDDLE...
THAT RIDDLE'S YOUR HOME-WORK.
NOW LEMME GET IN HERE... MM, YOU SMELL GOOD.
SNIFF
I-I JUST TOOK A BATH.
IS THAT WHY YOUR HAIR'S WET?
STROKE
YEAH... I LEFT TOO FAST TO DRY IT.
BACK OFF OR I'LL DRIP ON YOU.
OOH... I GET IT.

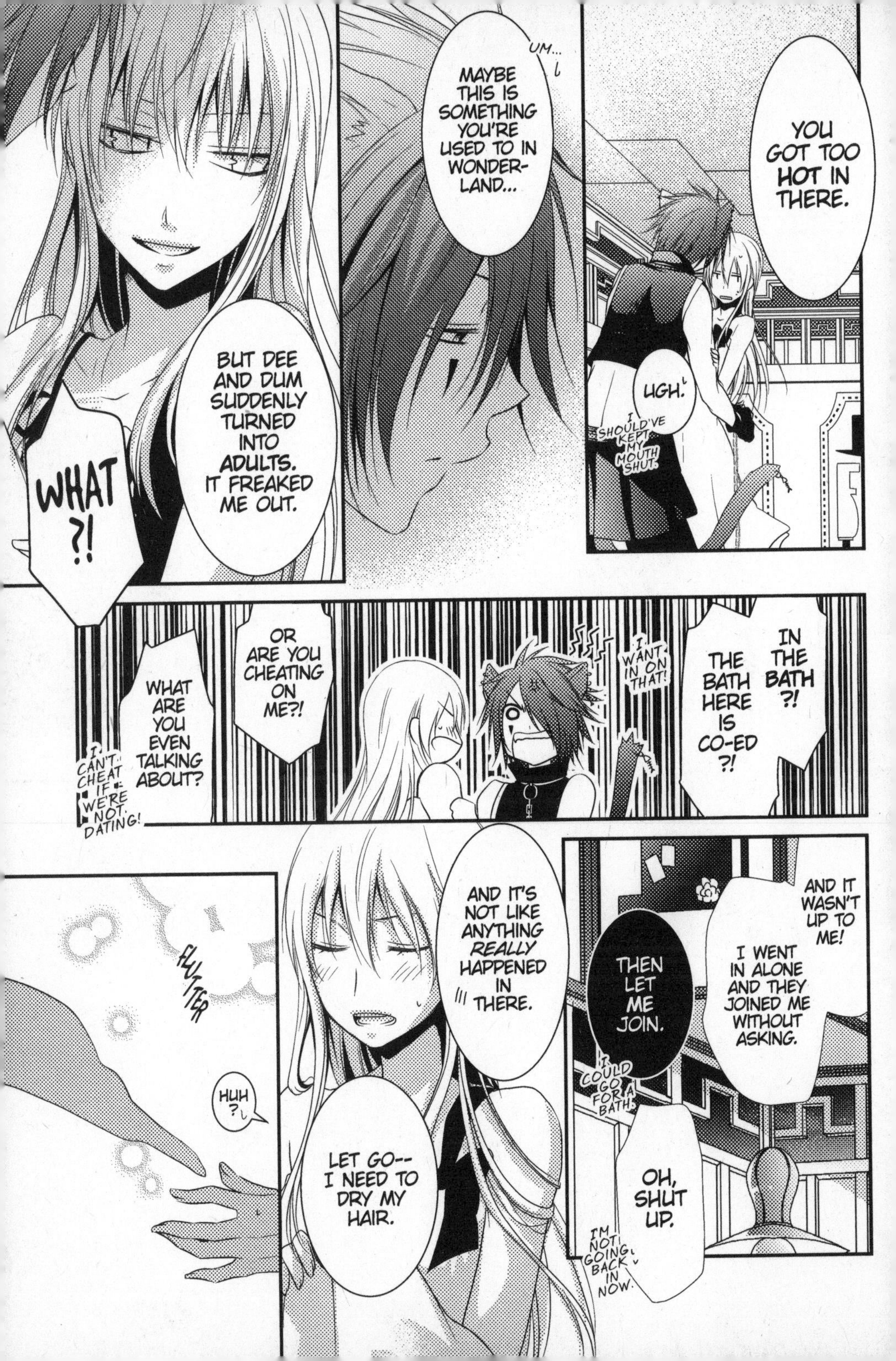
YOU GOT TOO HOT IN THERE.
UGH.
I SHOULD'VE KEPT MY MOUTH SHUT.
UM...
MAYBE THIS IS SOMETHING YOU'RE USED TO IN WONDERLAND...
BUT DEE AND DUM SUDDENLY TURNED INTO ADULTS. IT FREAKED ME OUT.
WHAT?!
IN THE BATH?!
THE BATH HERE IS CO-ED?!
I WANT IN ON THAT!
OR ARE YOU CHEATING ON ME?!
WHAT ARE YOU EVEN TALKING ABOUT?
I CAN'T CHEAT IF WE'RE NOT DATING!
AND IT WASN'T UP TO ME!
I WENT IN ALONE AND THEY JOINED ME WITHOUT ASKING.
THEN LET ME JOIN.
I COULD GO FOR A BATH.
OH, SHUT UP.
I'M NOT GOING BACK IN NOW.
AND IT'S NOT LIKE ANYTHING *REALLY* HAPPENED IN THERE.
LET GO-- I NEED TO DRY MY HAIR.
FLUTTER
HUH?

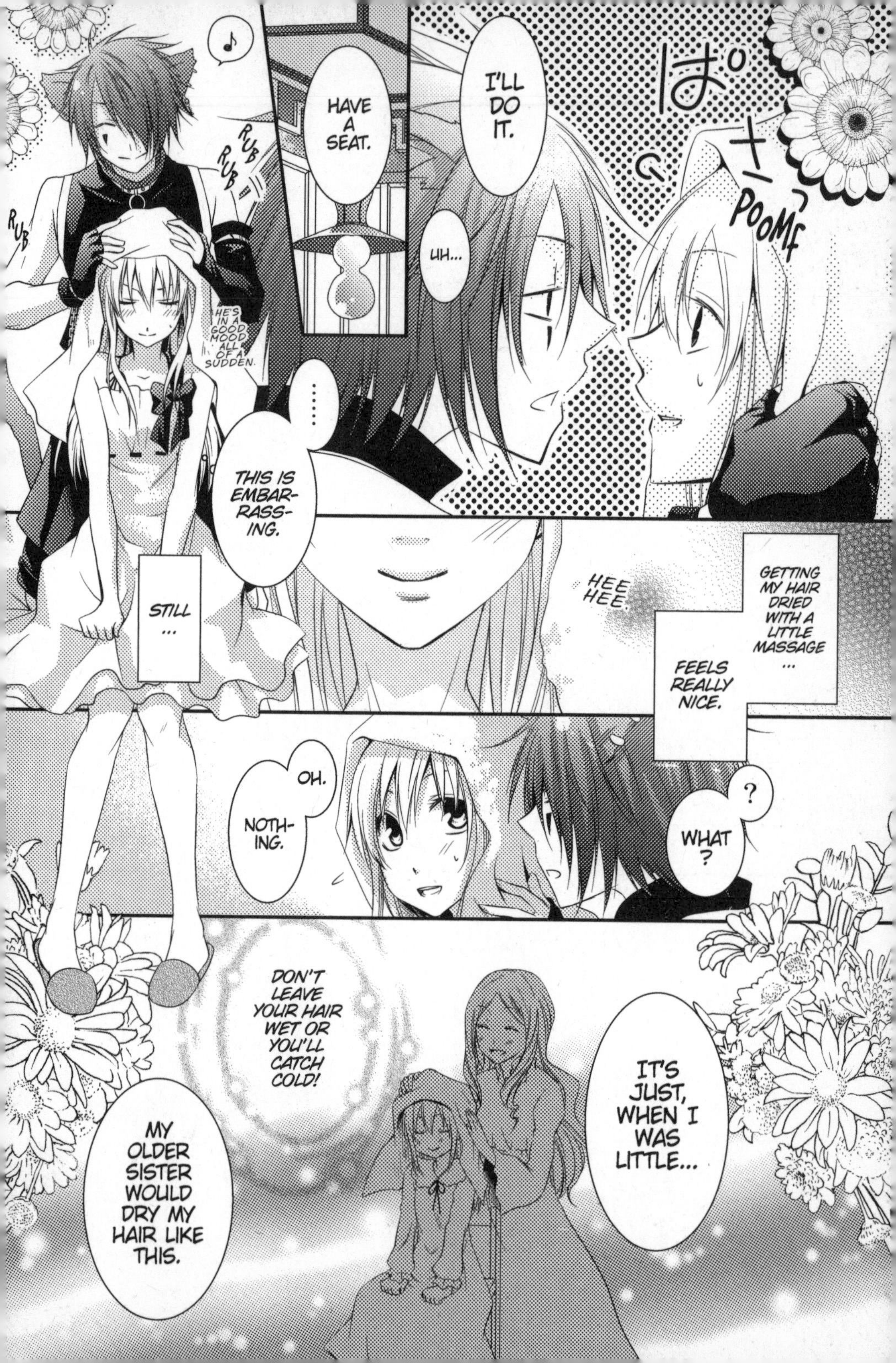

ぱさ
POOMF
I'LL DO IT.
UH...
......
HAVE A SEAT.
♪
RUB RUB
RUB
HE'S IN A GOOD MOOD ALL OF A SUDDEN.
THIS IS EMBARRASSING.
STILL...
GETTING MY HAIR DRIED WITH A LITTLE MASSAGE...
FEELS REALLY NICE.
HEE HEE.
?
WHAT?
OH.
NOTHING.
IT'S JUST, WHEN I WAS LITTLE...
DON'T LEAVE YOUR HAIR WET OR YOU'LL CATCH COLD!
MY OLDER SISTER WOULD DRY MY HAIR LIKE THIS.

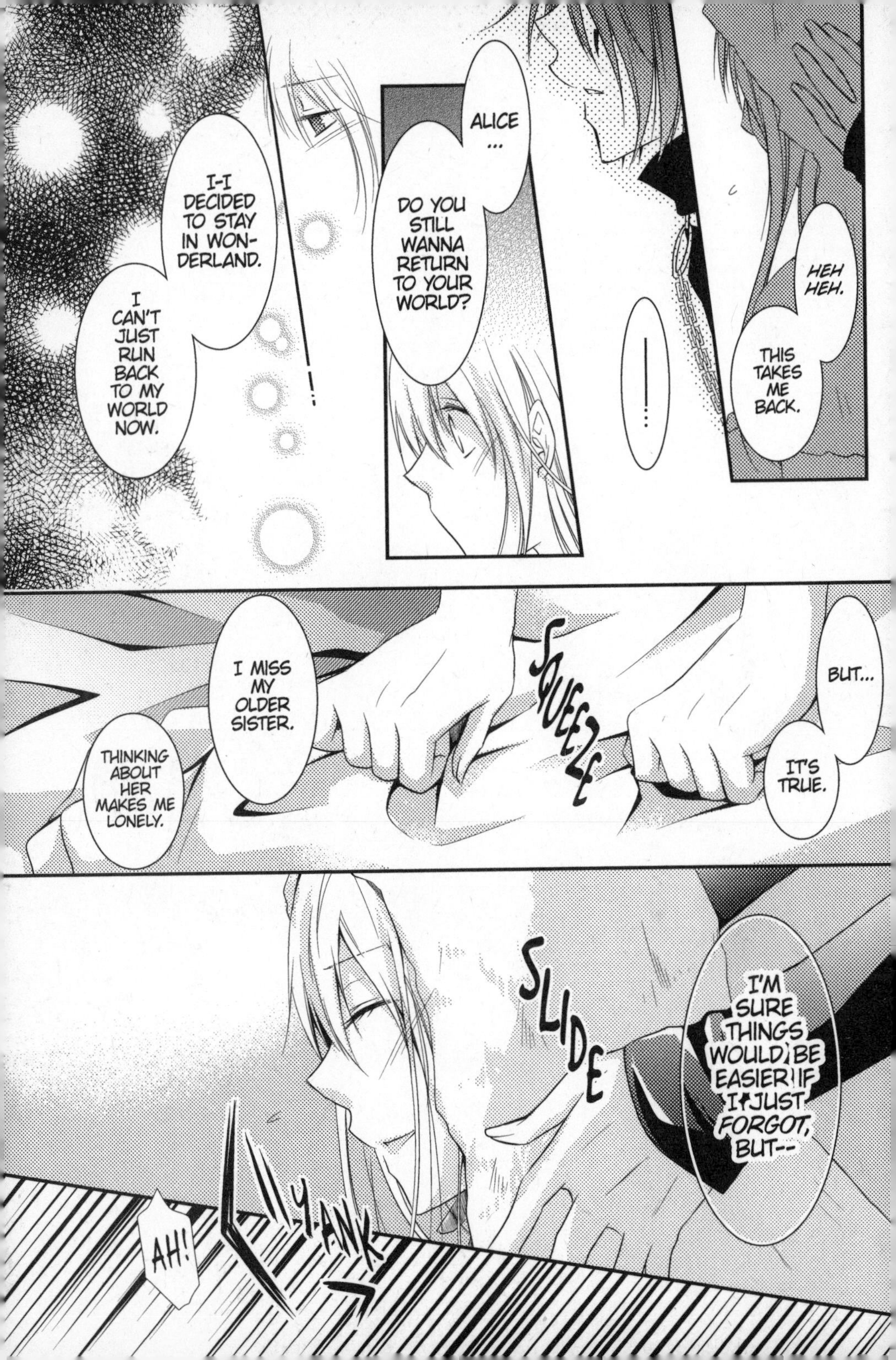
HEH HEH.
THIS TAKES ME BACK.
!...
ALICE...
DO YOU STILL WANNA RETURN TO YOUR WORLD?
I-I DECIDED TO STAY IN WONDERLAND.
I CAN'T JUST RUN BACK TO MY WORLD NOW.
BUT...
IT'S TRUE.
SQUEEZE
I MISS MY OLDER SISTER.
THINKING ABOUT HER MAKES ME LONELY.
I'M SURE THINGS WOULD BE EASIER IF I JUST FORGOT, BUT--
SLIDE
YANK
AH!

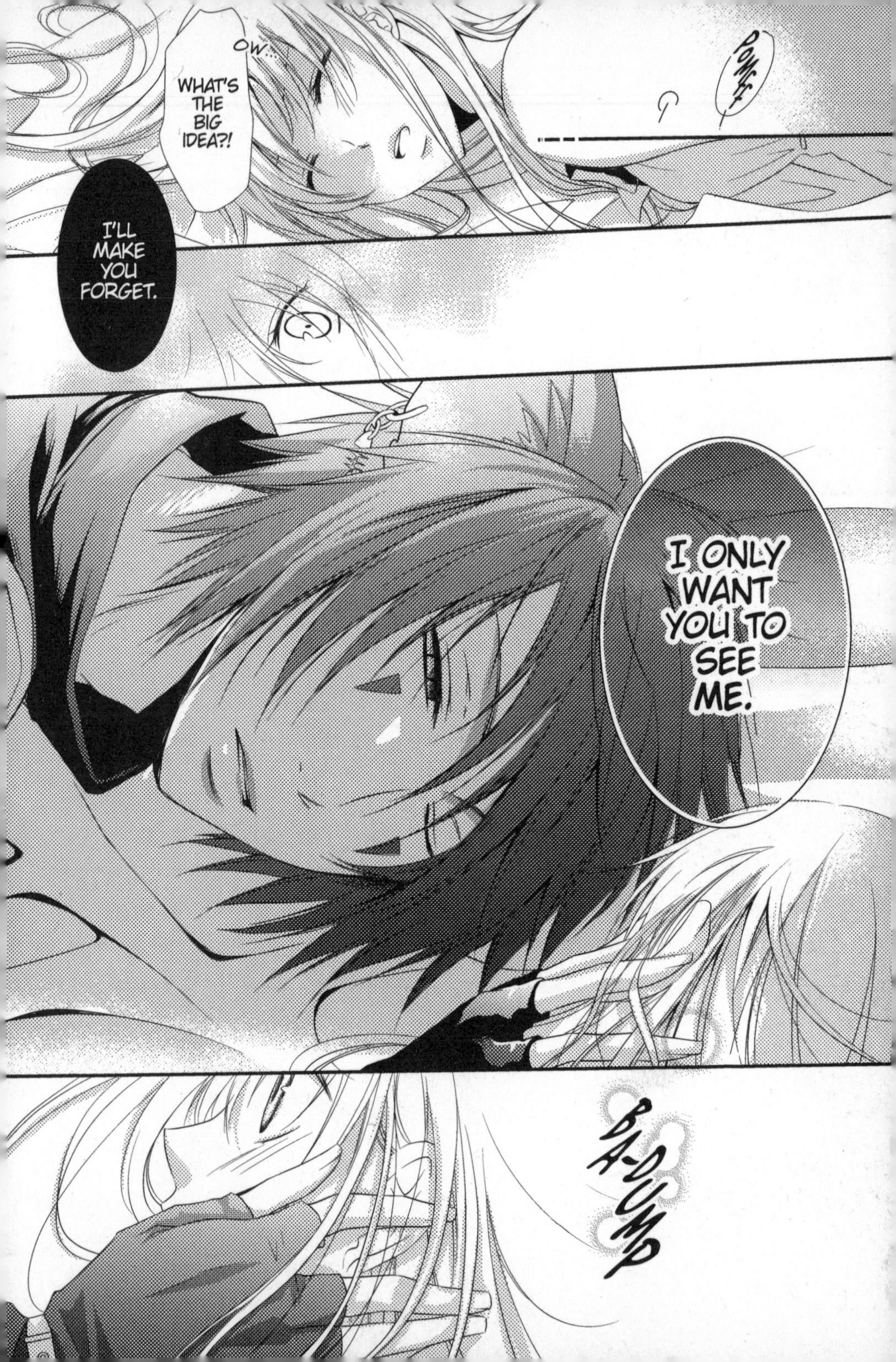
POMFF!
OW...
WHAT'S THE BIG IDEA?!
I'LL MAKE YOU FORGET.
I ONLY WANT YOU TO SEE ME.
BA-DUMP

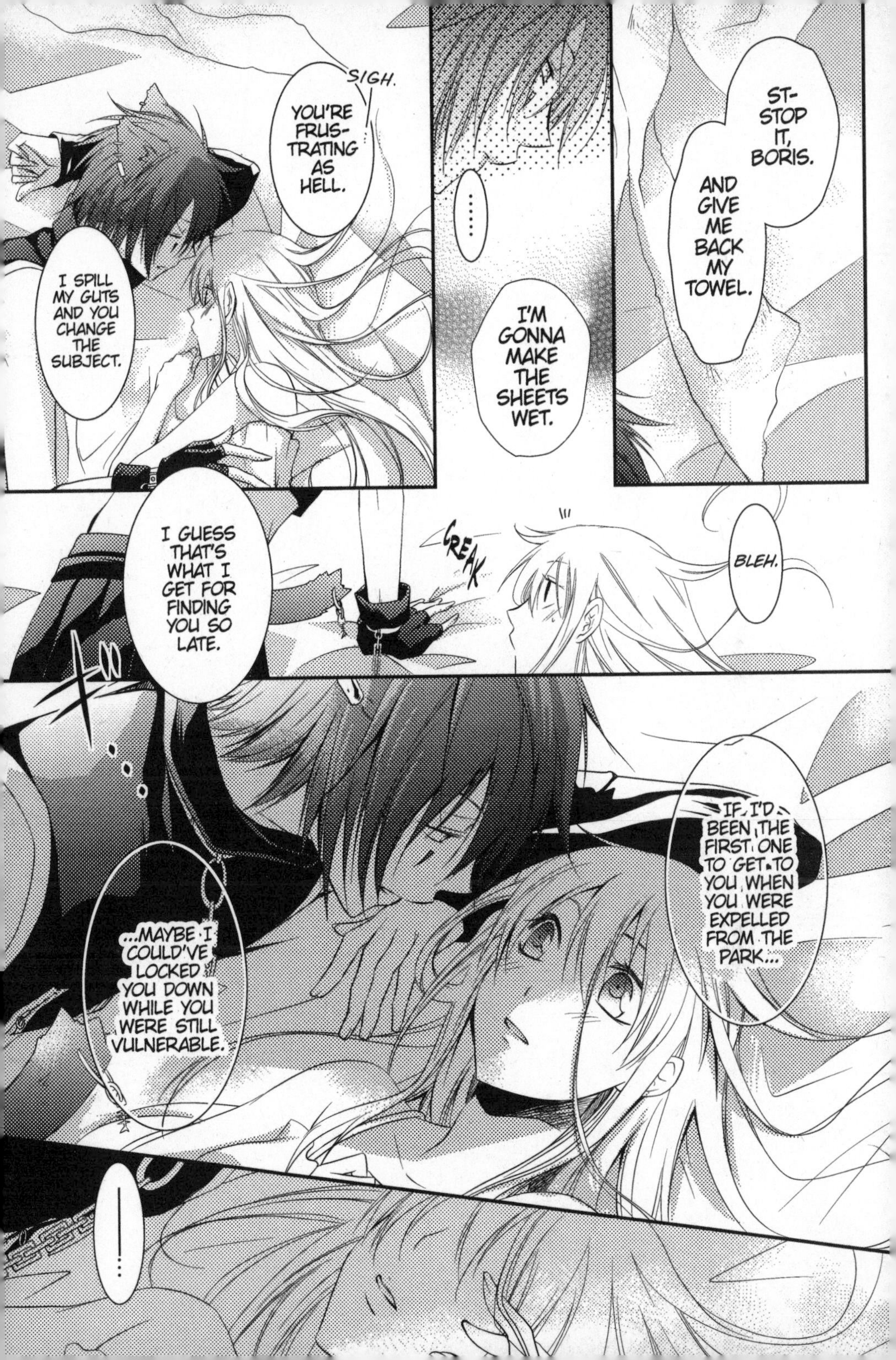
ST-STOP IT, BORIS.
AND GIVE ME BACK MY TOWEL.
......
I'M GONNA MAKE THE SHEETS WET.
SIGH.
YOU'RE FRUS-TRATING AS HELL.
I SPILL MY GUTS AND YOU CHANGE THE SUBJECT.
BLEH.
CREAK
I GUESS THAT'S WHAT I GET FOR FINDING YOU SO LATE.
IF I'D BEEN THE FIRST ONE TO GET TO YOU WHEN YOU WERE EXPELLED FROM THE PARK...
...MAYBE I COULD'VE LOCKED YOU DOWN WHILE YOU WERE STILL VULNERABLE.
!......

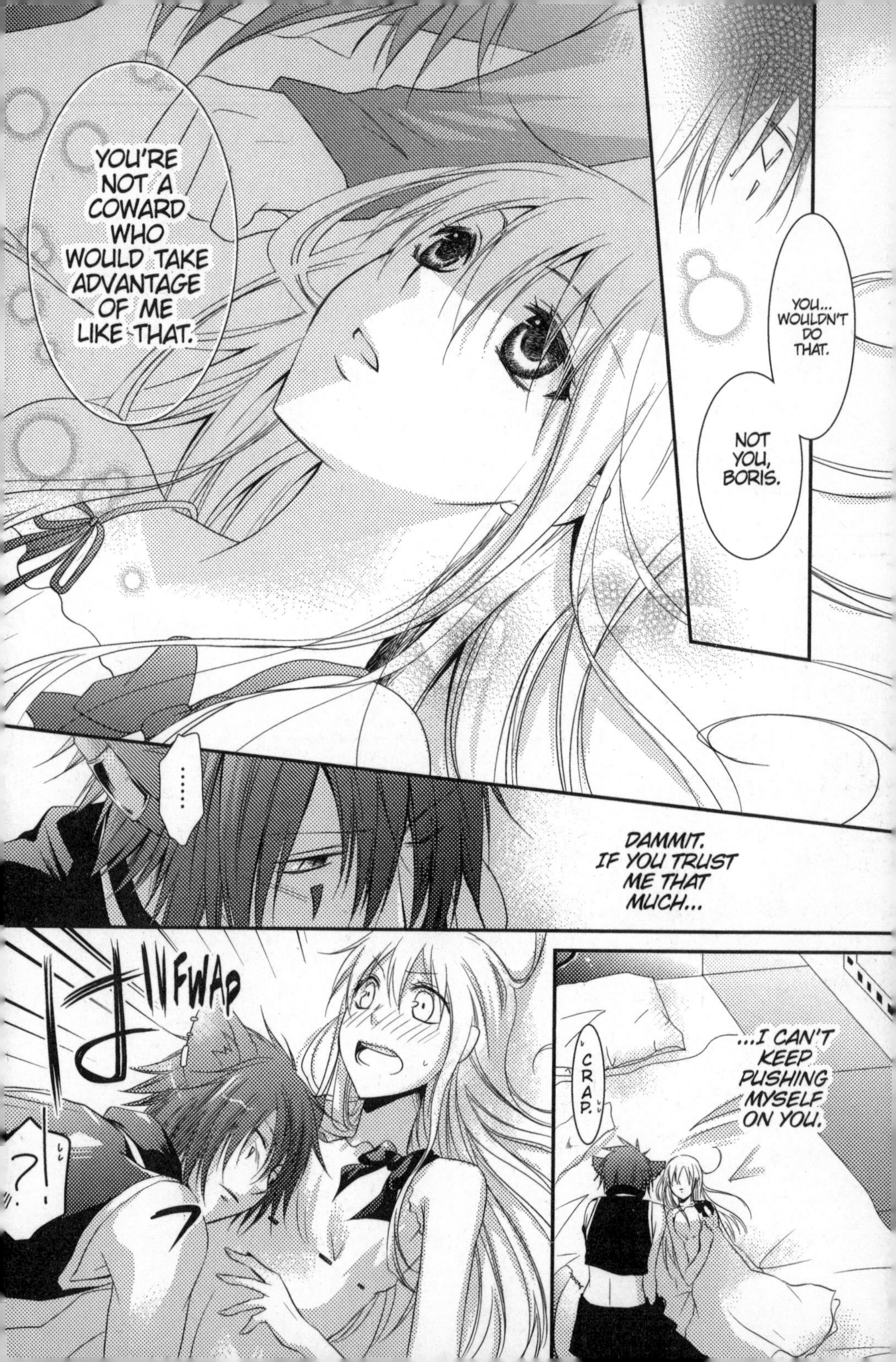
YOU... WOULDN'T DO THAT.
NOT YOU, BORIS.
YOU'RE NOT A COWARD WHO WOULD TAKE ADVANTAGE OF ME LIKE THAT.
......
DAMMIT. IF YOU TRUST ME THAT MUCH...
...I CAN'T KEEP PUSHING MYSELF ON YOU.
CRAP.
FWAP
?!

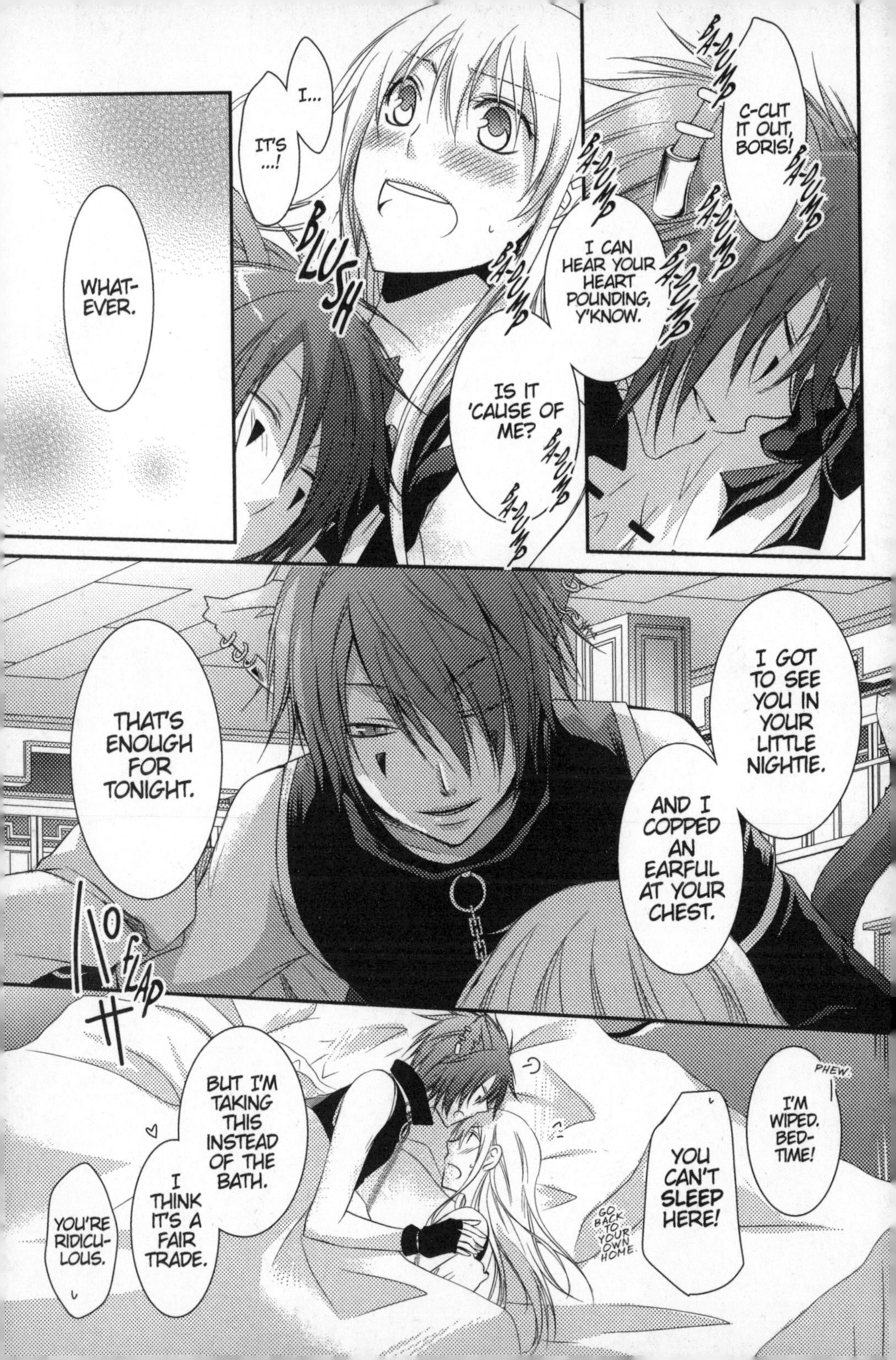
BA-DUMP
C-CUT IT OUT, BORIS!
BA-DUMP
BA-DUMP
BA-DUMP
I CAN HEAR YOUR HEART POUNDING, Y'KNOW.
BA-DUMP
IS IT 'CAUSE OF ME?
BA-DUMP
BA-DUMP
I...
IT'S ...!
BLUSH
WHATEVER.
I GOT TO SEE YOU IN YOUR LITTLE NIGHTIE.
AND I COPPED AN EARFUL AT YOUR CHEST.
THAT'S ENOUGH FOR TONIGHT.
FLAP
PHEW.
I'M WIPED. BEDTIME!
YOU CAN'T SLEEP HERE!
GO BACK TO YOUR OWN HOME.
BUT I'M TAKING THIS INSTEAD OF THE BATH.
I THINK IT'S A FAIR TRADE.
YOU'RE RIDICULOUS.

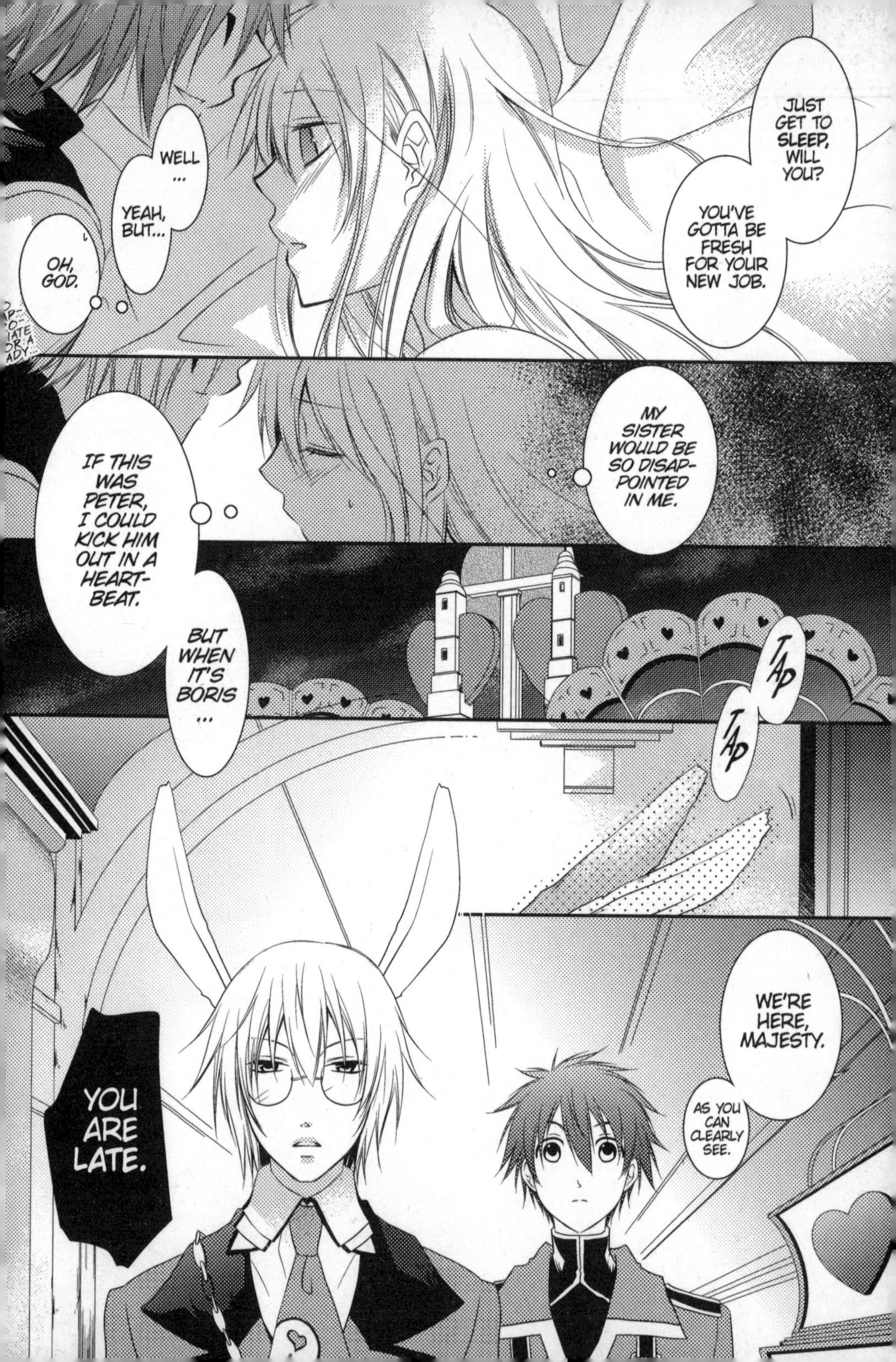
JUST GET TO SLEEP, WILL YOU?
YOU'VE GOTTA BE FRESH FOR YOUR NEW JOB.
WELL... YEAH, BUT...
OH, GOD.
MY SISTER WOULD BE SO DISAP-POINTED IN ME.
IF THIS WAS PETER, I COULD KICK HIM OUT IN A HEART-BEAT.
BUT WHEN IT'S BORIS...
TAP
TAP
WE'RE HERE, MAJESTY.
AS YOU CAN CLEARLY SEE.
YOU ARE LATE.

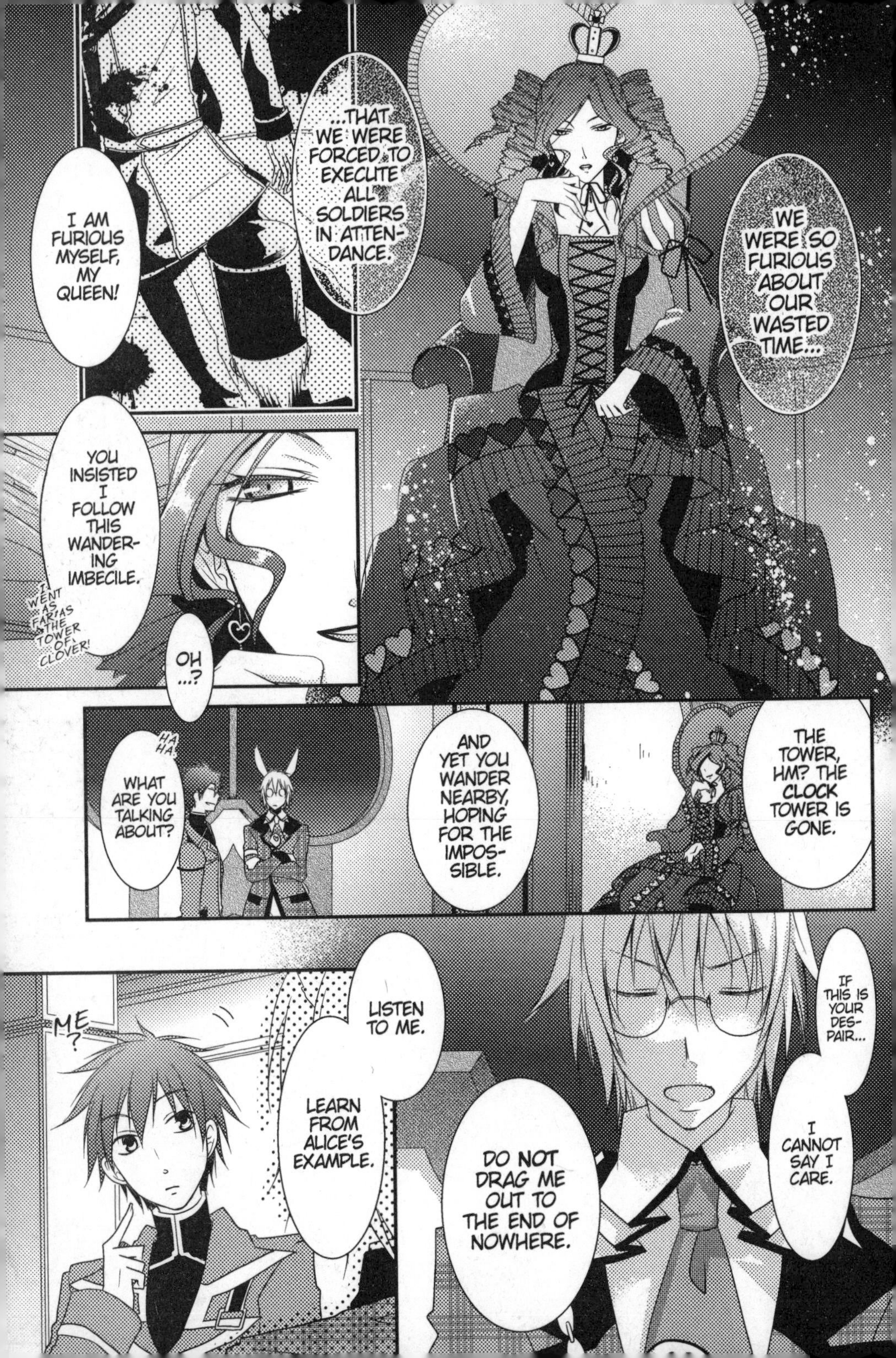

WE WERE SO FURIOUS ABOUT OUR WASTED TIME...
...THAT WE WERE FORCED TO EXECUTE ALL SOLDIERS IN ATTENDANCE.
I AM FURIOUS MYSELF, MY QUEEN!
YOU INSISTED I FOLLOW THIS WANDERING IMBECILE.
I WENT AS FAR AS THE TOWER OF CLOVER!
OH...?
THE TOWER, HM? THE CLOCK TOWER IS GONE.
AND YET YOU WANDER NEARBY, HOPING FOR THE IMPOSSIBLE.
HA HA
WHAT ARE YOU TALKING ABOUT?
IF THIS IS YOUR DESPAIR...
I CANNOT SAY I CARE.
DO NOT DRAG ME OUT TO THE END OF NOWHERE.
LISTEN TO ME.
LEARN FROM ALICE'S EXAMPLE.
ME?

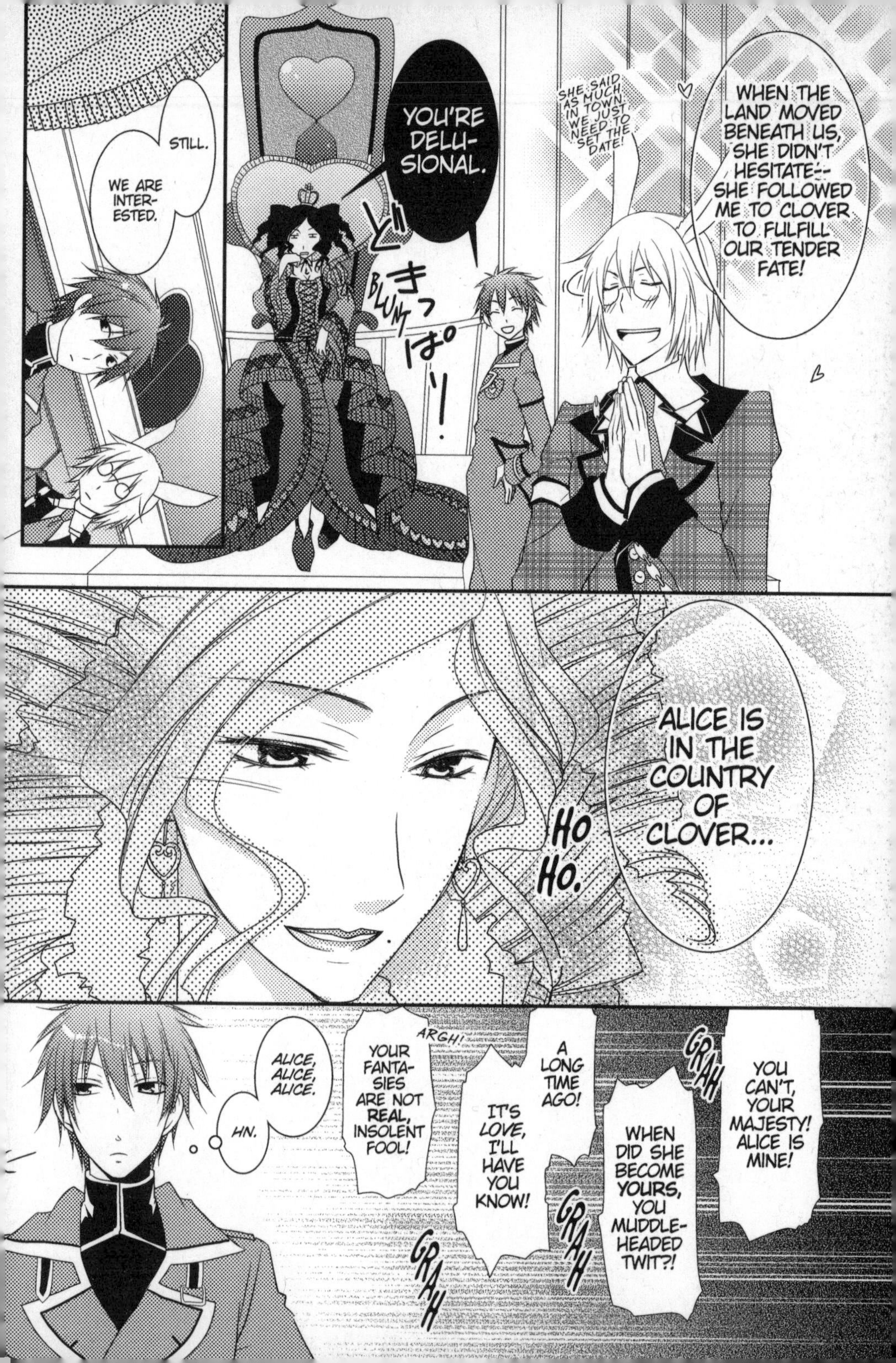
WHEN THE LAND MOVED BENEATH US, SHE DIDN'T HESITATE-- SHE FOLLOWED ME TO CLOVER TO FULFILL OUR TENDER FATE!
SHE SAID AS MUCH IN TOWN. WE JUST NEED TO SET THE DATE!
YOU'RE DELUSIONAL.
どきっぱり!
BLUNT
STILL.
WE ARE INTERESTED.
ALICE IS IN THE COUNTRY OF CLOVER...
HO HO.
YOU CAN'T, YOUR MAJESTY! ALICE IS MINE!
GRAH
WHEN DID SHE BECOME YOURS, YOU MUDDLE-HEADED TWIT?!
GRAH
A LONG TIME AGO!
IT'S LOVE, I'LL HAVE YOU KNOW!
ARGH!
YOUR FANTASIES ARE NOT REAL, INSOLENT FOOL!
GRAH
ALICE, ALICE, ALICE.
HN.

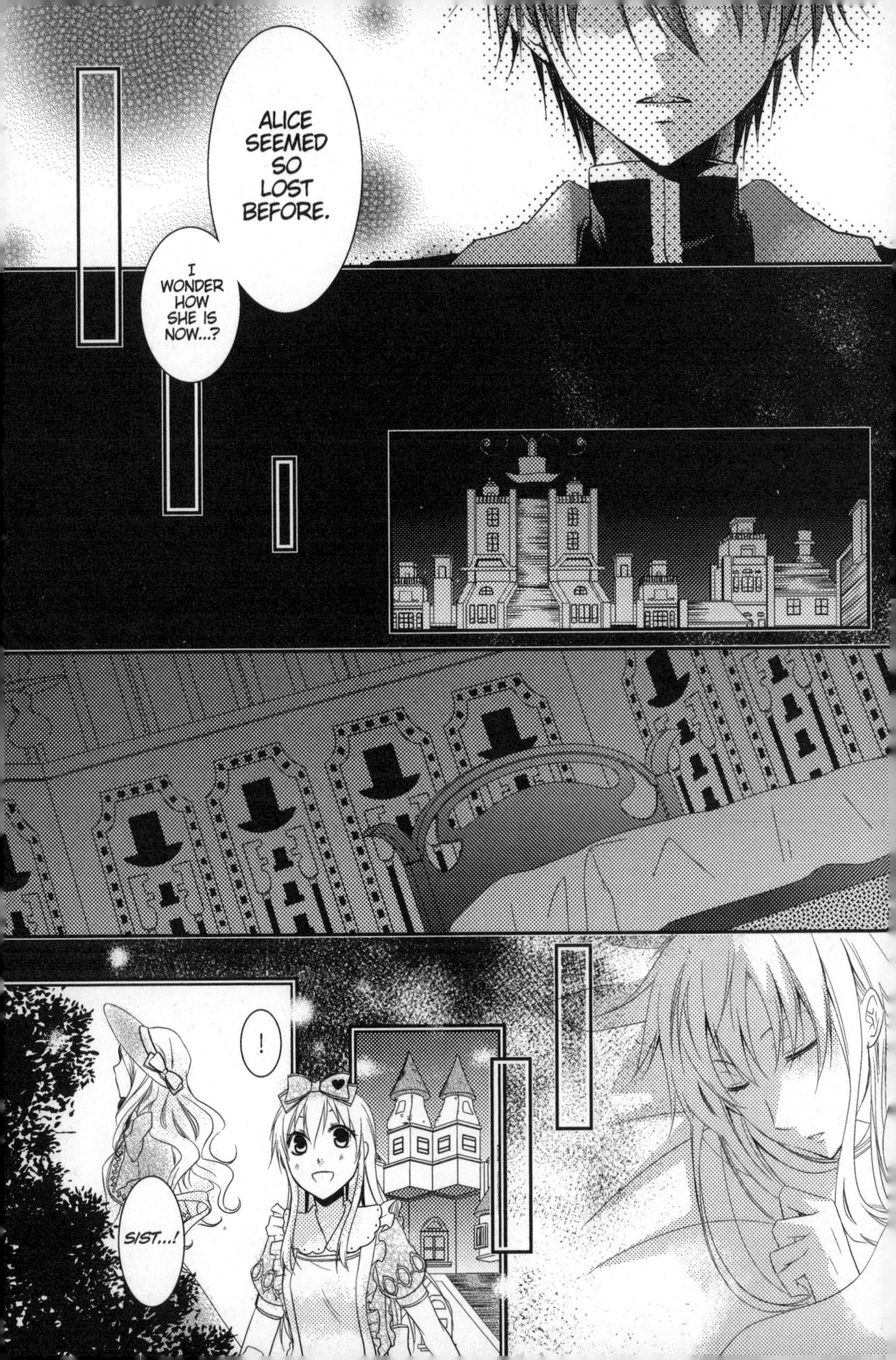
ALICE SEEMED SO LOST BEFORE.
I WONDER HOW SHE IS NOW...?
!
SIST...!

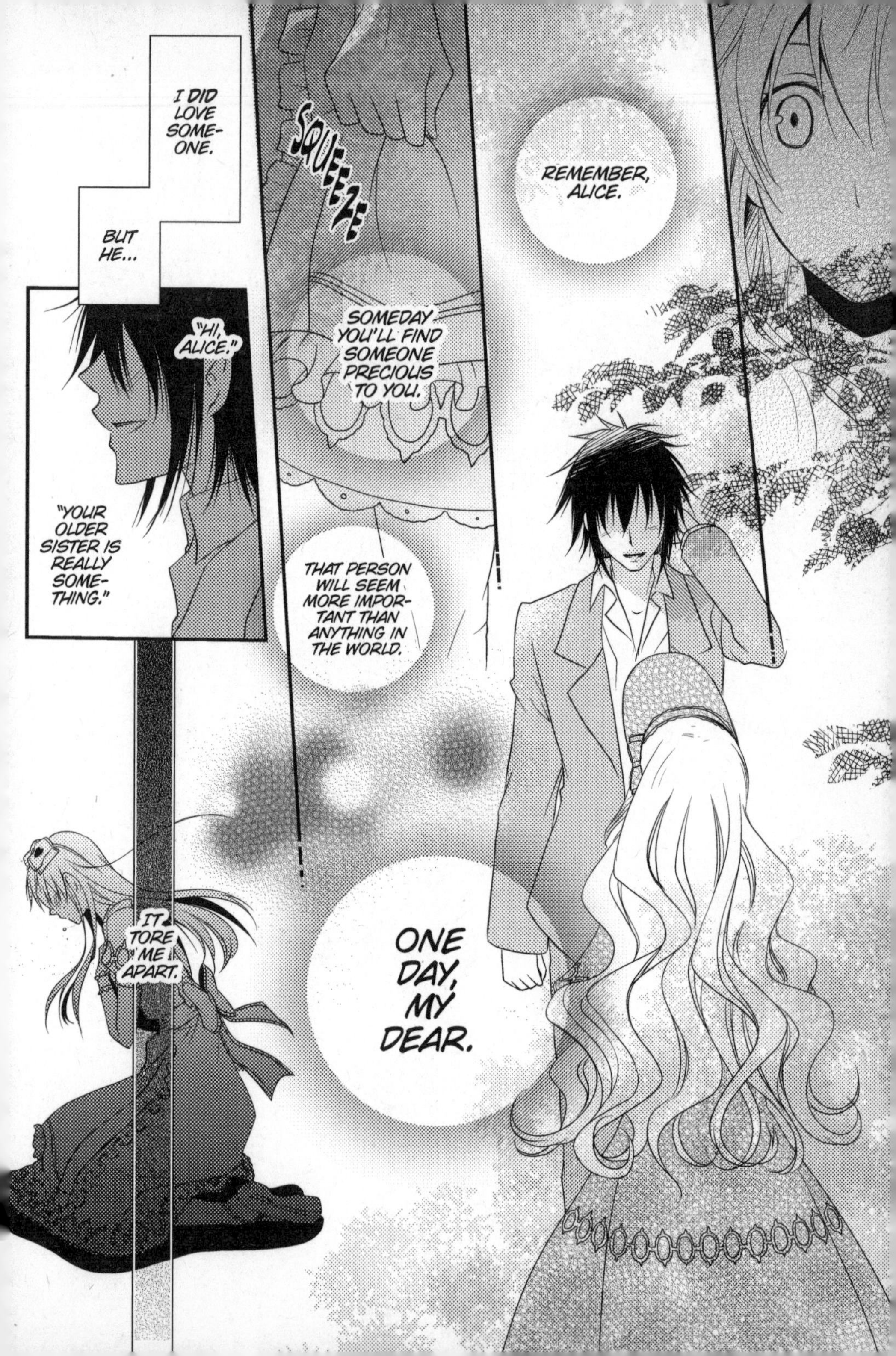
REMEMBER, ALICE.
SQUEEZE
SOMEDAY YOU'LL FIND SOMEONE PRECIOUS TO YOU.
THAT PERSON WILL SEEM MORE IMPORTANT THAN ANYTHING IN THE WORLD.
ONE DAY, MY DEAR.
I DID LOVE SOME-ONE.
BUT HE...
"HI, ALICE."
"YOUR OLDER SISTER IS REALLY SOME-THING."
IT TORE ME APART.

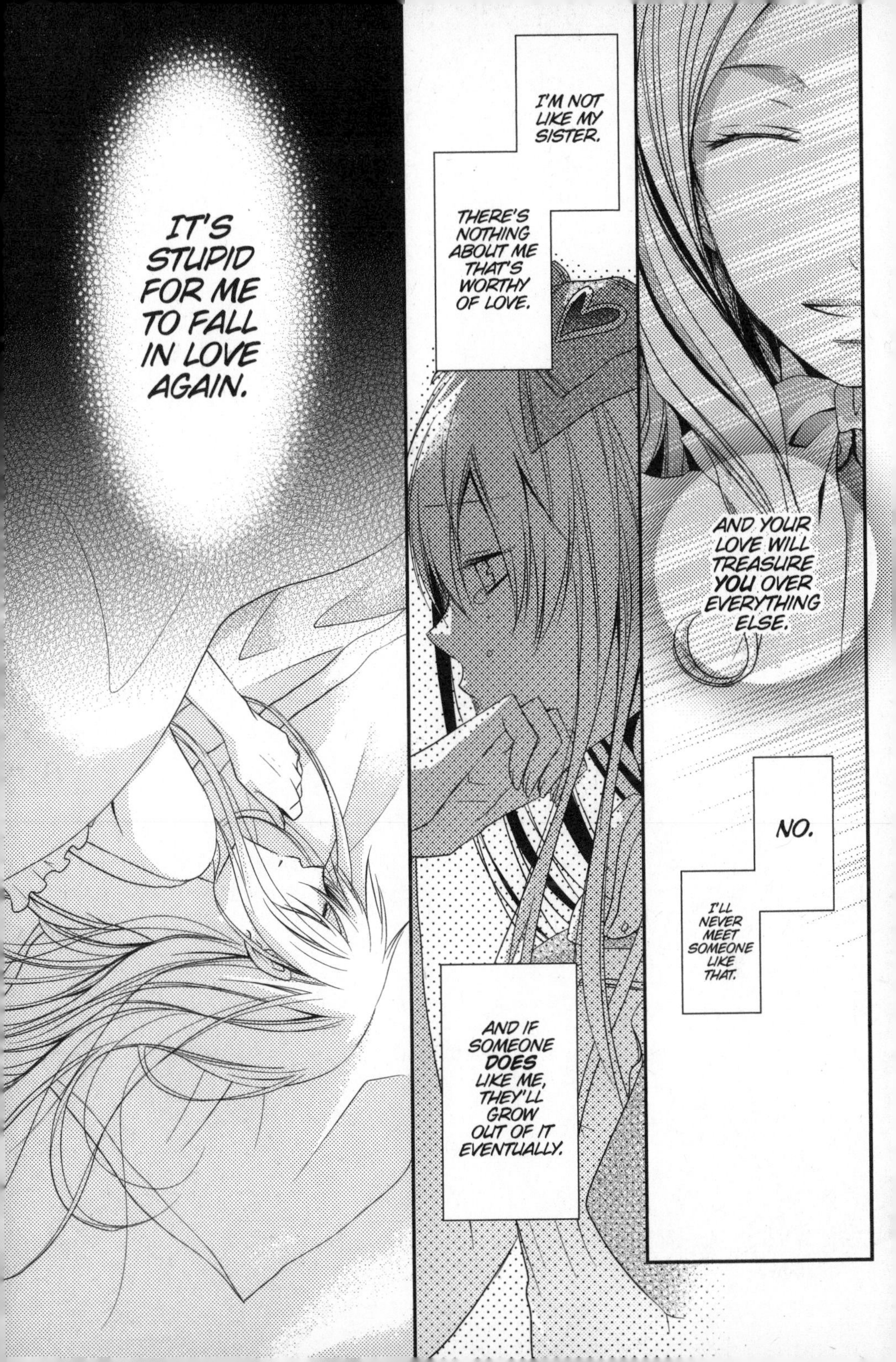
AND YOUR LOVE WILL TREASURE YOU OVER EVERYTHING ELSE.
NO.
I'LL NEVER MEET SOMEONE LIKE THAT.
I'M NOT LIKE MY SISTER.
THERE'S NOTHING ABOUT ME THAT'S WORTHY OF LOVE.
AND IF SOMEONE DOES LIKE ME, THEY'LL GROW OUT OF IT EVENTUALLY.
IT'S STUPID FOR ME TO FALL IN LOVE AGAIN.

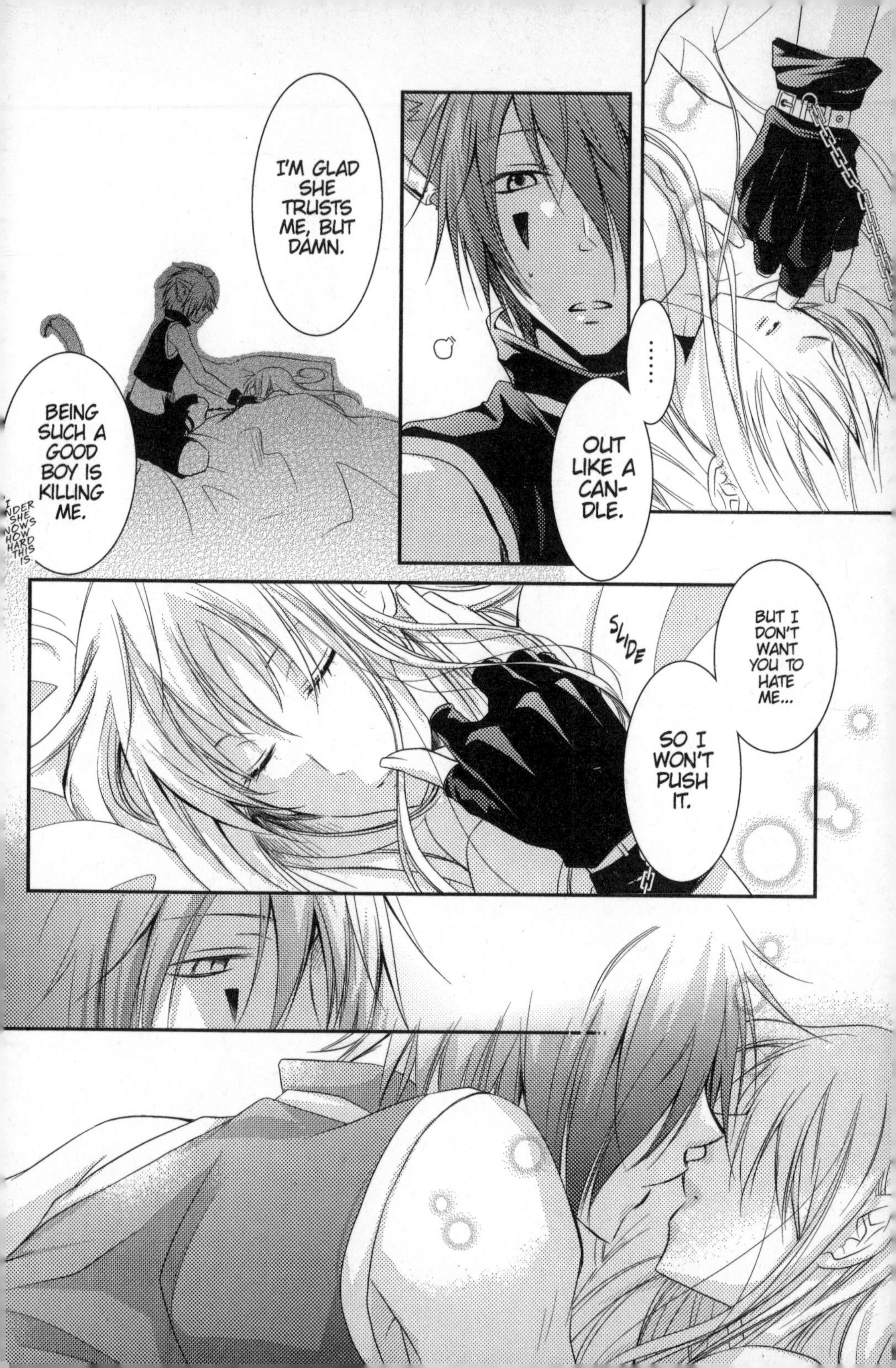
......
OUT LIKE A CAN-DLE.
I'M GLAD SHE TRUSTS ME, BUT DAMN.
BEING SUCH A GOOD BOY IS KILLING ME.
INDER SHE NOWS HOW HARD THIS IS.
SLIDE
BUT I DON'T WANT YOU TO HATE ME...
SO I WON'T PUSH IT.

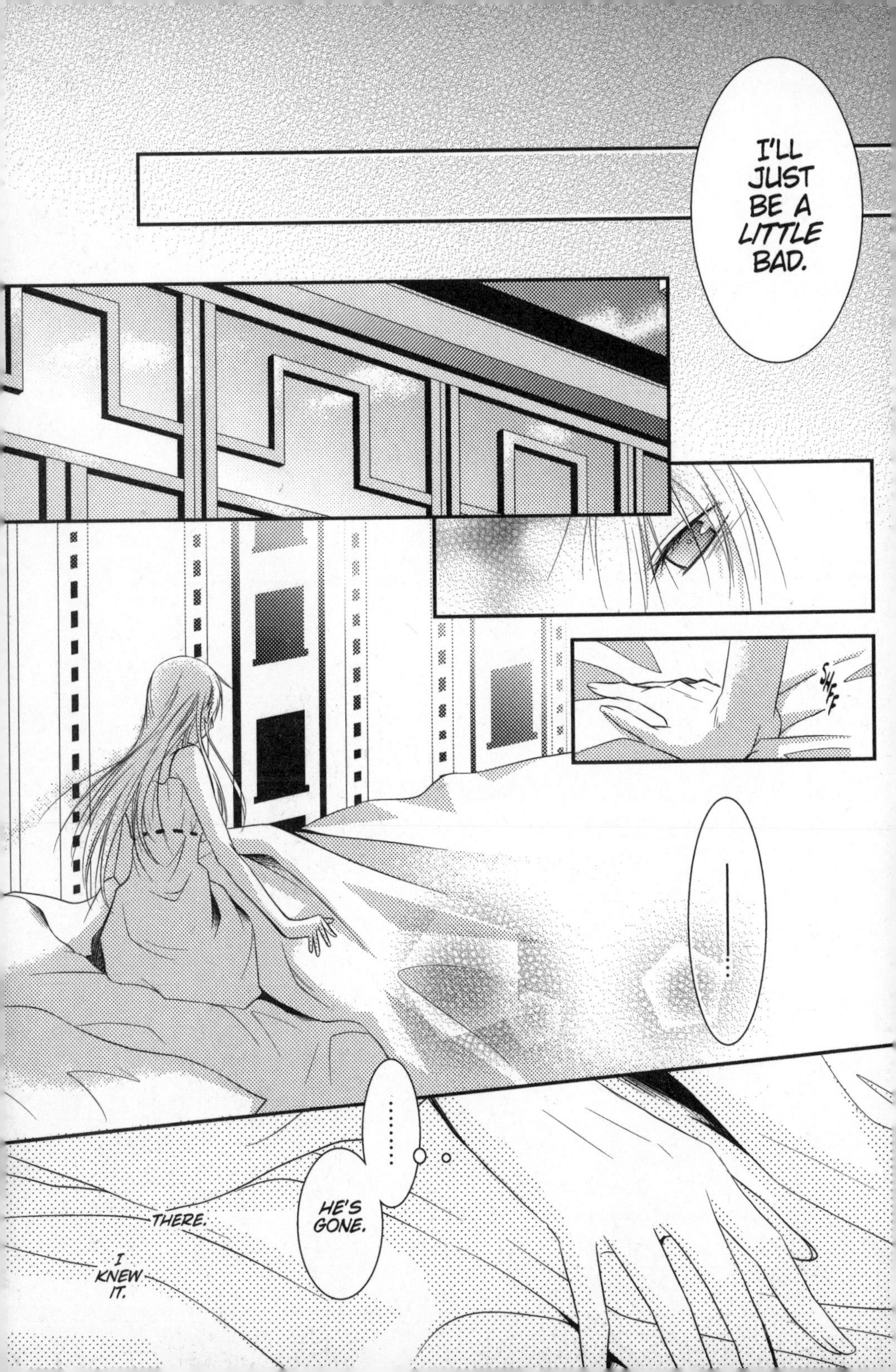
I'LL JUST BE A LITTLE BAD.
SHFF
—......
......
HE'S GONE.
THERE.
I KNEW IT.

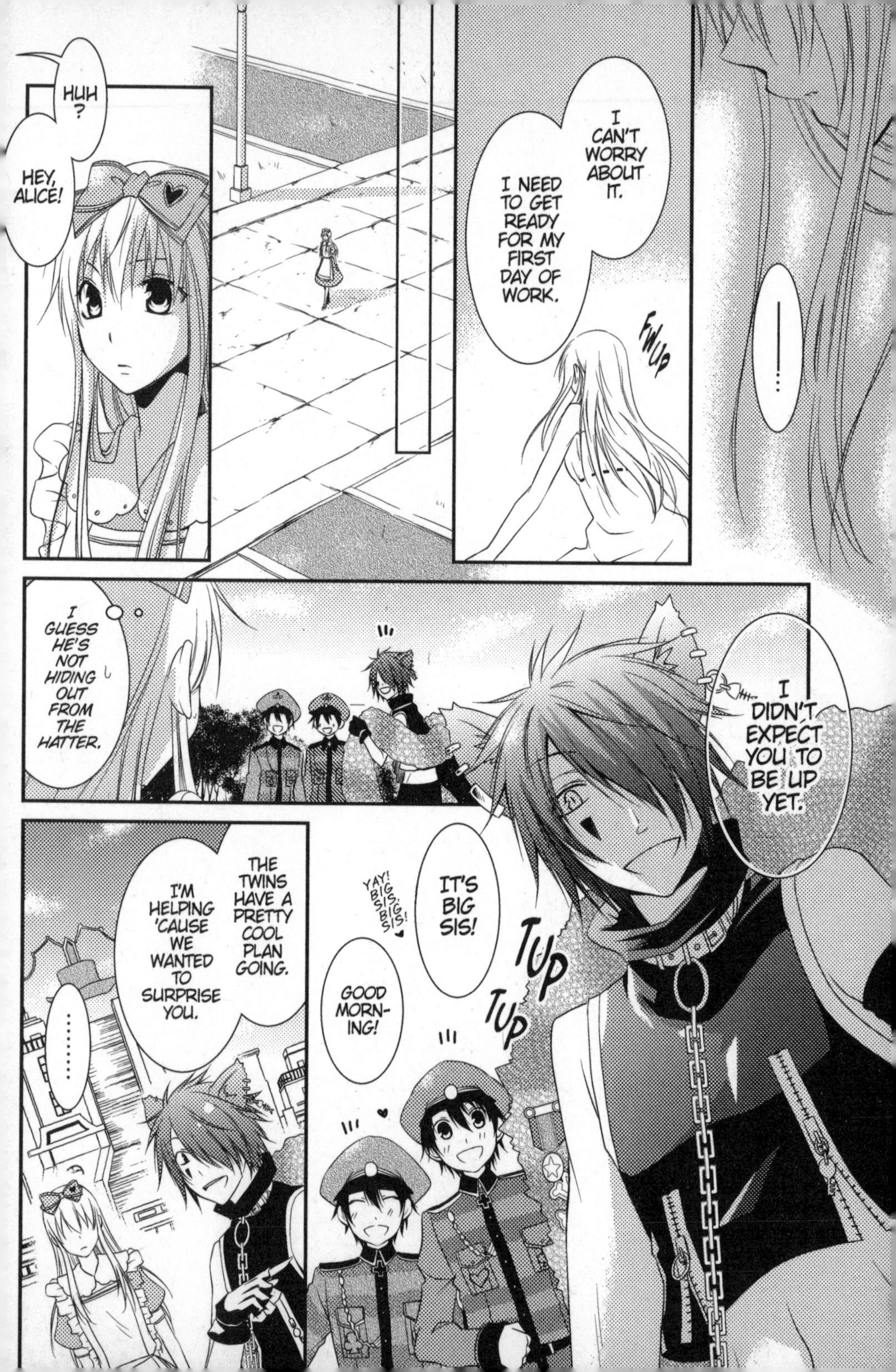
I CAN'T WORRY ABOUT IT.
I NEED TO GET READY FOR MY FIRST DAY OF WORK.
FWUP
HUH?
HEY, ALICE!
—......!
I DIDN'T EXPECT YOU TO BE UP YET.
I GUESS HE'S NOT HIDING OUT FROM THE HATTER.
TUP TUP
IT'S BIG SIS!
YAY! BIG SIS, BIG SIS!
GOOD MORNING!
THE TWINS HAVE A PRETTY COOL PLAN GOING.
I'M HELPING 'CAUSE WE WANTED TO SURPRISE YOU.
....

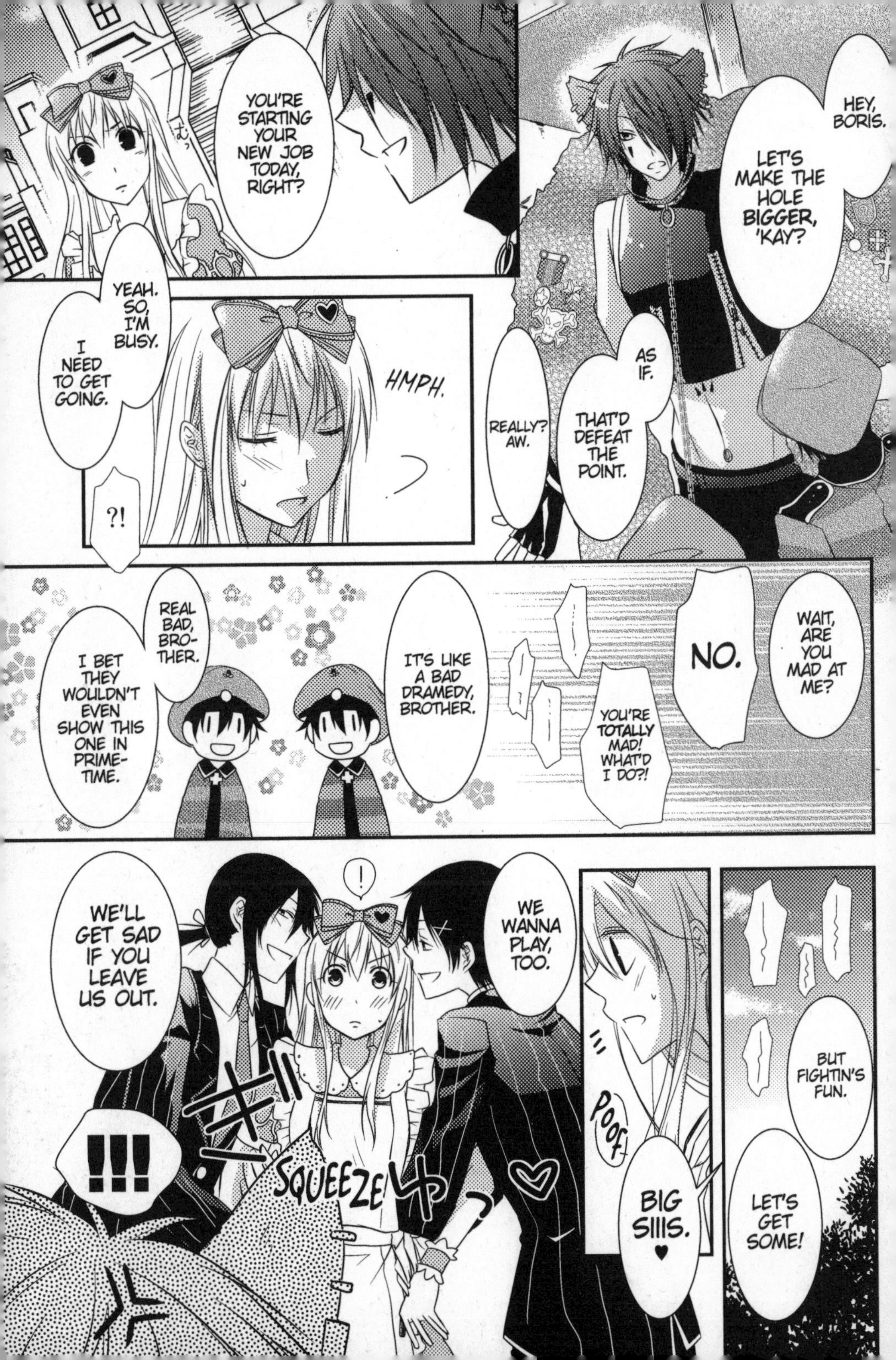
HEY, BORIS.
LET'S MAKE THE HOLE BIGGER, 'KAY?
AS IF.
THAT'D DEFEAT THE POINT.
REALLY? AW.
YOU'RE STARTING YOUR NEW JOB TODAY, RIGHT?
YEAH. SO, I'M BUSY.
I NEED TO GET GOING.
HMPH.
?!
WAIT, ARE YOU MAD AT ME?
NO.
YOU'RE TOTALLY MAD! WHAT'D I DO?!
IT'S LIKE A BAD DRAMEDY, BROTHER.
REAL BAD, BROTHER.
I BET THEY WOULDN'T EVEN SHOW THIS ONE IN PRIME-TIME.
BUT FIGHTIN'S FUN.
LET'S GET SOME!
BIG SIIIS. ♥
POOF
WE WANNA PLAY, TOO.
!
WE'LL GET SAD IF YOU LEAVE US OUT.
SQUEEZE
!!!

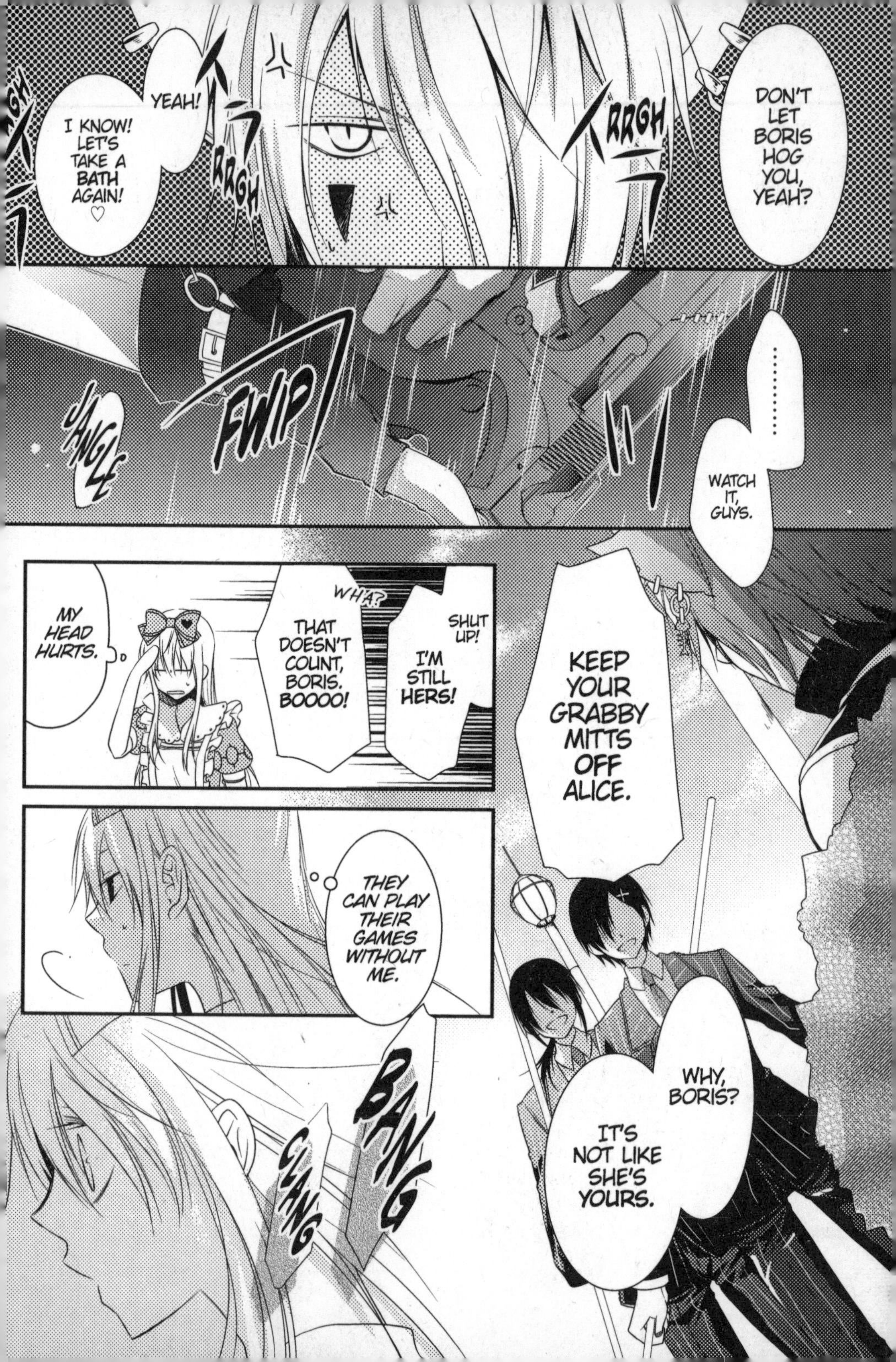

DON'T LET BORIS HOG YOU, YEAH?
RRGH
RRGH
YEAH!
I KNOW! LET'S TAKE A BATH AGAIN! ♡
......
WATCH IT, GUYS.
FWIP
JANGLE
KEEP YOUR GRABBY MITTS OFF ALICE.
WHY, BORIS? IT'S NOT LIKE SHE'S YOURS.
SHUT UP! I'M STILL HERS!
WHA?
THAT DOESN'T COUNT, BORIS. BOOOO!
MY HEAD HURTS.
THEY CAN PLAY THEIR GAMES WITHOUT ME.
BANG
CLANG

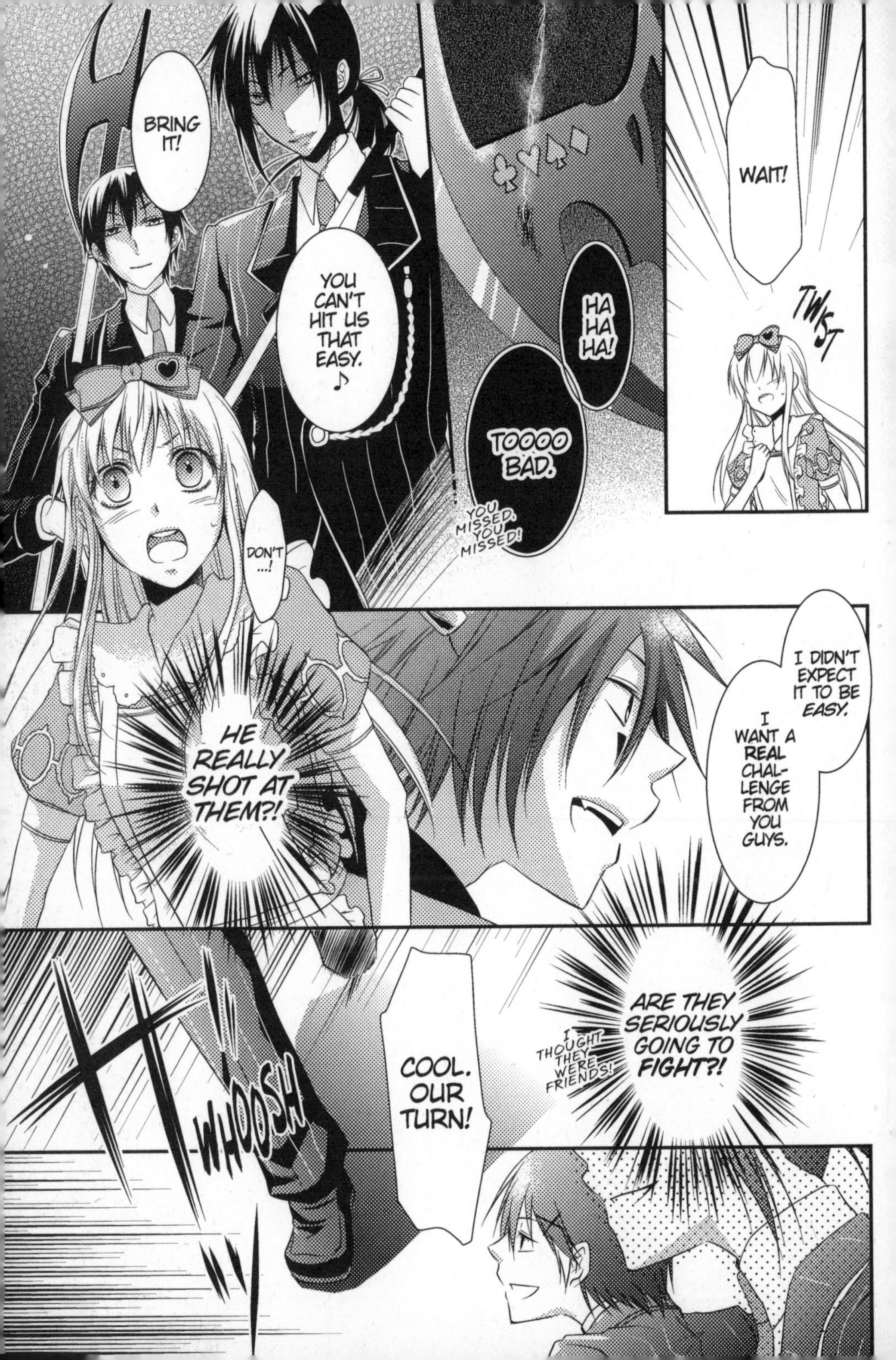
WAIT!
TWIST
HA HA HA!
TOOOO BAD.
YOU MISSED, YOU MISSED!
YOU CAN'T HIT US THAT EASY. ♪
BRING IT!
DON'T ...!
I DIDN'T EXPECT IT TO BE EASY.
I WANT A REAL CHAL-LENGE FROM YOU GUYS.
HE REALLY SHOT AT THEM?!
ARE THEY SERIOUSLY GOING TO FIGHT?!
I THOUGHT THEY WERE FRIENDS!
COOL. OUR TURN!
WHOOSH

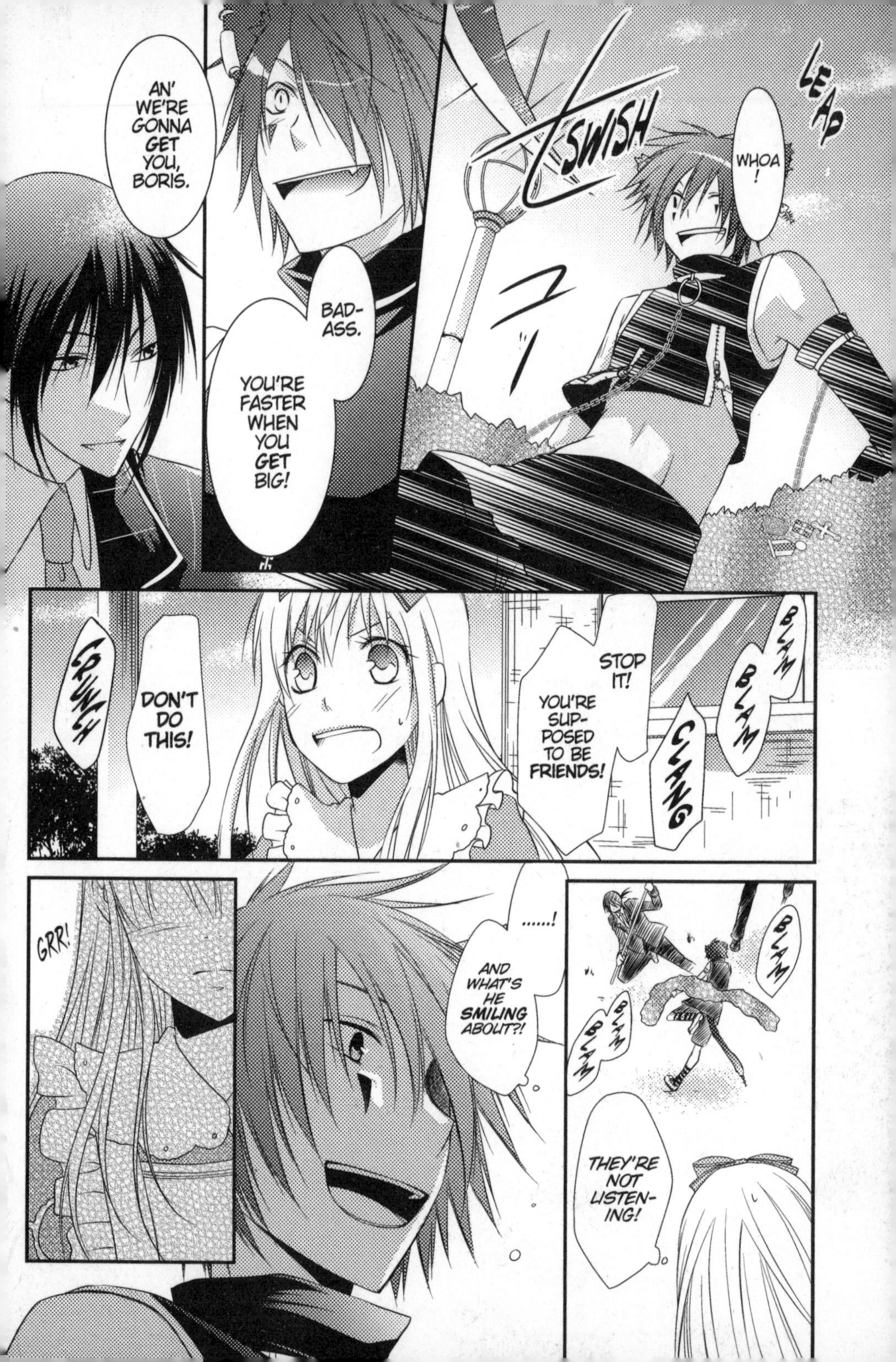
LEAP
WHOA!
SWISH
BAD-ASS.
YOU'RE FASTER WHEN YOU GET BIG!
AN' WE'RE GONNA GET YOU, BORIS.
BLAM
BLAM
CLANG
STOP IT!
YOU'RE SUP-POSED TO BE FRIENDS!
DON'T DO THIS!
CRUNCH
BLAM
BLAM BLAM
THEY'RE NOT LISTEN-ING!
......!
AND WHAT'S HE SMILING ABOUT?!
GRR!

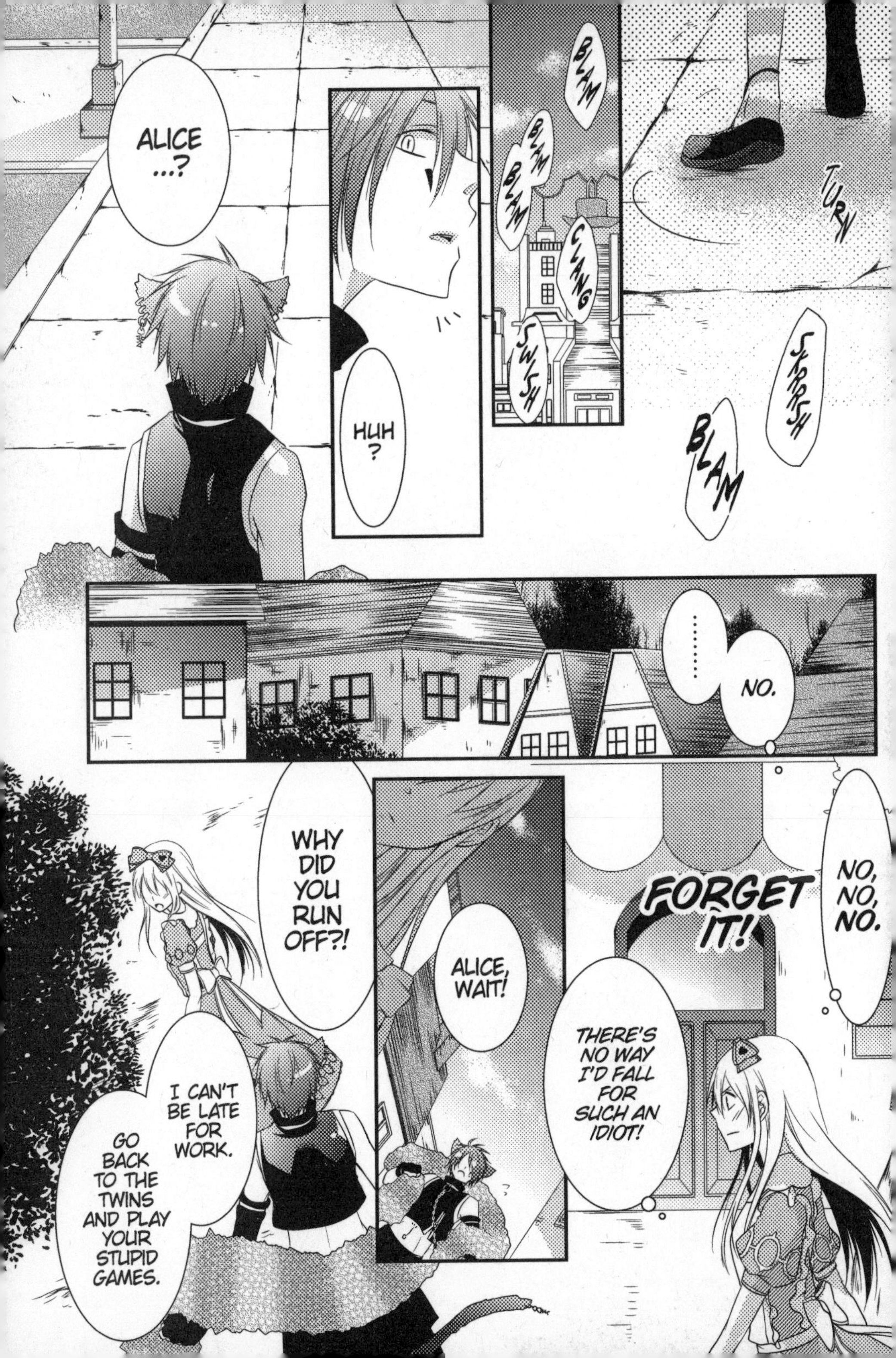
TURN
SKRRSH
BLAM
BLAM
BLAM
BLAM
BLAM
CLANG
SWISH
HUH?
ALICE ...?
......
NO.
NO, NO, NO.
FORGET IT!
THERE'S NO WAY I'D FALL FOR SUCH AN IDIOT!
ALICE, WAIT!
WHY DID YOU RUN OFF?!
I CAN'T BE LATE FOR WORK.
GO BACK TO THE TWINS AND PLAY YOUR STUPID GAMES.

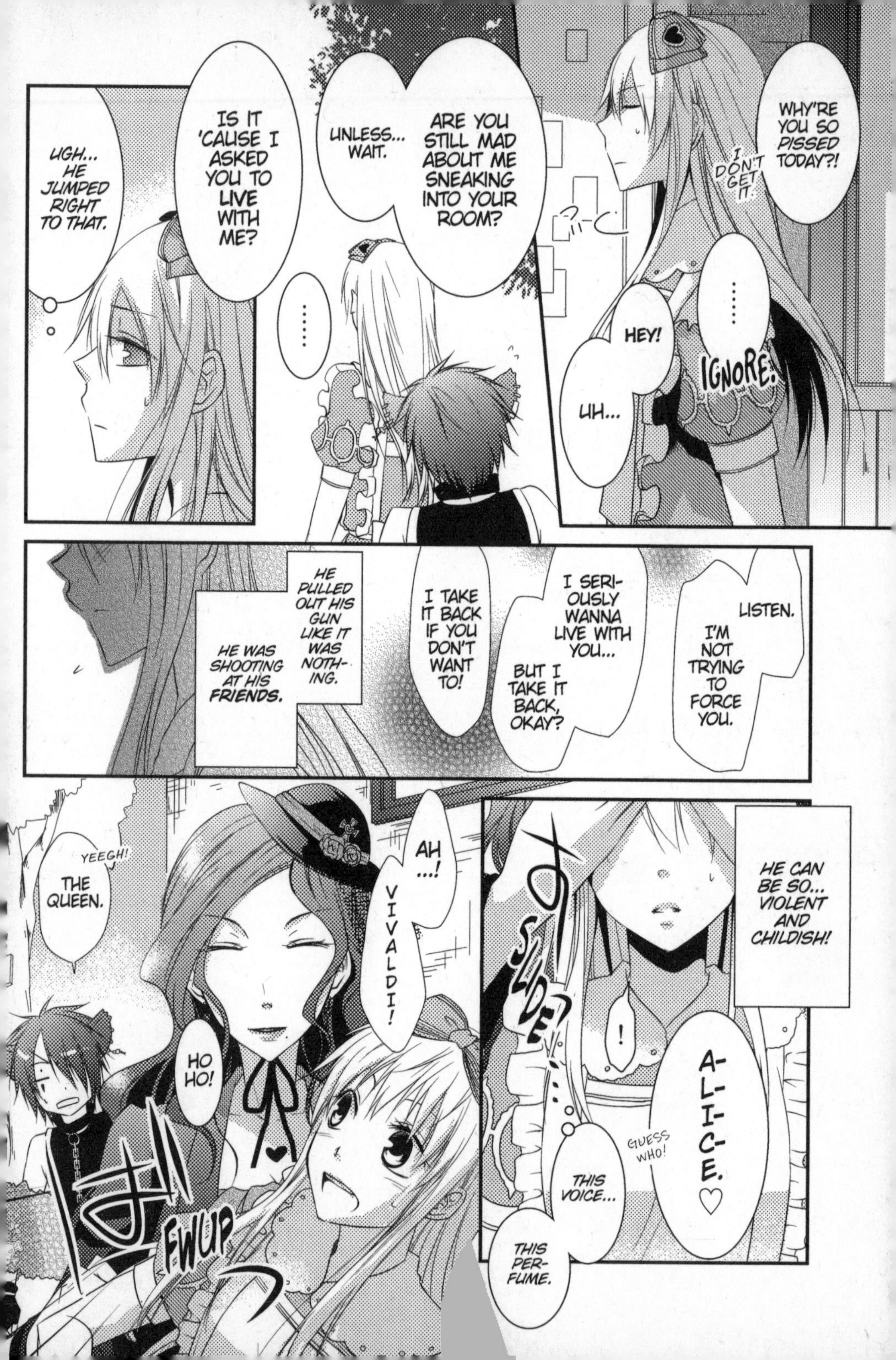
WHY'RE YOU SO PISSED TODAY?!
I DON'T GET IT.
......
HEY!
IGNORE
UH...
ARE YOU STILL MAD ABOUT ME SNEAKING INTO YOUR ROOM?
UNLESS... WAIT.
......
IS IT 'CAUSE I ASKED YOU TO LIVE WITH ME?
UGH... HE JUMPED RIGHT TO THAT.
LISTEN.
I'M NOT TRYING TO FORCE YOU.
I SERIOUSLY WANNA LIVE WITH YOU...
BUT I TAKE IT BACK, OKAY?
I TAKE IT BACK IF YOU DON'T WANT TO!
HE PULLED OUT HIS GUN LIKE IT WAS NOTHING.
HE WAS SHOOTING AT HIS FRIENDS.
HE CAN BE SO... VIOLENT AND CHILDISH!
SLIDE
!
A-L-I-C-E. ♡
GUESS WHO!
THIS VOICE...
THIS PERFUME.
AH...!
VIVALDI!
YEEGH!
THE QUEEN.
HO HO!
FWUP

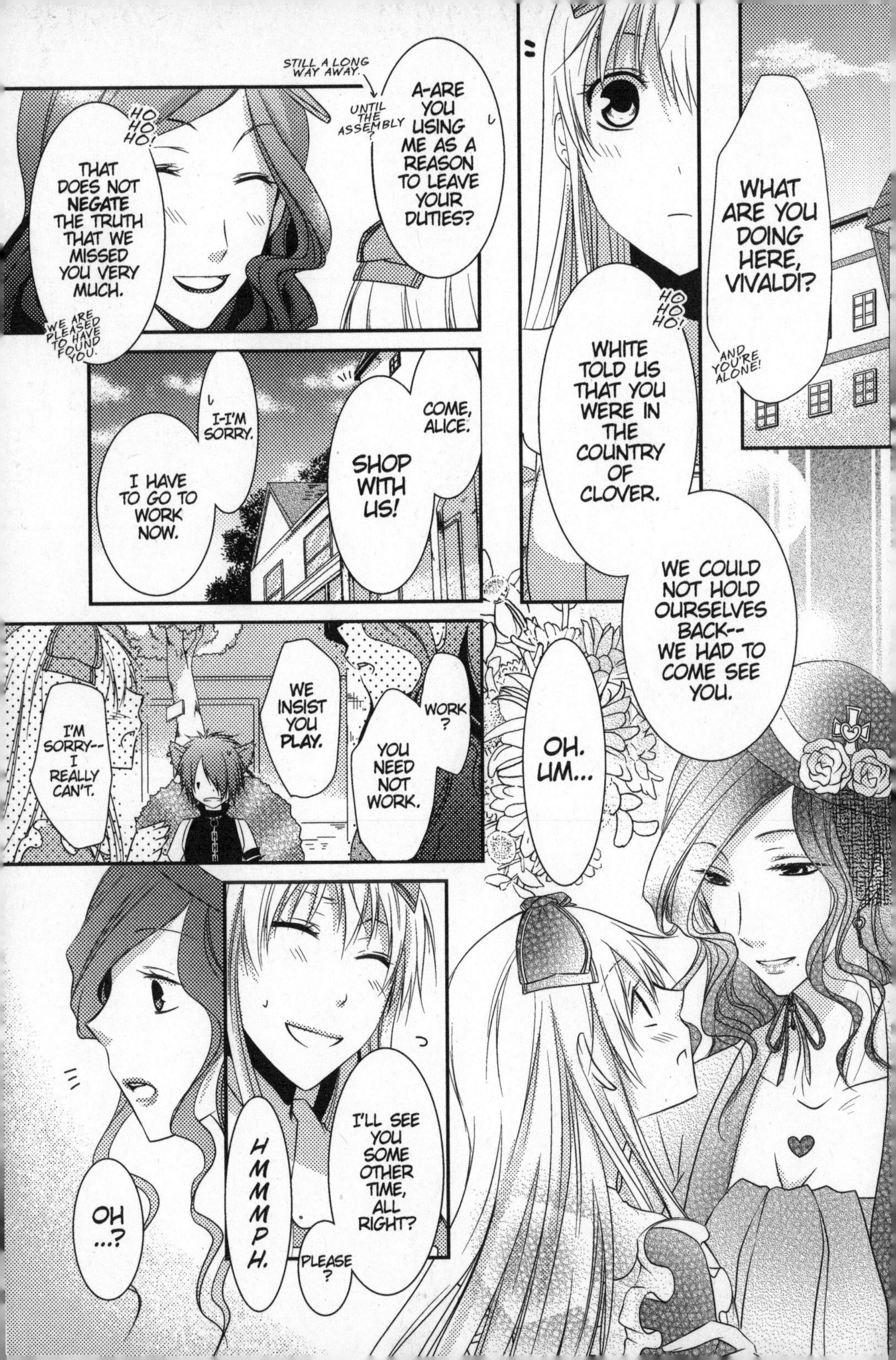
WHAT ARE YOU DOING HERE, VIVALDI?
AND YOU'RE ALONE!
HO HO HO!
WHITE TOLD US THAT YOU WERE IN THE COUNTRY OF CLOVER.
WE COULD NOT HOLD OURSELVES BACK-- WE HAD TO COME SEE YOU.
OH. UM...
A-ARE YOU USING ME AS A REASON TO LEAVE YOUR DUTIES?
UNTIL THE ASSEMBLY?
STILL A LONG WAY AWAY.
HO HO HO!
THAT DOES NOT NEGATE THE TRUTH THAT WE MISSED YOU VERY MUCH.
WE ARE PLEASED TO HAVE FOUND YOU.
COME, ALICE.
SHOP WITH US!
I-I'M SORRY.
I HAVE TO GO TO WORK NOW.
WORK?
YOU NEED NOT WORK.
WE INSIST YOU PLAY.
I'M SORRY-- I REALLY CAN'T.
I'LL SEE YOU SOME OTHER TIME, ALL RIGHT?
PLEASE?
HMMMPH.
OH ...?

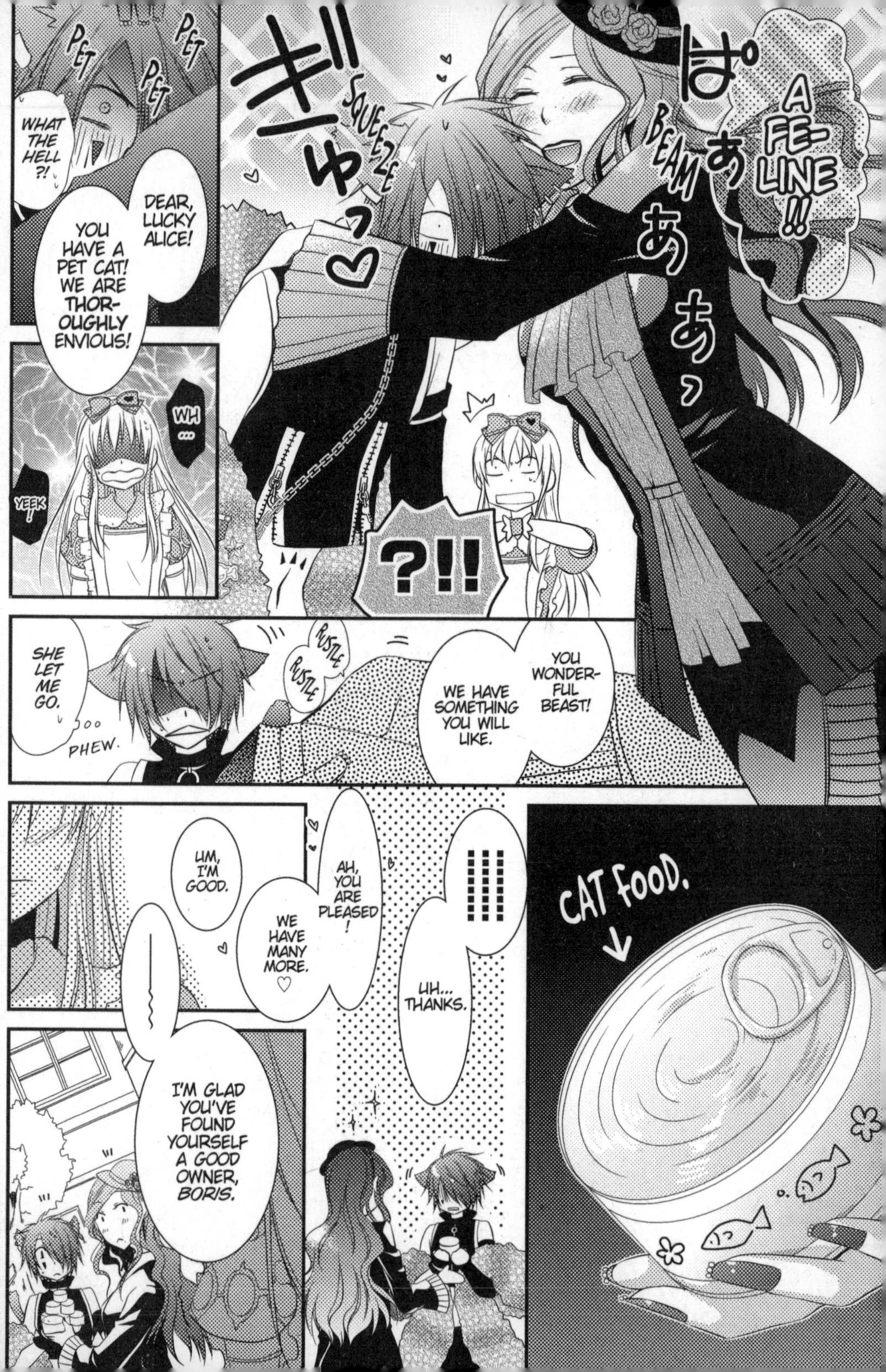

A FE-LINE!!
ぱあああっ
BEAM
ギュっ
SQUEEZE
?!!
PET PET PET
WHAT THE HELL ?!
DEAR, LUCKY ALICE!
YOU HAVE A PET CAT! WE ARE THOROUGHLY ENVIOUS!
WH ...
YEEK!
YOU WONDERFUL BEAST!
WE HAVE SOMETHING YOU WILL LIKE.
RUSTLE RUSTLE
SHE LET ME GO.
PHEW.
CAT FOOD.
!!!!
UH... THANKS.
AH, YOU ARE PLEASED!
WE HAVE MANY MORE.
UM, I'M GOOD.
I'M GLAD YOU'VE FOUND YOURSELF A GOOD OWNER, BORIS.

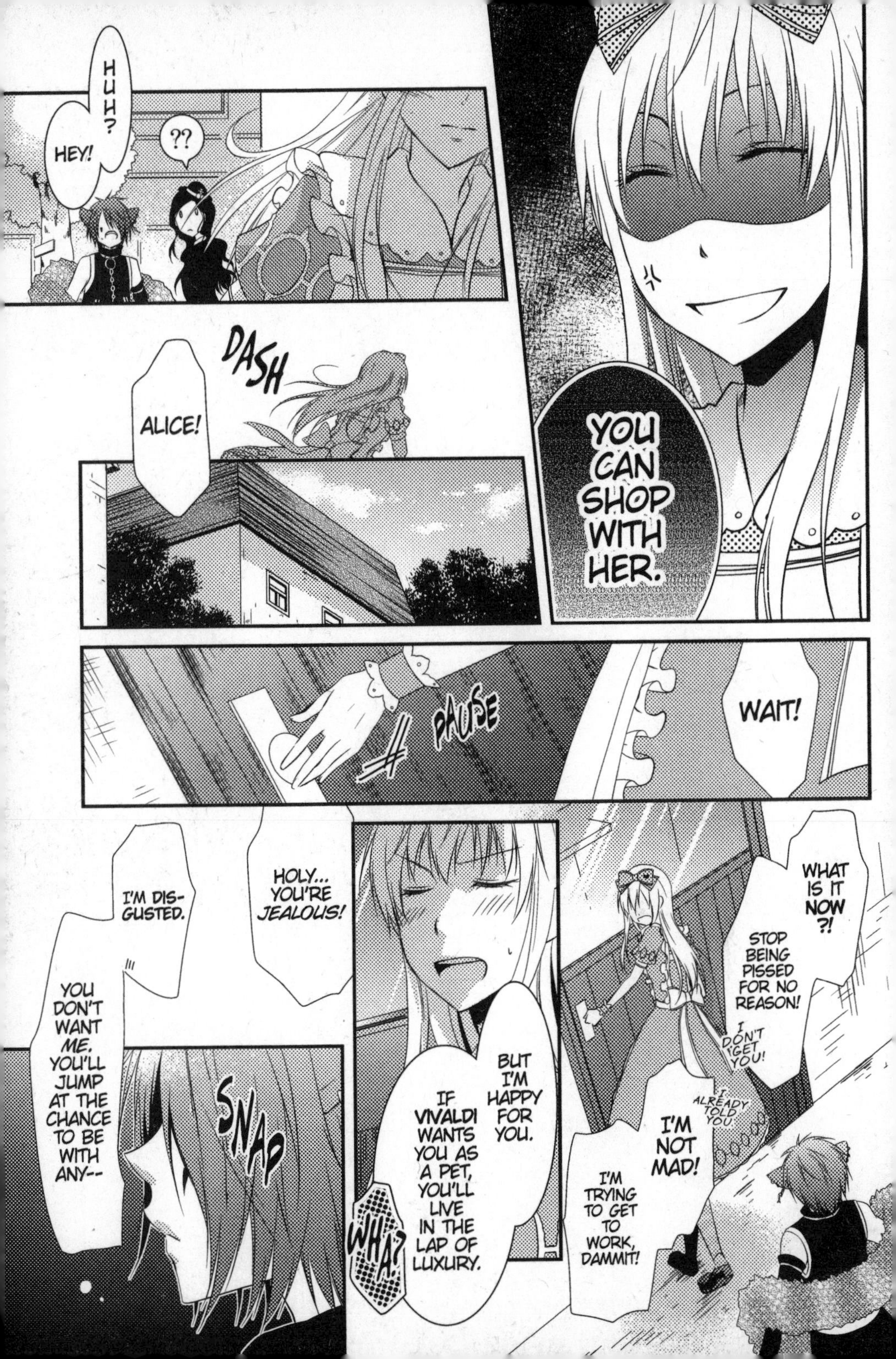

YOU CAN SHOP WITH HER.
HUH? HEY!
??
DASH
ALICE!
WAIT!
PAUSE
WHAT IS IT NOW?!
STOP BEING PISSED FOR NO REASON!
I DON'T GET YOU!
I ALREADY TOLD YOU.
I'M NOT MAD!
I'M TRYING TO GET TO WORK, DAMMIT!
HOLY... YOU'RE JEALOUS!
BUT I'M HAPPY FOR YOU.
IF VIVALDI WANTS YOU AS A PET, YOU'LL LIVE IN THE LAP OF LUXURY.
WHA?
I'M DIS-GUSTED.
YOU DON'T WANT ME. YOU'LL JUMP AT THE CHANCE TO BE WITH ANY--
SNAP

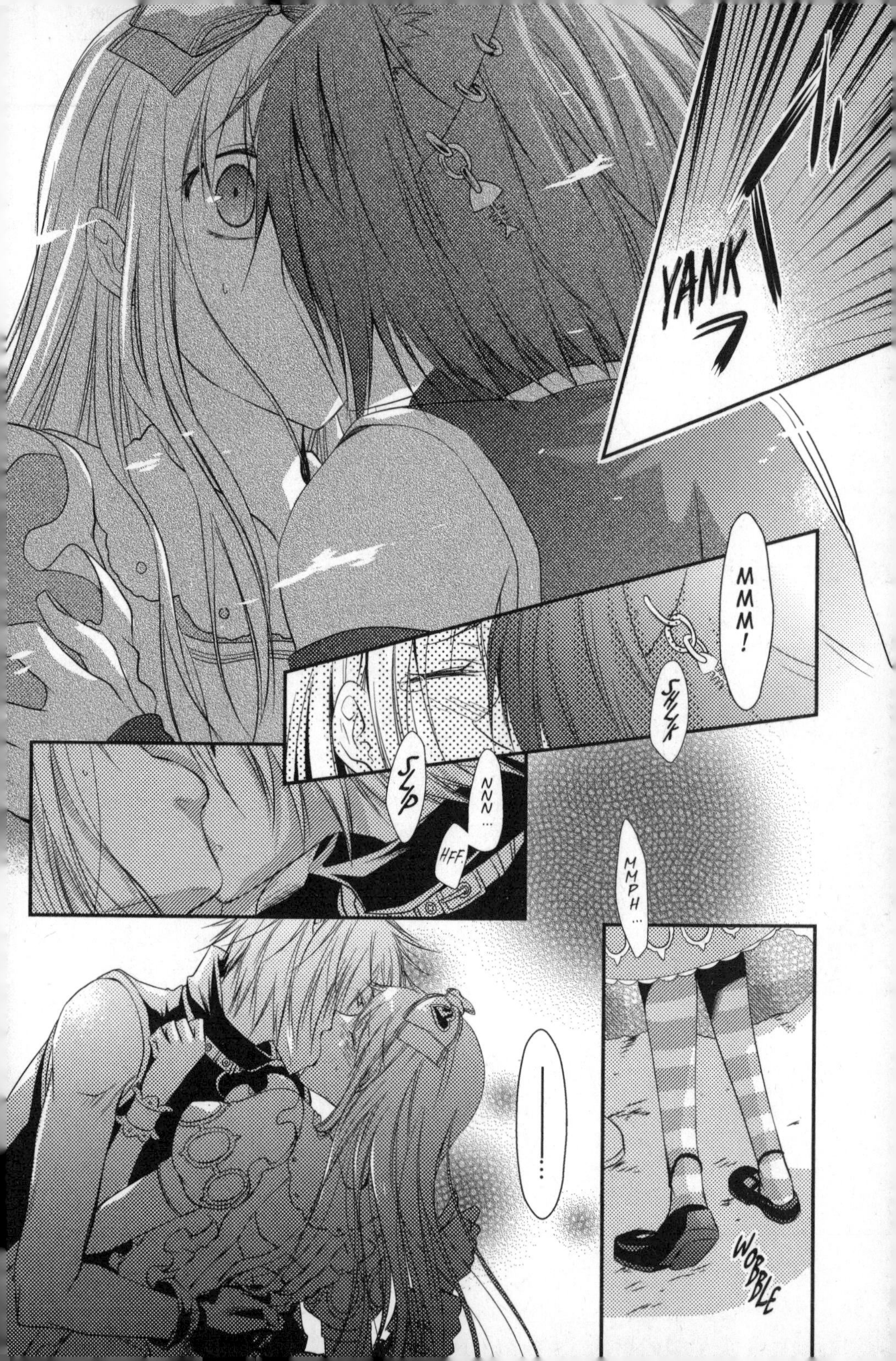
YANK
MMM!
SHLK
SLIP
NNN...
HFF.
MMPH...
WOBBLE
—!...

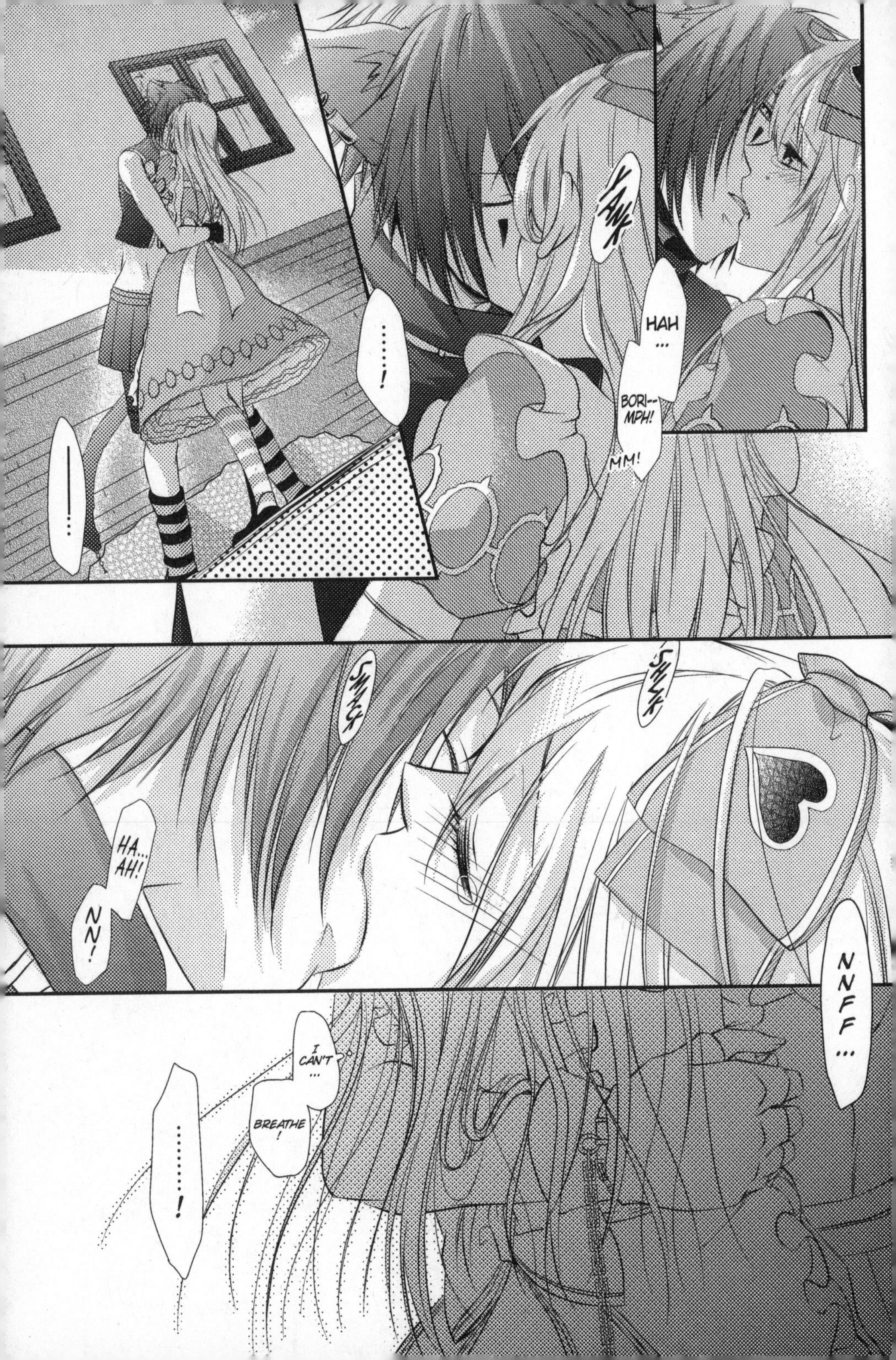
HAH ...
BORI--MPH!
MM!
YANK
......!
—...
SHLK
NNFF ...
SMACK
HA... AH!
NN!
I CAN'T ...
BREATHE!
......!

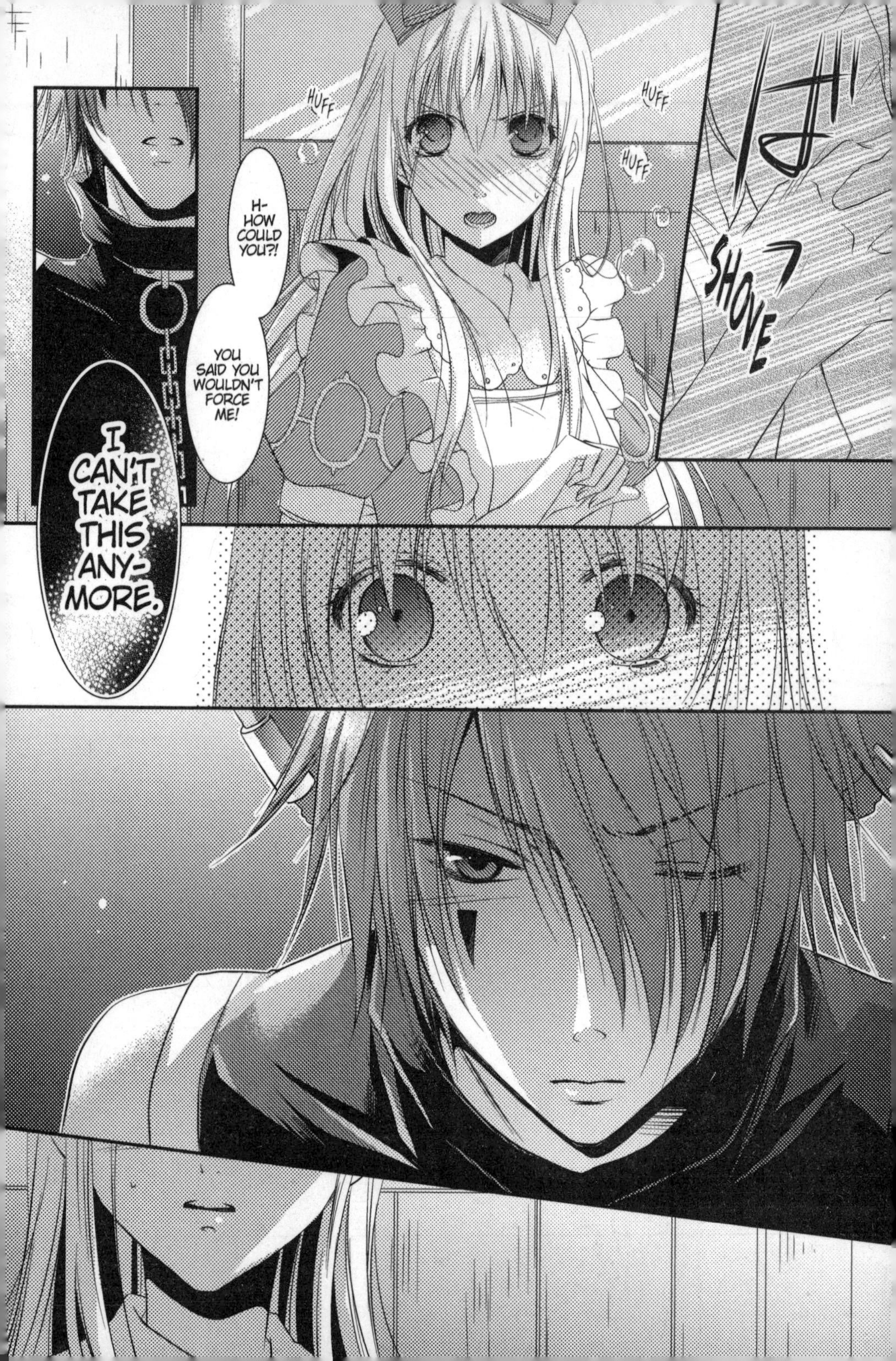
SHOVE
HUFF
HUFF
HUFF
H-HOW COULD YOU?!
YOU SAID YOU WOULDN'T FORCE ME!
I CAN'T TAKE THIS ANY-MORE.

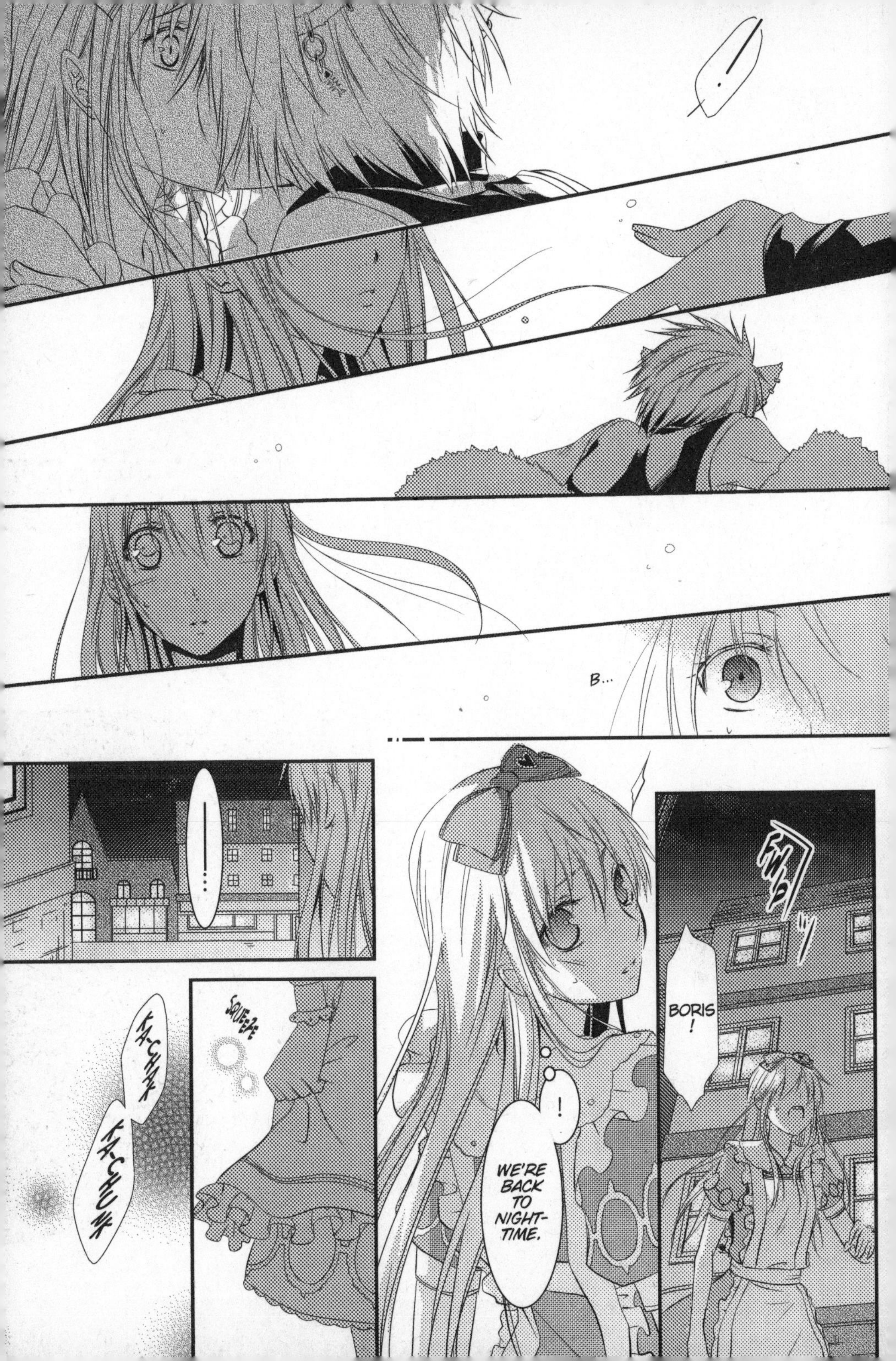

...!
B...
FWIP
BORIS!
!
WE'RE BACK TO NIGHT-TIME.
...!...
SQUEEZE
KA-CHUNK
KA-CHUNK

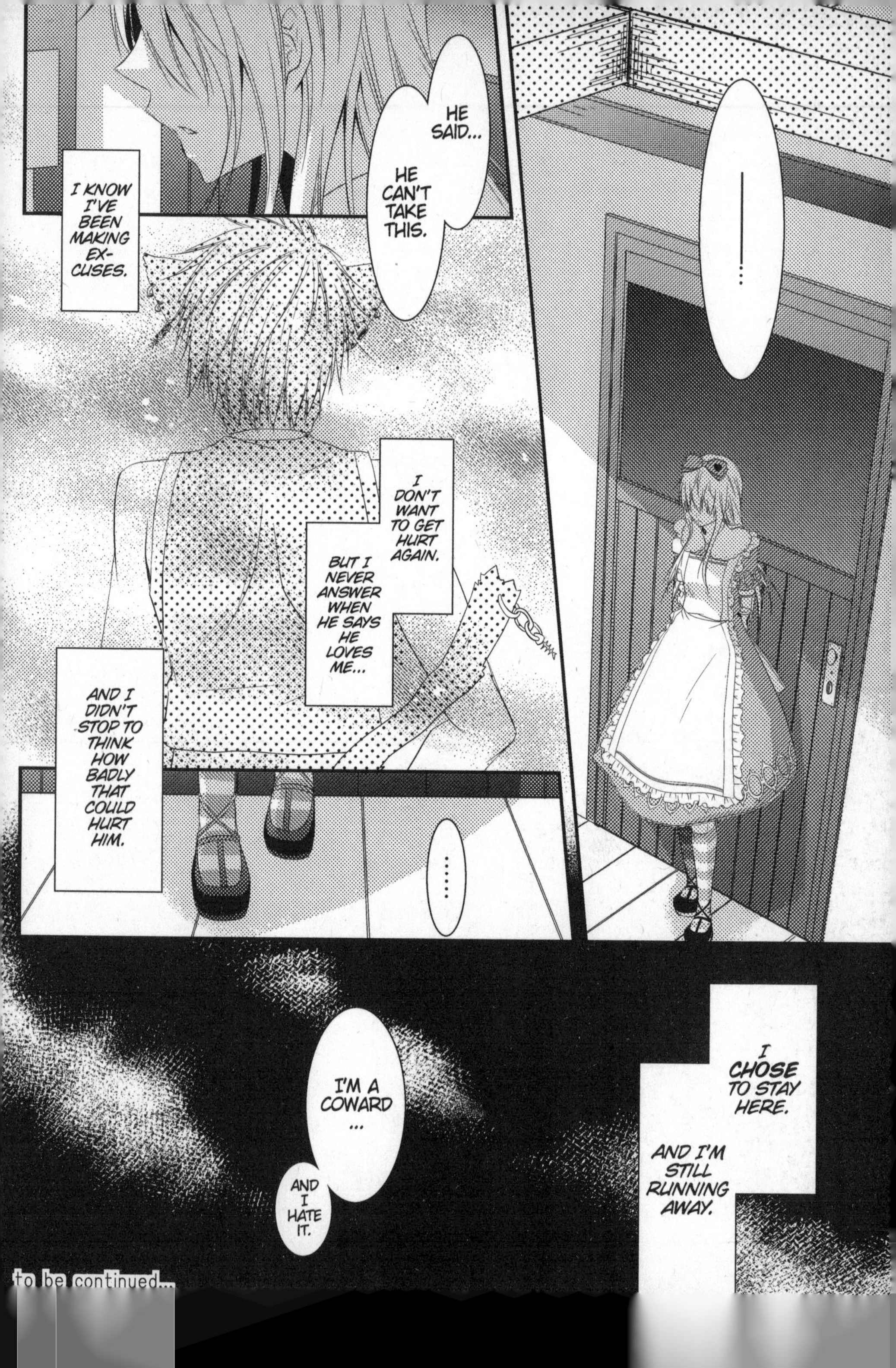
—......
HE SAID...
HE CAN'T TAKE THIS.
I KNOW I'VE BEEN MAKING EX-CUSES.
I DON'T WANT TO GET HURT AGAIN.
BUT I NEVER ANSWER WHEN HE SAYS HE LOVES ME...
AND I DIDN'T STOP TO THINK HOW BADLY THAT COULD HURT HIM.
......
I CHOSE TO STAY HERE.
AND I'M STILL RUNNING AWAY.
I'M A COWARD...
AND I HATE IT.
to be continued...

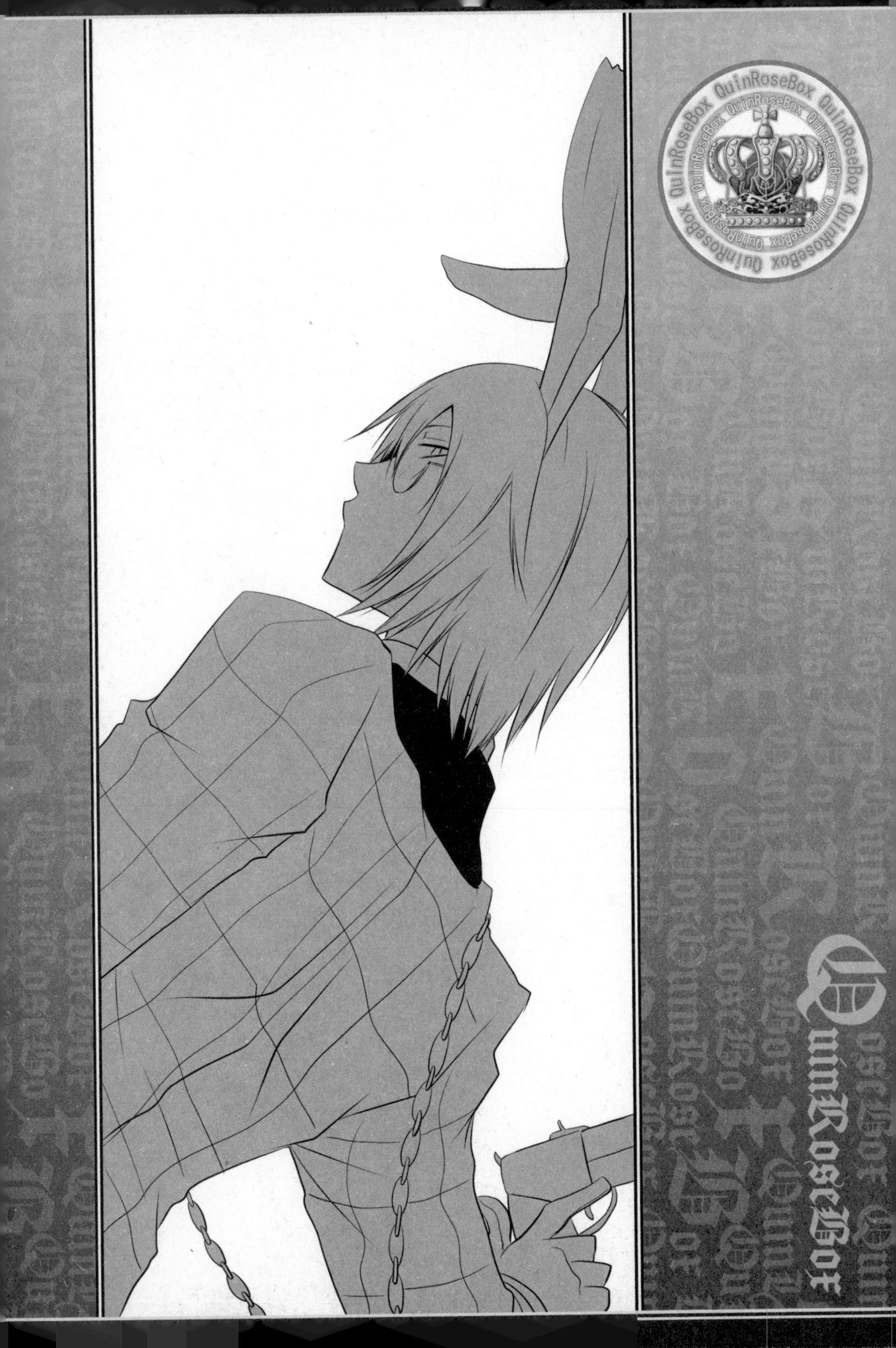
QuinRoseBox

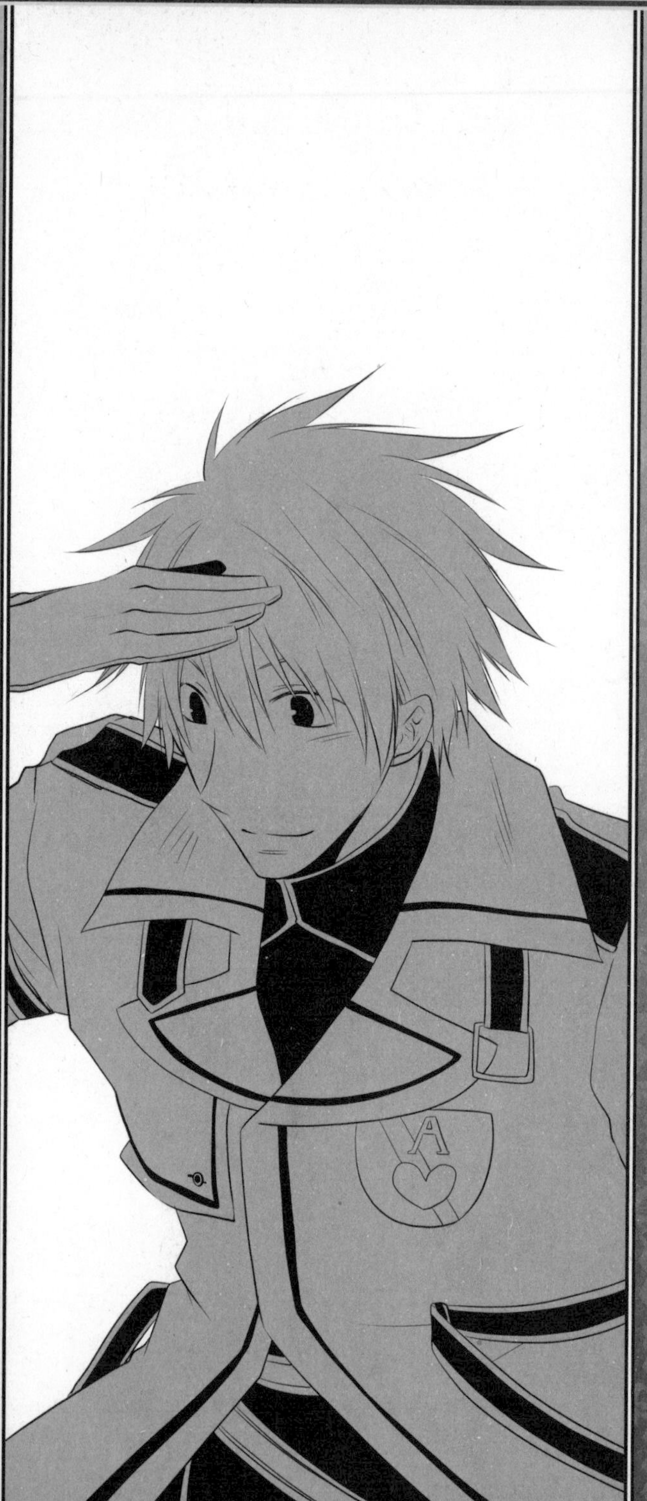

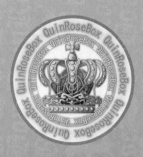

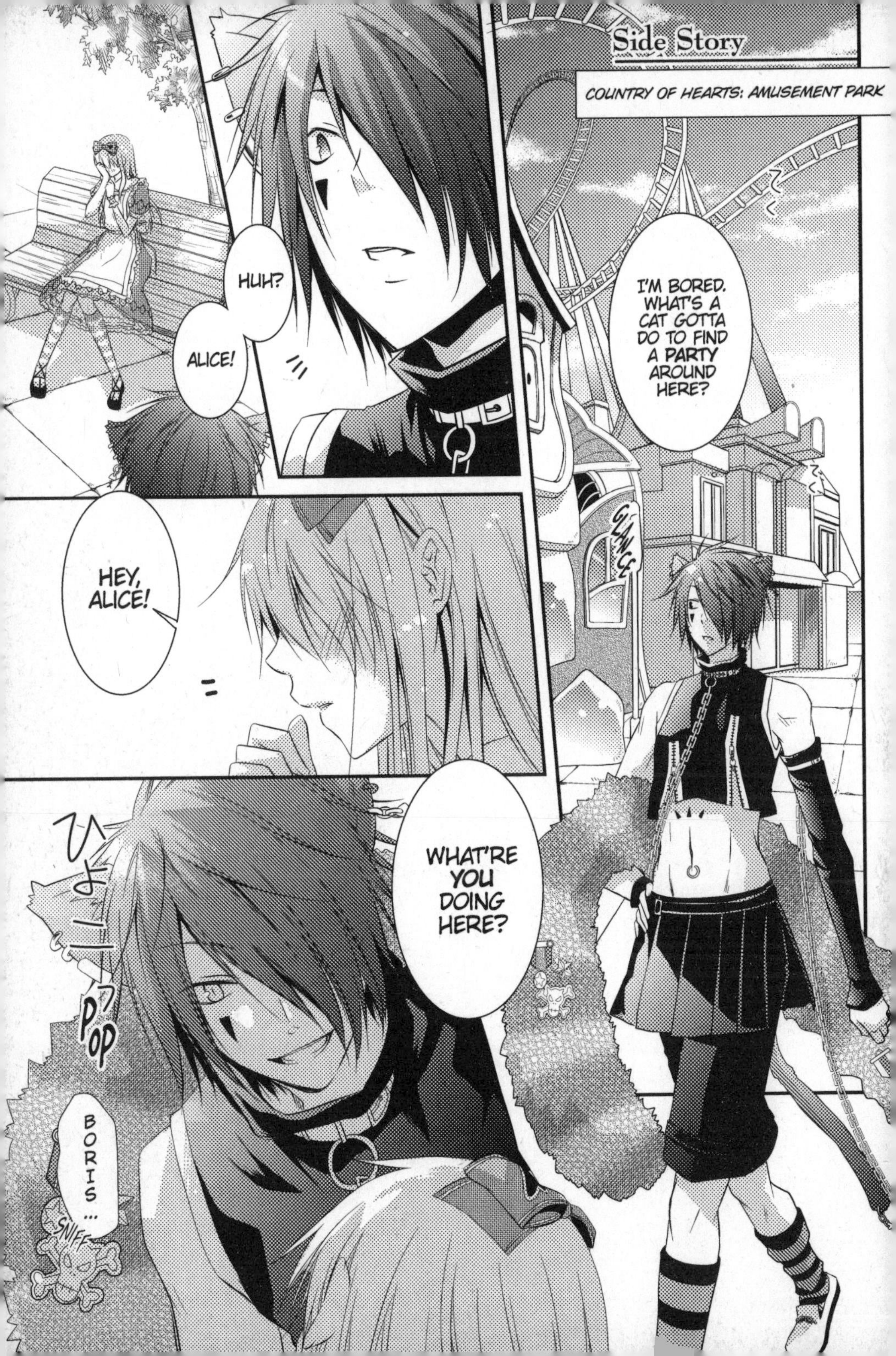

Side Story
COUNTRY OF HEARTS: AMUSEMENT PARK
I'M BORED. WHAT'S A CAT GOTTA DO TO FIND A PARTY AROUND HERE?
GLANCE
HUH?
ALICE!
HEY, ALICE!
WHAT'RE YOU DOING HERE?
POP
BORIS...
SNIFF

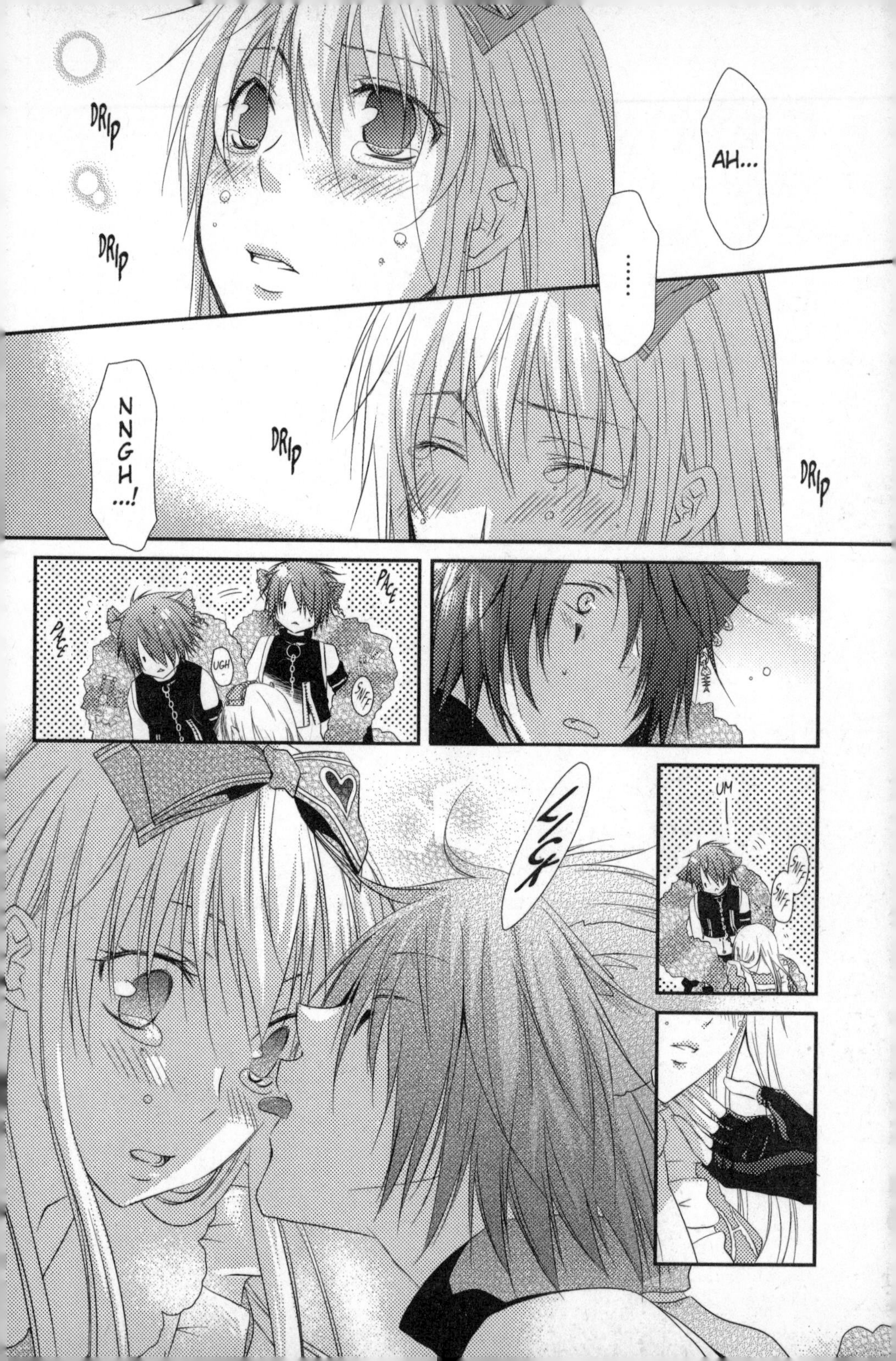
AH...
DRIP
DRIP
......
DRIP
NNGH...!
DRIP
PACE
SNIFF
UGH
PACE
UM
SNIFF
SNIFF
LICK

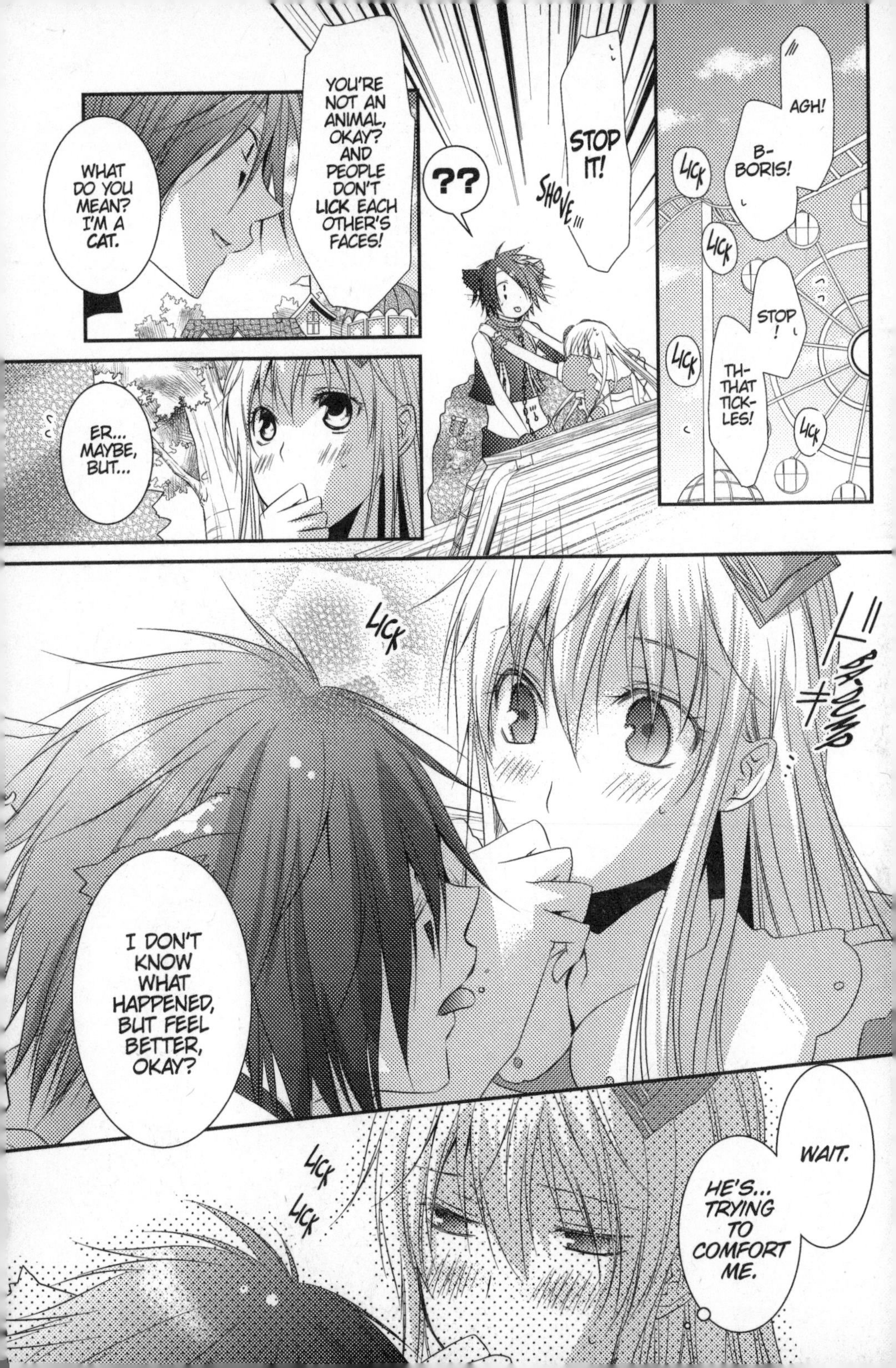
AGH!
B-BORIS!
LICK
LICK
STOP!
TH-THAT TICKLES!
LICK
LICK
STOP IT!
SHOVE
??
YOU'RE NOT AN ANIMAL, OKAY? AND PEOPLE DON'T LICK EACH OTHER'S FACES!
WHAT DO YOU MEAN? I'M A CAT.
ER... MAYBE, BUT...
BA-DUMP
LICK
I DON'T KNOW WHAT HAPPENED, BUT FEEL BETTER, OKAY?
WAIT.
HE'S... TRYING TO COMFORT ME.
LICK
LICK

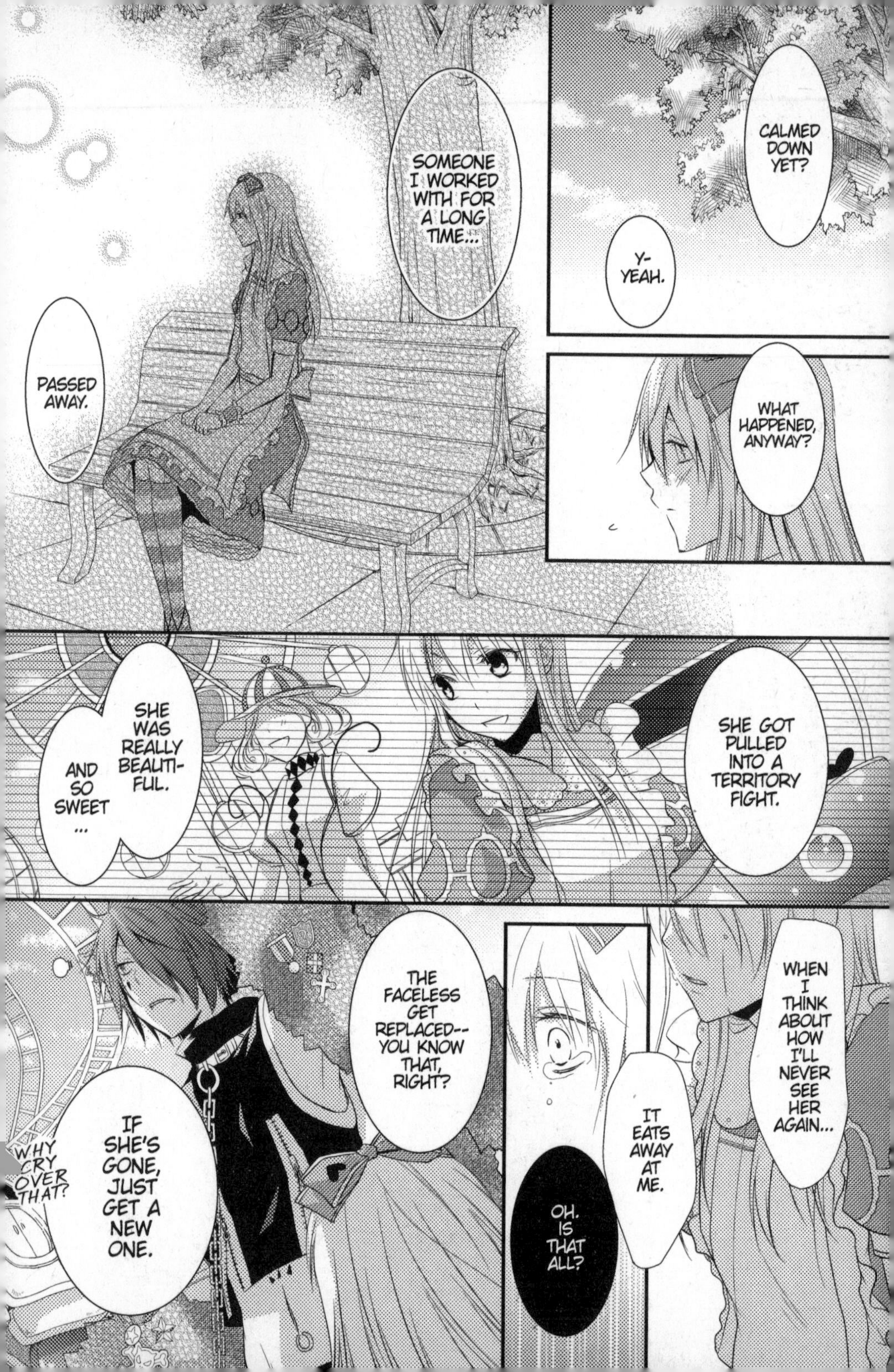
CALMED DOWN YET?
Y-YEAH.
WHAT HAPPENED, ANYWAY?
SOMEONE I WORKED WITH FOR A LONG TIME...
PASSED AWAY.
SHE GOT PULLED INTO A TERRITORY FIGHT.
SHE WAS REALLY BEAUTI-FUL.
AND SO SWEET ...
WHEN I THINK ABOUT HOW I'LL NEVER SEE HER AGAIN...
IT EATS AWAY AT ME.
OH. IS THAT ALL?
THE FACELESS GET REPLACED-- YOU KNOW THAT, RIGHT?
IF SHE'S GONE, JUST GET A NEW ONE.
WHY CRY OVER THAT?

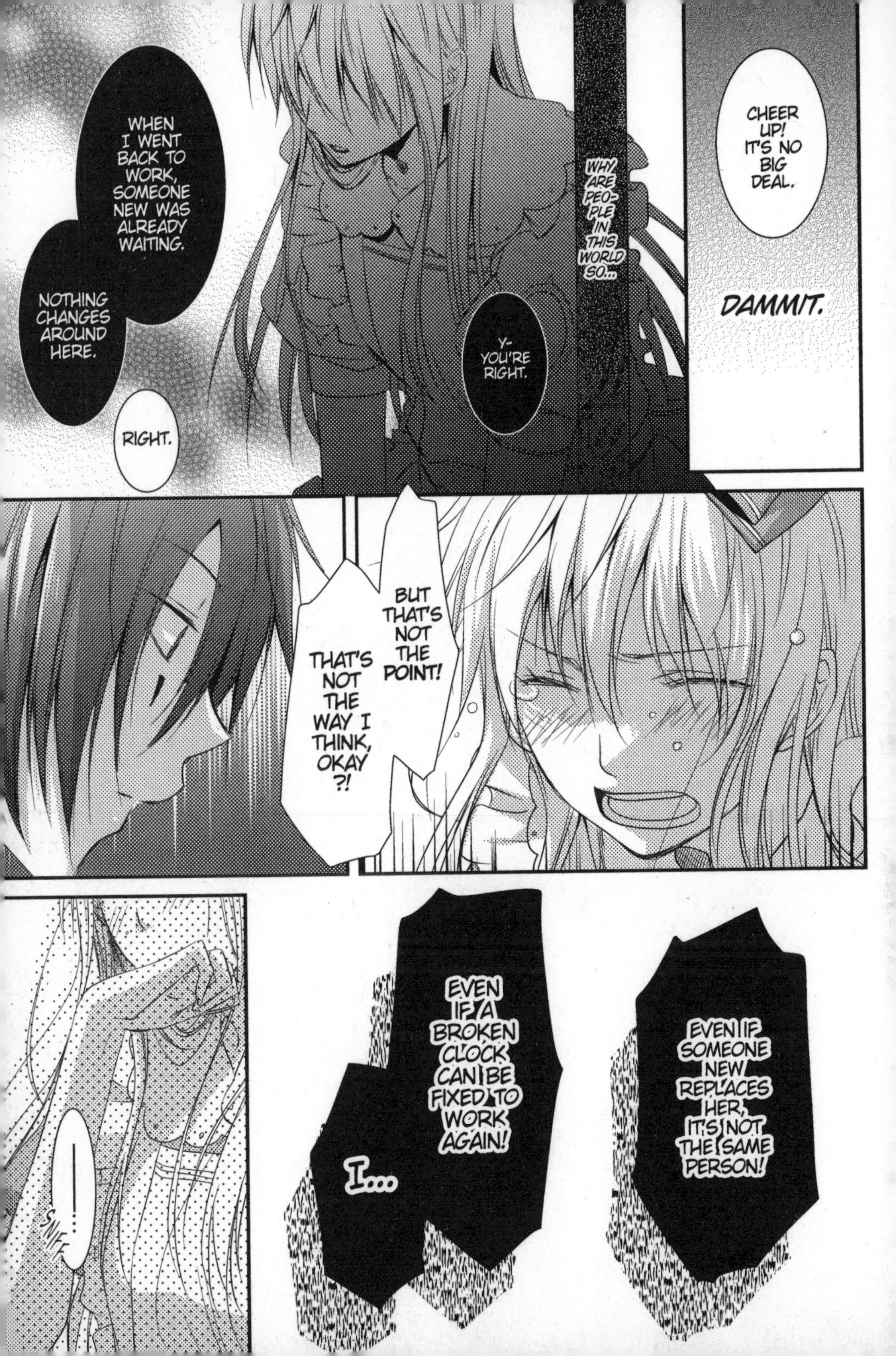
CHEER UP! IT'S NO BIG DEAL.
DAMMIT.
WHY ARE PEO-PLE IN THIS WORLD SO...
WHEN I WENT BACK TO WORK, SOMEONE NEW WAS ALREADY WAITING.
NOTHING CHANGES AROUND HERE.
Y-YOU'RE RIGHT.
RIGHT.
BUT THAT'S NOT THE POINT!
THAT'S NOT THE WAY I THINK, OKAY?!
EVEN IF SOMEONE NEW REPLACES HER, IT'S NOT THE SAME PERSON!
EVEN IF A BROKEN CLOCK CAN BE FIXED TO WORK AGAIN!
I...
......!
SNIFF

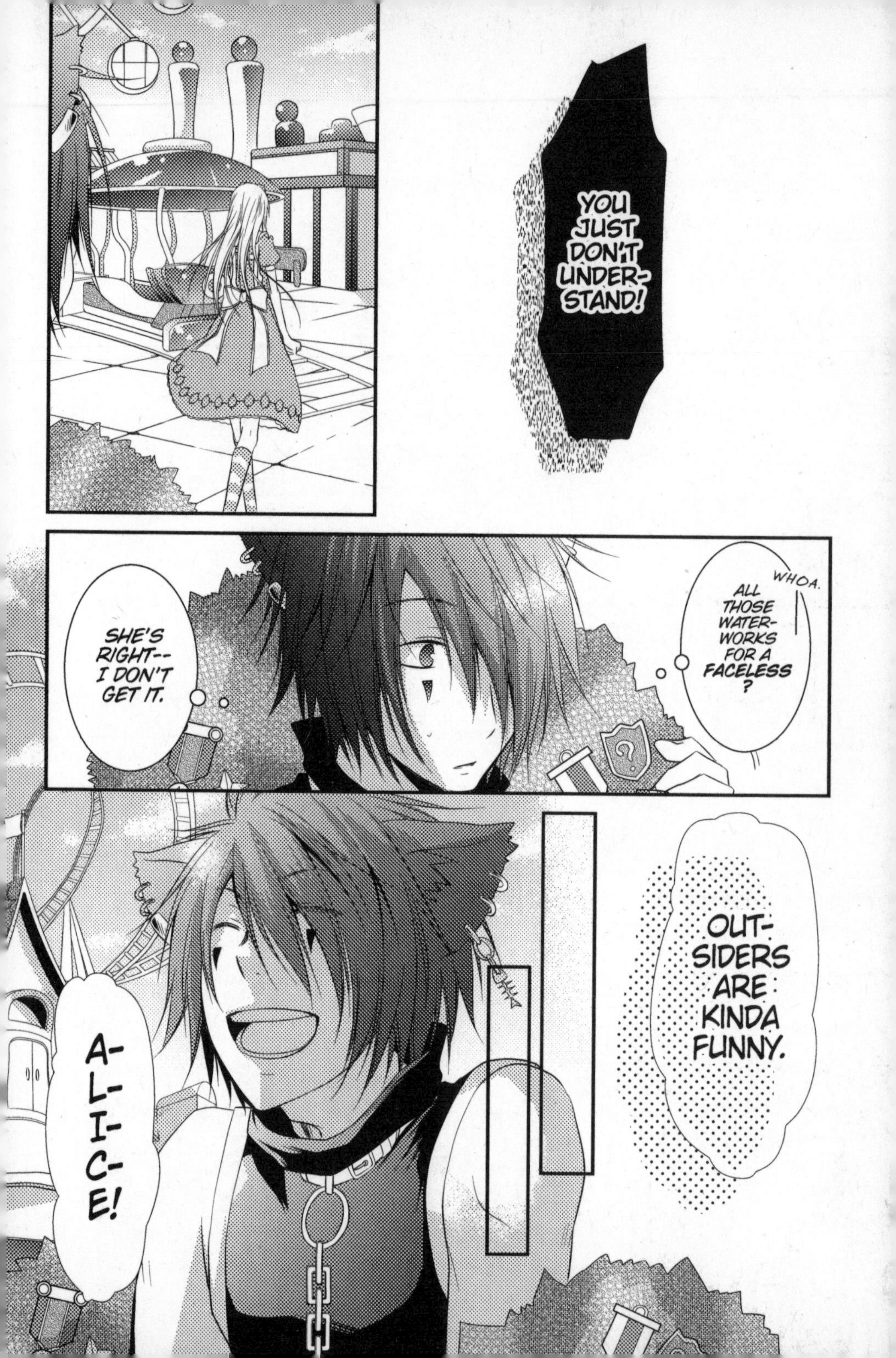
YOU JUST DON'T UNDER-STAND!
WHOA.
ALL THOSE WATER-WORKS FOR A FACELESS?
SHE'S RIGHT-- I DON'T GET IT.
OUT-SIDERS ARE KINDA FUNNY.
A-L-I-C-E!

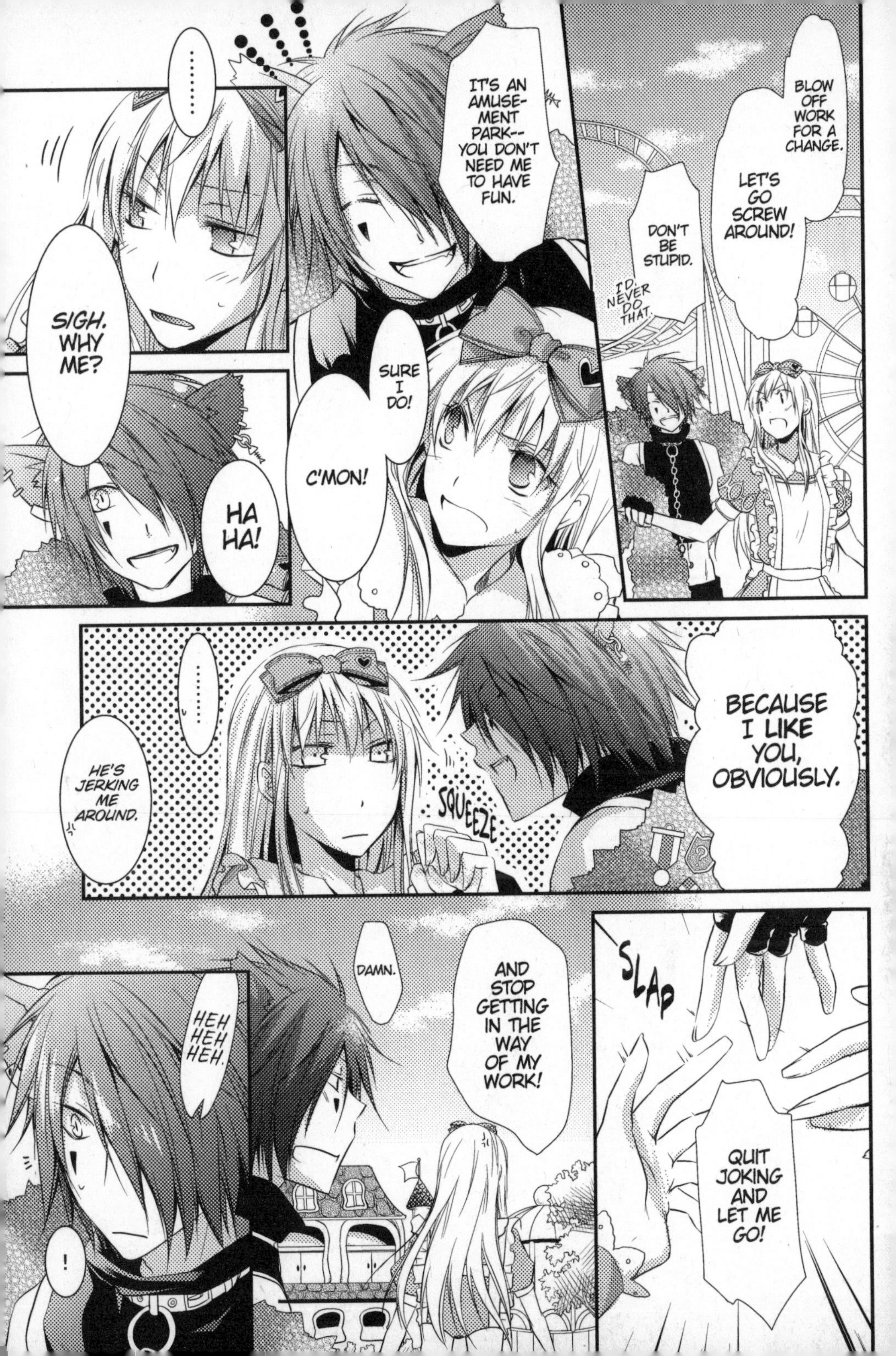
BLOW OFF WORK FOR A CHANGE.
LET'S GO SCREW AROUND!
DON'T BE STUPID.
I'D NEVER DO THAT.
IT'S AN AMUSEMENT PARK-- YOU DON'T NEED ME TO HAVE FUN.
SURE I DO!
C'MON!
......
SIGH. WHY ME?
HA HA!
BECAUSE I LIKE YOU, OBVIOUSLY.
SQUEEZE
......
HE'S JERKING ME AROUND.
SLAP
QUIT JOKING AND LET ME GO!
AND STOP GETTING IN THE WAY OF MY WORK!
DAMN.
HEH HEH HEH.
!

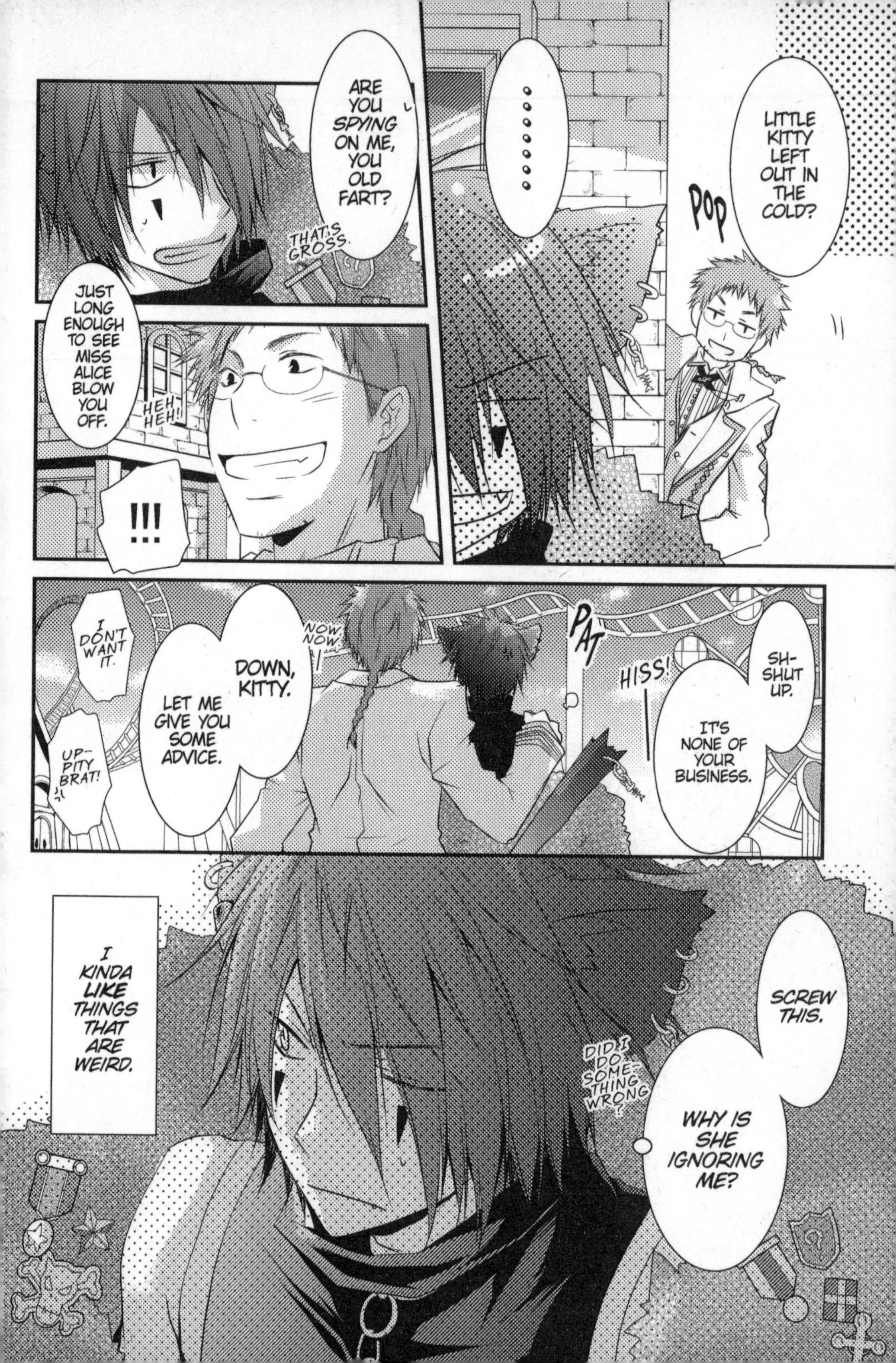
LITTLE KITTY LEFT OUT IN THE COLD?
POP
......
ARE YOU SPYING ON ME, YOU OLD FART?
THAT'S GROSS.
JUST LONG ENOUGH TO SEE MISS ALICE BLOW YOU OFF.
HEH HEH!
!!!
PAT
SH-SHUT UP.
IT'S NONE OF YOUR BUSINESS.
HISS!
DOWN, KITTY.
LET ME GIVE YOU SOME ADVICE.
NOW NOW!
I DON'T WANT IT.
UP-PITY BRAT!
SCREW THIS.
WHY IS SHE IGNORING ME?
DID I DO SOME-THING WRONG?
I KINDA LIKE THINGS THAT ARE WEIRD.

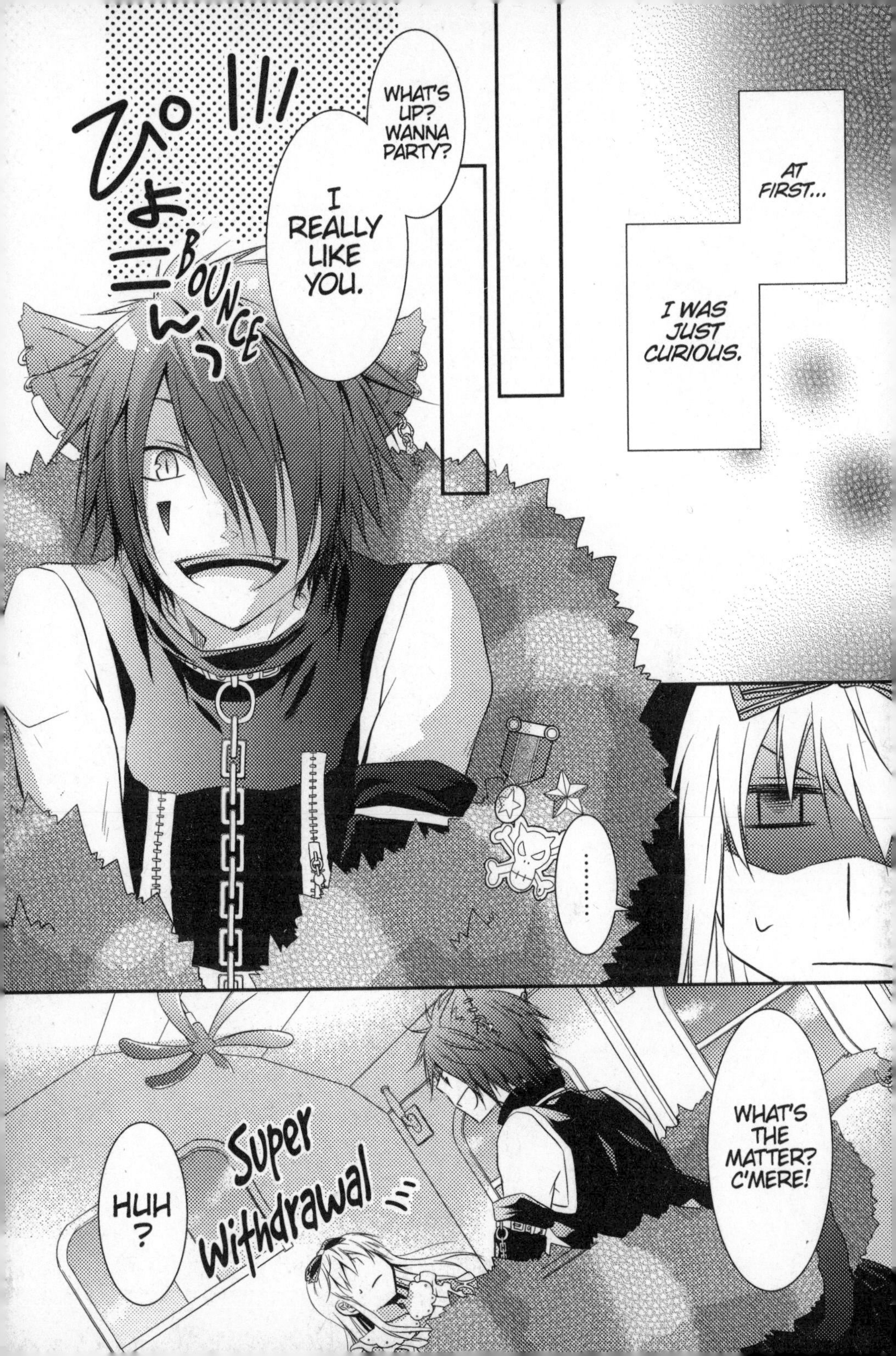
AT FIRST...
I WAS JUST CURIOUS.
WHAT'S UP? WANNA PARTY?
I REALLY LIKE YOU.
ぴょーん
BOUNCE
......
WHAT'S THE MATTER? C'MERE!
Super withdrawal
HUH ?

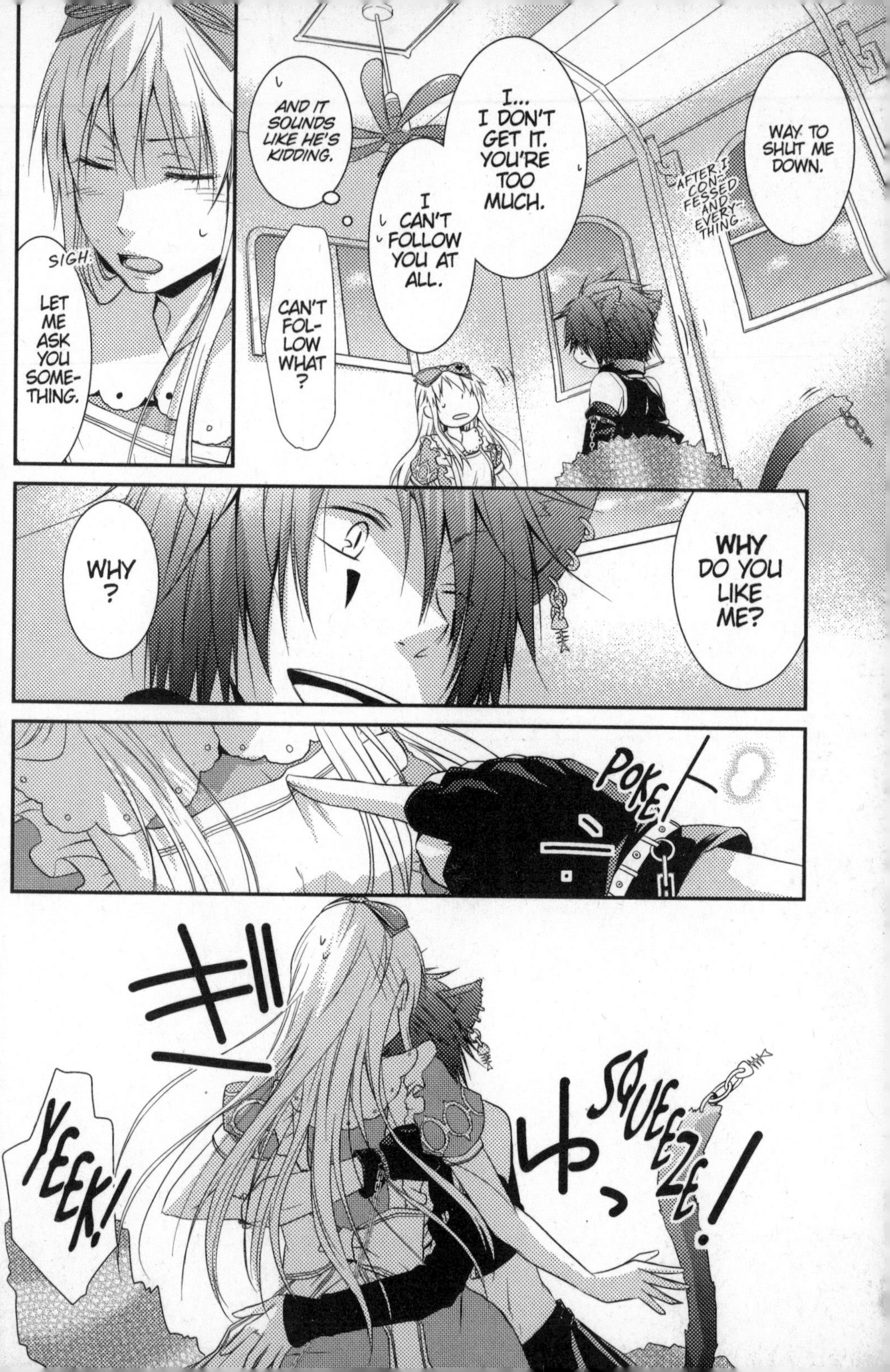
WAY TO SHUT ME DOWN.
AFTER I CONFESSED AND EVERYTHING...
I... I DON'T GET IT. YOU'RE TOO MUCH.
I CAN'T FOLLOW YOU AT ALL.
AND IT SOUNDS LIKE HE'S KIDDING.
CAN'T FOLLOW WHAT?
SIGH.
LET ME ASK YOU SOMETHING.
WHY DO YOU LIKE ME?
WHY?
POKE
SQUEEZE!
ギゅっ
YEEK!

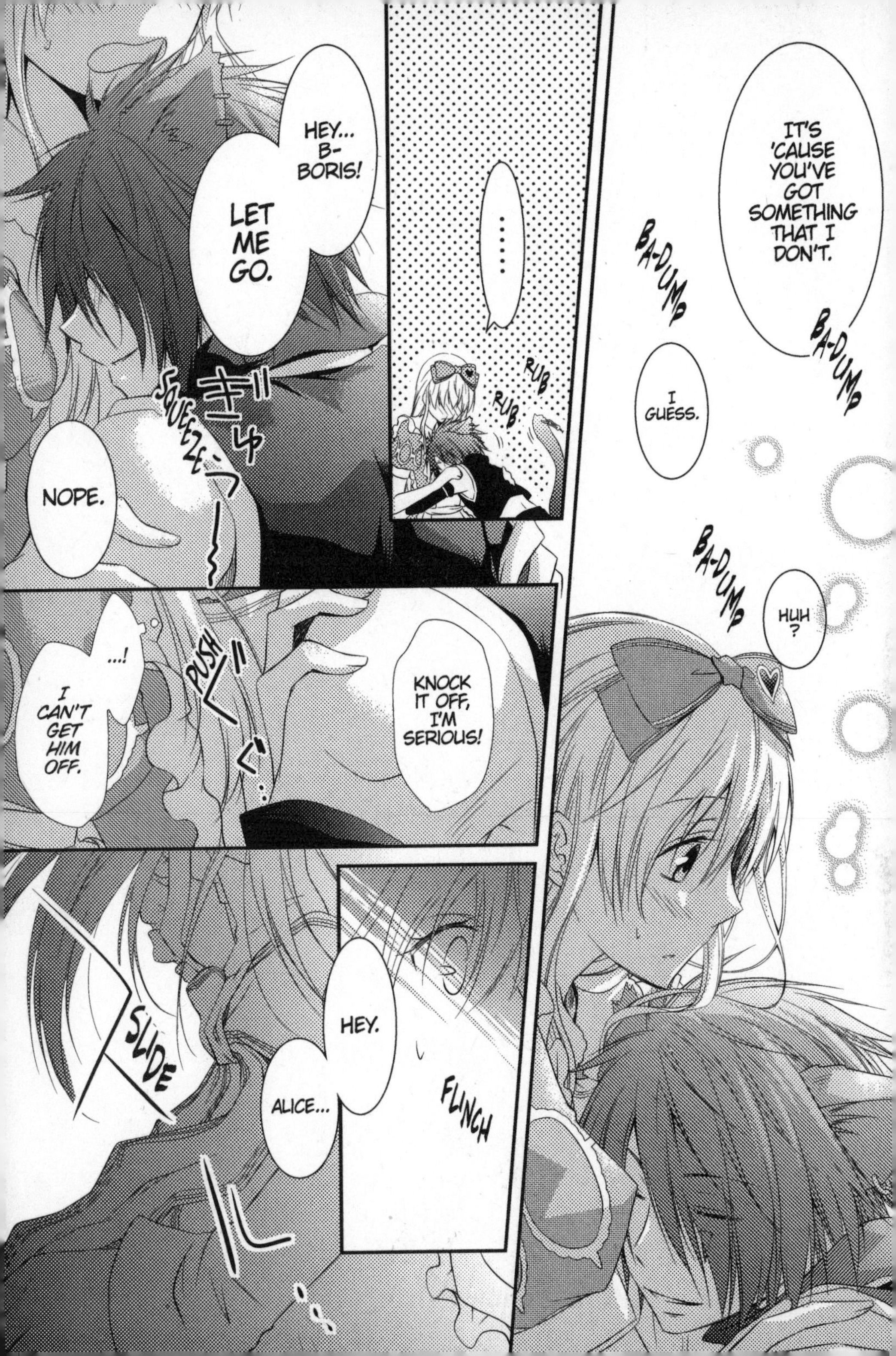

IT'S 'CAUSE YOU'VE GOT SOMETHING THAT I DON'T.
BA-DUMP
BA-DUMP
I GUESS.
BA-DUMP
HUH?
......
RUB
RUB
HEY... B-BORIS!
LET ME GO.
SQUEEZE
NOPE.
KNOCK IT OFF, I'M SERIOUS!
PUSH
...!
I CAN'T GET HIM OFF.
HEY.
ALICE...
FLINCH
SLIDE

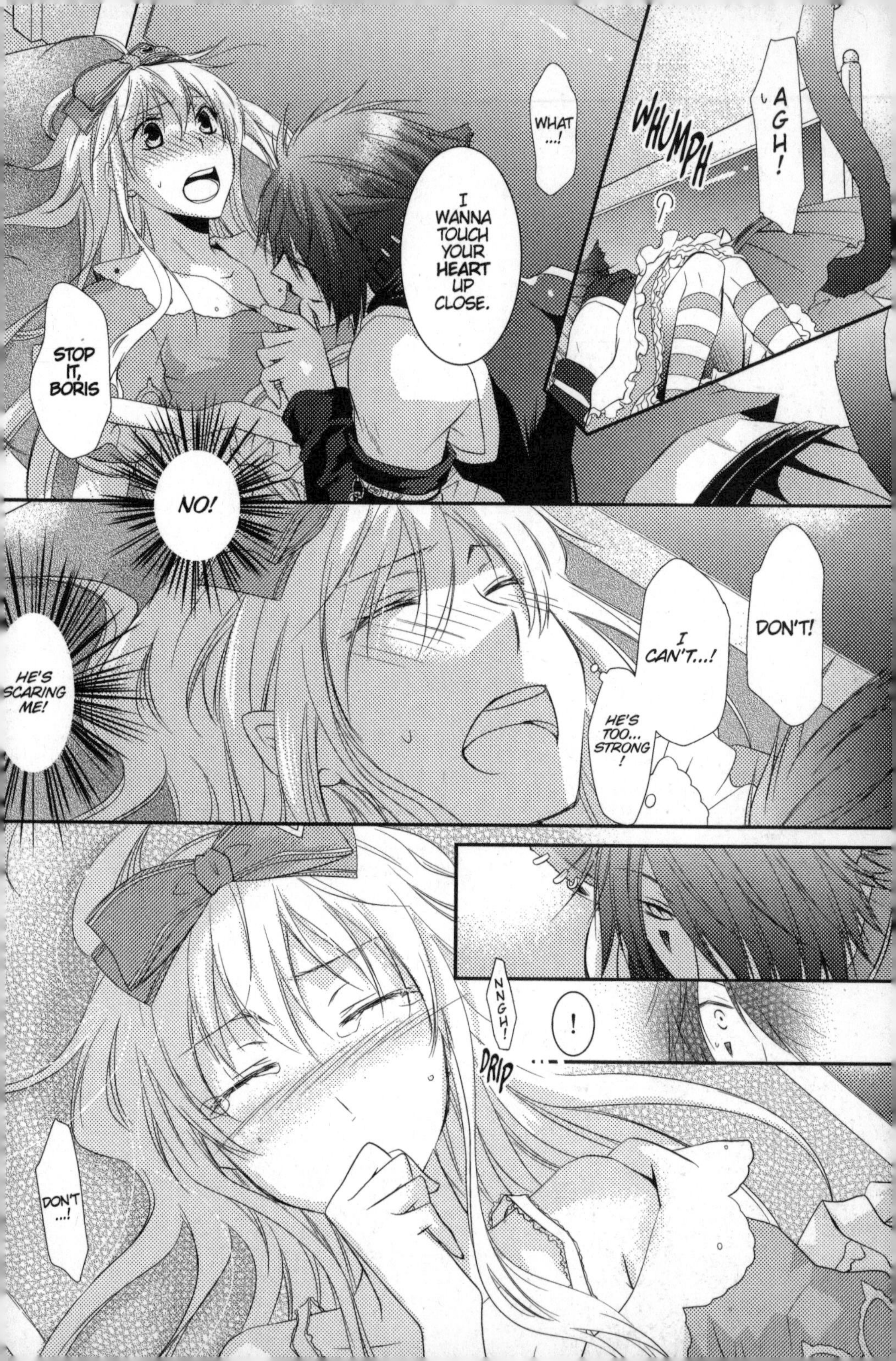
AGH!
WHUMPH
WHAT ...!
I WANNA TOUCH YOUR HEART UP CLOSE.
STOP IT, BORIS
DON'T!
I CAN'T...!
HE'S TOO... STRONG!
NO!
HE'S SCARING ME!
!
NNGH!
DRIP
DON'T ...!

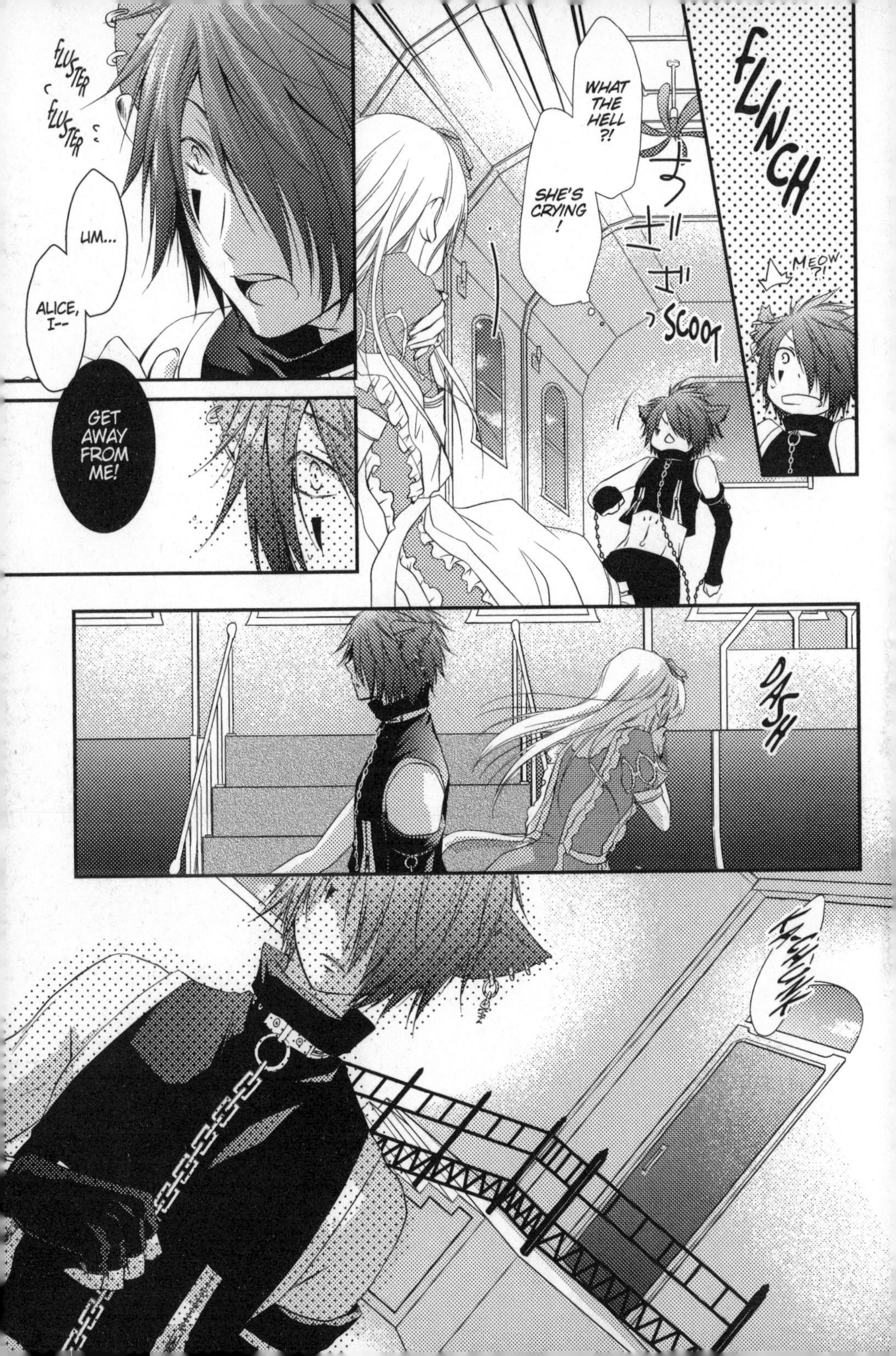

FLINCH
MEOW?!
WHAT THE HELL?!
SHE'S CRYING!
ずざざ
SCOOT
FLUSTER FLUSTER
UM...
ALICE, I--
GET AWAY FROM ME!
DASH
KA-CHUNK

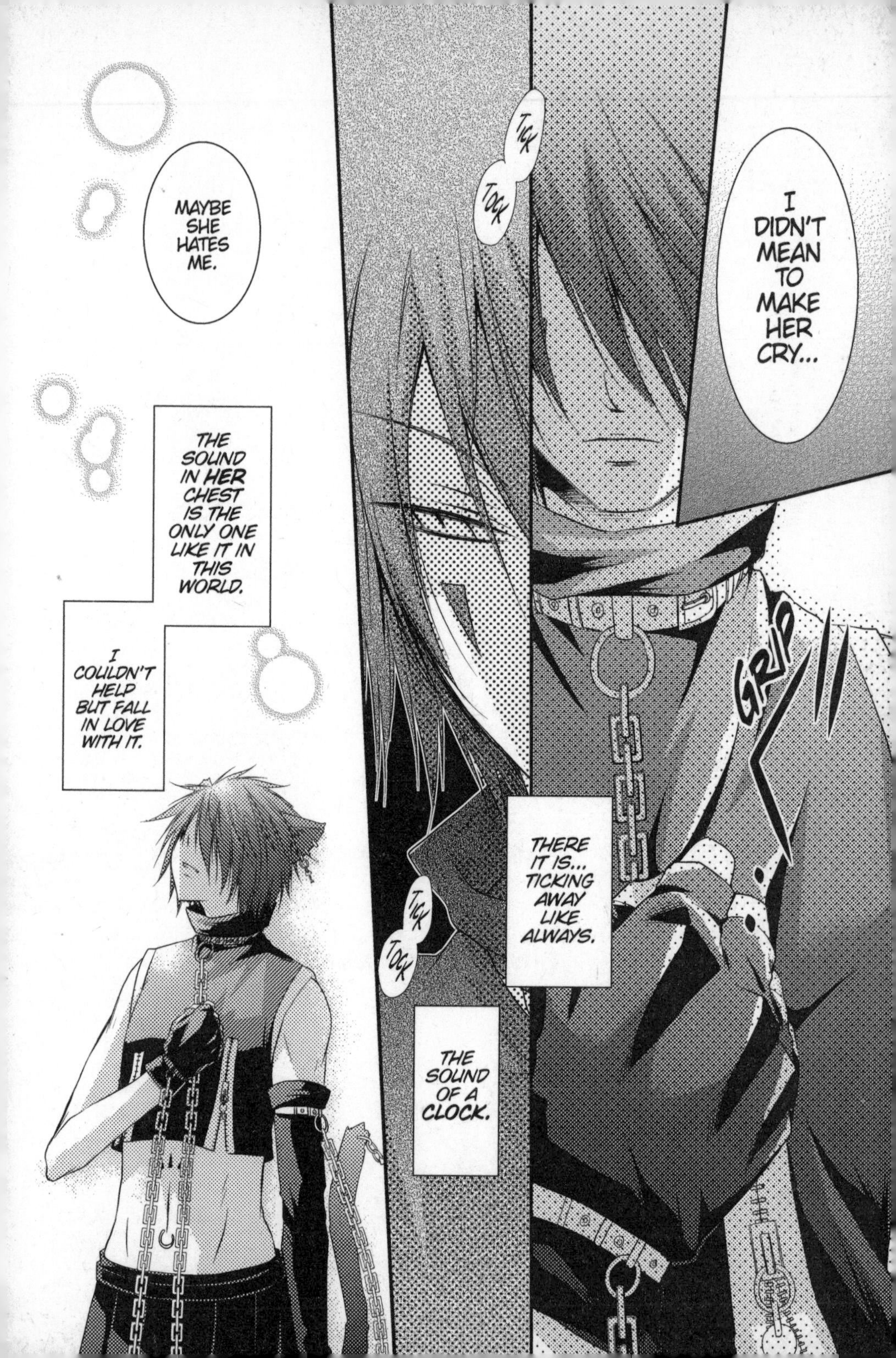

I DIDN'T MEAN TO MAKE HER CRY...
TICK
TOCK
GRIP
THERE IT IS... TICKING AWAY LIKE ALWAYS.
TICK
TOCK
THE SOUND OF A CLOCK.
MAYBE SHE HATES ME.
THE SOUND IN HER CHEST IS THE ONLY ONE LIKE IT IN THIS WORLD.
I COULDN'T HELP BUT FALL IN LOVE WITH IT.

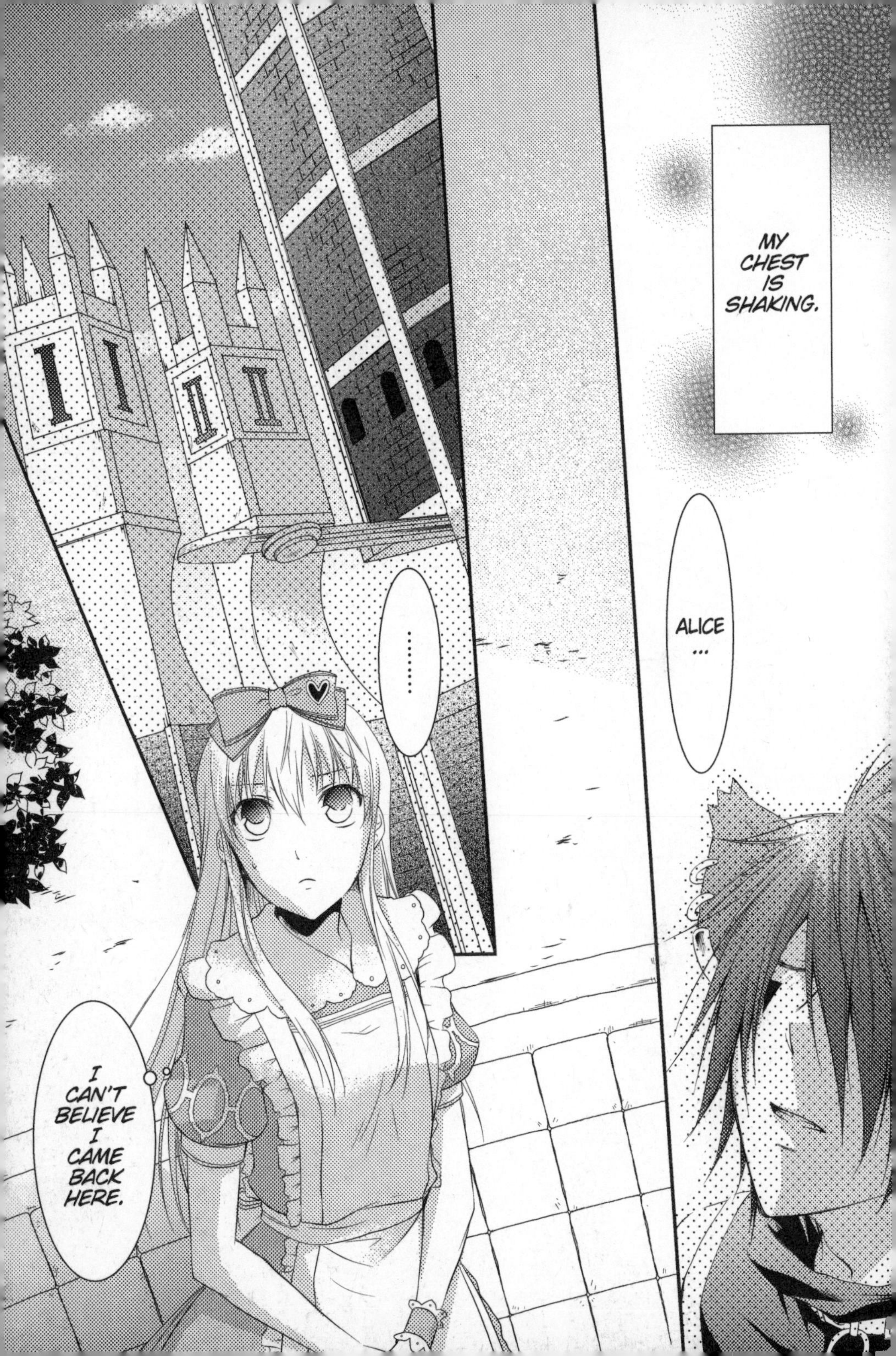
MY CHEST IS SHAKING.
ALICE ...
......
I CAN'T BELIEVE I CAME BACK HERE.

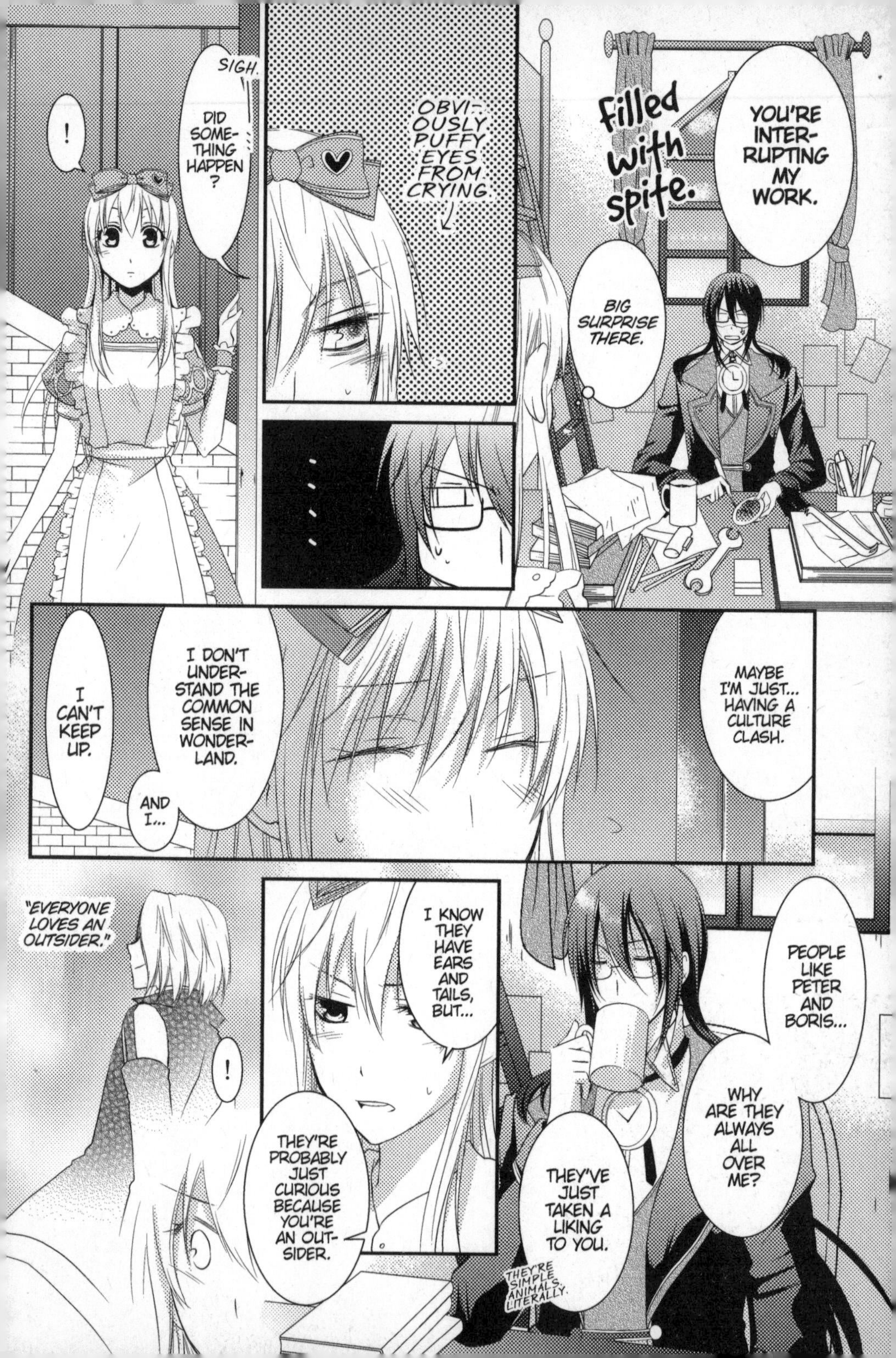
YOU'RE INTERRUPTING MY WORK.
Filled with spite.
BIG SURPRISE THERE.
OBVIOUSLY PUFFY EYES FROM CRYING.
SIGH.
DID SOMETHING HAPPEN?
!
MAYBE I'M JUST... HAVING A CULTURE CLASH.
I DON'T UNDERSTAND THE COMMON SENSE IN WONDERLAND.
AND I...
I CAN'T KEEP UP.
PEOPLE LIKE PETER AND BORIS...
WHY ARE THEY ALWAYS ALL OVER ME?
THEY'VE JUST TAKEN A LIKING TO YOU.
THEY'RE SIMPLE ANIMALS. LITERALLY.
I KNOW THEY HAVE EARS AND TAILS, BUT...
THEY'RE PROBABLY JUST CURIOUS BECAUSE YOU'RE AN OUTSIDER.
"EVERYONE LOVES AN OUTSIDER."
!

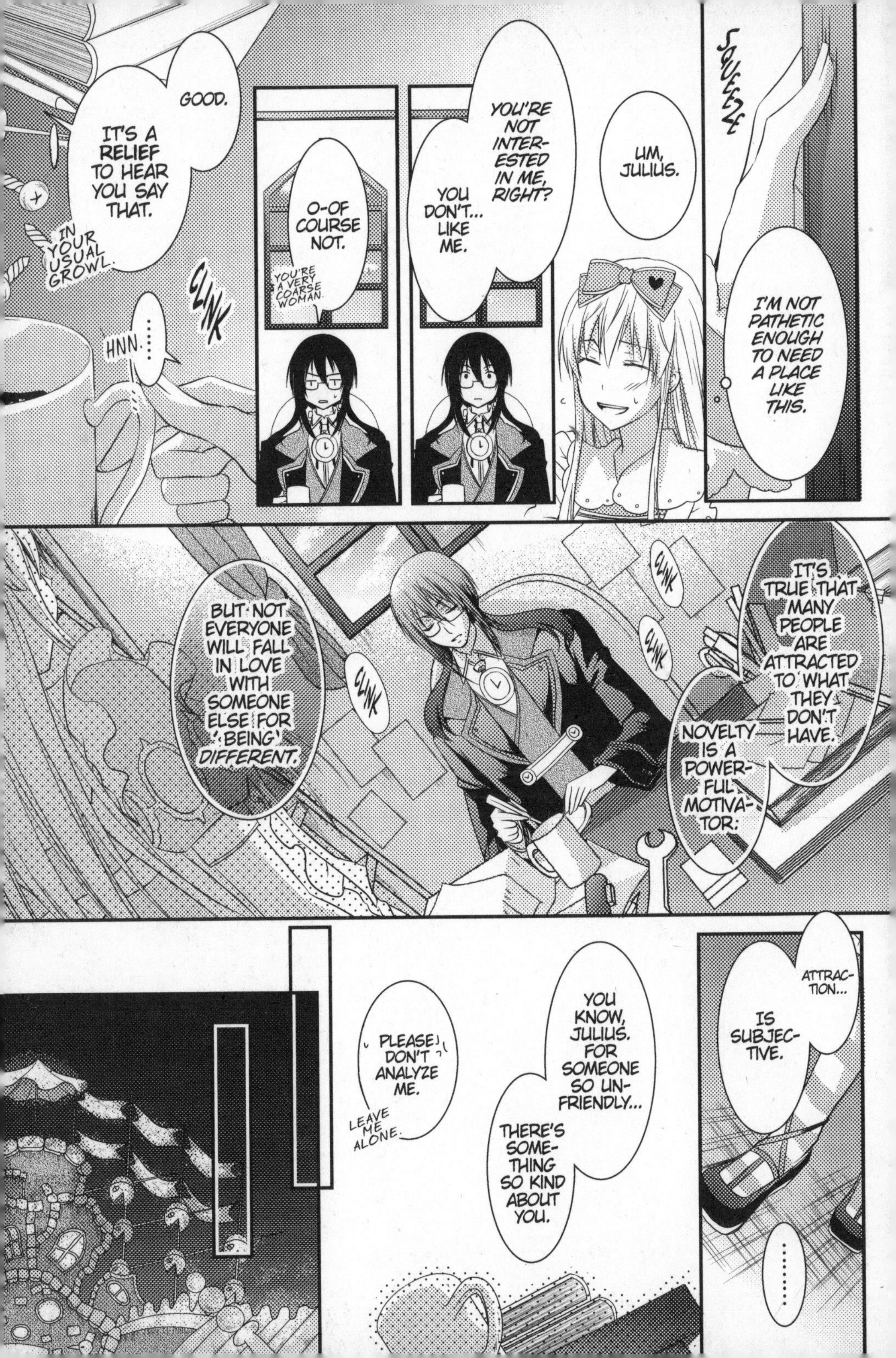
SQUEEZE
UM, JULIUS.
I'M NOT PATHETIC ENOUGH TO NEED A PLACE LIKE THIS.
YOU'RE NOT INTERESTED IN ME, RIGHT?
YOU DON'T... LIKE ME.
O-OF COURSE NOT.
YOU'RE A VERY COARSE WOMAN.
GOOD.
IT'S A RELIEF TO HEAR YOU SAY THAT.
IN YOUR USUAL GROWL.
CLINK
HNN......
IT'S TRUE THAT MANY PEOPLE ARE ATTRACTED TO WHAT THEY DON'T HAVE.
NOVELTY IS A POWERFUL MOTIVATOR.
CLINK
CLINK
CLINK
BUT NOT EVERYONE WILL FALL IN LOVE WITH SOMEONE ELSE FOR 'BEING' DIFFERENT.
ATTRACTION...
IS SUBJECTIVE.
......
YOU KNOW, JULIUS. FOR SOMEONE SO UNFRIENDLY...
THERE'S SOMETHING SO KIND ABOUT YOU.
PLEASE DON'T ANALYZE ME.
LEAVE ME ALONE.

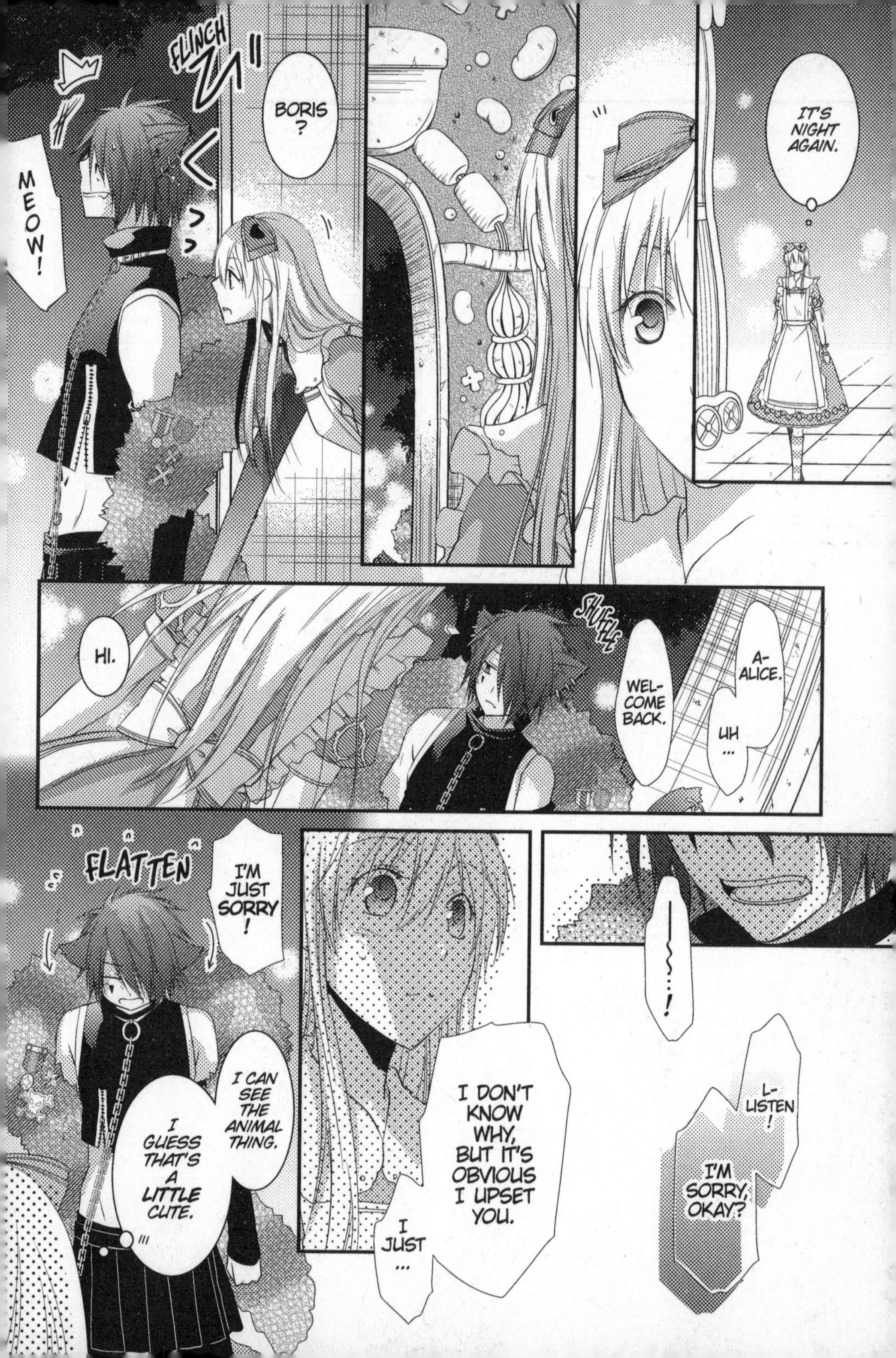
IT'S NIGHT AGAIN.
BORIS?
FLINCH
MEOW!
A- ALICE.
UH ...
WEL- COME BACK.
SHUFFLE
HI.
...!
L- LISTEN!
I'M SORRY, OKAY?
I DON'T KNOW WHY, BUT IT'S OBVIOUS I UPSET YOU.
I JUST ...
I'M JUST SORRY!
FLATTEN
I CAN SEE THE ANIMAL THING.
I GUESS THAT'S A LITTLE CUTE.

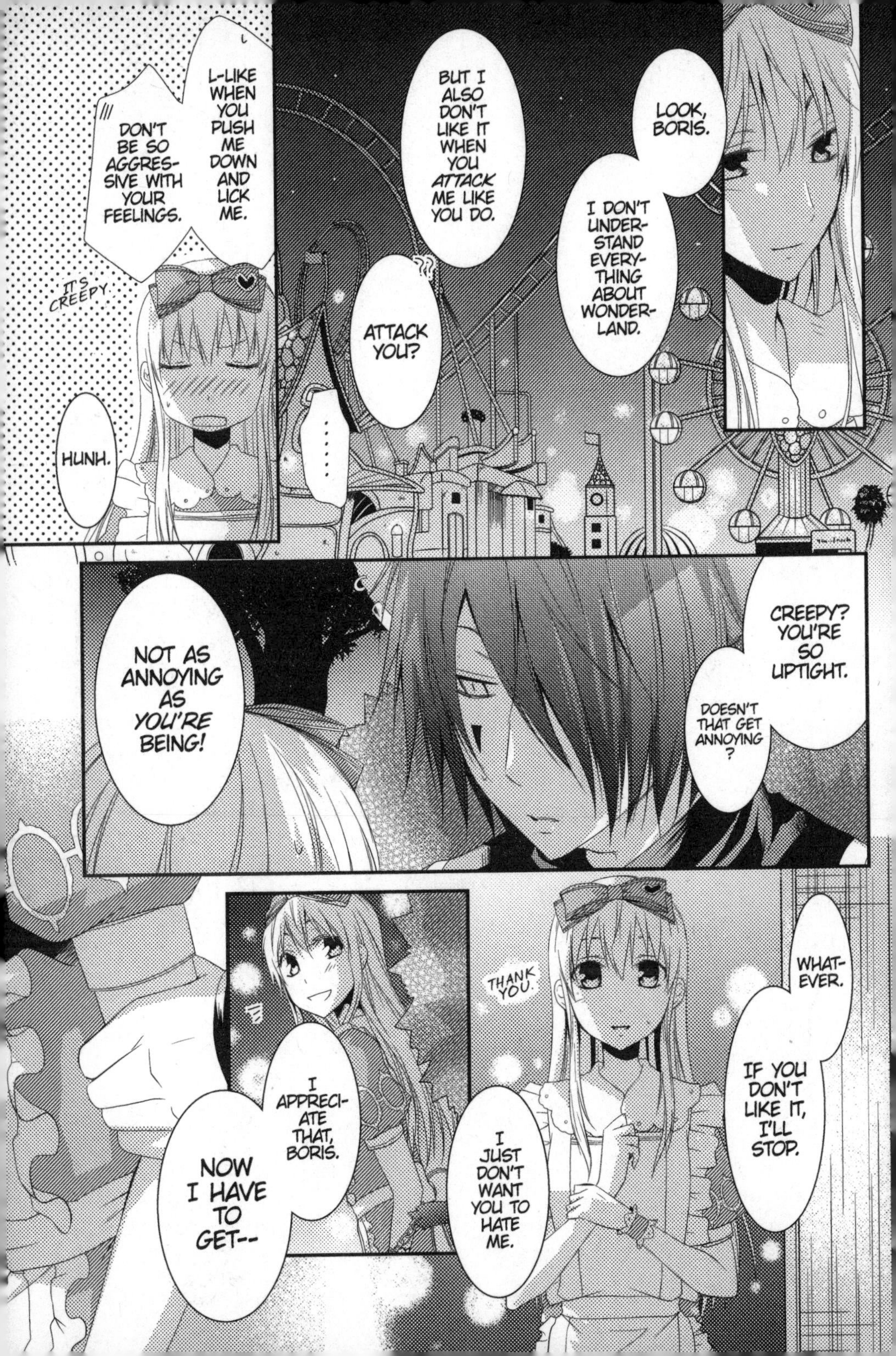
LOOK, BORIS.
I DON'T UNDERSTAND EVERYTHING ABOUT WONDERLAND.
BUT I ALSO DON'T LIKE IT WHEN YOU *ATTACK* ME LIKE YOU DO.
ATTACK YOU?
......
L-LIKE WHEN YOU PUSH ME DOWN AND LICK ME.
DON'T BE SO AGGRESSIVE WITH YOUR FEELINGS.
IT'S CREEPY.
HUNH.
CREEPY? YOU'RE SO UPTIGHT.
DOESN'T THAT GET ANNOYING?
NOT AS ANNOYING AS *YOU'RE* BEING!
WHATEVER.
IF YOU DON'T LIKE IT, I'LL STOP.
THANK YOU.
I JUST DON'T WANT YOU TO HATE ME.
I APPRECIATE THAT, BORIS.
NOW I HAVE TO GET--

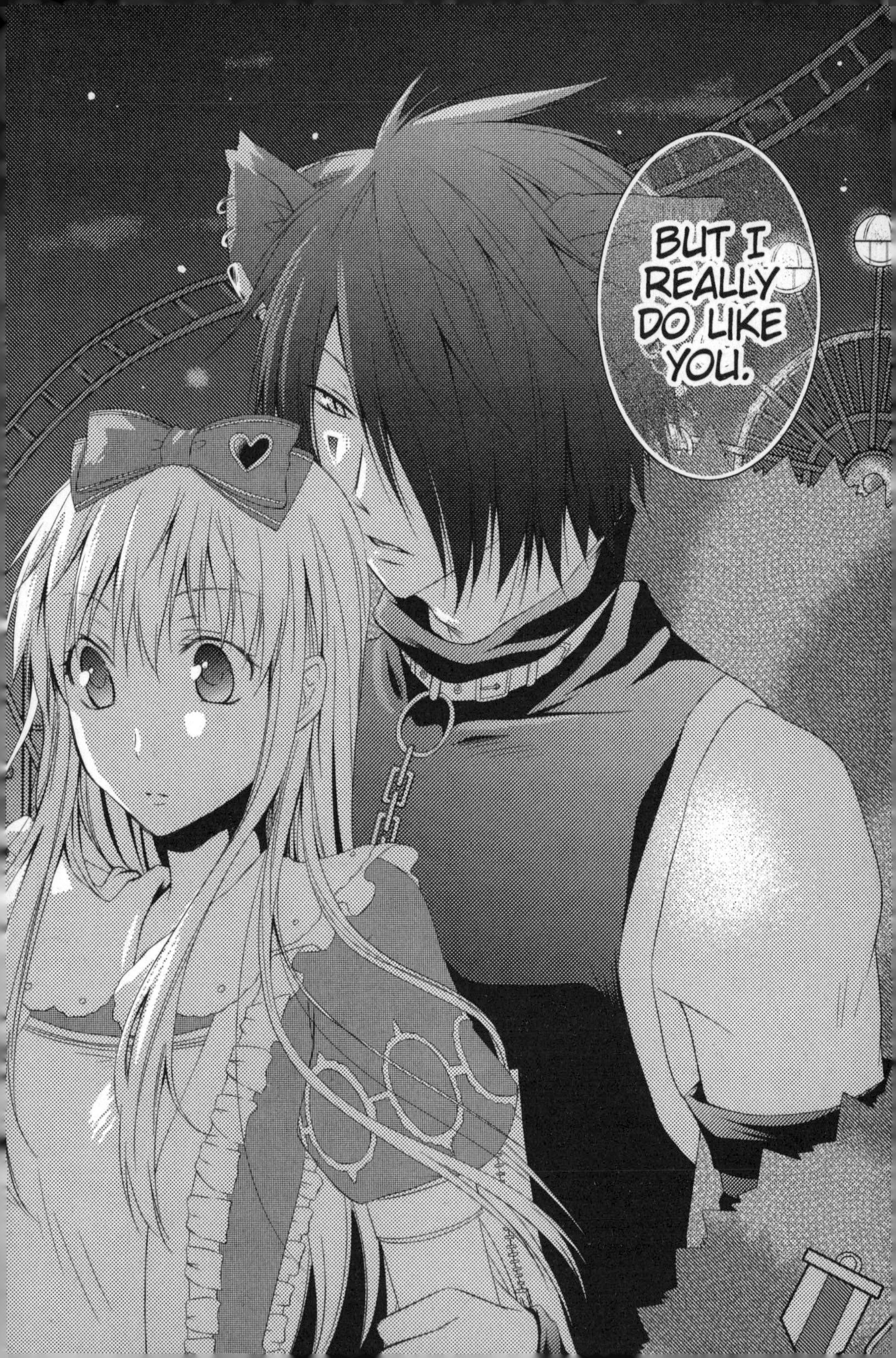
BUT I REALLY DO LIKE YOU.

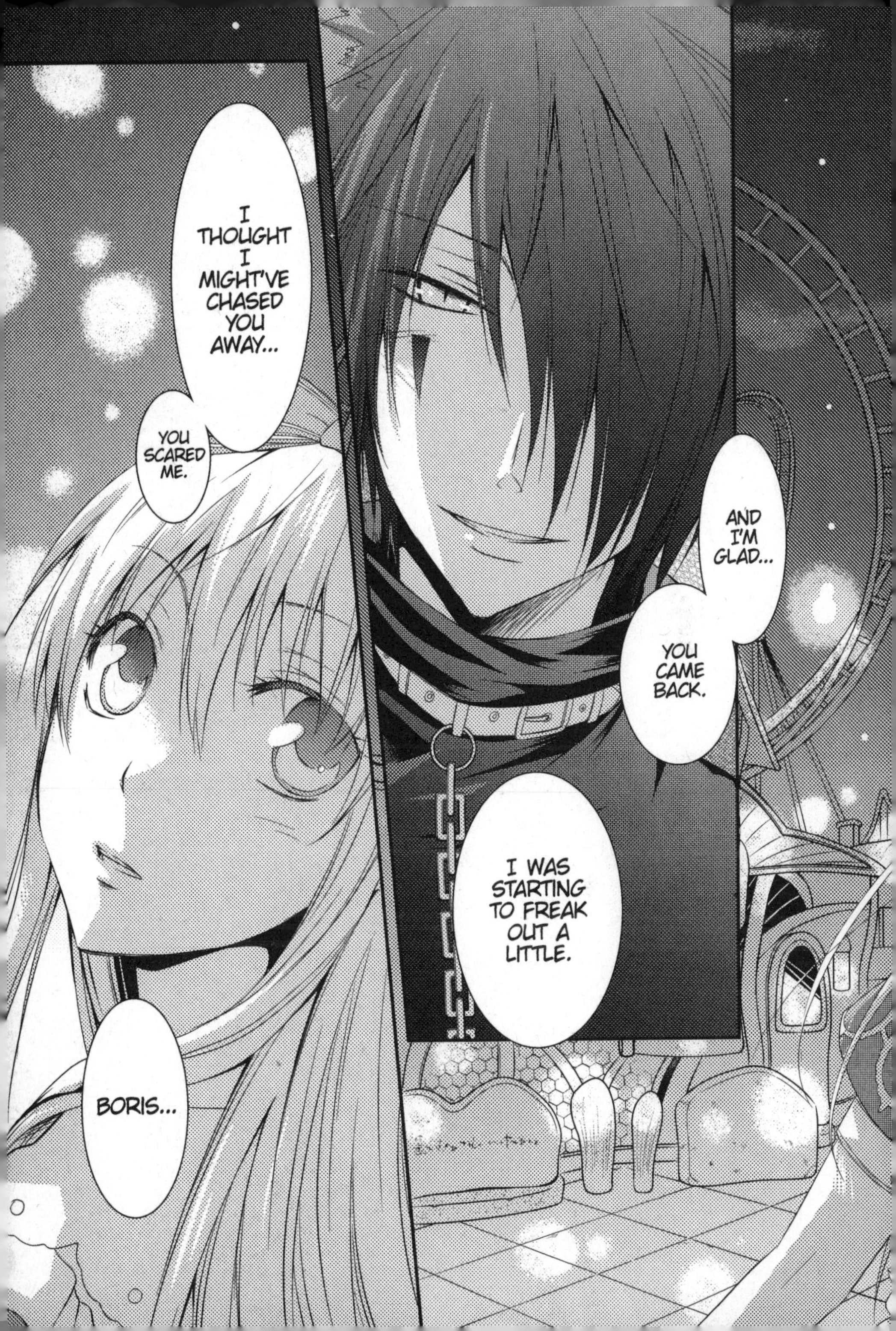
AND I'M GLAD...
YOU CAME BACK.
I WAS STARTING TO FREAK OUT A LITTLE.
I THOUGHT I MIGHT'VE CHASED YOU AWAY...
YOU SCARED ME.
BORIS...

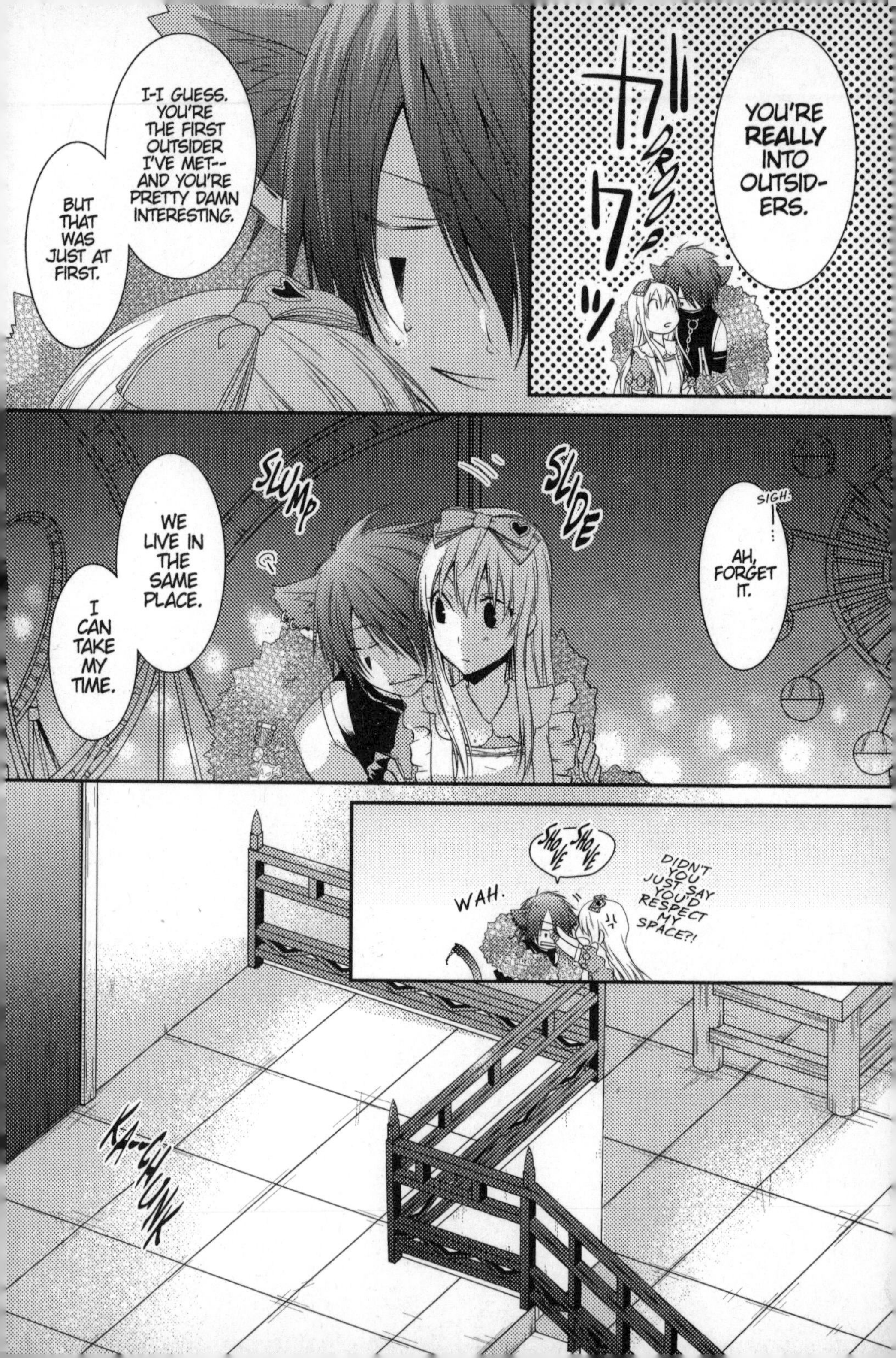
DROOP
YOU'RE REALLY INTO OUTSIDERS.
I-I GUESS. YOU'RE THE FIRST OUTSIDER I'VE MET-- AND YOU'RE PRETTY DAMN INTERESTING.
BUT THAT WAS JUST AT FIRST.
SIGH.
AH, FORGET IT.
SLIDE
SLUMP
WE LIVE IN THE SAME PLACE.
I CAN TAKE MY TIME.
DIDN'T YOU JUST SAY YOU'D RESPECT MY SPACE?!
SHOVE SHOVE
WAH.
KA-CHUNK

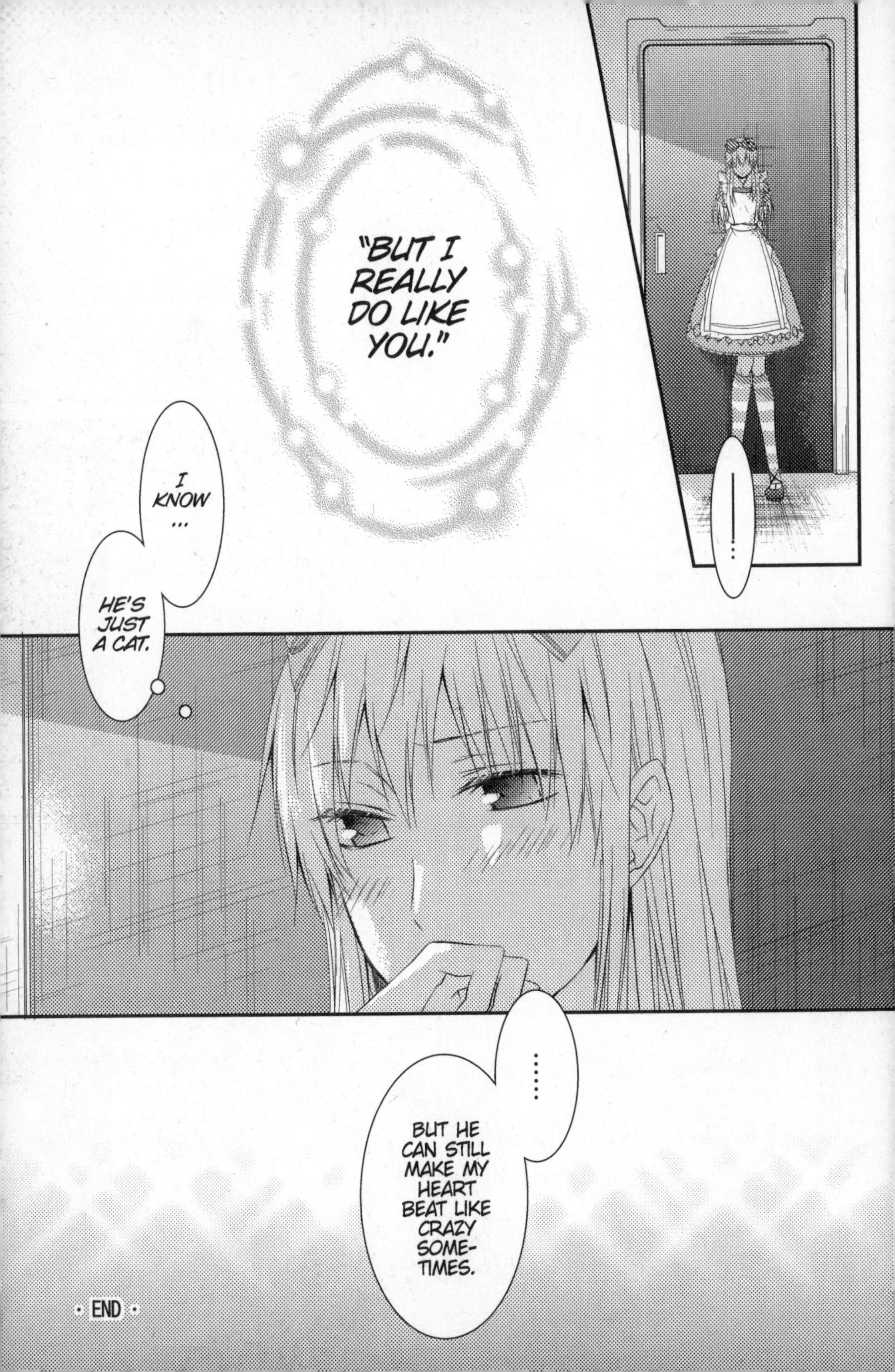
......
"BUT I REALLY DO LIKE YOU."
I KNOW ...
HE'S JUST A CAT.
......
BUT HE CAN STILL MAKE MY HEART BEAT LIKE CRAZY SOME-TIMES.
END

CHESHIRE CAT WALTZ: CHAPTER 3 - POST-MORTEM

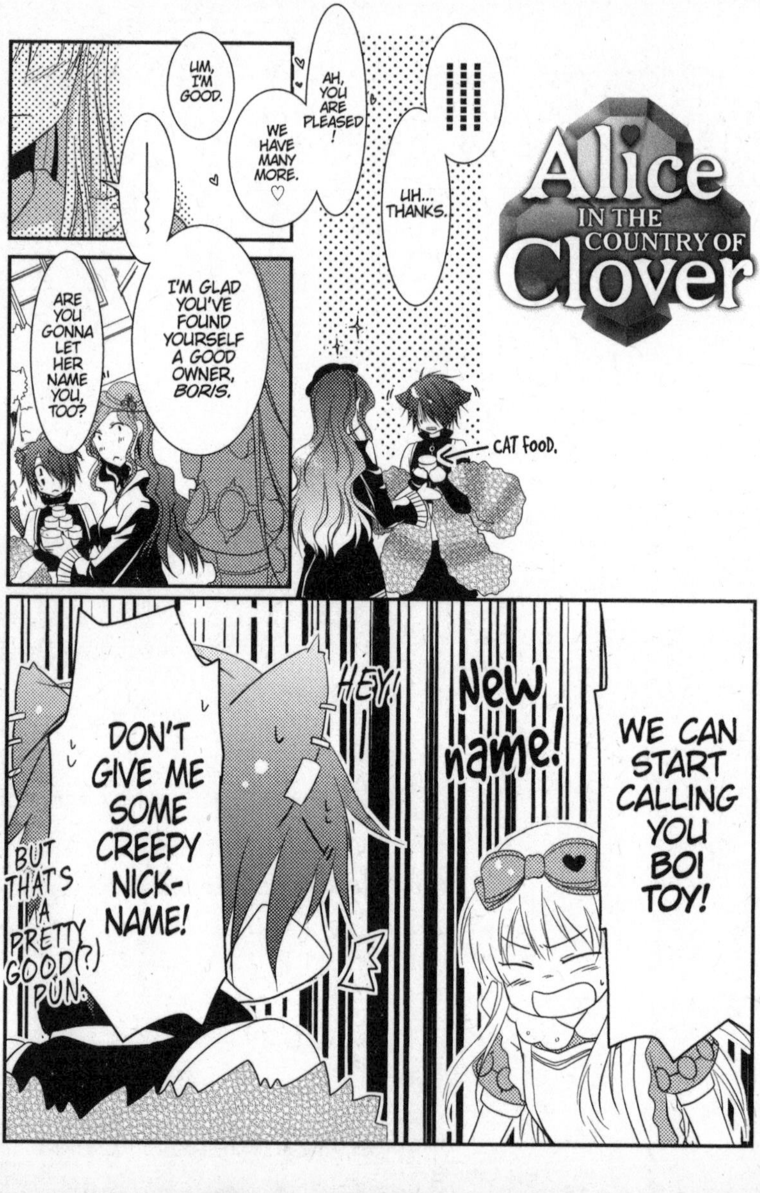
Alice in the Country of Clover
!!!!
UH... THANKS.
AH, YOU ARE PLEASED!
WE HAVE MANY MORE. ♡
CAT FOOD.
UM, I'M GOOD.
—!
I'M GLAD YOU'VE FOUND YOURSELF A GOOD OWNER, BORIS.
ARE YOU GONNA LET HER NAME YOU, TOO?
WE CAN START CALLING YOU BOI TOY!
New name!
HEY!
DON'T GIVE ME SOME CREEPY NICK-NAME!
BUT THAT'S A PRETTY GOOD(?) PUN.

CHESHIRE CAT WALTZ: SIDE STORY - POST-MORTEM

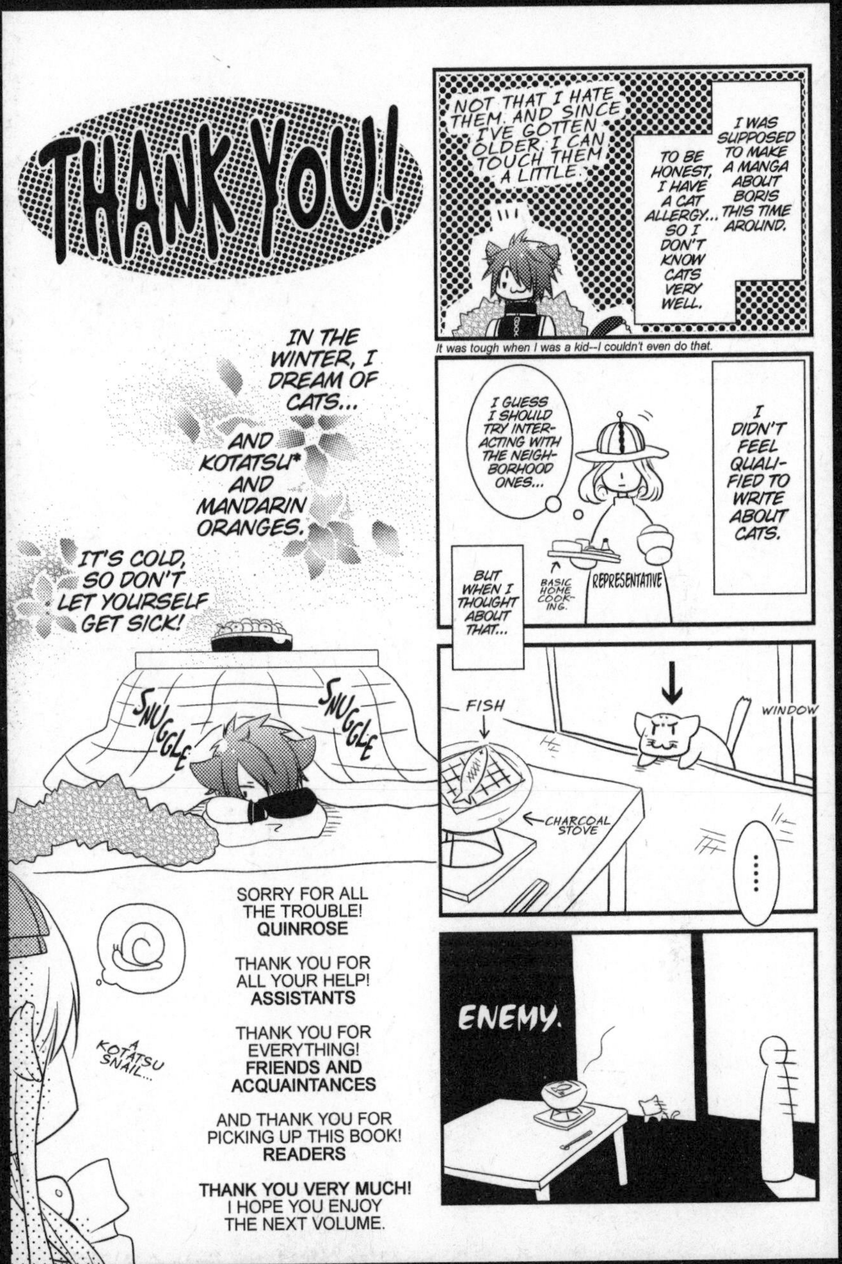
I WAS SUPPOSED TO MAKE A MANGA ABOUT BORIS THIS TIME AROUND.
TO BE HONEST, I HAVE A CAT ALLERGY... SO I DON'T KNOW CATS VERY WELL.
NOT THAT I HATE THEM. AND SINCE I'VE GOTTEN OLDER, I CAN TOUCH THEM A LITTLE.
It was tough when I was a kid--I couldn't even do that.
I DIDN'T FEEL QUALIFIED TO WRITE ABOUT CATS.
I GUESS I SHOULD TRY INTERACTING WITH THE NEIGHBORHOOD ONES...
REPRESENTATIVE
BASIC HOME COOKING.
BUT WHEN I THOUGHT ABOUT THAT...
WINDOW
FISH
CHARCOAL STOVE
......
ENEMY.
THANK YOU!
IN THE WINTER, I DREAM OF CATS... AND KOTATSU* AND MANDARIN ORANGES.
IT'S COLD, SO DON'T LET YOURSELF GET SICK!
SNUGGLE
SNUGGLE
SORRY FOR ALL THE TROUBLE! QUINROSE
THANK YOU FOR ALL YOUR HELP! ASSISTANTS
THANK YOU FOR EVERYTHING! FRIENDS AND ACQUAINTANCES
AND THANK YOU FOR PICKING UP THIS BOOK! READERS
THANK YOU VERY MUCH! I HOPE YOU ENJOY THE NEXT VOLUME.
A KOTATSU SNAIL...

*A Japanese table with a blanket over it and a heater inside. As it's rare for an entire house to have central heating, a kotatsu offers a warm place to spend time during a cold Japanese winter.

NEXT TIME...

Alice in the Country of Clover
CHESHIRE CAT WALTZ
2
STORY: QuinRose
ART: Mamenosuke Fujimaru

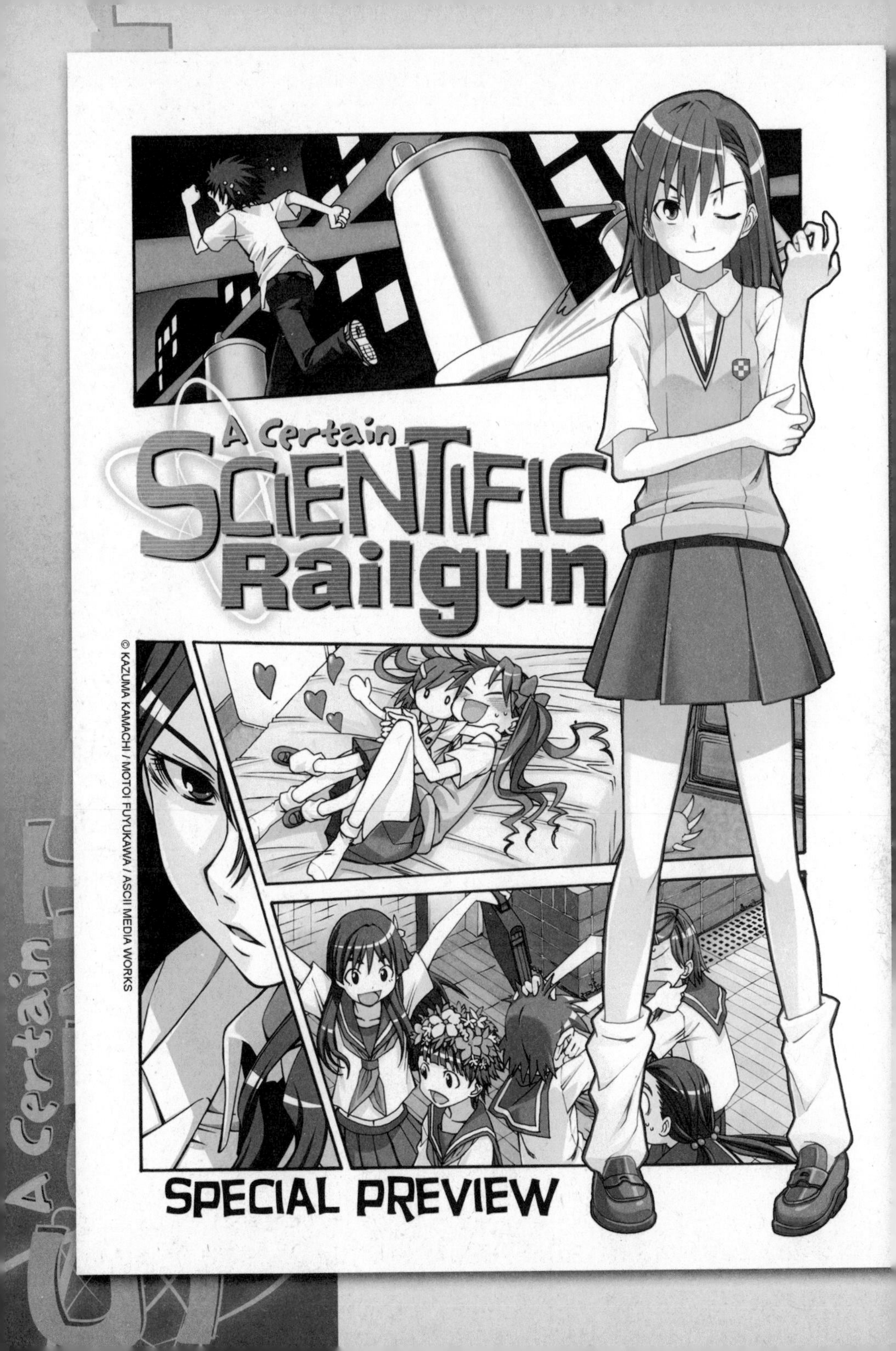
A Certain
SCIENTIFIC
Railgun
© KAZUMA KAMACHI / MOTOI FUYUKAWA / ASCII MEDIA WORKS
SPECIAL PREVIEW
A Certain

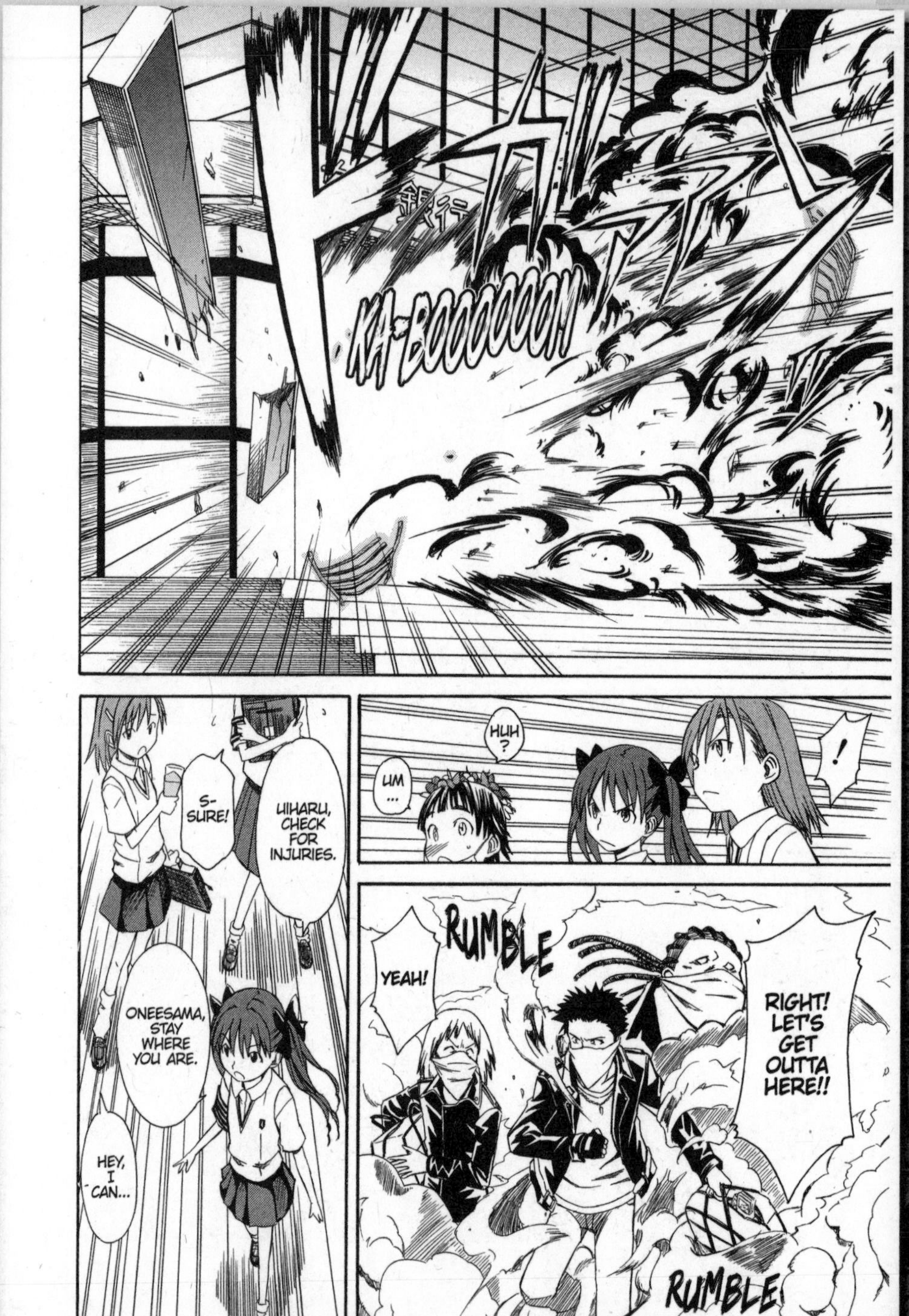

KA-BOOOOOOM
銀行
!
HUH?
UM...
RIGHT! LET'S GET OUTTA HERE!!
RUMBLE
YEAH!
RUMBLE
UIHARU, CHECK FOR INJURIES.
S-SURE!
ONEESAMA, STAY WHERE YOU ARE.
HEY, I CAN...

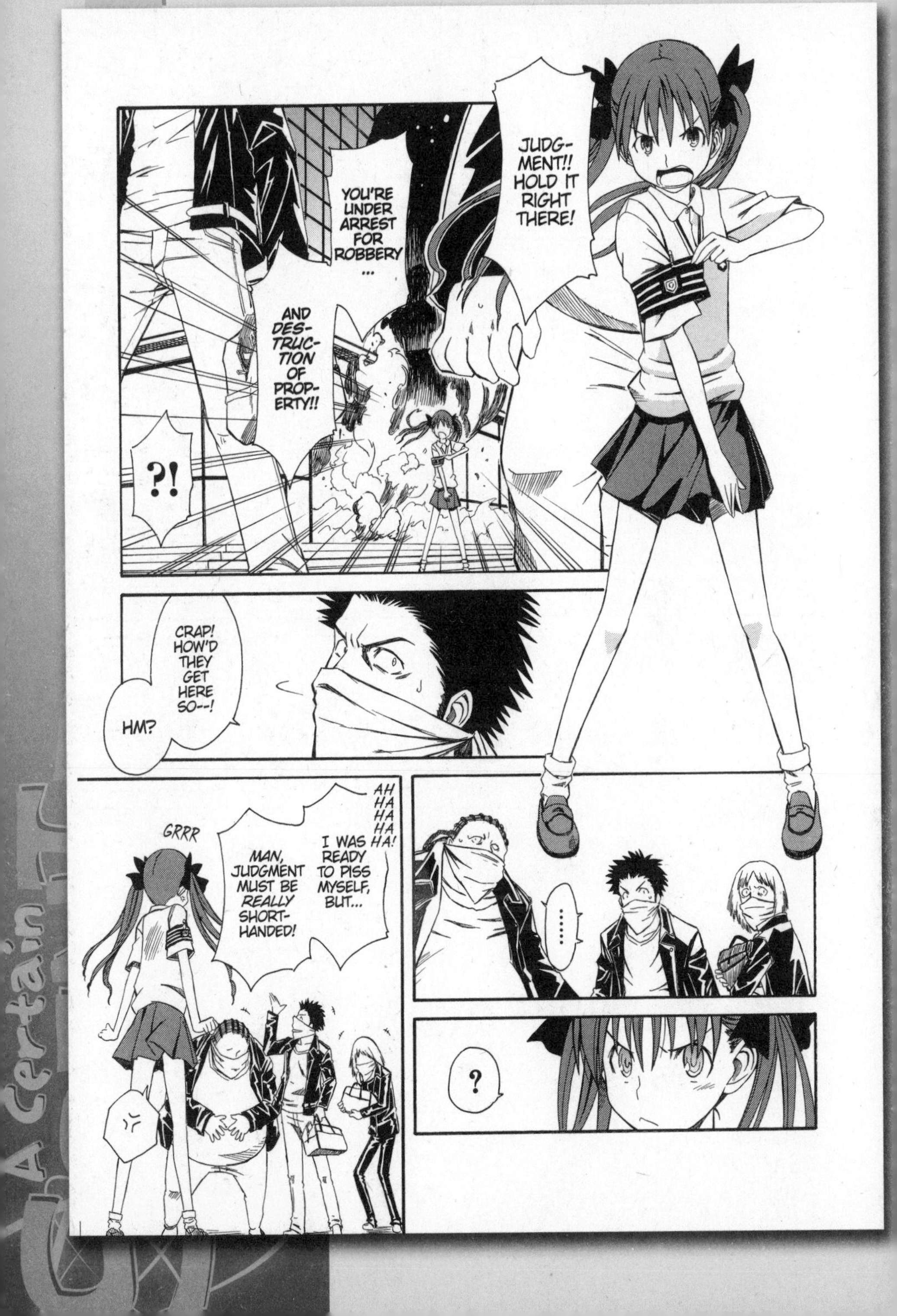
JUDG-MENT!! HOLD IT RIGHT THERE!
YOU'RE UNDER ARREST FOR ROBBERY...
AND DES-TRUC-TION OF PROP-ERTY!!
?!
CRAP! HOW'D THEY GET HERE SO--!
HM?
......
?
AH HA HA HA HA!
I WAS READY TO PISS MYSELF, BUT...
MAN, JUDGMENT MUST BE *REALLY* SHORT-HANDED!
GRRR

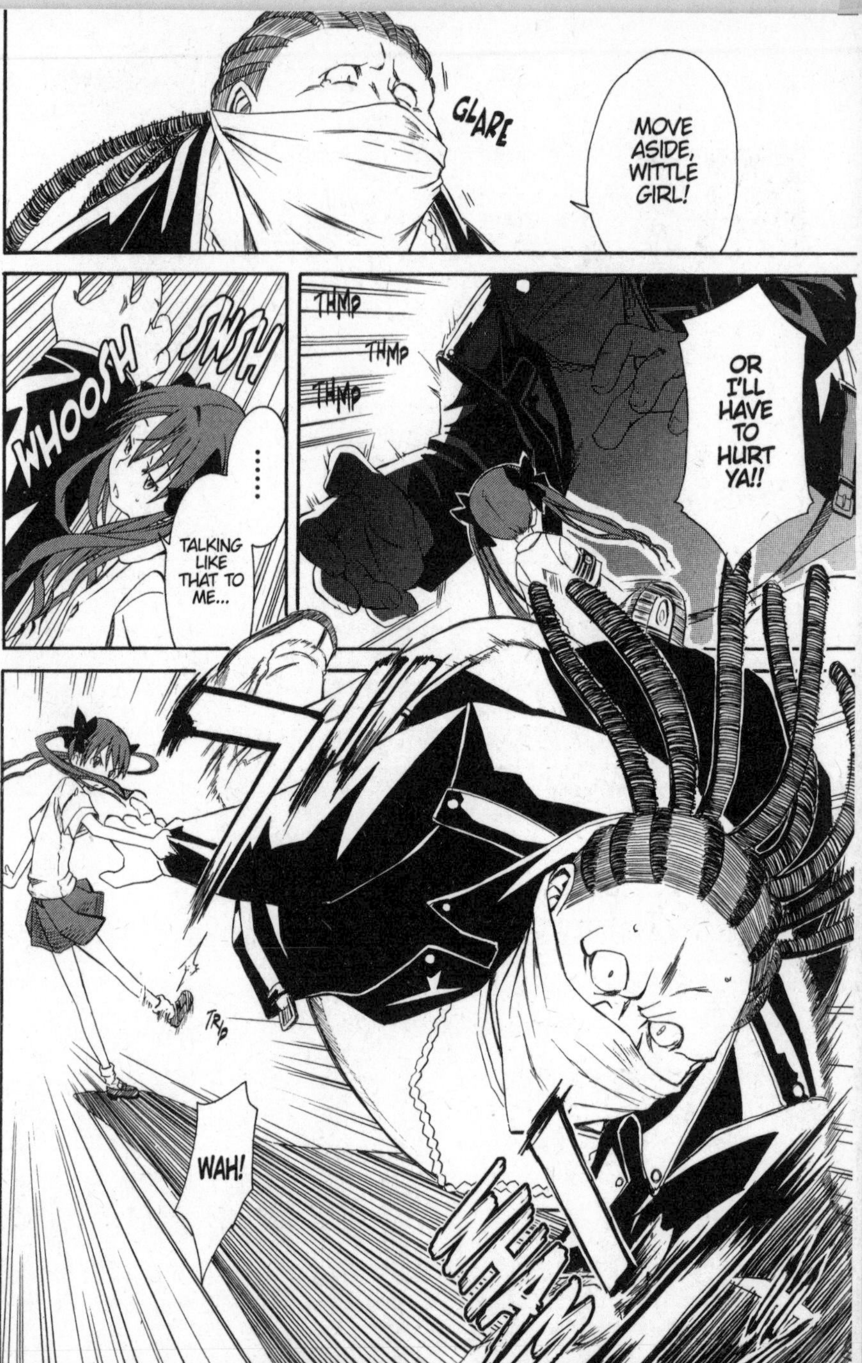
GLARE
MOVE ASIDE, WITTLE GIRL!
OR I'LL HAVE TO HURT YA!!
THMP
THMP
THMP
SWSH
WHOOSH
......
TALKING LIKE THAT TO ME...
TRIP
WAH!
WHAM

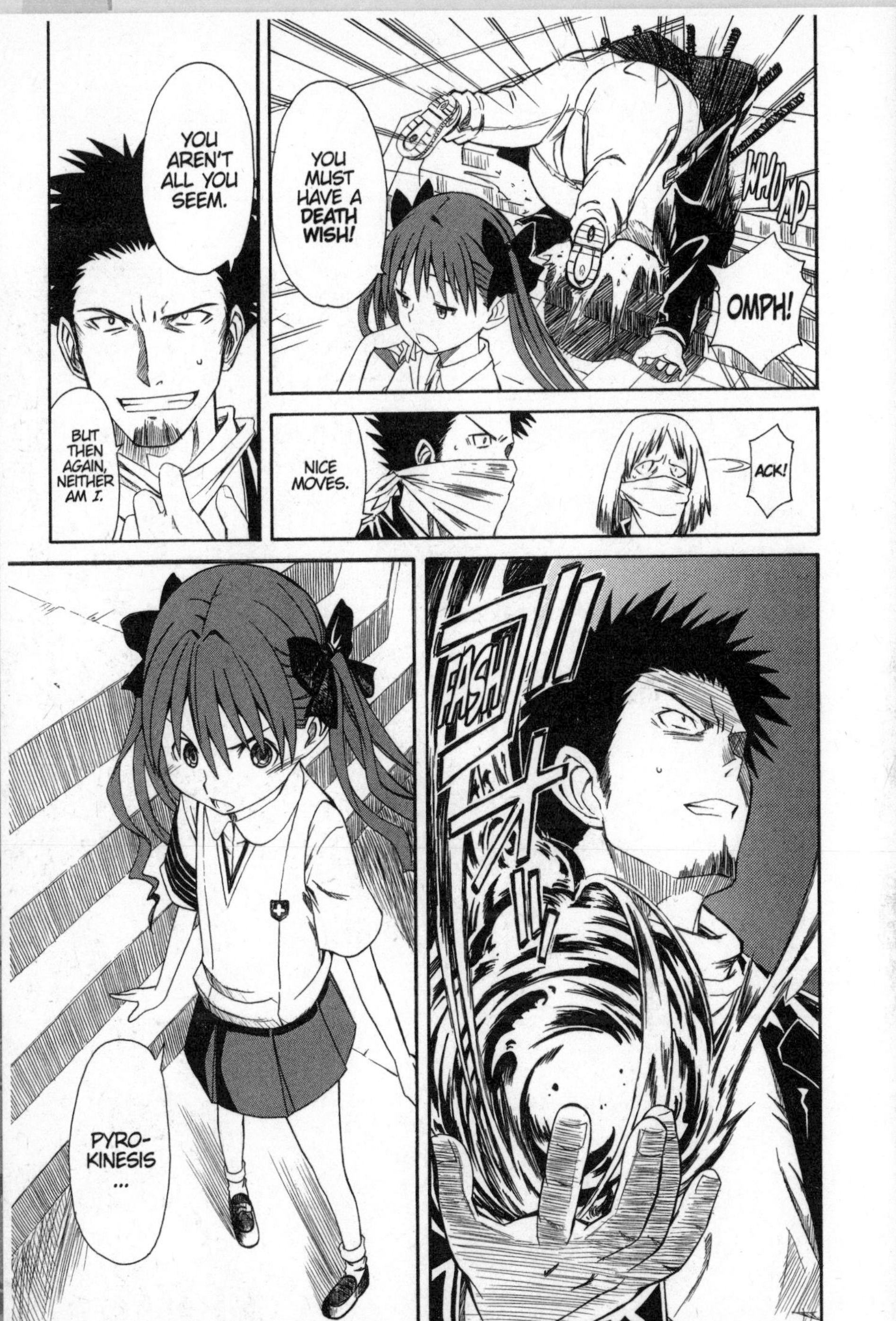
WHUMP
OMPH!
YOU MUST HAVE A DEATH WISH!
ACK!
NICE MOVES.
YOU AREN'T ALL YOU SEEM.
BUT THEN AGAIN, NEITHER AM I.
FASH
PYRO-KINESIS ...

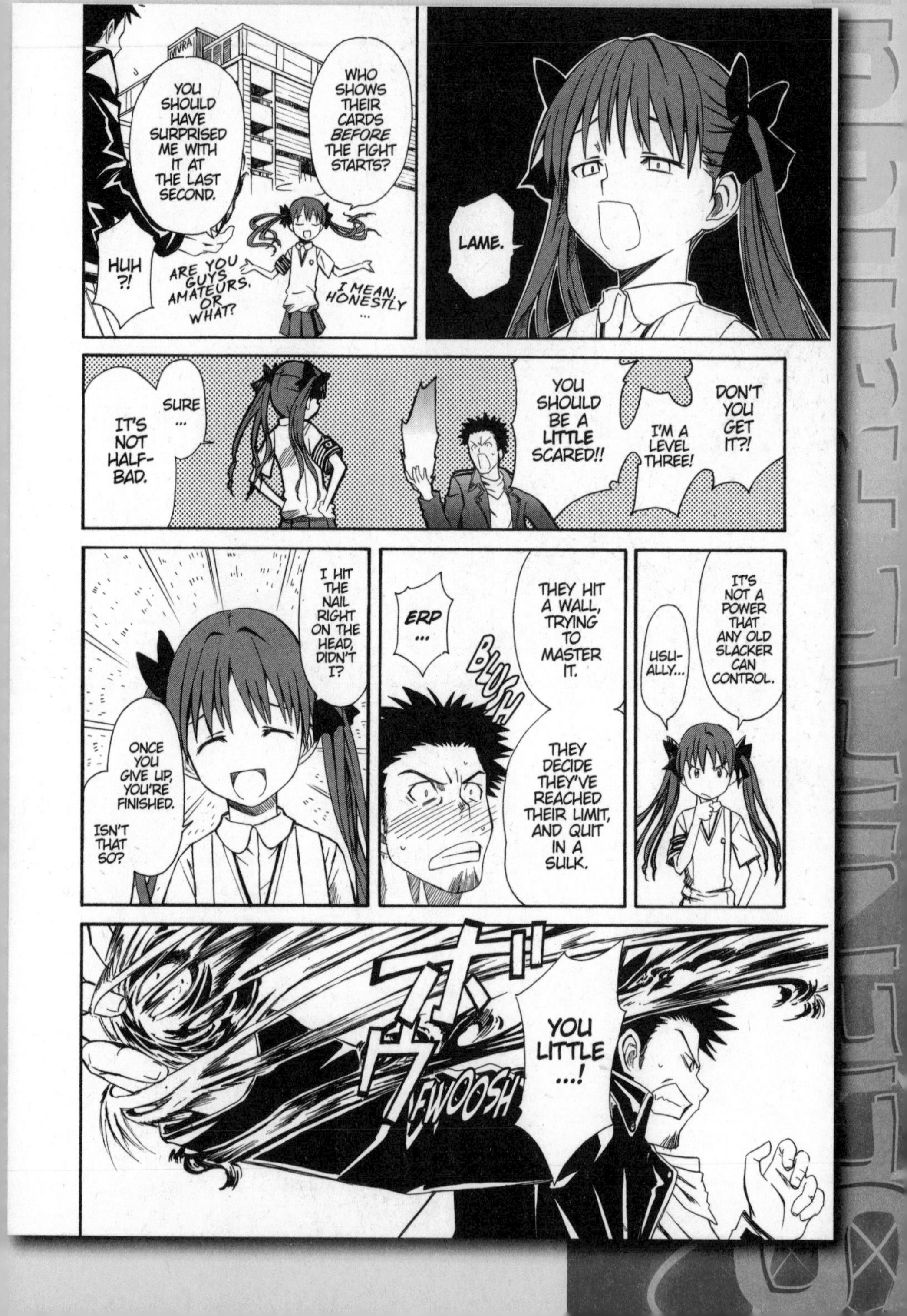
LAME.
WHO SHOWS THEIR CARDS *BEFORE* THE FIGHT STARTS?
VIVRA
YOU SHOULD HAVE SURPRISED ME WITH IT AT THE LAST SECOND.
I MEAN, HONESTLY ...
ARE YOU GUYS AMATEURS, OR WHAT?
HUH ?!
DON'T YOU GET IT?!
I'M A LEVEL THREE!
YOU SHOULD BE A LITTLE SCARED!!
SURE ...
IT'S NOT HALF-BAD.
IT'S NOT A POWER THAT ANY OLD SLACKER CAN CONTROL.
USU-ALLY...
THEY HIT A WALL, TRYING TO MASTER IT.
THEY DECIDE THEY'VE REACHED THEIR LIMIT, AND QUIT IN A SULK.
ERP ...
BLUSH
I HIT THE NAIL RIGHT ON THE HEAD, DIDN'T I?
ONCE YOU GIVE UP, YOU'RE FINISHED.
ISN'T THAT SO?
YOU LITTLE ...!
FWOOSH

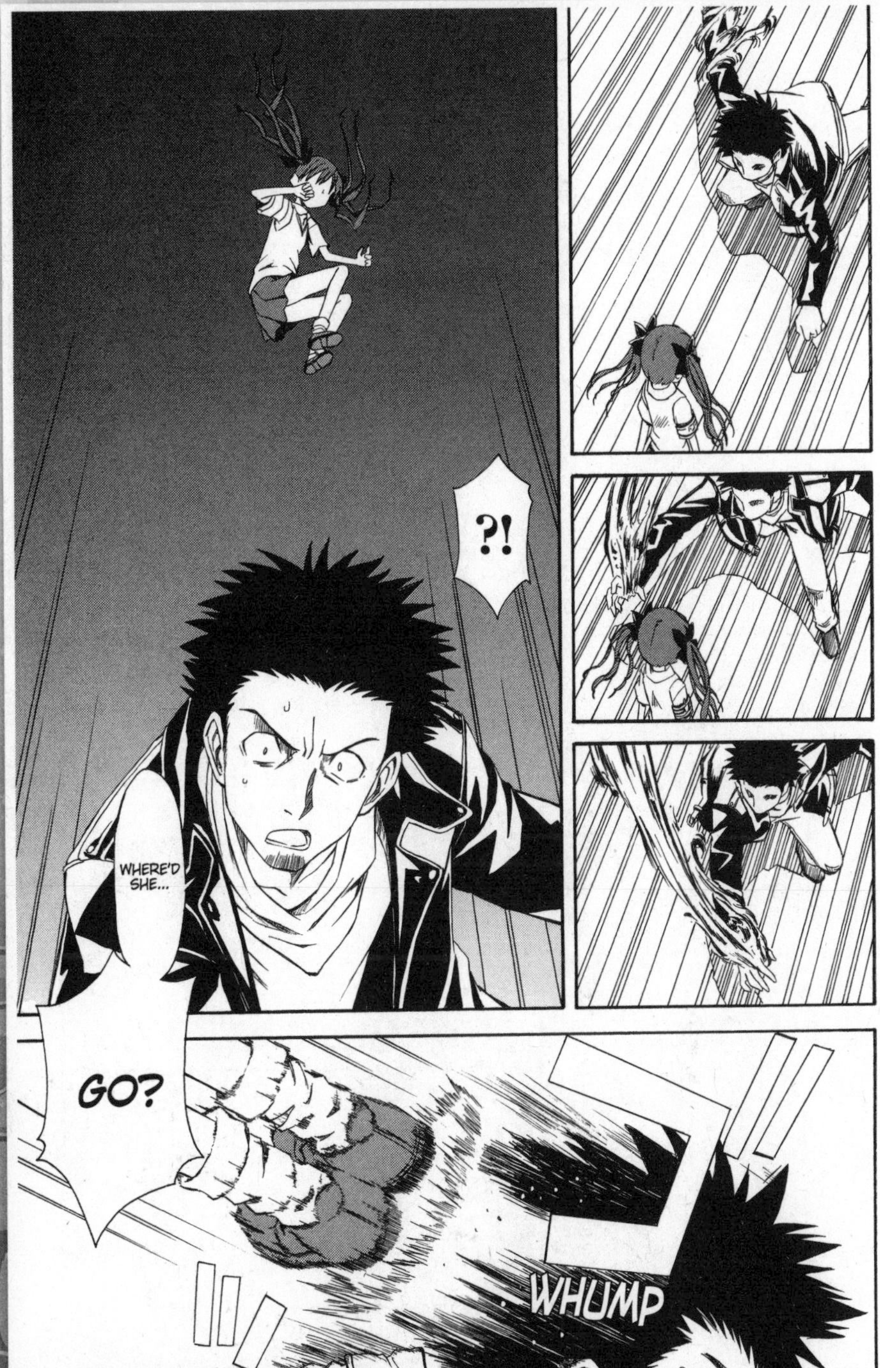
?!
WHERE'D SHE...
GO?
WHUMP

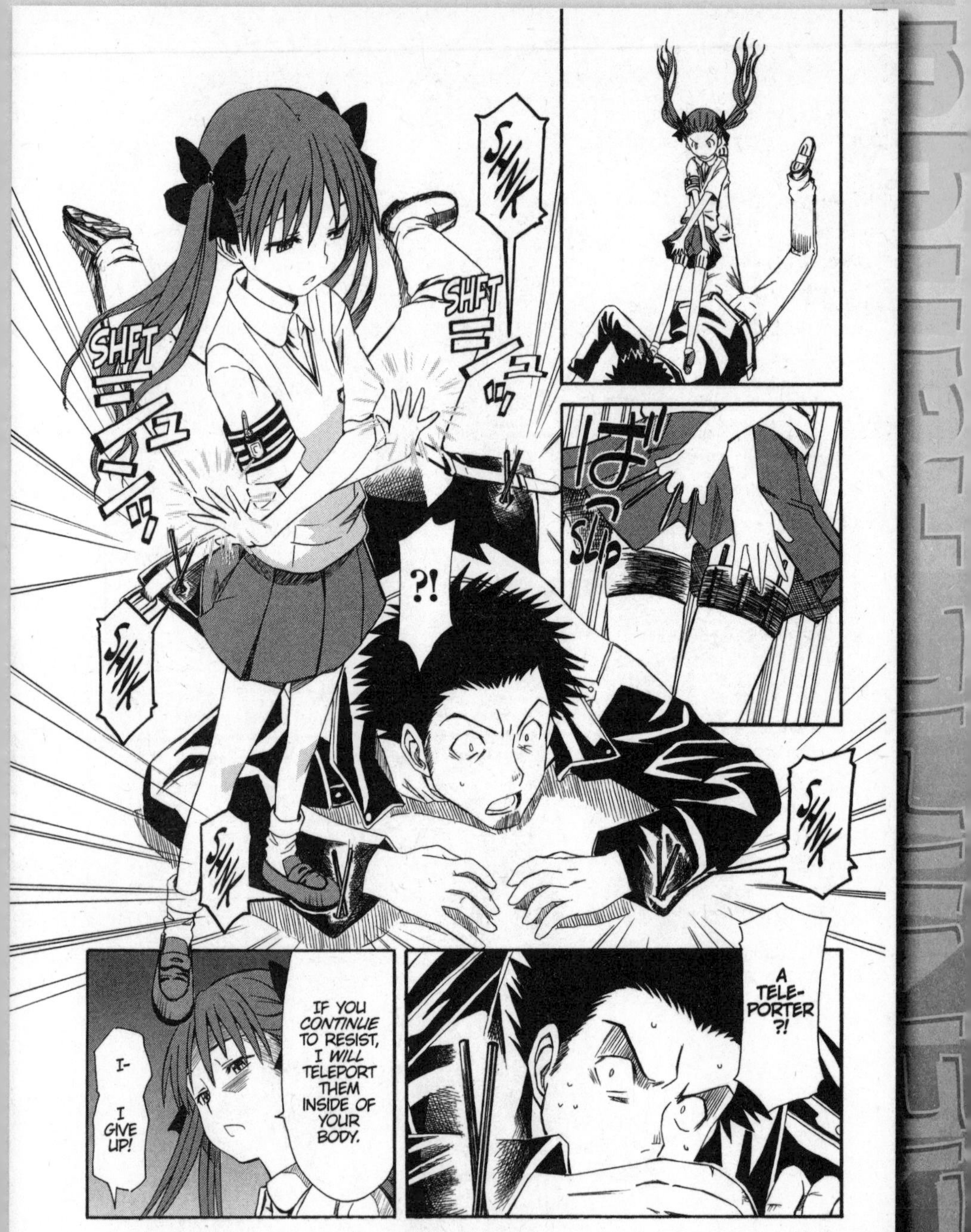

ぱっ
SLIP
SHNK
SHFT
ニュ
SHFT
ニュ
?!
SHNK
SHNK
SHNK
A TELE-PORTER ?!
IF YOU CONTINUE TO RESIST, I WILL TELEPORT THEM INSIDE OF YOUR BODY.
I- I GIVE UP!

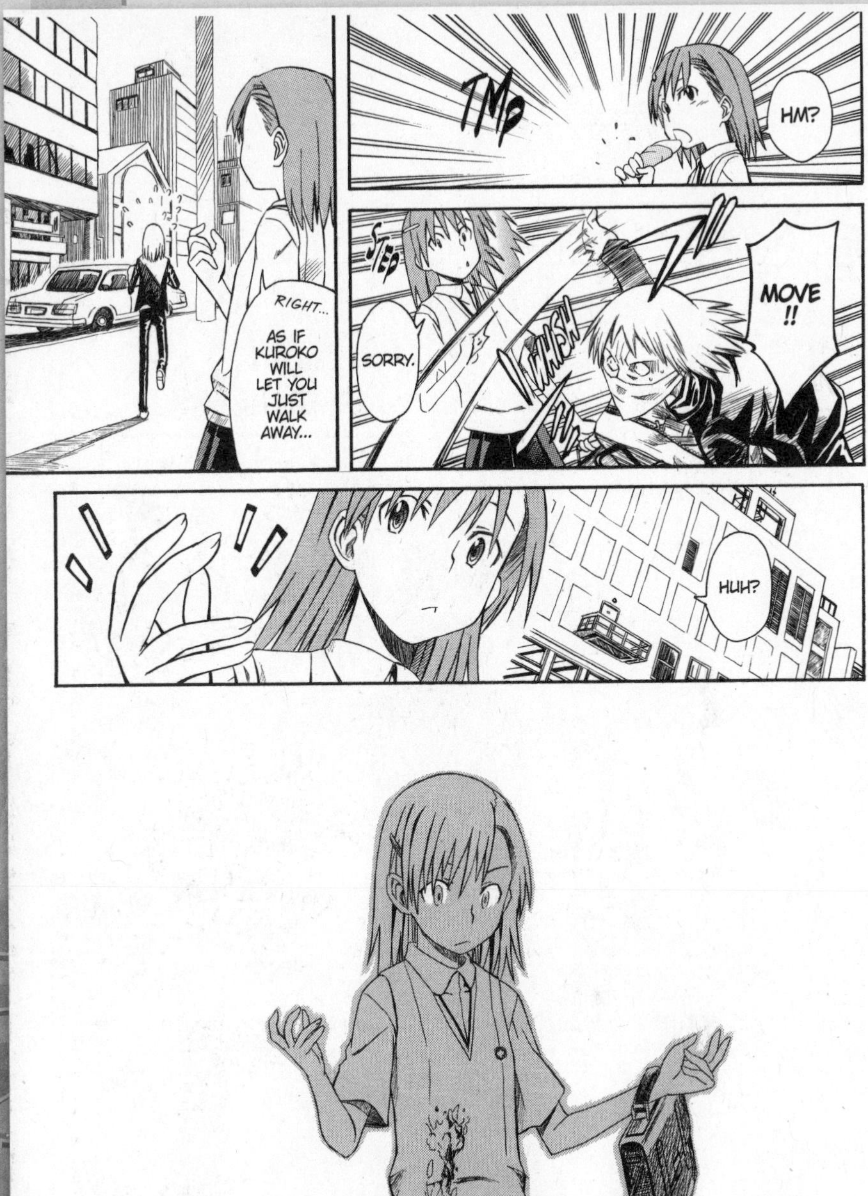
HM?
MOVE!!
WHISH
STEP
SORRY.
RIGHT...
AS IF KUROKO WILL LET YOU JUST WALK AWAY...
HUH?

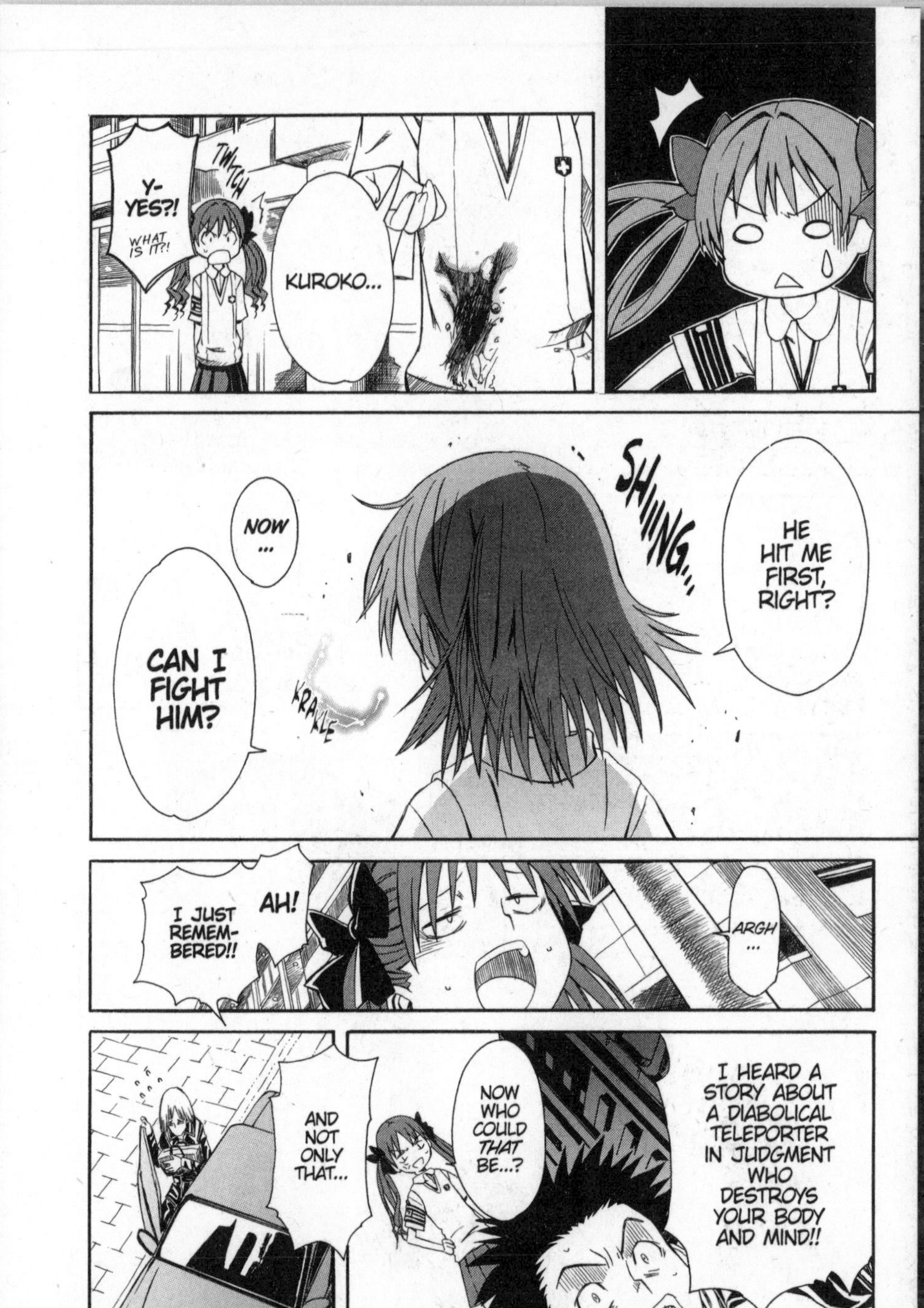
KUROKO...
TWITCH
Y-YES?!
WHAT IS IT?!
HE HIT ME FIRST, RIGHT?
SHIIING...
KRAKLE
NOW...
CAN I FIGHT HIM?
ARGH...
AH!
I JUST REMEMBERED!!
I HEARD A STORY ABOUT A DIABOLICAL TELEPORTER IN JUDGMENT WHO DESTROYS YOUR BODY AND MIND!!
NOW WHO COULD THAT BE...?
AND NOT ONLY THAT...

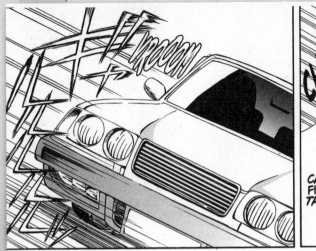

CHINK
GAH!
I CAN'T FIGHT THAT!
THE EVIL TELE-PORTER'S PARTNER...
IS THE STRONGEST ELECTRO-MASTER OUT THERE...
"THE RAILGUN"!!
I DON'T KNOW WHAT STORIES YOU'VE HEARD, BUT...
KRACKLE
KRACKLE
ELEC-TRIC-ITY...
THAT MEANS...!
YEP.

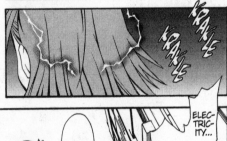

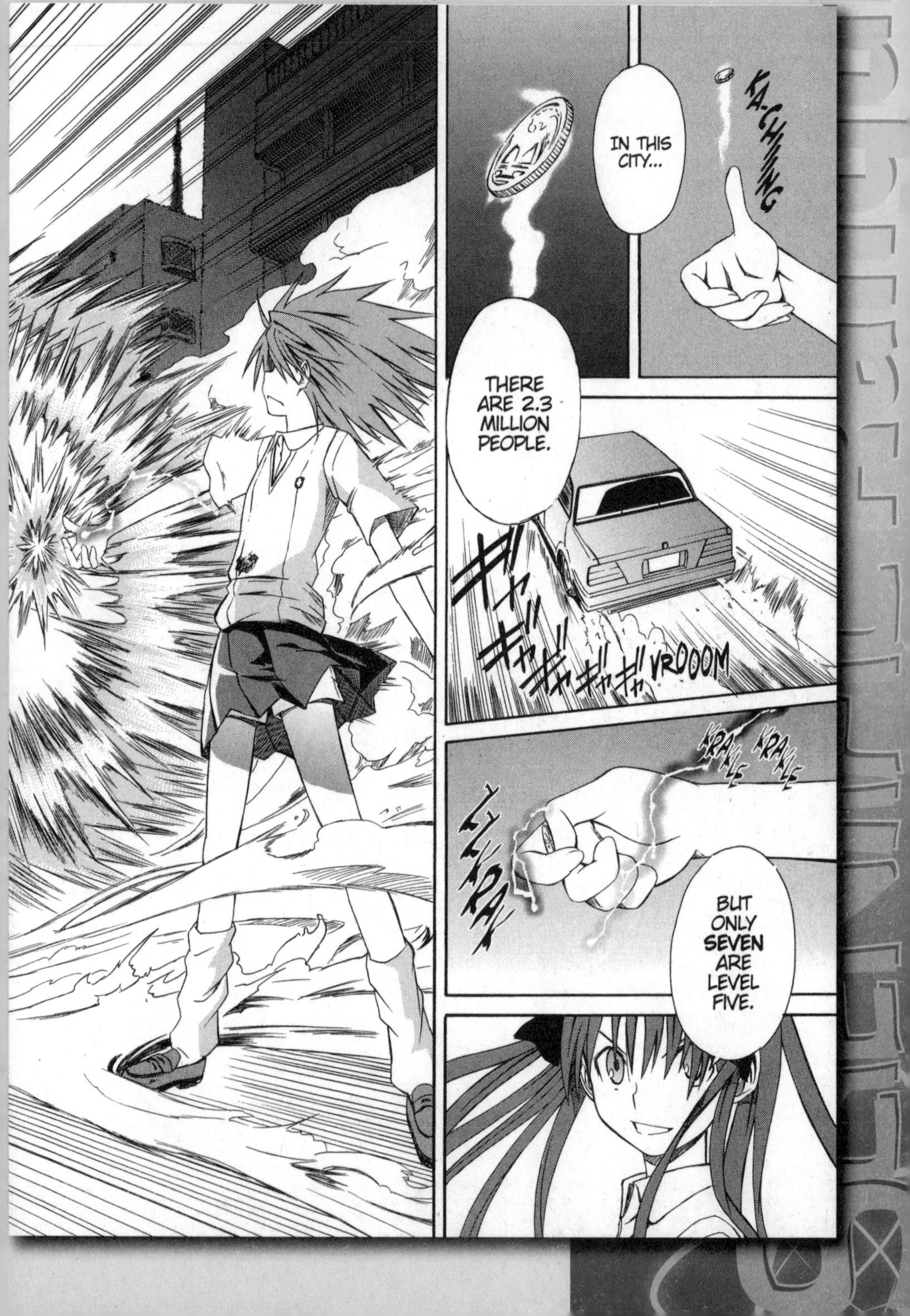
KA-CHING
IN THIS CITY...
THERE ARE 2.3 MILLION PEOPLE.
VROOM
KRAKLE KRAKLE
BUT ONLY SEVEN ARE LEVEL FIVE.

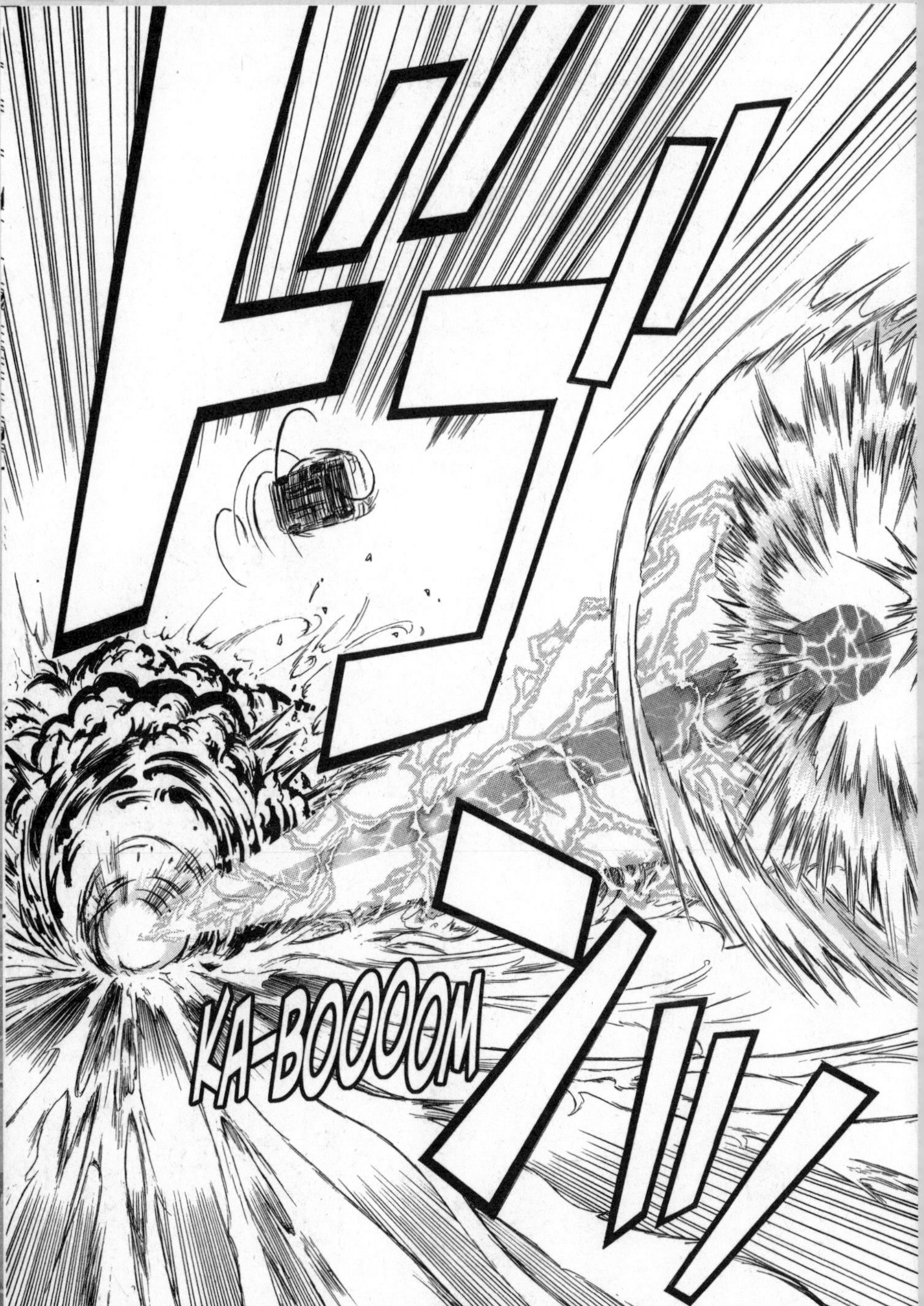
KA-BOOOOM

Continued in *A Certain Scientific Railgun* Vol. 1